SUCCESS SKILLS

Strategies for Study and Lifelong Learning

second edition

Abby Marks-Beale
Corporate Learning Specialist
The Reading Edge

SOUTH-WESTERN
THOMSON LEARNING

Australia • Canada • Mexico • Singapore • Spain • United Kingdom • United States

SOUTH-WESTERN

TM

THOMSON LEARNING

Success Skills: Strategies for Study and Lifelong Learning 2nd Edition
by Abby Marks-Beale

Eve Lewis: Executive Editor
Laurie Wendell: Project Manager
Patricia Matthews Boies: Production Manager
Colleen A. Farmer: Editor
Nancy A. Long: Marketing Manager
Linda Wasserman: Marketing Coordinator
Tippy McIntosh: Art and Design Coordinator
Kevin L. Kluck: Manufacturing Coordinator
Cover Design: Photonics Graphics
Internal Design: Photonics Graphics
Compositor: Career Solutions Training Group
Printer: Von Hoffman Graphics

Photo Credits:
Photo on page 111 © Abby Marks-Beale,
photos on pages 225 and 226 © South-Western.
All other photos © PhotoDisc, Inc.

International Division List

ASIA (Including India):
Thomson Learning
60 Albert Street, #15-01
Albert Complex
Singapore 189969
Tel 65 336-6411
Fax 65 336-7411

AUSTRALIA/NEW ZEALAND:
Nelson
102 Dodds Street
South Melbourne
Victoria 3205
Australia
Tel 61 (0)3 9685-4111
Fax 61 (0)3 9685-4199

LATIN AMERICA:
Thomson Learning
Seneca 53
Colonia Polanco
11560 Mexico, D.F. Mexico
Tel (525) 281-2906
Fax (525) 281-2656

CANADA:
Nelson
1120 Birchmount Road
Toronto, Ontario
Canada M1K 5G4
Tel (416) 752-9100
Fax (416) 752-8102

UK/EUROPE/MIDDLE EAST/AFRICA:
Thomson Learning
Berkshire House
168-173 High Holborn
London WC1V 7AA
United Kingdom
Tel 44 (0)20 497-1422
Fax 44 (0)20 497-1426

SPAIN (includes Portugal):
Paraninfo
Calle Magallanes 25
28015 Madrid
España
Tel 34 (0)91 446-3350
Fax 34 (0)91 445-6218

Continue down the path to success with South-Western's resources for lifelong learning.

SCANS 2000 Virtual Workplace Simulations

Each CD-ROM simulation presents users with a challenging interactive case study that promotes on-the-job problem solving and critical thinking skills. Check our online catalog for *Building a Problem Solving Team, Making Complex Decisions, Making a Technical Presentation* and more!

Personal Development for Life and Work

Develop the personal qualities today's employers seek and demand. This relevant and engaging text focuses on the successful attitudes, interpersonal skills, critical thinking skills, and work ethics needed for personal and career success.

Textbook   0-538-69795-4

Career Success: A Lifetime Investment

Make a lifetime investment in your personal success. Taking a unique lifelong learning approach, this dynamic text focuses specifically on self-understanding, self-acceptance, career information, and decision-making skills needed for career success in the 21st Century.

Textbook   0-538-69141-7

Quick Skills Series

Quickly sharpen essential skills with these quick-study guides. The *Quick Skills* series includes a full list of topics, such as *Self-Management and Goal Setting, Attitude and Self-Esteem, Reading in the Workplace, Decision Making and Problem Solving, How to Find and Apply for a Job,* and many more. Check our online catalog for a complete listing.

10-Hour Series

Become proficient in a variety of technical skill applications in a short amount of time. In just 10 hours each, you can learn how to do *Web Page Design, Online Resume and Job Search,* or *Electronic Presentations*. Check our online catalog for a complete listing!

Join Us On the Internet
www.swep.com

SOUTH-WESTERN

THOMSON LEARNING

Engage Student Interest

LEARNING BY DOING

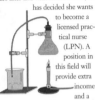

After Yvette finished high school, she took a job as a home health aide. Going directly to college was out of the question, as she needed to support herself. Now five years later and with an infant son, she has decided she wants to become a licensed practical nurse (LPN). A position in this field will provide extra income and a better family schedule. Though college will cost a great deal of time and money, she realizes it is an investment in the future.

Yvette successfully applies and is accepted at her local community college. Chemistry 101 is the first class she is scheduled to take as a part-time student. She is anxious, yet excited, to begin her training program.

During the first class, Yvette becomes worried because she has difficulty understanding the material.

Later she reads and rereads the textbook assignments, hoping they will begin to make sense. Then she learns she must complete experiments in the chemistry lab after only two more classes.

Since Yvette is not a quitter, she continues to go to class and attempts to do the homework, but she often hands in incomplete assignments. She becomes more and more frustrated and starts to feel inadequate. She desperately wants to make it through her college program but is feeling quite helpless.

What advice do you have for Yvette?

In This Chapter

1.1 Distinguishing Between Active and Passive Learning
1.2 Advantages of Active Learning
1.3 On Becoming an Active Learner

Chapter Goals

After studying and working with the information in this chapter, you should be able to:

♦ Distinguish between active and passive learning.
♦ Recognize the advantages to becoming an active learner.
♦ Understand how active learning skills can help you now and in the future.
♦ Identify ways to develop a more positive attitude toward learning.
♦ Develop methods to become an active participant in your learning.

Chapter Intro
Presents a short case study and previews the content and issues found in the chapter.

Chapter Goals
Begin each lesson with clear objectives and learning outcomes.

In This Chapter
Identifies the topics and sections of the chapter.

...first exposure to ...endent work ...udying was ...ime around the ...rade. You were ...cted to go ..., complete your ... and bring it ...he next day. As ...ars progressed, ...your assignments became more challenging in both scope and content. Out of necessity, you probably figured out on your own how to get the work done.

Some learners are more successful with their self-taught learning skills than others. Many learners spend more time studying than is necessary because they use ineffective study skills.

When people continue formal learning beyond high school, many find that their self-taught learning skills are not enough. Whether in college or on the job, they work hard to learn what they need to know. Just as a car's engine may run for years with little maintenance, so, too, can some people make it through high school while giving little attention to learning skills. Learning in college or the workplace, however, proves to be quite a different story!

Only when a car gets a tune-up and a person acquires effective learning skills do they function efficiently. Any learning *is* work, but learning can be a lot easier when the proper skills are applied. *Working harder or longer is not the same as working smarter.*

This chapter (1) identifies the differences between active and passive learning, (2) provides simple ideas and strategies for becoming an active learner, and (3) encourages you to create your own action plan for learning success.

When you're learning, you're making use of many tools available to you. What tools do *you* use for learning?

3.1 YOUR LEARNING INFLUENCES

A **learning influence** is something that affects how well you concentrate while trying to learn. Some are physical; others are mental. Some influences are helpful in keeping your concentration, while many others are distracting. The helpful ones are considered positive, while the distracting ones are considered negative.

ACTIVITY 1

Below is a list of common influences that can affect your concentration. Think about how each of the influences affects the way you concentrate; and decide whether it is positive/helpful (+), negative/unhelpful (-), or sometimes helpful/sometimes unhelpful (=). For example, if you find yourself very focused when you are under time pressure, place a plus (+) in the blank. If you find you are continually distracted by time pressure with little ability to focus, place a minus (-) in the blank. However, if you find you are both focused and distracted equally, place an equal (=) in the blank. Add other influences that can affect your concentration.

Location
___At your desk
___At a table
___On a couch
___On a recliner
___In bed
___Other:_____

State of Mind/Being
___Interested
___Not interested
___Alert
___Sleepy
___Relaxed
___Stressed
___Time-pressured
___Not time-pressured
___Preoccupied
___Tired

___Well rested
___Hungry
___Other:_____

External Environment
___Warm
___Cool
___Well lit
___Dimly lit
___Noisy
___Quiet
___Other:_____

Distractions
___Other people
___Telephone
___e-mail
___Television
___Radio
___Other:_____

Type of Written Material
___Familiar content
___Unfamiliar content
___Wide columns
___Narrow columns
___Large print size
___Small print size
___Good copy quality
___Poor copy quality
___Other:_____

Delivery of Information
___Lecture
___Discussion
___Reading
___Writing
___On computer screen
___One-on-one instruction
___Group interaction

___Research
___Hands-on learning
___Visual demonstration
___Other:_____

Purpose/Usability
___For a meeting
___For your boss or instructor
___For a presentation
___For a test
___For pleasure
___For background knowledge
___Other:_____

Chapter 3: Creating Concentration (55)

Activities

Challenge learners to recall information, think critically about chapter concepts, and analyze their own study habits.

Factoids

Highlight interesting facts, findings, and trends in the areas of reading, studying, and lifelong learning.

Mind Wandering: The Enemy of Concentration

[The] mind must focus before it can learn. When [focused], you concentrate on the learning [material] and content. **Mind wandering,** on the [other] hand, is the enemy of concentration. Also [known] as daydreaming, mind wandering is a [momen]tary lack of mental concentration or [focus]. It can last a second, five seconds, thirty seconds, or longer. It is natural—and necessary for learning. Most human beings daydream.

When you read or study, some mind wandering may be helpful. If you are building a mental bridge of knowledge from the new information to the old, then mind wandering can be productive. For example, if you are learning about the installation of electrical sockets, your mind may wander to the time you got an electrical shock as a child when you stuck your finger in a socket; that thought is important for your learning.

But if, while installing the sockets, your mind wanders to your plans for the coming weekend, that thought is not productive. Nonproductive thoughts break your concentration, slow down and interrupt your learning process, and ultimately affect your ability to understand the information you are trying to comprehend.

It is important to be aware of the mental thoughts that cause your mind to wander and break your concentration.

Which photo more closely resembles your learning area?

Concentration Factoid

According to the research of Becky Patterson, Ph.D., Professor Emeritus of the University of Alaska and author of *Concentration: Strategies for Attaining Focus*, an average [co]llege student's concentration period while reading is only 16 minutes. Other research suggests young children have concentration periods that last for just 20 seconds! It is amazing that we ever learn anything with such small intervals of concentration.

(56)

Success Skills

Special Features Enhance Learning

Checkpoint 3.1

1. What is a learning influence?
2. What influences you positively when you learn?
3. What influences you negatively?

Checkpoint

Short questions at the end of each chapter section assist with review and comprehension of key concepts.

> To furnish the means of acquiring knowledge is . . . the greatest benefit that can be conferred upon mankind.
>
> —John Quincy Adams
> Sixth president of the United States

Quotations

Quotes from authors, leaders, and celebrities add relevance, humor and motivational thoughts.

WEB LINK

www.utexas.edu/student/lsc/handouts/1442.html

This is a page entitled "Concentration and Your Body" from the University of Texas at Austin. It reinforces and supplements the information in this chapter. Access the main site to search other learning skills pages.

Web Links

Address technology issues and suggest web sites to visit for additional information on lifelong learning subjects.

Focus on Ethics

You have a job working for a great boss who challenges you and makes you feel valued. Of your many job functions, you check your boss's e-mail when she travels and only forward those messages that are of the most importance. You have been told not to open messages marked "personal." This day, your mind wanders and you inadvertently open a personal message. It is from a recruiting firm providing job openings outside of your company that she might have interest in. As you stare at the screen, you must decide whether or not to pass this message along. you do? Why?

Focus on Ethics

Presents situational ethical dilemmas for analysis and problem solving.

Smart Tip

According to R. Alec MacKenzie, a time management guru, for every minute you plan, you save two minutes in execution. For example, if you take 15 minutes at the end of each day to plan the following day, you would then save 30 minutes that next day because of the forethought and planning. How might this

Smart Tip

Highlights interesting facts, findings, and trends in the areas of reading, studying, and lifelong learning.

Key Terms and Concepts

Provide an opportunity for learners to test recall of new terms and ideas.

Key Terms and Concepts

arm-swing rule	learning environment	mind wandering
concentration	learning influences	physical learning environment
effective learning environment	mental learning environment	physiology
ineffective learning environment		

Assessment and Review

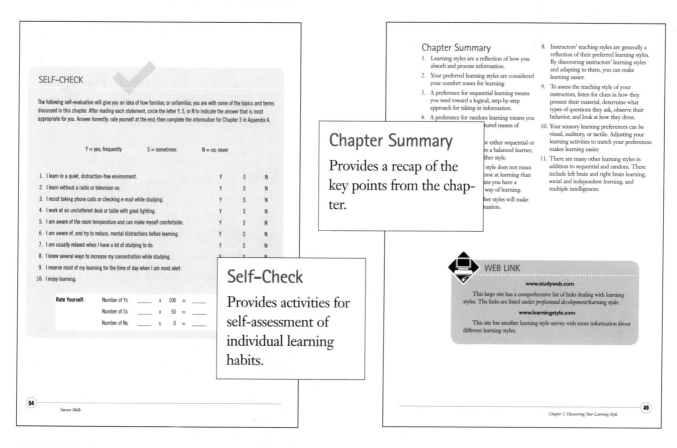

The following self-evaluation will give you an idea of how familiar, or unfamiliar, you are with some of the topics and terms discussed in this chapter. After reading each statement, circle the letter Y, S, or N to indicate the answer that is most appropriate for you. Answer honestly; rate yourself at the end; then complete the information for Chapter 3 in Appendix A.

Y = yes; frequently   S = sometimes   N = no; never

1. I learn in a quiet, distraction-free environment.   Y   S   N
2. I learn without a radio or television on.   Y   S   N
3. I resist taking phone calls or checking e-mail while studying.   Y   S   N
4. I work at an uncluttered desk or table with good lighting.   Y   S   N
5. I am aware of the room temperature and can make myself comfortable.   Y   S   N
6. I am aware of, and try to reduce, mental distractions before learning.   Y   S   N
7. I am usually relaxed when I have a lot of studying to do.   Y   S   N
8. I know several ways to increase my concentration while studying.   Y   S   N
9. I reserve most of my learning for the time of day when I am most alert.   Y   S   N
10. I enjoy learning.

Rate Yourself: Number of Ys _____ x 100 = _____
                    Number of Ss _____ x 50 = _____
                    Number of Ns _____ x 0 = _____

Self–Check

Provides activities for self-assessment of individual learning habits.

Chapter Summary

1. Learning styles are a reflection of how you absorb and process information.
2. Your preferred learning styles are considered your comfort zones for learning.
3. A preference for sequential learning means you tend toward a logical, step-by-step approach for taking in information.
4. A preference for random learning means you [...] structured means of
[...] either sequential or [...] a balanced learner, [...] her style. [...] style does not mean [...] rse at learning than [...] ns you have a [...] way of learning. [...] her styles will make [...] tion.

8. Instructors' teaching styles are generally a reflection of their preferred learning styles. By discovering instructors' learning styles and adapting to them, you can make learning easier.
9. To assess the teaching style of your instructors, listen for clues in how they present their material, determine what types of questions they ask, observe their behavior, and look at how they dress.
10. Your sensory learning preferences can be visual, auditory, or tactile. Adjusting your learning activities to match your preferences makes learning easier.
11. There are many other learning styles in addition to sequential and random. These include left brain and right brain learning, social and independent learning, and multiple intelligences.

Chapter Summary

Provides a recap of the key points from the chapter.

WEB LINK

www.studyweb.com

This large site has a comprehensive list of links dealing with learning styles. The links are listed under *professional development/learning styles.*

www.learningstyle.com

This site has another learning style survey with more information about different learning styles.

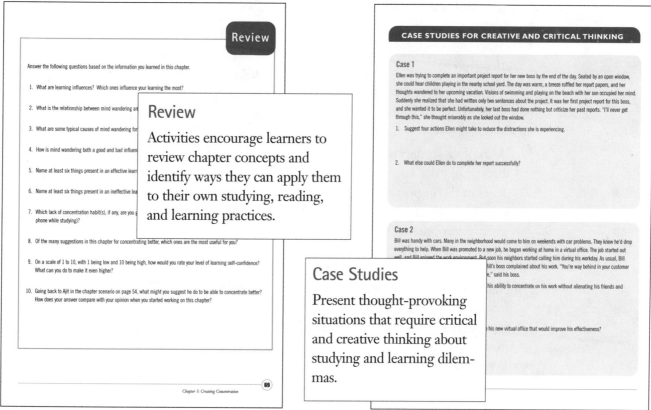

Review

Answer the following questions based on the information you learned in this chapter.

1. What are learning influences? Which ones influence your learning the most?
2. What is the relationship between mind wandering an[...]
3. What are some typical causes of mind wandering for [...]
4. How is mind wandering both a good and bad influen[...]
5. Name at least six things present in an effective lear[...]
6. Name at least six things present in an ineffective lea[...]
7. Which lack of concentration habit(s), if any, are you g[...] phone while studying)?
8. Of the many suggestions in this chapter for concentrating better, which ones are the most useful for you?
9. On a scale of 1 to 10, with 1 being low and 10 being high, how would you rate your level of learning self-confidence? What can you do to make it even higher?
10. Going back to Ajit in the chapter scenario on page 54, what might you suggest he do to be able to concentrate better? How does your answer compare with your opinion when you started working on this chapter?

Review

Activities encourage learners to review chapter concepts and identify ways they can apply them to their own studying, reading, and learning practices.

CASE STUDIES FOR CREATIVE AND CRITICAL THINKING

Case 1

Ellen was trying to complete an important project report for her new boss by the end of the day. Seated by an open window, she could hear children playing in the nearby school yard. The day was warm, a breeze ruffled her report papers, and her thoughts wandered to her upcoming vacation. Visions of swimming and playing on the beach with her son occupied her mind. Suddenly she realized that she had written only two sentences about the project. It was her first project report for this boss, and she wanted it to be perfect. Unfortunately, her last boss had done nothing but criticize her past reports. "I'll never get through this," she thought miserably as she looked out the window.

1. Suggest four actions Ellen might take to reduce the distractions she is experiencing.

2. What else could Ellen do to complete her report successfully?

Case 2

Bill was handy with cars. Many in the neighborhood would come to him on weekends with car problems. They knew he'd drop everything to help. When Bill was promoted to a new job, he began working at home in a virtual office. The job started out well, and Bill enjoyed the work environment. But soon his neighbors started calling him during his workday. As usual, Bill [...] Bill's boss complained about his work. "You're way behind in your customer [...]e," said his boss.

[...] his ability to concentrate on his work without alienating his friends and

[...] his new virtual office that would improve his effectiveness?

Case Studies

Present thought-provoking situations that require critical and creative thinking about studying and learning dilemmas.

*S*uccess Skills: Strategies for Study and Lifelong Learning equips users with the learning and study skills required in today's academic and workplace environments. With a focus on learning how to learn, critical thinking, reading comprehension, and managing information, this text-workbook prepares users to make successful learning an ongoing part of their academic and career development.

This totally new edition of Abby Marks-Beale's *Study Skills: The Tools for Active Learning* emphasizes key areas that are vital to successful lifelong learning:

- learning how to learn
- managing time and tasks
- building reading comprehension
- effective listening and note-taking
- improving memory and concentration
- successful test taking
- thinking critically and creatively
- gathering information and writing effectively

Thirteen newly-organized chapters offer a fresh design with engaging instructional features:

- Workplace scenarios and examples throughout the text engage students in the importance of ongoing learning in both academic and work environments.
- Numerous self-check, critical thinking, and review activities challenge learners to recall information, think critically about chapter concepts, and analyze their own study habits.
- Web Links apply technology to learning processes and suggest web sites to visit for additional information on lifelong learning subjects.
- Case Studies present thought-provoking situations that require critical and creative thinking about studying and learning dilemmas. These cases illustrate the importance of good learning habits both in school and at work.
- Focus on Ethics presents ethical dilemmas for analysis and problem solving. These features consider the ethical implications in managing time, using technology, and working with others in a learning or working environment.

Supplementary Materials

Success Skills: Strategies for Study and Lifelong Learning is supported by extensive tools that make instruction easier:

- The updated Instructor's Manual provides general guidelines for instruction and specific suggestions pertaining to each chapter. Also included are suggestions for guiding discussion, facilitating activities, and working through case problems.
- An Electronic Test Bank contains questions for comprehensive review and assessment. The software allows for easy generation of tests and editing of individual questions.
- A new Instructor Resource CD-ROM provides PowerPoint presentation slides, links to helpful web sites, additional readings and study scenarios, and a free trial version of Ace Reader software for improving reading speed and comprehension.

A Word from the Author

CONGRATULATIONS! By picking up this book, you have expressed a desire to discover how to make your learning easier.

You may have this book because an instructor required it or you may have picked it up out of curiosity. For whatever reason, you probably have a very personal need to learn from this book. Think about what you want to know or do as a result of working with this book, what you want from your formal education, and the kinds of jobs or careers you envision yourself having. You might want to write your thoughts down and keep them in a safe place to refer back to from time to time while you go through this book. They will remind you of your personal desire for learning more about how-to-learn.

This book is intended to honor and identify who you are currently as a learner. It is also geared to provide you with the awareness, knowledge, and tools you need to build the skills for lifelong learning. Ultimately, it will guide you in understanding what you can do to be a more efficient and effective learner.

The learning strategies discussed in this book are meant to be used for learning tasks in school, at work, and in your personal life. You will find, however, there is a strong emphasis on academic learning. If you can learn to use it for school, you can learn to use it in life and work.

Because I know there is no one best way to learn, I have provided you with a buffet of learning strategies from which to choose. Your job is to try them all and find those that work best for you. To help me help others, I would appreciate knowing what works or doesn't work for you.

Please send your feedback via e-mail to Abby@AbbyLearn.com or via snail mail to Abby Marks-Beale, The Reading Edge, PO Box 4212, Yalesville, CT 06492.

Keep in mind that the road to knowledge begins with the turn of a page. Enjoy learning!

Acknowledgments

I am grateful for many people who helped make this book come to life. To all of the following contributors, I am extremely appreciative of their skillful sharing of time, expertise, and experience:

- **Charlotte J. Foster**, founder of *Multivariant Learning Systems Corporation*, and **Dr. Thomas G. McCain**, president of *Learning Builders*, contributed the foundation for Chapter 2 on Discovering Your Learning Style.

- **Louise Loomis, Ed.D.**, founder and Executive Director of *The Thinking Center for Creativity and Problem Solving* (www.thethinkingcenter.com) in Hartford, CT, contributed her insightful ideas about thinking to Chapter 11 on Using Your Critical and Creative Mind. Her "brain-wise" workshops make knowledge about thinking and learning useable for the general public.

- **Charles Seiter, Ph.D.** makes Finding Information on the Web easier with his contributions to Chapter 12. He has written twenty books on computing topics. A former chemistry professor, he got caught up in the personal computer revolution and the rise of the Web and writes regularly for *PC World* and *Macworld*.

- **Mel Lane Donoghue, Ed.D.**, founder and director of QED & Associates, created the Cases for Creative and Critical Thinking found at the end of each chapter. She teaches college courses in creative thinking and problem solving as well as other personal and professional development topics.

- I am indebted to **Nancy Leary**, my trusty office assistant, who diligently read through every chapter and provided valuable feedback. Thanks also to **Pamela Mullan** who expertly surfed the web locating appropriate web links.
- I am grateful for the creative feedback and insightful additions from Fran Castiello, Anita Cazenave, T.T. Tok, Vanda North of The Buzan Centre, Ajit Gopalakrishnan, and Bill Roland and the students at Gateway Community College.
- To all of the authors of the books I researched (listed in the bibliography) as well as those I haven't yet found, thank you for your significant contributions to this important field.
- And last, but certainly not least, I am most thankful to my husband Christopher, who is always there for me with love, support, and friendship. I dedicate this book to him and to my two sons, Jonathan and Michael.

Abby Marks-Beale

Reviewers

The publisher and author gratefully acknowledge the contributions of the following manuscript reviewers:

James M. Anderson
Notre Dame School
Wichita Falls, Texas

Pamela Donehew-Lambert
West Georgia Technical College
LaGrange, Georgia

Shelly Grevillius
Dunwoody Institute
Minneapolis, Minnesota

Jonathan Keiser
Dunwoody Institute
Minneapolis, Minnesota

Susan Pehl
Modesto Junior College
Modesto, California

Thomas Young Smith, Sr.
West Georgia Technical College
LaGrange, Georgia

About the Author

Abby Marks-Beale is the founder of The Reading Edge, a speaking, training and consulting business that specializes in helping busy professionals, educators, and students to read, learn, and do more in less time. Her extensive client list includes Fortune 500 companies, small businesses, schools, universities, associations and individuals. She is a member of the ASCD Faculty (Association of Supervision and Curriculum Development), an exclusive team of expert consultants who craft, design, and deliver individualized professional development programs for educators. Abby is also the author of *10 Days to Faster Reading* (Warner Books, 2001). Abby holds a B.A. in Spanish from Boston University and an M.S. in Adult Learning from Southern Connecticut State University. She believes one's formal education is just a continuation of the lifelong process in learning how to learn. For more information, check out Abby's web site at www.AbbyLearn.com.

How to Use the Self-Check Feature

The Self-Check in each chapter, provided it is answered honestly and accurately, is one of the most important tools of this text. You will use it to evaluate your learning habits at the beginning of every chapter and to then re-evaluate them at the end of the book in the Final Self-Check located in Appendix A. The objective of the exercise is to assess your current skills and habits and then hopefully see improvement based on what you learned.

After each chapter introduction, under the subheading of Self-Check, there are ten statements. You are asked to respond with one of the three choices: "yes/frequently," "sometimes," or "no/never." Your response should be based on your current knowledge, experience, and habits. The following Self-Check for Chapter One includes one student's sample responses.

After responding to all ten statements, first count the number of Y's you have circled and place that number in the appropriate blank in the "Rate Yourself" section located at the end of the exercise box. Then do the same for the S's and then the N's. Now multiply the number of responses by the number next to it.

> **"** Success has always been easy to measure. It is the distance between one's origins and one's final achievements. **"**
>
> —Michael Korda
> Contemporary author

One Student's Sample Response to Chapter One Self-Check

SELF-CHECK

The following self-evaluation will give you an idea of how familiar, or unfamiliar, you are with some of the topics and terms discussed in this chapter. After reading each statement, circle the letter Y, S, or N to indicate the answer that is most appropriate for you. Answer honestly; rate yourself at the end; then complete the information for Chapter 1 in Appendix A.

Y = yes; frequently   S = sometimes   N = no; never

1.	I generally have a positive attitude while learning.	(Y)	S	N
2.	I sit near the instructor or meeting leader.	Y	(S)	N
3.	I actively and fearlessly participate in discussions.	Y	S	(N)
4.	I listen carefully and take good notes.	Y	(S)	N
5.	I work or study in an appropriate environment for learning.	Y	(S)	N
6.	I take good notes and write questions while reading.	Y	(S)	N
7.	I am prepared and complete my work on time.	Y	(S)	N
8.	I keep a calendar and follow a schedule.	Y	S	(N)
9.	I ask for and get help when needed.	Y	(S)	N
10.	I learn from my mistakes.	(Y)	S	N

Rate Yourself:

Number of Ys	2	x	100	=	200	
Number of Ss	6	x	50	=	300	
Number of Ns	2	x	0	=	0	Total 500

Rate Yourself Sample

The highest number you can have is 1,000 (10 x 100) and the lowest is 0 (0 x 10). Getting the highest number is NOT the objective here—showing honest improvement from beginning to end is.

Once you have completed the "Rate Yourself" section, turn to the Self-Check Progress Chart in Appendix A at the end of this text. Take your total number of points and fill in the bar graph above "Begin" for Chapter 1 as shown in the sample.

Sometime during your course of study, depending on your instructor's syllabus, you may be asked to complete all or parts of the "Final Self-Check" found in Appendix A. The "Final Self-Check" is all of the self-check statements from all 13 chapters, separated by chapter number and name. There are 130 statements in all. If you have completed all of the chapters, then you may eventually be responding to all of the statements. If you have not worked with all of the chapters, then you will only be responding to those chapter statements that you have completed.

After you have finished responding to the statements in the Final Self-Check, you follow the same procedure for completing the bar graph except this time fill in the bar graph above End for each chapter. See sample on the right.

Compare your beginning and ending bar graphs. Hopefully, you will see a rise in your graph from beginning to end. The more Y's you have, the more efficient and effective learner you have become. The S's are habits you are working on and put to use as needed. The N's that still remain are areas you need to pay attention to and continue to work on.

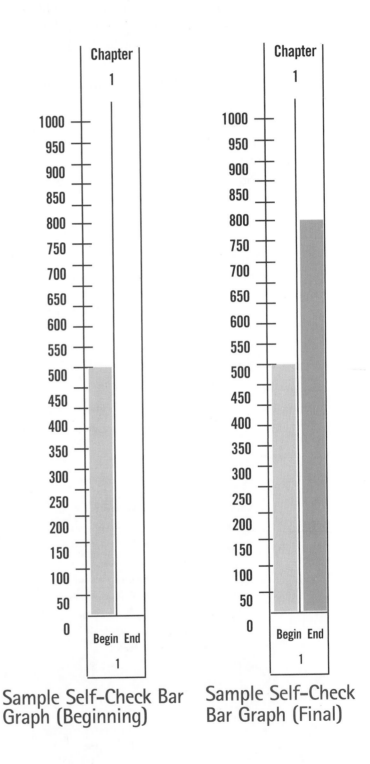

Sample Self-Check Bar Graph (Beginning)

Sample Self-Check Bar Graph (Final)

Success Skills

CONTENTS

Chapter 4: Learning Time Management 71

Chapter 5: Study Smart 106

Success Skills

Chapter 13: Writing In The Real World 322

Appendices

Success Skills

After Yvette finished high school, she took a job as a home health aide. Going directly to college was out of the question, as she needed to support herself. Now five years later and with an infant son, she has decided she wants to become a licensed practical nurse (LPN). A position in this field will provide extra income and a better family schedule. Though college will cost a great deal of time and money, she realizes it is an investment in the future.

Yvette successfully applies and is accepted at her local community college. Chemistry 101 is the first class she is scheduled to take as a part-time student. She is anxious, yet excited, to begin her training program.

During the first class, Yvette becomes worried because she has difficulty understanding the material. Later she reads and rereads the textbook assignments, hoping they will begin to make sense. Then she learns she must complete experiments in the chemistry lab after only two more classes.

Since Yvette is not a quitter, she continues to go to class and attempts to do the homework, but she often hands in incomplete assignments. She becomes more and more frustrated and starts to feel inadequate. She desperately wants to make it through her college program but is feeling quite helpless.

What advice do you have for Yvette?

In This Chapter

1.1 Distinguishing Between Active and Passive Learning
1.2 Advantages of Active Learning
1.3 On Becoming an Active Learner

Chapter Goals

After studying and working with the information in this chapter, you should be able to:

♦ Distinguish between active and passive learning.
♦ Recognize the advantages to becoming an active learner.
♦ Understand how active learning skills can help you now and in the future.
♦ Identify ways to develop a more positive attitude toward learning.
♦ Develop methods to become an active participant in your learning.

> ❝ The illiterate of the future are not those who can't read or write, but those who cannot learn, unlearn, and relearn. ❞
>
> —Alvin Toffler
> Futurist

Your first exposure to independent work and studying was sometime around the first grade. You were instructed to go home, complete your work, and bring it back the next day. As the years progressed, your assignments became more challenging in both scope and content. Out of necessity, you probably figured out on your own how to get the work done.

Some learners are more successful with their self-taught learning skills than others. Many learners spend more time studying than is necessary because they use ineffective study skills.

When people continue formal learning beyond high school, many find that their self-taught learning skills are not enough. Whether in college or on the job, they work hard to learn what they need to know. Just as a car's engine may run for years with little maintenance, so, too, can some people make it through high school while giving little attention to learning skills. Learning in college or the workplace, however, proves to be quite a different story!

Only when a car gets a tune-up and a person acquires effective learning skills do they function efficiently. Any learning *is* work, but learning can be a lot easier when the proper skills are applied. *Working harder or longer is not the same as working smarter.*

This chapter (1) identifies the differences between active and passive learning, (2) provides simple ideas and strategies for becoming an active learner, and (3) encourages you to create your own action plan for learning success.

When you're learning, you're making use of many tools available to you. What tools do *you* use for learning?

Success Skills

SELF-CHECK

The following self-evaluation will give you an idea of how familiar, or unfamiliar, you are with some of the topics and terms discussed in this chapter. After reading each statement, circle the letter Y, S, or N to indicate the answer that is most appropriate for you. Answer honestly; rate yourself at the end; then complete the information for Chapter 1 in Appendix A.

Y = yes; frequently	S = sometimes	N = no; never

1. I generally have a positive attitude while learning.	Y S N
2. I sit near the instructor or meeting leader.	Y S N
3. I actively and fearlessly participate in discussions.	Y S N
4. I listen carefully and take good notes.	Y S N
5. I work or study in an appropriate environment for learning.	Y S N
6. I take good notes and write questions while reading.	Y S N
7. I am prepared and complete my work on time.	Y S N
8. I keep a calendar and follow a schedule.	Y S N
9. I ask for and get help when needed.	Y S N
10. I learn from my mistakes.	Y S N

Rate Yourself:

Number of Ys	_____	x	100	=	_____
Number of Ss	_____	x	50	=	_____
Number of Ns	_____	x	0	=	_____ Total_____

1.1 DISTINGUISHING BETWEEN ACTIVE AND PASSIVE LEARNING

The terms *active* and *passive* are opposites of each other. Being **active** simply means *doing something* or *being conscious and mindful*, while being **passive** means *doing nothing* or *being unconscious* and *mindless*. Though you can sometimes learn mindlessly and unconsciously, those who are mindful and conscious are far more effective and successful in their learning.

The process of *osmosis* is a helpful example in demonstrating the difference between active and passive learning. **Osmosis** is a passive process by which a person learns information or ideas *without conscious effort*. As an example, you might have learned how bees make honey simply by tuning into a program on television.

If, however, you place a book under your pillow before going to sleep, the information contained in the book will not absorb into the pillow nor into your head. In this case, the passive process of osmosis doesn't work, so you must become more active in your learning process to absorb the material in the book.

> **"** To furnish the means of acquiring knowledge is . . . the greatest benefit that can be conferred upon mankind. **"**
>
> —John Quincy Adams
> Sixth president of the
> United States

Read the following list of learning habits. Put a P on the line next to those habits that you think are passive and an A next to those you think are active. At the bottom of the list, add three more passive and three more active habits. Feel free to work with a partner.

_____ Frequently daydreaming about a non-related topic

_____ Mentally relating what you know to the new information

_____ Doing a half-hearted job

_____ Ignoring deadlines

_____ Comparing notes with someone else

_____ Documenting from written material

_____ Not asking for help (or knowing when to ask)

_____ Sharing with others what you are learning

_____ Not participating in discussions

_____ Sitting far from the speaker

_____ Waiting until the last minute to do the work

_____ Listening carefully and/or taking notes

_____ Reading at a time of day when you are most tired

_____ Learning from mistakes

P _____

P _____

P _____

A _____

A _____

A _____

Throughout this book, more detailed explanations will be given about each of the active habits listed above, as well as others. Each explanation will help you better understand how and why being more active in the learning process is better than being passive. As you attend classes or meetings, read and take notes, and perform other learning functions, be aware of how active or passive you are. The more active, the better!

Checkpoint 1.1

1. Do you think most people are passive learners or active learners? Why?

2. Do you think you are mostly an active or passive learner? Why?

3. What do you want to learn from this chapter?

1.2 ADVANTAGES OF ACTIVE LEARNING

Many people are able to make it through their schooling with self-taught learning skills. Some of these people are *observers* while others are *participants* in the learning process. **Observers** learn by paying careful attention to what they see, while **participants**

learn by getting involved in the learning process.

Beginning electricians can learn a lot by observing someone with more experience install a light switch, but that does not necessarily mean they will be able to perform the same task successfully the first time on their own. If, however, they participate in the installation, instead of simply observing it, they will probably be more successful when they try it on their own. Similarly, first-time computer users learn faster and understand more if they are able to work on a computer while learning about it.

Because active learners are involved in their learning process, they understand more when new information is introduced. As a result, they learn with less effort and in less time. The Chinese proverb in the box above describes the value of active learning.

Becoming an active learner is a simple and rewarding way to gain knowledge without wasting valuable time and money. The information in this chapter will provide specific steps you can take to become more involved in your learning process.

> " Tell me and I will forget;
> show me and I may remember;
> involve me and I will understand. "
>
> —Chinese Proverb

Checkpoint 1.2

1. What is the difference between an observer and a participant? Which are you?

2. Based on the Chinese proverb in the box at the top of this page, describe the best way to learn to change a tire?

3. Which learning skills identified in the chapter titles on page 8 do you already know?

4. Which of these learning skills do you need to learn more about?

Think about something you recently learned how to do. It could have been learning a new computer program, balancing a checkbook, or trying a new recipe. Now respond to the following questions.

What did you learn to do?_____

How did you learn it?_____

Which learning method(s) was used: *told, shown,* or *involved in the process*?_____

In your opinion, what are the differences between each type of learning method?

Telling: _____

_____

Showing:_____

_____

Involving:_____

_____

Which methods do you prefer to learn by? Why?_____

_____

Why Learning Skills Are So Important

Developing learning-how-to-learn skills is essential in this technology age because companies continue to use advanced technologies that require a high level of skill from employees. Work processes are being reorganized so people work in teams toward higher and more efficient performance.

This requires a work force that is highly adaptable to gaining new knowledge. A company is considered successful when it has an abundance of **intellectual capital**, or a smart work force that is able to continuously learn and improve.

Learning-how-to-learn skills are the keys to your success in life. Possessing and using

effective and efficient learning skills means that (1) you feel confident in your ability to learn and (2) you spend less time learning more. Not only do these skills help you achieve academic success, but they also lead to career and family success.

You may wonder how all of this relates to your future. In Figure 1, you will see chapter by chapter how each of the learning skills discussed in this textbook can be used in the future. You may want to return to this information later to reinforce your learning.

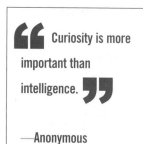

> Curiosity is more important than intelligence.
>
> —Anonymous

Figure 1-1 How Learning-How-To-Learn Skills Relate to the Future

No.	Chapter Title	Relationship to the Future
1	Learning by Doing	Active learning is useful for all types of life activities, including job hunting, career development, taking care of your health, and raising a family.
2	Discovering Your Learning Style	Understanding that people learn differently enables you to (1) understand your learning abilities and (2) adapt better to others.
3	Creating Concentration	In order to read or learn effectively, you need concentration. This involves gaining control over your work environment to keep your mind focused.
4	Learning Time Management	Effective and efficient people use some form of time management system, most commonly a calendar, to schedule time for school, work, and family activities. Without it, many things may not get done.
5	Study Smart	Knowing how to study smart means you know the factors necessary for success in the real world, such as being prepared and learning from your mistakes.
6	Taking Notes from Lecture	Organizing information on paper is a useful skill for school and business activities, such as lectures, meetings, and training workshops.
7	Taking Notes from Reading Material	Organizing information on paper is a useful skill for school and business activities including report writing, and project tracking.
8	Reading Comprehension Skills	Reading professional journals, newspapers, magazines, and textbooks will increase your reading comprehension and retention. Having a good vocabulary helps you read, speak, and write better, making you a more desirable candidate for many professions.
9	Survival Reading Skills	Knowing how to read effectively and faster will enable you to read more in less time.
10	Mastering Tests	Tests are not only taken in a school setting. Many professions offer certificate programs that require passing a series of tests. Other types of tests are necessary for gaining or keeping employment.
11	Using Your Creative and Critical Mind	Using your creative mind allows you to unleash possibilities for better problem solving and global thinking. Using your critical mind is important for all the decisions you will ever make, including those for your career, your family, and yourself.
12	Finding Information on the Web	In this technology age, using computers is essential to locating information you can also use computers to you research schools and career opportunities.
13	Writing in the Real World	Writing is a part of most careers. Becoming good at it will help you to perform your job more effectively.

Success Skills

1.3 ON BECOMING AN ACTIVE LEARNER

Active learners can be described as people who are **empowered**. They feel capable and confident in their ability to learn anything they  want, know what they have to do in order to learn, ask when they don't know, and then proceed to learn. Active learners continually seek ways to make learning easy and rewarding. They want to learn as much as they can in the least amount of time. Most important, active learners possess a feeling of self-confidence and high self-esteem as a result of their involvement in learning. Anyone can become an active learner once they know how.

To become an active learner, read carefully the remaining sections of this chapter. After reading each section, you will have the option of checking one of the following statements in the question mark box.

❑ I understand this section and have no questions.

❑ I don't understand or I need to know more and will ask about _____

If you understand what you read, place a check mark (✓) next to the statement "I understand this section and have no questions." If, after reading, you are unsure about what you just read or have a question about it, place a check mark (✓) next to the statement "I don't understand or I need to know more and will ask

about . . . ." Then write your question(s) in the blank. At the end of this chapter, you will be asked to use the information you have read to work on an action plan.

Know Your Purpose and Responsibility

With every learning activity, you have a purpose and a responsibility. Your **purpose** is the reason *why* you are doing the activity, and your **responsibility** is *how* you are accountable for it. For example, let's say your instructor assigns 15 pages of material to read and 10 questions to answer. What is the purpose? Why are you reading it? Here are several possible responses:

♦ You want to learn about the topic.

♦ The reading was assigned.

♦ You know you are going to discuss the material in class tomorrow and you want to be prepared.

Your responsibility, besides being ready for the discussion, is to answer the ten assigned questions. It might help to take notes so you can review the information for a test later in the term. You also need to think about how else you might use the information, such as for a paper, for a job interview, or for some future project.

Do you understand ?

❑ I understand this section and have no questions.

❑ I don't understand or I need to know more and will ask about _____

_____

ACTIVITY 3

In your job at a retail store, you are asked to learn a new procedure for documenting refunds. You have been given a five-page memo to read, which gives you the details for performing this new procedure.

What is your purpose for reading the memo? _____

What is your responsibility? _____

You just bought an ear thermometer to use in taking your child's temperature. Before using it, you need to read the instructional brochure enclosed with the thermometer. _____

What is your purpose for reading the brochure? _____

What is your responsibility? _____

By taking a few moments to get yourself mentally prepared to do the work, you are identifying a reason to begin working (your purpose) as well as identifying a point at which you are finished (your responsibility). People who keep their purpose and responsibility in mind while doing a learning activity find that they not only concentrate better but also learn and retain more.

ACTIVITY 4

Think of a learning activity you have to do for school or work, and consider your purpose and responsibility. Fill in your answers to each of the following questions.

Learning Activity 1 _____

What is your purpose? _____

What is your responsibility? _____

Learning Activity 2 _____

What is your purpose? _____

What is your responsibility? _____

Writing down your purpose and responsibility is not necessary once you have trained yourself to mentally ask the questions.

Success Skills

Work in a Conducive Environment

In Chapter 3, the ingredients of a good working environment for improving concentration are discussed in detail. For now, start thinking about your own work environment and how it compares to the conditions suggested below.

♦ A quiet, distraction-free place

♦ A comfortable chair at a clutter-free desk or table

♦ A comfortable room temperature

♦ Good lighting

♦ The materials you need, including writing utensils, highlighter, reading materials, notepaper

Sometimes working outside your regular work area (such as in a school library, an empty office, or a conference room) can improve your concentration.

Develop a Positive Belief in Yourself

You may not be aware of it, but every time you become involved in a learning situation, you begin with a predetermined attitude or belief in your ability to do the activity. What is your attitude about your ability level?

Your confidence in your ability to learn can make your learning either easier or more difficult. If you believe the work is easy and you can do it, then it will be easy. If you believe the work is too hard or that you can't do it, then it will be hard. A negative attitude encourages you to give up.

If, on the other hand, you are determined to learn as much as you can, no matter how hard the work or how much of it, you will learn more easily. A positive attitude provides you with the persistence you need to continue until you succeed.

If you believe in yourself—in the fact that you can learn anything you want—you will possess the confidence necessary to succeed in all aspects of life. You can begin to gain this confidence by learning to replace failure words with success words.

Do you understand ?

❑ I understand this section and have no questions.

❑ I don't understand or I need to know more and will ask about _____

_____

ACTIVITY 5

Provide the success word that means the opposite of each failure word.

Failure Words	Success Words
1. can't	1. _____
2. fail	2. _____
3. impossible	3. _____
4. no	4. _____

Now create a typical statement using each of the failure words; then rewrite the statement using the success word. For example, "I can't read that much in a night" becomes "I can read that much in a night."

1. _____

_____

2. _____

_____

3. _____

_____

4. _____

_____

Think about the difference between each failure and success statement you wrote. Which is a more typical statement for you? Are success words part of your vocabulary? If so, good for you! If not, why not start using them now?

A middle step on the way to a more positive attitude is to use a coping attitude. A **coping attitude** is neither positive nor negative, but one that helps you deal with the work or situation.

> In order to succeed, you must know what you are doing, like what you are doing, and believe in what you are doing.
>
> —Will Rogers

Think about or discuss with others the differences each attitude brings to your ability to learn. In the first column, list some of your negative attitudes. In the second column, rewrite the negative attitudes into positive or coping attitudes.

Negative Attitudes

I can't do it.

I have too much work to do.

I dislike my instructor or boss.

The work is too hard.

I don't have time to study.

_____

_____

_____

_____

_____

_____

_____

Positive or Coping Attitudes

I can do it. I can deal with it.

I need to set aside more time today to do my work.

_____

_____

_____

_____

_____

_____

_____

_____

_____

_____

With any attitude, be aware that *you* make the choice to think either positively or negatively about your abilities and work load.

If you find that you didn't do as well on a test as you had hoped, which of the following statements is closest to your attitude?

Positive: *What a great opportunity to learn from my mistakes!*

Coping: *How can I do better next time?*

Negative: *I'm a failure. The test was too hard.*

Developing a more positive attitude overnight may not be realistic. But by the time you complete this textbook, you will have new approaches to all kinds of learning tasks that will make it easier to think positively about your abilities as a student.

The late Earl Nightingale, a popular speaker on personal development said, "You go in the direction of your most dominant thoughts." This means that if you think negatively, you will more likely end up with negative results. If you think positively, you will more likely end up with positive results. Remember, the choice is yours.

In reaction to each of the following situations, create a positive, coping, and negative response.

You find out a week in advance that you have two tests in one day.

Positive: _____

Coping: _____

Negative: _____

Your boss gives you an extra project on top of your already heavy work load.

Positive: _____

Coping: _____

Negative: _____

You have trouble learning a new computer program.

Positive: _____

Coping: _____

Negative: _____

You have to write a résumé, but you are not sure how to do it.

Positive: _____

Coping: _____

Negative: _____

Do you understand ?

- ❏ I understand this section and have no questions.

- ❏ I don't understand or I need to know more and will ask about _____

  _____

Engage in Your Learning Process

Most people have mastered "the look"—where you stare blankly at someone while trying to act interested. In reality, your mind is wandering more than listening or learning. It could be that the person speaking is not very interesting or that you are just tired or unmotivated that day.

No matter the situation, it is your responsibility to understand what the person is saying. In a learning situation, the key is to engage with the speaker. To engage means to get either mentally or physically involved and to actively participate. Active participation (1) increases concentration, (2) improves listening, (3) seems to make the time go quicker, and (4) positively affects overall learning.

How can you actively take part in a learning situation? Five key ways to engage in your learning process are discussed in the following sections.

Be there and do it

One obvious way to increase your potential for learning is to be physically and mentally present. Whether you are learning in a classroom or lab or searching the Internet, learning sessions are a very important part of the learning process.

Since learning is an individual activity, there is no substitute for being there.

In every learning situation, you have the choice of acting like a sponge or a rock. Learners who act like sponges soak up the information through active participation, demonstrate a positive learning attitude, and possess an eagerness to learn. On the other hand, learners who act like rocks generally have a negative learning attitude and are, in effect, just occupying space. It should be no surprise that sponges learn more than rocks.

Do you understand ?

❑ I understand this section and have no questions.

❑ I don't understand or I need to know more and will ask about _____

_____

Who are you? Are you an active learner, like the sponge who soaks up knowledge, or a passive learner, like the rock who expects knowledge to come to it?

PASSIVE

ACTIVE

Sit close to the action

This is an easy way to ensure your participation in the learning process. Sitting up front limits distractions from others and gives you a clear view of the speaker and the speaker a clear view of you. Learners in front usually sit up taller than those in the back and thus appear more eager and ready to learn. Though you may feel a little uncomfortable at first, try sitting in front in your next class. You just might find yourself concentrating better and learning more.

Do you understand

- ❏ I understand this section and have no questions.
- ❏ I don't understand or I need to know more and will ask about _____

_____

Fearlessly ask and answer questions

To ask an intelligent question and to respond intelligently, you have to be listening and concentrating. Too many learners feel that asking questions makes them look stupid. Actually, learners who don't ask questions don't learn nearly as much or as easily as those who do.

Remember that you aren't expected to know it all; that's why you are studying—to learn. Your job is to ask questions so you can learn more. In the workplace, active questioning is essential for clarifying work tasks and communicating efficiently with others.

Questions, of course, can be asked during the learning activity but also after it, during office hours, or during a scheduled appointment.

As long as the question gets answered, it doesn't matter where it is asked. Remember to make a list of your questions; otherwise, you may forget them.

Not all questions need to be asked aloud. Just being curious about a topic can help you learn more. Create your own list of questions about a topic; then actively seek the answers to them as you study and learn.

Questions are easy to ask when you use the **5Ws** and **H**: who, what, when, where, why, and how. For example, if you are taking a computer course and the day's topic is "Font Styles and When to Use Them," you might think about any or all of the following questions:

1. Who uses the fonts?
2. What are the font styles?
3. When should the font be changed?
4. Where do I get fonts?
5. Why should fonts be used?
6. How many fonts are available?

Think of yourself as a young child, a curious student of the entire world. By learning to ask questions, you will understand the world better while learning more in less time.

Do you understand

- ❏ I understand this section and have no questions.
- ❏ I don't understand or I need to know more and will ask about _____

_____

Success Skills

If you are taking an electronics course and the day's topic is "Measuring with an Oscilloscope," what questions might you ask? Remember to use the 5Ws and H listed on page 18 to help you come up with your questions.

1. _____
2. _____
3. _____
4. _____
5. _____
6. _____
7. _____
8. _____

If you are taking a travel or tourism course and the day's topic is "Handling Cancellations," what questions might you ask? Remember to use the 5Ws and H listed on page 18 to help you come up with your questions.

1. _____
2. _____
3. _____
4. _____
5. _____
6. _____
7. _____
8. _____

If you are taking a learning skills course and the day's topic is "Active Participation for More Learning," what questions might you ask? Remember to use the 5Ws and H listed on page 16 to help you come up with your questions.

1. _____
2. _____
3. _____
4. _____
5. _____
6. _____

Take notes

Taking effective notes is like taking a picture for later reference of what you saw, heard, or read. Learners who take notes are more focused, have information to study from, and—most importantly—daydream less. Even if you are not required to take notes, creating your own notes will help you learn more.

Knowing how to take good notes will transform the act of reading—which for many individuals is a passive activity—into an active process. Note taking while reading forces you to concentrate because you are actively seeking out important information to write. *More concentration means less mind wandering. Less mind wandering means more learning in less time.*

An example of notes from part of a chapter of the text *Civil Litigation for the Paralegal* is shown below. Notice that the notes are written in an easy-to-read format and in the learner's own words. When it comes time to study, the learner will not have to reread the chapter, but only refer back to the notes. In Chapters 6 and 7, how to take effective notes will be discussed in more detail. In the meantime, take notes as best you can to promote active participation in learning.

Get help

Even the most active learners need help. Assistance can come from your instructor, boss, or fellow learners. The time to ask for help is *not* the day of or the day before an exam or a project deadline. Starting to prepare at least a week ahead will ensure that the help you need will be available when you want it. Classroom instructors generally do not have a lot of sympathy for students who wait until the last minute to ask for help. Bosses have even less tolerance for employees who wait to ask for help.

Do you understand ?

- ❏ I understand this section and have no questions.

- ❏ I don't understand or I need to know more and will ask about _____

		9/24/02
pp 3-22	1-1 _What Civil Litigation Is_	
Civil Litigation	=	resolving private disputes thru courtesy
Trial or hearing	=	parties present evidence to judge
		or jury
Litigation attys &		
assts.	=	gather & analyze facts/research law
		— legal doc's prep'd & filed
		— witnesses interviewed
		— other evidence identified & located

Where to Look for Help

Though it may seem like you are all alone in your quest for learning success, know that you are not. There are many people you can talk to, places you can go, and materials you can read to help you reach your goals.

People you can talk to

There are plenty of people with whom you can talk who will be able to provide you with the information you need regarding school-related issues, work-related issues, and personal issues. In the following chart, you will see a list of these people and descriptions of how they can help you. Most are specialists whose job is to give you assistance and advice.

Figure 1–2   People You Can Go To for Help

People You Can Talk To	How They Can Help You
Course Instructor	♦ Answers questions about the course ♦ Helps you manage course requirements
Other students in class	♦ Provides an academic support system ♦ Provides a network of friends
Academic Advisor or Guidance Counselor	♦ Helps you select courses you need to graduate ♦ Helps you decide on a major ♦ Lends support for personal problems
Career Counselor	♦ Evaluates where your interests lie ♦ Provides information about careers ♦ Assesses your employment opportunities ♦ Sets up internships ♦ Provides information on available jobs
Tutor	♦ Provides extra academic assistance
Librarian	♦ Helps you find answers to questions
Head of Department	♦ Assists with problems related to a course
Department Secretary	♦ Answers questions about department requirements and course offerings
Boss	♦ Provides feedback on skills you can improve upon for career growth
Resident Assistant (if you live on campus)	♦ Advises on campus services and student activities ♦ Lends support for academic problems
Athletic Coach (if you are on an athletic team)	♦ Lends support for personal issues

Chapter 1: Learning by Doing

Places you can go

There will probably be times when you have a question or problem and you don't know where to go for assistance. Be assured that many places are available to help you. Each school or business has a staff of knowledgeable people who are there to assist you. To find the specific addresses or phone numbers of their locations, look in a school or company catalog, in a campus directory, on a web site, or in a telephone directory.

Figure 1-3   Places You Can Go for Information

Places You Can Go	How They Can Help You
Learning Skills Center	◆ Assists in the development of reading, writing, math, or study skills that help you meet course requirements
Tutoring Center	◆ Provides assistance for your course work
Library	◆ Provides you with resources to answer questions
Human Resources Department	◆ Provides advice about career growth ◆ Provides information on jobs available within a company
Training Department	◆ Gives information on training programs available for further education
Student Activities Office	◆ Provides information about what is happening on campus
Student Government Office	◆ Provides information about campus events, clubs, and organizations
Career Development Center	◆ Provides information on careers; also evaluates your interests and skills
Computer Lab	◆ Assists with computer course work. Also helps you learn how to use a word processor
Academic Advising or Guidance Counselor Office	◆ Helps you choose your courses and manage your academic life
Registrar's Office	◆ Handles applications, registrations, grades, and transcripts of the courses you have taken
Financial Aid, Academic Assistance Office, or Bank	◆ Assists with money matters
Health Office/Infirmary	◆ Provides medical advice and help

Success Skills

Materials you can read

In addition to people you can talk to and places you can go, there are also materials you can read to find the information you seek. A school or company handbook will contain a wealth of information about policies, programs, services, and requirements. The school catalog usually contains a calendar that lets you know when classes begin and end, when holidays occur, when drop and add periods end, and when final exams are scheduled. The company handbook usually contains the company's mission statement, policies and services, and a list of training workshops or courses.

A course catalog, usually found in the admissions or registrar's office of a college or the training department of a company, will list all the information you need to register for a course, including dates and times and who the instructor will be. A school newspaper or company newsletter will provide you with information about upcoming events and other news. Bulletin boards and web sites are probably your best source for the most current information.

Learn from Your Mistakes

If you ask successful people how they got to where they are now, they will most likely tell you that while they did a lot of things right, they also made many mistakes along the way. Mistakes are a vital part of becoming successful, as long as you learn from your experiences.

Have you ever been unprepared for a class or a meeting? To prevent this from happening again, use a calendar to keep track of your responsibilities (see Chapter 4 for more information) and find a working partner who can be relied upon. People can and do make mistakes; but the key is to recognize that you have made a mistake and then act to prevent it from happening again.

Do you understand ?

- ❏ I understand this section and have no questions.
- ❏ I don't understand or I need to know more and will ask about _____

_____

List at least five common mistakes that learners make. By being aware of them, you can prevent them!

1. _____

2. _____

3. _____

4. _____

5. _____

Take Good Care of Yourself

Your health, or lack of it, greatly influences your ability to learn. The more mentally and physically prepared you are, the easier it is to learn. The more tired and stressed out you are, the harder it is to learn. You have the ability to control how well and how easily you learn by getting enough sleep, eating nutrition-packed meals, and exercising. Health problems increase with habits such as smoking and drinking alcohol, so it is advisable to avoid them. If you don't take good care of yourself, no one else will. (See Chapter 3 for more information.)

Checkpoint 1.3

1. Without looking back, list five active learning habits.

2. Which active learning habits have you already mastered?

3. Which do you want to master?

Smart Tip

You have now read a chapter's worth of information about active learning. Though reading about active learning is interesting, doing something with it is more rewarding.

On page 27, you will find an easy-to-use Awareness and Action Plan for building awareness toward active learning. Tear the page out. Photocopy as many as you need to complete one for each learning activity. This plan is meant to help you become aware of what you do, or not do, in your own learning process. The idea is to encourage changes in your habits so you can move from passive to active learning.

Chapter Summary

1. The terms *active* and *passive* are opposites. Being an active learner means you do something to make learning happen, while being a passive learner means you do nothing to make learning happen. Though you can sometimes learn from doing nothing, doing something makes learning more effective and successful.

2. Advantages of becoming an active learner include learning more in less time and knowing how to learn anything you want. Active learners also possess feelings of self-confidence and high self-esteem as a result of their involvement in learning.

3. Learning how-to-learn skills can help you succeed in school, at work, and at home.

4. With every learning task, you have a purpose and a responsibility. By giving yourself a reason to begin working (your purpose) as well as a point at which you are finished (your responsibility), you will concentrate better and learn and remember more of what you are working on.

5. If you believe in your ability to learn, you will possess the confidence necessary to succeed in any area of your life. You can begin to gain this confidence in yourself by replacing failure words with success words and negative attitudes with positive and coping attitudes.

6. This chapter describes many ways to be active in your learning. They include being there and doing it, sitting close to the action, fearlessly asking and answering questions, taking notes, getting help, and learning from your mistakes.

7. Every school and every company has resources you can turn to for help in answering questions or solving problems. These resources include people, places, and reading materials.

8. Your health, or lack of it, greatly influences your ability to learn. The more mentally and physically prepared you are, the easier it is to learn. Being tired and stressed out makes learning more difficult.

Key Terms and Concepts

5W's and H	intellectual capital	passive
active	observer	purpose
coping attitude	osmosis	responsibility
empowered	participant	

Focus on Ethics

You've been assigned to work on a project with a group of people you don't know very well. Most members of the team work hard, except for Tom. He seems unprepared, forgets important meetings, doesn't volunteer to help, rarely asks questions or contributes to discussions, and always seems tired. You've tried to be patient with him, but he doesn't seem to want to take responsibility for his part of the work.

How would you react? What could be the cause of his behavior? What can you suggest to Tom to help him take more responsibility for your group's success?

WEB LINK

Technology can be both something you need to learn for your job and a valuable source of learning on your own. But don't overlook the Internet as a valuable source on information on a wide range of topics.

Online universities make courses available electronically. Searches for business and organizations related to your work can help you learn more about the field you're in. Powerful search engines, such as www.metacrawler.com, or human-guided search resources, such as www.about.com or www.looksmart.com can help you find information on almost any topic, field, or industry.

Awareness and Action Plan

Name _____ Date _____

Learning Activity _____ Instructor's Name _____

Topic(s) of Discussion _____ Meeting Time: From _____ To _____

Today's Format (check those that apply)

_____Lecture _____Discussion _____AV Presentation _____Internet Class _____Other _____

1. Did I sit close to the action? (circle one)   Yes   No

    If yes, what did I notice about my learning? _____

    If no, what did I notice about my learning? _____

2. Did I actively participate in the discussion? (circle one)   Yes   No

    If yes, what did I do? _____

    What did I notice about my learning? _____

    If no, what did I notice about my learning? _____

3. Did I take notes? (circle one)   Yes   No

    If yes, what did I notice about my learning? _____

    If no, what did I notice about my learning? _____

4. Was I prepared (e.g., doing the work as assigned)? (circle one)   Yes   No

    If yes, what did I do to be prepared? _____

    What did I notice about my learning? _____

    If no, what did I notice about my learning? _____

5. Did I have a positive attitude about learning? (circle one)   Yes   No

    If yes, why did I have this attitude? _____

    What did I notice about my learning? _____

    If no, why did I have this attitude? _____

    What did I notice about my learning? _____

6. Did I make any mistakes? (circle one)   Yes   No

    If yes, what happened?_____

    What did I learn from it?_____

After the Learning Activity

7. Did I choose an appropriate working environment? (circle one)   Yes   No

    If yes, what did I notice about my learning?_____

    If no, what did I notice about my learning? _____

8. While reading, did I take notes or write down questions? (circle one)   Yes   No

    If yes, what did I notice about my learning?_____

    If no, what did I notice about my learning?_____

9. In general, as a learner today, I was_____

10. Next time I plan to_____

Based on the information you learned in this chapter, answer the following questions using your own words and thoughts.

1. What is a passive learner?

2. What is an active learner?

3. What are the benefits of becoming an active learner? List as many as you can.

4. What is your purpose and responsibility when doing an assignment? How do you go about identifying them?

5. What helps you build confidence in your ability to learn? Why is it important to believe in yourself?

6. Describe at least five ways to take part in your learning process.

7. What are the 5Ws and H? How can they be used to increase active participation and learning?

8. What are you going to do to become more involved in your learning?

9. If you were to improve one thing about the way you take care of yourself, what would it be? How might you make it happen?

10. What was the most important piece of information you learned from this chapter?

Case 1

Maria and Ken were told by their supervisor to attend a company class in telephone skills. Before the class started, Ken confided to Maria his anxiety about attending. "I've never been much of a student," he said. "I know if I'm called on for an answer, I'll sound really stupid." Maria agreed she was a little nervous, but she was looking forward to learning new skills that would help her with her job in customer service. "Well, I don't know why I have to go," Ken said. "They'll probably cover all the things I already do. It will be boring. I've got better things to do with my time," he complained.

1. If you were Maria, what suggestions would you make to Ken?

2. Where could Ken look for help to reduce his nervousness and make this a successful learning experience?

Case 2

Newly hired employees were attending an orientation seminar designed to introduce them to their new company. An agenda was distributed to all the new hires before the orientation started. It outlined the topics of the seminar, which included benefit options, company guidelines, basic work procedures, the performance evaluation process, and other useful information. One of the new hires, John, read through the agenda and, on a pad he brought with him, jotted down questions about several of the topics. Another new employee, Miranda, spent the time talking on her cell phone. When it was time to go into the seminar, John took a seat in the second row. Miranda was the last one into the room and sat in the back looking out the window.

1. What did John do to help himself be an active, not a passive, learner? What more could he do?

2. What might Miranda's new manager suggest to help her become a more active learner on the job?

DISCOVERING YOUR LEARNING STYLE

Jamal and Luke live near each other and are good friends. Since they met in the fourth grade, they have been on the same baseball and soccer teams, taken karate lessons together, and sat through many of the same classes in school. They attend the same college, but are majoring in different subject areas. Jamal wants to learn computers, specifically graphic design, while Luke wants to become an accountant. Though both programs require a basic science course, Jamal and Luke have different instructors with widely varying teaching styles.

On the first day of class, Jamal's instructor took attendance, reviewed the course syllabus, and lectured to the class for over an hour. No one asked any questions, and Jamal's hand hurt from taking so many notes. Homework consisted of reading the textbook and answering questions. The instructor said she would give a quiz based on the previous night's reading.

Luke's instructor passed around a sign-in sheet, asked the students about their experiences with science, and led a class discussion focusing on the students' opinions about the environment. Homework consisted of going online to search out environmental sites to share with the class the next day.

After class, Jamal and Luke met in the cafeteria to talk about their first classroom experiences and impressions. Neither Jamal nor Luke liked his class or his instructor.

Chapter Goals

After studying and working with the information in this chapter, you should be able to:

♦ Define learning style.
♦ Identify several of your preferred learning styles.
♦ Explain the importance of knowing your instructors' teaching styles.
♦ Assess the teaching styles of your instructors.
♦ Identify the benefits of adapting to different learning styles.
♦ Apply the information in this chapter to learning situations.

What do you think this scenario says about the way Jamal prefers to learn? About the way Luke prefers to learn?

In This Chapter

2.1 What Are Learning Styles?

2.2 Sequential or Random: Which Are You?

2.3 Identifying Teaching Styles

2.4 Your Senses and Learning

2.5 Other Learning Styles

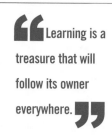

From the moment you were born, you've been learning. Learning is a natural process of all species—including human beings. Before the age of five, you were able to learn faster than at any other time in your life. And you learned in a very skillful and effortless way. You were so successful that you learned a whole language without any formal instruction. You learned athletic abilities that you will use for the rest of your life. You also learned how to read and react to the expressions on other people's faces, and you learned social skills that you still use today. You learned none of these skills in a classroom, and yet they may be counted among your most significant achievements.

As you continued to learn about the world around you, you began to develop your own preferences for learning—those that were comfortable and effective. These learning preferences, or styles, are entirely personal and entirely right for you. They are both different from and similar to the styles of others. More importantly, they are *yours*, and the more you know about your styles of learning, the better you can adapt them for success in the classroom and the real world.

There are many different learning styles. In this chapter, you will learn (1) how to recognize several of your learning styles and (2) how to understand what these learning differences mean. You'll also learn how to identify your instructors' teaching styles. Throughout this book, you will be given a variety of strategies that will enable you to learn more easily.

We all have learning preferences. Do you know the ways you prefer to learn?

SELF-CHECK

The following self-evaluation will give you an idea of how familiar, or unfamiliar, you are with some of the topics and terms discussed in this chapter. After reading each statement, circle the letter Y or N to indicate the answer that is most appropriate for you. Answer honestly; rate yourself at the end; then complete the information for Chapter 2 in Appendix A.

Y = yes   N = no

1. I know what learning styles are.	Y	N
2. I know my learning style preferences.	Y	N
3. I am familiar with how a sequential learner prefers to learn.	Y	N
4. I am familiar with how a sequential instructor prefers to teach.	Y	N
5. I am familiar with how a random learner prefers to learn.	Y	N
6. I am familiar with how a random instructor prefers to teach.	Y	N
7. I know if I am a more visual, auditory, or tactile learner.	Y	N
8. I know several learning strategies that will help me learn best.	Y	N
9. I am aware of the learning styles of others.	Y	N
10. I know how to adjust my learning styles to the teaching styles of my instructors.	Y	N

Rate Yourself: Number of Ys _____ x 100 = _____

Number of Ns _____ x 0 = _____   **Total_____**

2.1 WHAT ARE LEARNING STYLES?

Learning is a natural and constant process of gathering and processing information. The term **learning styles** refers to how you prefer to gather information and then what you do with the information. How you do a lot of things in life—such as where live, how you dress, what you do for a living, and how you arrange your home—are a reflection of your learning styles.

Observers and participants are two kinds of learners with different learning styles. The observer, or more thoughtful learner, prefers to *think* about what is being taught, while the participant, or more involved learner, prefers to *experience* learning firsthand. For example, in a driver's education course, the observer would be content to listen to a lecture or watch a movie. The participant would prefer to sit in the car, play with the knobs and buttons, and begin driving as soon as possible.

You have probably been aware of differences in people for as long as you can remember. You may have a friend who is "neat as a pin" and who keeps a very orderly apartment or bedroom. On the other hand, your house or bedroom may look like a violent storm just hit it. For you, this may be comfortable, but for others who live with you, this disorderliness may be annoying and result in tension and friction. People who are less neat cannot seem to figure out the concern for neatness.

How you approach the matter of neatness is, to some extent, a reflection of your learning styles. Your learning styles are a reflection of how you absorb information from your world and how you process that information. Your way

of dealing with your course work, work life, and living space quite naturally reflects that style.

If you are an instructor, teaching either in a formal classroom or in an informal setting, your teaching style will match your preferred learning styles. As a student, if you know your preferred learning styles and recognize your instructor's teaching style, you can adjust your learning skills to meet that instructor's demands. This ensures greater learning success. If you do not adjust to your instructor's teaching, your learning success will be affected negatively.

The same holds true in the workplace. If you know your boss' and coworkers' preferences and provide them with what they want (regardless of what you want), you will be more successful working with them.

Learning styles are only preferences for the way people learn. One preference is no better or worse than any other. Your preferred learning styles may be considered your comfort zone for learning.

> " Whatever is received, is received according to the nature of the recipient. "
>
> —St. Thomas Aquinas
> 13th century Italian philosopher and theologian

Checkpoint 2.1

1. What is meant by "learning styles"?
2. Why do you think it would be helpful to know about learning styles?
3. Why might you want to determine the learning styles of your instructors?

2.2 SEQUENTIAL OR RANDOM: WHICH ARE YOU?

The learning styles assessment that follows will help you understand whether you prefer the sequential or random learning style. Both styles will be further explained after the exercise. Remember that one style is no better than another.

If you have a higher number on the left side, you are a sequential-preferenced learner. A higher number on the right means you are a random-preferenced learner. If your numbers are the same, you are an equal-preferenced, or balanced, learner.

ACTIVITY I

As you read the two lists below, notice that the quality on the left is opposite the quality on the right. Compare the first quality on the left and the first quality on the right; then place a check mark (✓) next to the one that sounds most like you. Do not skip any qualities. Go with your first impression. Do not think too much about each response, as there are no right or wrong answers. When you are done, count the number of check marks you have on the left and on the right. Place each total at the bottom of the column.

Sequential Preferences	**Random Preferences**
_____ Organized	_____ Disorganized
_____ Enjoy learning and playing with theories	_____ Enjoy comparisons and examples
_____ Want order and structure in life	_____ Like creativity and dislike authority
_____ Want details	_____ Want big picture (first)
_____ See play as a waste of time	_____ Enjoy play
_____ Want intellectual recognition	_____ Want personal attention and feedback
_____ Have difficulty with improvisation	_____ Enjoy improvisation
_____ Find speculation difficult	_____ Have vivid imagination
_____ Prefer math	_____ Prefer art, music, sports
_____ Show high regard for time	_____ Show little regard for time
_____ Good at making decisions	_____ Good at considering possibilities
_____ Prefer to work on one project at a time	_____ Prefer to work on several projects at a time
_____ Like one correct answer	_____ Like several possible answers
_____ Like routine	_____ Like impulsive activities
_____ Prefer reading and lecture	_____ Prefer role-playing, open discussion, and small group work
_____ Learn well independently	_____ Learn well through discussion, collaboration, and participation
_____ **Total check marks**	_____ **Total check marks**

The Sequential Learner

If you possess several of the qualities listed on the left of Activity 1, you have the preferences of a **sequential learner**. You probably also possess some random qualities from the right that tone down your sequential nature. High sequential-preferred learners tend toward a more logical, step-by-step approach to solving problems and taking in information. If this is your type, you most likely enjoy theory and want order in all things, including your living area, your study area, and even your notebooks. You take pride in submitting neat papers and projects. You are a planner and require structure in your life. When you are under stress, you stick firmly to your sequential learning preference because it is most comfortable for you.

So what might this mean in real life? If a friend tells you about a recent party, you probably want all the details—a complete description of who was there, what they were wearing, what time everyone left—and you want the description delivered in an orderly, sequential way. You might feel impatient if your friend rambles, telling you a little of this and a little of that. Most likely, to keep things on track and in *your* sense of order, you'll start asking questions that guide and control the conversation. At work, when discussing a project with a coworker, you might feel you are wasting time if the person does not "get to the point" as quickly as you would like.

Sequential learners tend to think in one-two-three order. They find formal school structure and traditional instruction comfortable. Many successful American businesses also place a high value on sequential thinking. Can you think of careers where sequential preferences would be valued?

> " What we perceive comes as much from inside our heads as from the world outside. "
>
> —William Jones
> Successful businessperson

The Random Learner

If you possess many of the qualities listed on the right side of Activity 1, then you have the preferences of a **random learner**. You probably also possess some sequential qualities that tone down your random nature. You tend to learn better in a less structured manner. This means that math may not have been one of your favorite subjects in school, since it is a sequential subject. Your English papers may have been returned with comments such as "lacks organization," "good ideas, but you fail to order them or develop them fully," and "you didn't follow the assignment." At work, you are probably involved in discussions of current events and sports.

As a random learner, you need examples and comparisons to make the facts stick in your mind (and if the analogy or example is in story form, so much the better). You often have a gut sense as to when something is right but are unable to support your feelings with details or facts. When you read, you frequently study and remember

Chapter 2: Discovering Your Learning Style

the illustrations. When you are under stress, you stick firmly to this preference because it is most comfortable for you.

Random learners frequently go off in many directions at once and are accused of being disorganized. If, as a random learner, you describe the party in the earlier example to a sequential-preferred friend, your friend may get annoyed when you jump from topic to topic. The sequential-preferred friend will probably ask you for factual details.

Random learners tend to skip around in their thinking. They are not as comfortable as sequential learners with formal school structure and traditional instruction. To be successful in a sequential-demanding world, they must force themselves to act disciplined and orderly. After a while, however, acting sequential becomes easier. Some people are surprised to discover they are random-preferenced learners because they have adapted so well to the demands of a sequential world.

Sequentially preferred learners often can be identified by their neat, organized desks, while random preferred learners can often be

identified by their less organized work space.

Research shows that you can change or adjust your learning style to different tasks. More importantly, doing so expands your

thinking capability. (Random learners, in fact, are well ahead of the sequential ones who didn't have to adjust so much in high school.) Imagine what it's like for sequential learners when they enter a random classroom!

Can you think of careers where random preferences would be valued?

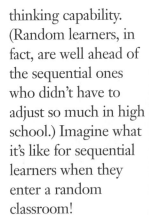

The Balanced Learner

If you have close to the same number of check marks in each of the two columns of Activity 1, you can consider yourself an equal-preferenced, or **balanced learner**. You are balanced between the two styles and possess both sequential and random preferences.

You are able to adapt to either style and can do it better and more easily than individuals who definitively fall into one of the two preferences. You probably get along well with others because you can match their styles as needed. When under stress, you tend to become unbalanced and lean toward one or the other preference. If you can identify which preference you lean toward, you might be able to figure out your true learning style preference.

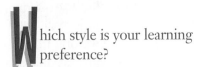

Which style is your learning preference?

Learning to Flex to Other Styles

In addition to sequential and random, we use many other styles of thinking and learning. Several of them will be explained later in this chapter. Being aware of your preferences and learning to adapt to others makes you think and recall more efficiently. In fact, *using both styles benefits memory and thinking*.

The most challenging part of flexing to other styles is overcoming the discomfort of thinking differently. The more you do it, the easier it becomes!

Practicing a style that is not your preference is like learning to use your nondominant hand. On the first line below, write your full name. On the second line, write your full name using your other hand.

_____

_____

Chances are, when you wrote with your dominant hand—your natural hand—the writing was easy. When you wrote with your nondominant hand, the writing probably felt awkward, unnatural, and may not have looked as neat. Though you prefer writing with your dominant hand, with practice, you would be able to adapt and get comfortable with your nondominant one.

Learning to adapt to your nondominant learning style preference helps you become a more balanced learner. You will always retain your natural preferences, but you can stretch your mind and enhance your ability to understand the styles of others. Practicing a style that is not your own allows you to develop the ability to face all styles with equal success.

> " To the man who only has a hammer, everything he encounters begins to look like a nail. "
>
> —Abraham H. Maslow
> American psychologist

Checkpoint 2.2

1. Identify someone you know who you think possesses sequential preferences. What do you think makes them sequential?

2. Identify someone you know who you think possesses random preferences. What do you think makes them random?

3. Which learning style do you think is best? Why?

2.3 IDENTIFYING TEACHING STYLES

Whether you are learning at work, in class, or at home, it should not matter who instructs you. The fact remains that *your job is to learn and succeed in every learning situation*. Every person instructs differently. Some will be easy to understand, while others will be difficult. Some will be likeable, others not. The best strategy is to first observe your instructors, learn as much as possible about their teaching styles and habits, and then find ways to adapt to each style.

While it is your instructor's responsibility to understand you, it is also your responsibility to understand your instructor. Think of a current learning situation you are involved in. Is your instructor's information organized or disorganized? Is information presented verbally, on handouts, or on the board? Are you only given theories, or are you able to get first-hand experience with the subject matter? Are the work assignments useful for class discussions, or are they just preparation for tests? How are you evaluated? What are your instructor's expectations of you? Answers to these and other questions can help you gather information about your instructors.

It is important to realize that instructors' teaching styles are mostly an extension of their learning styles. Most instructors teach the same way they learn.

Before continuing, stop for a moment and think about your past instructors. Recall one or two with whom you really felt in tune. Did you always know exactly what they wanted? Did you enjoy their teaching? What did they do to make their classes enjoyable? When they asked questions, did they want just one correct answer, or did they want your thoughts and opinions? Think also of one or two instructors with whom you felt at odds, never knowing exactly what they wanted or never being able to give them quite what they expected. What made their teaching difficult to understand?

> " Do what you can, with what you have, where you are. "
>
> —David Sarnoff
> American radio and television pioneer

Descriptions of the two types of instructors are given on pages 40 and 41. If you are a sequential learner, you may prefer to skip this activity and get right to the descriptions. Don't! Complete the activity; it is good practice for getting into a random mode of thinking—imagining, recalling how a class felt, having a gut sense of information. Go with it—go random for a moment to improve your thinking skills.

A past instructor to whom I could relate was _____

This instructor used presentation methods like _____

_____

_____

This instructor asked questions like _____

_____

_____

This instructor did things like _____

_____

_____

This instructor dressed like _____

_____

_____

A past instructor to whom I could not relate was _____

This instructor used presentation methods like _____

_____

_____

This instructor asked questions like _____

_____

_____

This instructor did things like _____

_____

_____

This instructor dressed like _____

_____

_____

The Sequential Instructor

Characteristics of a sequential instructor, quite

naturally, are similar to those of a sequential learner. These instructors may also demonstrate several random characteristics, but they are clearly more sequential. From the list of sequential characteristics below, see if you recognize an instructor, a coworker, a friend, or a boss.

♦ Is idealistic, systematic, and organized

♦ Likes facts and details

♦ Values sequential thinking

♦ Shows more interest in data than people

♦ Prefers informational forms of instruction, such as reading or a lecture

♦ Can sometimes be completely unaware of the emotional climate in a room

♦ Seeks efficiency

♦ Is a decision maker

♦ Works in a job that requires sequential thinking

♦ Has well-planned learning activities

♦ Tends to be a firm disciplinarian

♦ Grades answers as right or wrong (no partial credit); stresses correctness and facts

The Random Instructor

Characteristics of the random instructor, as you can surely guess, are similar to the random learner. These instructors may also demonstrate several sequential characteristics, but they are clearly more random. See if you recognize an instructor, a coworker, a friend, or a boss with these random characteristics:

♦ Enjoys people

♦ Is nonjudgmental and supportive (values others' opinions)

♦ Prefers role-playing, open discussion, and small group work

♦ Will often individualize instruction

♦ Prefers to create own course of study

♦ Gives imaginative assignments

♦ Assumes learning is a function of interest

♦ Prefers self-discovery, experience, and a variety of instructional modes

♦ Tends to follow what he or she feels like doing rather than a structured lesson plan

♦ Works in a job that requires random thinking

♦ Displays a learning environment that sequential instructors may view as disorderly

♦ Stresses concepts and conclusions

The Balanced Instructor

Characteristics of a balanced instructor show an equal mix from the sequential and the random preferences. These instructors are generally well liked because they attract both styles. Because the traditional role model for teaching is a sequential instructor, the balanced instructor may tend more toward the sequential style than the random style.

Balanced instructors are challenging to both the sequential and random learner because they require each type of learner to adapt to the other style while providing some comfort in his or her preferred style. Can you guess with some certainty the styles of the two instructors you described in Activity 2? You will most likely relate to an instructor with the same preference as you.

Quick Ways to Assess Your Instructor's Style

The following four guidelines may also help you identify the preferred learning style, and teaching styles, of your instructors. Apply them to several instructors in your life. Do you get a clearer picture of these people?

1. Listen for clues in how they present their material.

2. Determine what kinds of questions they ask.

3. Observe their behavior.

4. Look at how they are dressed.

Listen for clues in how your instructor presents the material

Sequential-preferred instructors generally deliver content in specific order by lecture, probably use a lot of outlined notes and rarely deviate, may speak in a monotone voice with very little humor (remember that they are apt to see play as wasteful), and always stick to the topic. They make clear connections to relevant topics and do not allow you to wander far off the topic.

Random-preferred instructors tell stories; use metaphors, analogies and humor, and allow for "wanderings" during a lecture. During a computer lesson, they might tell the "story of computers" and describe and develop its characters. Such a lesson may sound more like a conversation than a lecture.

Instructors who are balanced in their learning preferences tend to use both styles of delivery. However, since most of the teaching models in traditional education are sequential, balanced instructors may lean in that direction.

> " . . . Dominance is part and parcel of the normal human condition . . as a result, we are handed, footed, eyed and—in a general sense—brained. "
>
> —Ned Herrmann
> Contemporary author and educator on brain

Determine what kinds of questions your instructor asks

Sequentials ask questions that require you to recall and recite facts, data, and specific theories. They tend not to ask for your opinion, especially if they are the type of sequential who is comfortable with only one correct answer. The test formats they prefer are those that require you to pick one correct answer (such as multiple choice, true or false, and matching).

Randoms ask questions that ask you to interpret, give an opinion, suggest an application, form a connection to some other subject area, and provide for multiple answers. The test formats they prefer include more writing, (such as short answer and essay), where you have to provide your thoughts and opinions. Those who are balanced in their learning preferences tend to use both styles of questioning.

Observe your instructor's behavior

Sequentials are formal and will stand behind a lectern or table. They will write notes on the board in outline form, using few abbreviations. If they use an overhead projector, they'll use a black pen only—no other colors. Their lecture delivery tone will be restrained and, at the worst, will consist of one-word utterances. They will have a low tolerance for students who want to sit anywhere but at desks or tables in straight rows—"classroom style."

Randoms will wander around the room and gaze out the window—or better yet, sit on the window sill and play with the venetian blind cord. They will scribble fragments of ideas on the board, use arrows to connect one fragment to another, and use abbreviations or even pictures to illustrate ideas. Randoms will gesture with their hands, and their vocal tone will vary from soft to animated. They might even tolerate students sitting on the floor or propping their feet up.

Those who are balanced in their learning preferences tend to use both styles of behavior.

Look at how your instructor is dressed

Sequentials are more inclined to wear muted colors that blend and match with every part of their outfit. They dress in "sets," or outfits, and one outfit usually doesn't get mixed with another.

Randoms tend to wear more relaxed, colorful, and casual clothing. Randoms don't like boredom.

Those who are balanced in their learning preferences tend to mix both styles. They may dress more formally on the days they are feeling sequential and more casually on the days they are feeling random.

All three teaching styles have a place in instructional settings. More than likely, you will not encounter any one instructor who is purely sequential or random. As you read through the previous descriptions, you could probably recall

past teachers who demonstrated each style. Use the preceding descriptions to help you identify individual teaching styles so you can plan your learning strategy now and in the future.

sequential learner develop creativity through those imaginative assignments that ask for concept development and conclusion. Recent research shows creativity is part of the truly successful learning experience.

Sequential instructors can help a random learner develop the discipline to get a job done more easily and quickly, thereby reducing the unnecessary work that results when the random learner wanders off.

Experiencing and adapting to both styles will definitely help your learning and thinking and will instill in you a tolerance for and appreciation of differences. The more you are able to adjust your style to that of your instructor, the more success you will have as a learner.

Learning from Style Differences

It can be to your advantage if your instructor teaches in a style different from your preference. For example, a random instructor can help a

Checkpoint 2.3

1. Why is it important to identify the learning styles of your instructors?

2. What can you do to identify your instructor's preferred learning styles?

3. Would it be a good idea to try to find instructors who match your learning style? Why or why not?

2.4 YOUR SENSES AND LEARNING

There is another set of personal learning preferences called **sensory learning preferences**. These are visual, auditory and tactile. John Grinder and Richard Bandler have researched and written about this theory.

Visual learners prefer to use their eyes to learn. They learn best by seeing information, either through demonstration, visual aids, or in their mind's eye. They prefer to see information on the board, and they like to write things down—otherwise, they tend to forget. Visual learners tend to use statements such as, "I see what you mean," "Show it to me," or "I get the picture."

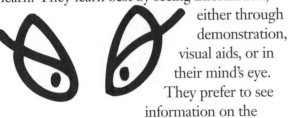

Auditory learners prefer to use their ears to learn. They learn best by hearing information, either by listening or speaking. They do not have a great need to write things down because they tend to be comfortable relying on what they hear. They also work well in partners and teams. Auditory learners tend to use statements such as, "I hear you," "That sounds good to me," or "I'm glad you mentioned that."

Kinesthetic or **tactile learners** prefer to use their bodies to learn. They prefer to be involved physically in their learning. Being comfortable is important to tactile learners. As a result, they tend to move around a lot, fidgeting and slouching in their chairs. Tactile learners express themselves through their body language. They tend to use statements such as, "I grasp what you mean," "You're on the right track," or "That really tickles my funny bone."

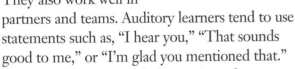

Many people have a combination of more than one of these preferences. For example, a visual-tactile learner learns best by watching and experiencing, while an auditory-tactile learner learns best by listening and experiencing. If you had to pick one of these three to identify yourself, which would you be? Remember, as with any learning style preference, one preference is not better than another.

> ❝I desire that there be as many different persons in the world as possible; I would have each one be very careful to find out and preserve his own way.❞
>
> —Henry David Thoreau
> Poet

Success Skills

A quick way to assess your sensory learning preferences is shown below. Read each statement and, if it sounds like you, place a checkmark (√) on the line to the left. If the statement doesn't sound like you, leave the line blank. Total your checkmarks for each section.

Visual

_____ I prefer reading more than listening or doing.

_____ I learn more easily when I see a demonstration of what is being discussed.

_____ I learn how to spell better by seeing words written on paper or in my mind's eye.

_____ Seeing my notes is helpful for recalling what was discussed in class or a meeting.

_____ I would rather read a newspaper than watch the news on television.

_____ I remember people's faces better than their names.

_____ I remember telephone numbers or e-mail addresses after seeing them once or twice.

_____ **Total Visual Preferences**

Auditory

_____ I prefer listening more than reading or doing.

_____ I learn how to spell by saying words aloud before writing them down.

_____ I remember better when I explain what I am learning to someone else.

_____ I learn best when I study with other people.

_____ I learn more when I watch the news than when I read about it.

_____ I remember better when I am told something.

_____ I remember people's names better than their faces.

_____ **Total Auditory Preferences**

Tactile (or Kinesthetic)

_____ I prefer doing more than reading or listening.

_____ I prefer to learn through real-life experiences.

_____ I have a hard time sitting still while working independently.

_____ I take notes to help me concentrate and remember.

_____ Rewriting my notes helps me learn.

_____ If given a choice, I'd rather complete a project than write a report.

_____ I like to doodle pictures in my notes.

_____ **Total Tactile (or Kinesthetic) Preferences**

Total each sensory learning preference section so you can see which preferences are stronger and weaker. You probably have some preferences in all three areas. You can apply many learning strategies to accommodate your sensory learning preferences. Using strategies from all of the preferences will help you learn more. Read the list of strategies below, then create your own "Master List of Personal Learning Strategies." If you think of other strategies that work for you, add them to your list.

Figure 2-1   Sensory Learning Strategies

Visual Strategies

- Take good notes for reference later.
- Read notes and use flash cards repeatedly.
- Read instructions rather than listen to someone describe how to do something.
- Review the reading material to be covered in class the next day.
- Write reminders to yourself on sticky notes.
- Look up new vocabulary in a dictionary or glossary, and then write the words.
- Visualize the spelling of people's names when you meet them, and match the names to their faces.
- Write the names of people you meet, documenting where and when you met them.
- Set up and use a calendar and assignment planner.
- Sit close to the action so you can see more easily.
- Close your eyes and "see" what you need to remember.
- Watch educational TV on topics related to the content you are learning.
- Reduce test anxiety by picturing yourself in control of the information.
- Reduce your learning anxiety by picturing yourself mastering the information.
- Color code your notes and files for visual remembering.
- Keep a separate notebook or file for each topic area.
- Figure numbers by visualizing them in your head (when possible).

Auditory Strategies

- Read out loud when possible. (This will take longer than silent reading.)
- Listen to a tape of yourself reviewing the material you are learning.
- Work and review material with a partner or small study group.
- Ask the meaning of something when you don't understand.
- When recalling information, create a rhythm or song.
- Tape record your instructor as a reinforcement of your notes or class discussions.
- Use a tape recorder to ask yourself questions.

Figure 2-1 continued   Sensory Learning Strategies

- Repeat names immediately after hearing them.
- Ask questions of the instructor.
- Ask yourself questions while studying.
- Problem solve out loud.
- Memorize content using self-created rhythms.
- Pretend you are the instructor, and "teach" the material aloud.
- Reduce test anxiety by saying positive things to yourself.

Tactile (Kinesthetic) Strategies

- Make flash cards for important concepts and vocabulary.
- Place a 3"x 5" card below the line you are reading.
- While reading, run your finger down the left margin, using it to mark your place.
- Read with a pen or pencil in your hand, and write down what is important.
- Create your own abbreviations, either words or symbols, while taking notes.
- Rewrite or recopy your notes.
- Say the information aloud while writing it.
- Highlight notes or make margin notes directly on reading material.
- Use highlighters when reviewing notes.
- Use a calculator or computer.
- Make sure your work area allows you to move around while you study.
- Take short movement breaks.
- Pay attention to the real-world applications of what you are learning.

Learning Style Preferences and the Computer

Whether fair or not, computers are heavily biased toward visual, tactile, and random learners. Using a computer is a hands-on and eyes-on experience where you learn by seeing and doing. No matter how many formal classes about computers you take, you will not learn to use a computer unless you actually put your hands on it and work with it. Connecting to a computer is also a highly tactile experience. Unless you are working with an interactive or multimedia CD-ROM, which plays sound, auditory learners are not accommodated at all.

There are few rules when surfing the Web and researching on the Internet, which delights the random learner but frustrates the sequential learner. Randoms love to explore the Web and patiently search for information. Sequentials want efficiency and prefer to go to the one site that will help them. Randoms may enjoy searching many related sites to answer one question, but sequentials tend to feel overwhelmed. Sequentials do, however, enjoy the step-by-step process in programming.

More and more, people are using the Internet to take courses because of its convenience and availability. The ability to take a course at any time and at any place a computer is located appeals to busy people. Online courses at present, however, are only visual and tactile, not auditory. They require the learner to read a sequence of screens (just like a book on screen) and then interact with an instructor or expert by keying questions and reading the answers. When streamlined video with sight and sound becomes more popular and affordable, auditory learners will be more comfortable with their computers.

Be aware that many auditory and sequential learners manage just fine with their computers. They have figured out how to adapt their styles to manage the technology.

Focus on Ethics

Janelle, a preferred random learner, is usually a law-abiding citizen. One late night she was driving through her quiet town. She was singing along to the radio and digging through her purse for a piece of gum when the traffic light ahead of her turned yellow. She could have stopped in time for the light, but when her impulsive nature took over, she put her foot on the gas and ran a red light. After all, she thought, no one was around.

Did Janelle break the law? Explain your answer. In what ways could her random preferences have contributed to her behavior?

Checkpoint 2.4

1. What are some preferences of a visual-auditory learner?

2. What are some preferences of an auditory-tactile learner?

3. Which of the three sensory preferences would you guess is the most universal? Why?

2.5 OTHER LEARNING STYLES

In addition to sequential and random styles of learning, there are several other learning styles worth mentioning. If you would like more information about any of these learning style theories, consult your local library or search the Web. Look under the key words *psychology, the brain,* or *learning styles.*

Left Brain/Right Brain Theory

Left brain/right brain theory, also known as **hemisphericity**, is closely related to the sequential and random learning theories previously discussed. This theory says that the brain has two hemispheres, a left side and a right side. Each side represents certain qualities. In effect, a left-brain person tends to resemble a sequential learner, while a right-brain person tends to resemble a random learner. Roger Sperry, Kenneth and Rita Dunn, Ned Herrmann, and many others have researched and written about this theory.

Social and Independent Learning Theories

Social and independent learning theories say that some people prefer to learn independently while others prefer to learn in a group. If you prefer to learn independently, you are called an **independent learner**. It is possible you are also introverted and prefer to rely on your own thoughts and feelings. If you prefer to learn in a group, you are called a **social learner**. It is possible you are also extroverted and prefer to rely on others' thoughts and feelings.

Multiple Intelligences

Howard Gardner of Harvard University has identified eight natural intelligences, also called **multiple intelligences**. People can be strong in one or more of these areas. Many schools have begun using his model to enhance students' learning. The eight intelligences are listed below with brief descriptions of each. See if you can identify your type of intelligence.

1. Logical/Mathematical—deals with inductive and deductive thinking, questioning and reasoning, numbers, and the recognition of abstract patterns

2. Visual/Spatial—relies on the sense of sight and being able to visualize an object or a picture

3. Body/Kinesthetic—relates to physical movement

4. Musical/Rhythmic—based on the recognition of tonal patterns and sensitivity to rhythm, beats, and music

5. Interpersonal—relies primarily on socializing and person-to-person relationships and communication

6. Intrapersonal—relates to being alone and inner states of being, self-reflection, metacognition (or thinking about thinking), and awareness of spiritual realities

7. Verbal/Linguistic—relates to words and language, both written and spoken

8. Naturalist—relates to the recognition, appreciation, and understanding of the natural world around us

With a partner or in a small group, make a list of several famous people who are strong in each of these eight areas. For example, Oprah Winfrey, a successful talk show host, is strong in interpersonal intelligence. Albert Einstein, the Father of Physics, was strong in logical mathematical intelligence. You can locate names on the Internet using the key word *multiple intelligences*.

Checkpoint 2.5

1. Name the three learning theories discussed in this section.

2. Do you think you are a social or independent learner? Why?

3. Which of the multiple intelligences are your strongest?

Smart Tip

You have heard the expression *opposites attract*. In some long-term intimate relationships, you will find one person who possesses many sequential qualities while the other has more random qualities. People, in essence, have found a balance of styles.

Key Terms and Concepts

auditory learner
balanced learner
hemisphericity
independent learner

learning styles
multiple intelligences
random learner
sensory learning preferences

sequential learner
social learner
tactile learner
visual learner

Chapter Summary

1. Learning styles are a reflection of how you absorb and process information.

2. Your preferred learning styles are considered your comfort zones for learning.

3. A preference for sequential learning means you tend toward a logical, step-by-step approach for taking in information.

4. A preference for random learning means you tend toward a less structured means of taking in information.

5. No strong preference for either sequential or random indicates you are a balanced learner, most able to adapt to either style.

6. Your preferred learning style does not mean you are any better or worse at learning than anyone else. It only means you have a preference for a certain way of learning.

7. Learning to adapt to other styles will make learning easier in any situation.

8. Instructors' teaching styles are generally a reflection of their preferred learning styles. By discovering instructors' learning styles and adapting to them, you can make learning easier.

9. To assess the teaching style of your instructors, listen for clues in how they present their material, determine what types of questions they ask, observe their behavior, and look at how they dress.

10. Your sensory learning preferences can be visual, auditory, or tactile. Adjusting your learning activities to match your preferences makes learning easier.

11. There are many other learning styles in addition to sequential and random. These include left brain and right brain learning, social and independent learning, and multiple intelligences.

 **WEB LINK**

www.studyweb.com

This large site has a comprehensive list of links dealing with learning styles. The links are listed under *professional development/learning styles*.

www.learningstyle.com

This site has another learning style survey with more information about different learning styles.

Review

Based on the information you learned in this chapter, answer the following questions using your own words and thoughts.

1. a. Is your preferred learning style sequential or random?

    b. What does this style mean about the way you learn?

2. If your learning style is random, how can you learn in sequential style (and vice versa)?

3. a. Which sensory learning preference do you lean toward—visual, auditory, or tactile?

    b. What does this style mean about the way you learn?

4. List at least eight learning strategies that accommodate your sensory learning preference.

5. Based on your sensory learning preference, what do instructors do that help you learn?

6. How do you learn an instructor's preferred teaching styles?

7. Why do you think it's important to know an instructor's preferred teaching styles?

8. What are some things you can do if an instructor's style does not match yours?

9. a. Which of the multiple intelligences are your strongest?

    b. How might you gain strength in the weaker ones?

10. After studying this chapter, what do you know about the way you learn? What can you do to make your learning more successful?

Case 1

Joyce watched as several large packages were delivered to her apartment. They contained the new wall storage unit she had ordered. As she opened each of the boxes and placed the contents on the floor, she started to feel apprehensive. There were so many pieces of wood and bags of hinges and bolts. "I've never put something like this together," she worried. She found the directions and looked at the illustrations. While she was still confused, she could match some of the pieces with the drawings. That made her feel a little bit better. "What should I do next?" she wondered as she looked at the items spread over the floor.

1. What conclusions can you draw about Joyce's preferred learning style?

2. What might a visual, auditory, or tactile learner do to accomplish the task of putting the unit together?

Case 2

David and Carlos were taking a real estate course as part of their training to become agents. Carlos, who was an active participant in the discussions and even volunteered to role-play as a difficult client, enjoyed the course. David found it frustrating. Carlos was so involved in the activities he lost track of time. David, on the other hand, felt unprepared for the activities and pressed the instructor for the correct answers to the situations being discussed by the group. On his evaluation of the course, Carlos stated he liked the many viewpoints expressed. David's evaluation listed several suggested improvements, among which were more lecture and reading materials, detailed, accurate answers to questions, and clear, step-by-step instructions.

1. What learning style does David prefer? What might he do to develop his nonpreferred learning style?

2. What learning style does Carlos prefer? What might he do to develop his nonpreferred learning style?

Ajit, who is taking an insurance course on the Internet, has completed the curriculum and is now preparing for the final exam. As a computer repair technician, he has little time during the day to study. His nights are not much better, as he volunteers at the fire department and spends time with his girlfriend.

If things are quiet at work during his 45-minute lunch, he pulls out his study materials. Inevitably, the phone rings, the e-mail message alert beeps, or a coworker stops by to chat. When it's time to get back to work, Ajit is frustrated because he spent most of his time communicating and eating, but not studying.

When he finds time to study at home, he usually begins after 9 p.m. His typical study place is in bed with the television on. If he gets interested in the study material, he will roll over on his side and ignore the TV. Sometimes he sits in a recliner or on the couch with music playing. Occasionally he gets telephone calls or his cat begs for attention by sitting on top of his study material.

Finally, two weeks after the recommended test date, Ajit is "ready" to take the exam.

What might Ajit do at work and at home to be able to concentrate better during the short time he has for studying?

Chapter Goals

After studying and working with the information in this chapter, you should be able to:

♦ Identify the influences that affect the way you concentrate.
♦ Identify distractions that cause your mind to wander.
♦ Understand the effects of mind wandering.
♦ Specify ways to increase your concentration.
♦ Identify the makeup of an effective physical learning environment.
♦ Identify the ingredients of an effective mental learning environment.
♦ Begin to improve concentration while learning.

In This Chapter

3.1 Your Learning Influences

3.2 Your Learning Environments

Concentration is the art of being focused, the ability to pay attention. Without concentration, you have no memory of what you hear, see, and read. Concentration is a frame of mind that enables you to stay centered on the activity or work you are doing. You know when you're concentrating because time seems to go by quickly, distractions that normally take you off task don't bother you, and you have a lot of mental or physical energy for the task. Your mind and body are naturally "going with the flow."

You have probably experienced intense concentration—a time when you were so focused on what you were doing that you didn't hear someone approach and jumped in surprise when he or she touched you or spoke. Maybe you played, or watched, a play-off game where the outcome came down to the final seconds. You were probably quite focused at that time!

Good concentration is a result of being active, mindful, and conscious. Knowing how to concentrate is directly related to your ability to learn. Many influences affect concentration—the amount of time and energy you spend in the learning process. The influences discussed in this chapter are those that specifically affect your concentration.

An **effective learning environment** is one where concentration comes easily and more learning occurs. An **ineffective learning environment** causes you to waste time and makes learning difficult. You can learn how to increase your concentration by being aware of and choosing the appropriate physical and mental learning environment.

In this chapter, you will learn about (1) becoming aware of the influences in your learning environment, (2) understanding how these influences affect you, and (3) creating an effective learning environment for improving your overall learning. You will also discover the available opportunities that make your learning easier and more enjoyable.

What does good concentration feel like for you? When does it happen?

SELF-CHECK

The following self-evaluation will give you an idea of how familiar, or unfamiliar, you are with some of the topics and terms discussed in this chapter. After reading each statement, circle the letter Y, S, or N to indicate the answer that is most appropriate for you. Answer honestly; rate yourself at the end; then complete the information for Chapter 3 in Appendix A.

Y = yes; frequently	S = sometimes	N = no; never

1.	I learn in a quiet, distraction-free environment.	Y	S	N
2.	I learn without a radio or television on.	Y	S	N
3.	I resist taking phone calls or checking e-mail while studying.	Y	S	N
4.	I work at an uncluttered desk or table with good lighting.	Y	S	N
5.	I am aware of the room temperature and can make myself comfortable.	Y	S	N
6.	I am aware of, and try to reduce, mental distractions before learning.	Y	S	N
7.	I am usually relaxed when I have a lot of studying to do.	Y	S	N
8.	I know several ways to increase my concentration while studying.	Y	S	N
9.	I reserve most of my learning for the time of day when I am most alert.	Y	S	N
10.	I enjoy learning.	Y	S	N

Rate Yourself:

Number of Ys	_____	x	100	=	_____	
Number of Ss	_____	x	50	=	_____	
Number of Ns	_____	x	0	=	_____	**Total** _____

3.1 YOUR LEARNING INFLUENCES

A **learning influence** is something that affects how well you concentrate while trying to learn. Some are physical; others are mental. Some influences are helpful in keeping your concentration, while many others are distracting. The helpful ones are considered positive, while the distracting ones are considered negative.

ACTIVITY I

Below is a list of common influences that can affect your concentration. Think about how each of the influences affects the way you concentrate; and decide whether it is positive/helpful (+), negative/unhelpful (-), or sometimes helpful/sometimes unhelpful (=). For example, if you find yourself very focused when you are under time pressure, place a plus (+) in the blank. If you find you are continually distracted by time pressure with little ability to focus, place a minus (-) in the blank. However, if you find you are both focused and distracted equally, place an equal (=) in the blank. Add other influences that can affect your concentration.

Location
____At your desk
____At a table
____On a couch
____On a recliner
____In bed
____Other:_____

State of Mind/Being
____Interested
____Not interested
____Alert
____Sleepy
____Relaxed
____Stressed
____Time-pressured
____Not time-pressured
____Preoccupied
____Tired

____Well rested
____Hungry
____Other:_____

External Environment
____Warm
____Cool
____Well lit
____Dimly lit
____Noisy
____Quiet
____Other:_____

Distractions
____Other people
____Telephone
____e-mail
____Television
____Radio
____Other:_____

Type of Written Material
____Familiar content
____Unfamiliar content
____Wide columns
____Narrow columns
____Large print size
____Small print size
____Good copy quality
____Poor copy quality
____Other:_____

Delivery of Information
____Lecture
____Discussion
____Reading
____Writing
____On computer screen
____One-on-one instruction
____Group interaction

____Research
____Hands-on learning
____Visual demonstration
____Other:_____

Purpose/Usability
____For a meeting
____For your boss or instructor
____For a presentation
____For a test
____For pleasure
____For background knowledge
____Other:_____

Mind Wandering: The Enemy of Concentration

Your mind must focus before it can learn. When you focus, you concentrate on the learning material and content. **Mind wandering,** on the other hand, is the enemy of concentration. Also known as daydreaming, mind wandering is a momentary lack of mental concentration or focus. It can last a second, five seconds, thirty seconds, or longer. It is natural—and necessary for learning. Most human beings daydream.

When you read or study, some mind wandering may be helpful. If you are building a mental bridge of knowledge from the new information to the old, then mind wandering can be productive. For example, if you are learning about the installation of electrical sockets, your mind may wander to the time you got an electrical shock as a child when you stuck your finger in a socket; that thought is important for your learning.

But if, while installing the sockets, your mind wanders to your plans for the coming weekend, that thought is not productive. Nonproductive thoughts break your concentration, slow down and interrupt your learning process, and ultimately affect your ability to understand the information you are trying to comprehend.

It is important to be aware of the mental thoughts that cause your mind to wander and break your concentration.

Which photo more closely resembles your learning area?

Concentration Factoid

According to the research of Becky Patterson, Ph.D., Professor Emeritus of the University of Alaska and author of *Concentration: Strategies for Attaining Focus,* an average college student's concentration period while reading is only 16 minutes. Other research suggests young children have concentration periods that last for just 20 seconds! It is amazing that we ever learn anything with such small intervals of concentration.

Think about the wandering thoughts that break your concentration when you read, work, or study. List below as many specific thoughts as you can.

1. *Being hungry*
2. _____
3. _____
4. _____
5. _____
6. _____
7. _____
8. _____
9. _____
10. _____

11. _____
12. _____
13. _____
14. _____
15. _____
16. _____
17. _____
18. _____
19. _____
20. _____

Once you have listed as many thoughts as possible in Activity 2, compare them with your classmates' answers. You may remind each other of items you forgot. Continue to add to your list as you remember thoughts that interfere with your concentration. You should get a clear picture of just how many miscellaneous thoughts cross your mind when you believe you are concentrating.

From Activity 2, did you discover any mental distractions you would like to eliminate forever? Unfortunately, you may be able to avoid them only temporarily. For example, you can stop thinking about how hungry you are by eating a snack, but eventually you will be hungry again. Mind wandering can be reduced, but not totally eliminated. Now that you're aware of what breaks your concentration, you have a fighting chance of doing something about it.

Effects on learning

So what happens when your mental thoughts get your mind offtrack? If your mind wanders on your way home, you might miss your stop, drive past your exit, or (even worse) get into an accident. When your mind wanders while you are reading, working, or studying, your ability to learn is being affected.

With a partner or on your own, consider the effects of mind wandering on learning. Summarize your discussion on the lines below. *Remember, mind wandering is effective only when it relates to the material you are learning.*

_____

_____

_____

_____

_____

_____

_____

_____

_____

_____

_____

_____

_____

Ways to Improve Concentration

Since mind wandering is a natural and human characteristic, you can never get rid of it forever. If you were asked to never daydream again while reading or studying, could you do it? The honest answer is no! Nonetheless, if you recognize the fact that you are daydreaming, you can at least learn how to reduce it. The very first step in reducing mind wandering is to catch yourself doing it. Then you can do something about it. By reducing mind wandering, you will be able to learn more in less time with better concentration.

> " Hold yourself responsible to a higher standard than anybody else expects of you. "
>
> —Henry Ward Beecher
> Preacher and abolitionist

With a partner or on your own, consider what you can do to reduce mind wandering while learning. Keep track of your strategies below. As you continue to work through this book and learn more ways to develop good concentration, refer to this list and add more items. If you run out of room, use another piece of paper. *Remember, mind wandering cannot be eliminated, only reduced.*

1. _Catch myself when I start daydreaming!_____
2. _____
3. _____
4. _____
5. _____
6. _____
7. _____
8. _____
9. _____
10. _____
11. _____
12. _____
13. _____
14. _____
15. _____

Checkpoint 3.1

1. What is a learning influence?
2. What influences you positively when you learn?
3. What influences you negatively?

3.2 YOUR LEARNING ENVIRONMENTS

As human beings, we react to our environment. When it is warm, we get sleepy. When it is noisy, we become distracted. When we have a lot on our minds, we have a hard time concentrating. A **learning environment** is the combination of influences that are present while you are learning or working.

There are two learning environments: physical and mental. Your physical environment includes external surroundings, such as room type, lighting, and noise level. Your mental environment is your internal state, which includes your attitude, how you feel, and what you are thinking about.

Both the physical and mental environments *directly* affect how well you can concentrate when learning or working. In turn, how well you concentrate directly affects how much you learn and how much time you have to spend in the learning process.

What's Around You?

Your **physical learning environment** is the place where you choose to read and study. It may be in your bedroom or kitchen, at the library, or at work. You could be seated in a reclining chair, on a couch, or at a desk or table. The room could be noisy or quiet. It could be filled with clutter or be neat and organized.

ACTIVITY 5

To understand physical influences that can affect learning, look at the sample floor plan below. Working in a group, discuss the influences that increase concentration and those that hinder it. A desk might promote concentration, while a bed might cause sleepiness. If an influence affects concentration negatively, brainstorm ways to make it positive.

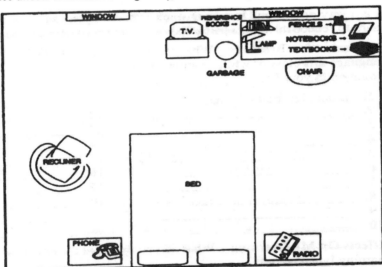

Now visualize the place (or places) in which you read, study, and learn. It could be some place at work or at home. Then using the sample diagram above as an example, sketch a simple floor plan of the space you learn in. Place an X or other marking that indicates where you are in the room. Make sure to include where the following items are as they pertain to your location. Identify what you can do to make your personal learning environments more conducive for learning.

desks and tables	chairs	bed	television	radio
dictionary	windows	other people	writing instruments	doorways/doors
computer	textbooks	lighting sources	food/drink	telephone

15 Options for Achieving Concentration

You are ultimately in charge of how well you concentrate. As you read through the following strategies for increasing your focus while learning, mark the strategies you think are most useful so you can refer to them later.

1. Choose a workplace.

Consider the following equation:

If a Bed = Sleep
and a Desk = Work,
then a Bed ≠ Work.

For years, learners have chosen a bed, the floor, a couch, or a comfortable chair as places to study. Yet, we associate these locations with relaxing or sleeping. A desk or table, on the other hand, is a place that we associate with working. If you think about it, that's why schools and libraries are filled with tables and desks, not beds! If you try to study in a place where you usually relax, you will find learning to be more challenging and time-consuming.

By moving to a desk or table to do your studying, you can concentrate better, thereby getting more work done in less time. A desk or table also has a convenient writing surface and plenty of space to spread out. At the other locations, you are often distracted either because you want to move to a different body position or you need to balance the learning material.

2. Manage your clutter.

Your desktop or tabletop should be clear of clutter, except for the materials you need for studying. You should have enough room for your elbows, reading material, a notebook, and any other necessary items. If your desk or table is cluttered, try the **arm-swing rule**; that is, gently sweep a semi-circle of clear space in front of you using the length of space from your elbow to your fingertips. You may end up with a clutter fortress piled up around the semi-circle, but nothing directly in front of you. When you have learning to do, clutter is a distraction.

3. Ensure good lighting.

Some people require a bright space, while others prefer a dimmer environment. It is easier to learn when the lighting is just right for your eyes. For example, if fluorescent lights bother you, place a lamp on your table, or sit by natural sunlight. If outside light bothers you, draw the curtains.

Getting work done in the least amount of time requires concentration. Which of these illustrations looks like a better situation for learning? Why?

4. Feed your body right.

What you eat plays an important role in how well or how poorly you concentrate. Protein foods (such as cheese, meat, fish, and vegetables) keep the mind alert, while carbohydrates (such as pasta, bread, and processed sugars), make you sleepy. Caffeine (commonly found in coffee, tea, soft drinks, and chocolate) acts as a stimulant in low doses. In high doses, it can cause jitters, heart palpitations, diarrhea, and sleeplessness. So when you want to concentrate, eat more protein in relation to your carbohydrates, and limit your caffeine.

5. Avoid food.

Food and serious learning don't mix well. Think about it. When you try to eat and study at the same time, which gets more of your concentration? The food, of course! You will be more effective if you eat first, then study. If you want to study while you eat, review material or read background information that requires less concentration.

6. Create room temperature comfort.

Room temperature is also important. You know that a too hot room makes you sleepy, while a too cold one makes you think about getting warm. You end up focusing more on how warm or cold you are than on your learning. Getting comfortable in a fixed temperature environment may mean putting on a sweater or turning on a fan. By working in a room that's a comfortable temperature, your concentration will improve, resulting in more effective studying.

7. Listen to your own thoughts.

Listening to anything but your own thoughts interferes with good concentration. Eliminating distractions such as vocal music, television, telephones, e-mail beeps, and other people can greatly increase the amount of studying you can accomplish.

8. Listen to Mozart.

Though you may disagree, listening to music with words does interfere with your ability to learn. You may think you are "tuning it out," but when you hear a song that you like, you may find yourself tapping your feet, humming along, or daydreaming. When your brain has to focus on two activities instead of one, your concentration is affected. If you need music while studying, try classical music. Recent research shows that playing classical music softly in the background, especially Mozart, may boost your brain while you are studying. Classical music helps you focus and concentrate better than music with words.

Focus on Ethics

You have a job working for a great boss who challenges you and makes you feel valued. Of your many job functions, you check your boss's e-mail when she travels and only forward those messages that are of the most importance. You have been told not to open messages marked "personal." This day, your mind wanders and you inadvertently open a personal message. It is from a recruiting firm providing job openings outside of your company that she might have interest in. As you stare at the screen, you must decide whether or not to pass this message along. What would you do? Why?

Success Skills

During your next learning session, work without music for ten minutes. Then turn your favorite music on at your usual volume, and work for another ten minutes. Listen to classical music for another ten minutes. In which ten-minute period did you get more done or learn more? Some say that silence is more distracting than music, but that too can be tuned out with a little practice. Write a few sentences to describe the more effective learning situation.

_____

_____

_____

_____

_____

_____

_____

_____

9. Turn off the television.

Watching television also interferes with your concentration when studying. Instead of focusing on just learning, you are adding listening and watching. In a half-hour period, if you do your work only at the commercial breaks, you might be lucky to accomplish five minutes of work. Even if you can hear a television in another room, you will be distracted. Your concentration should be on your learning, so it is a good idea to stay away from the television when trying to learn.

10. Hold all calls.

Receiving telephone calls during your study time is both distracting and time-consuming. Thanks to other human beings and answering devices, you have the ability to hold your calls until you complete your work. If you choose to study between 7:00 and 8:30 in the evening, you can leave a message on your answering machine or you can tell the person answering the phone to let your callers know that you will return their calls after 8:30. This will provide uninterrupted time for studying and you won't miss any phone calls.

11. Let e-mail wait.

Checking e-mail is just like answering the phone. If you choose to wait until you are done with your work, your concentration will stay on track.

12. Move to a quieter place.

Reading or working when other people are around can make concentrating difficult. If you do your reading or working in a public place such as a library, it may be quiet, but other people will always be moving around. If you read or work at home, your family may interrupt you more often than necessary. If you read at work, your boss or coworkers will inevitably interrupt you. In all cases, you have the ability to prevent these distractions. At the library, find a quiet corner of the building where few people go. At home, explain to your family your need for uninterrupted time, and move to a room where you can close the door. You will have a better chance of increasing your concentration. At work, move to a place where no one will find you, such as an empty conference room or the cafeteria during off-hours. These options provide more uninterrupted work time and a better chance of increasing your concentration.

13. Dump your to-do list.

If while you are reading or working, you find yourself thinking of other things you need to be doing, try writing them on a piece of paper. At inappropriate times your mind will almost always wander to things you need to do. Keeping track of your thoughts on paper and referring to the paper from time to time can be very effective for clearing your mind and focusing on your task.

14. Take short, frequent breaks.

Since people concentrate for about 20 minutes or less at a time, it would make sense to capitalize on your natural body rhythms and take a short break every 20 to 30 minutes. If you feel you are fully concentrating and involved in a task, then work until a natural break occurs. Generally, do some activity other than reading or learning.

15. Set a time goal.

If you know you have only 25 minutes to work on a project and you want to get through half of it, you will be more apt to finish if you stick to a time frame. Another example of this occurs when you naturally set goals by saying you will read until you reach the end of a chapter or an article. It may help motivate you to keep going.

What's On Your Mind?

What your mind thinks about while you are learning is called your **mental learning environment.** As you have already discovered, you often have many things on your mind that are unrelated to the learning task. You also have natural breaks in your concentration. It is during the breaks that you sometimes talk to yourself.

You may say negative or nonproductive statements such as, "I don't know how I'm going to finish all of this tonight" or "I'm going to fail the test tomorrow." You might say positive or productive statements, such as, "I really learned a lot today" or "I'm glad I've kept up with my work." The kind of self-talk you choose is based on your attitude and your physiology.

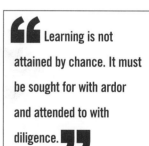

Developing positive self-talk

To take on the task of learning means you accept that you don't know everything. It means you will make mistakes along the way in the quest to find what you need. Accepting this reality will greatly enhance your self-confidence and your ability to develop positive self-talk. You will no longer dread mistakes, but welcome them.

A high level of confidence in your ability to try new things and think new thoughts will make your learning easier. In Chapter 1, you learned how important it is to develop a positive belief in yourself. You were also given the opportunity to begin to think positively. (You may want to take time now to go back and review Chapter 1.) Making the commitment to be a lifelong learner is a positive step toward a successful future. There is every reason in the world to believe that you can achieve anything you want.

Developing a positive attitude about your ability to learn makes the amount of time and energy you spend more enjoyable. Only you are in charge of your own attitude and learning!

Becoming aware of your physiology

Your **physiology,** simply defined as how your body feels, affects your thoughts and concentration while studying. Here are a few things to consider when you want to learn.

1. *Get Enough Sleep.* If you are feeling tired or ill, you will daydream and think more about getting sleep than about the work in front of you. You may try to continue to study, but you will waste a lot of time and find learning difficult. When you are really exhausted, you may wisely decide to put off the learning activity in favor of getting some sleep so that you don't waste your time or do more work than necessary. Your best option is to find a way to get enough sleep on a regular basis.

2. *Learn at Your Peak Time(s) of Day.* Your physiology changes throughout the day, with certain times of the day better for learning than others. Your ability to concentrate is easier when you feel fully awake and more difficult when you do not. Some individuals consider themselves morning people, while others consider themselves night owls. Planning your study time around your peak times of the day or when you feel best will make the time you spend more effective.

> ❝ Learning is not attained by chance. It must be sought for with ardor and attended to with diligence. ❞
>
> —Abigail Adams
> 2nd First Lady of the United States

3. *Take Care of Human Needs.* If you are hungry, need to use the bathroom, or feel ill, your concentration will be interrupted with these basic human functions. Do what you can to take care of them so your comfort level will be maximized for good concentration.

ACTIVITY 7

Complete the blanks below to explain how each item affects your ability to learn.

If I am tired, I_____

If I am rested, I_____

If I am hungry, I _____

If I am not hungry, I_____

If I feel ill, I_____

If I feel well, I _____

Compare your responses with those of others in your class, and discuss the effects of each. Talk about what you might do to improve your concentration in all of the above situations.

_____

_____

_____

_____

WEB LINK

www.utexas.edu/student/lsc/handouts/1442.html

This is a page entitled "Concentration and Your Body" from the University of Texas at Austin. It reinforces and supplements the information in this chapter. Access the main site to search other learning skills pages.

Taking Control of Your Concentration

Blaming external or internal factors for your inability to concentrate is easy to do. However, you can take an active role in setting up a learning environment that maximizes your concentration needs.

In Activity 1, you created a list of learning influences and decided whether each influence was positive, negative, or both. Using the columns below and the information you learned in this chapter, rearrange your learning influence list into two categories: *Mind wandering is a result of* and *Concentration is a result of.* (Hint: The negative influences are usually on the mind-wandering side, and the positive influences are usually on the concentration side.) You are encouraged to add more influences to either side of your list as you think of them. Review your two lists. Do you now know what you need to eliminate or add to create an effective learning environment? Remember to add to your list on page 61, Activity 4.

Mind wandering is a result of

Being tired

Learning late at night

Concentration is a result of

Being well rested

Learning early in the day

Checkpoint 3.2

1. What in your physical environment distracts you the most?

2. What in your mental environment distracts you the most?

3. What can you do right now to ensure better concentration for reading, learning, and working?

Key Terms and Concepts

arm-swing rule
concentration
effective learning environment
ineffective learning environment

learning environment
learning influences
mental learning environment

mind wandering
physical learning environment
physiology

Chapter Summary

1. Many influences affect the way you learn. Some are positive, and others are negative.

2. Concentration is vital to learning. Mind wandering is the enemy of concentration. Distractions are the primary cause of mind wandering.

3. You lose concentration and waste time when your mind wanders. Mind wandering can prevent you from understanding what you are trying to learn.

4. Mind wandering is effective only when it relates to the material you are learning.

5. Reducing mind wandering is the same as increasing concentration. There are many ways to improve your concentration while trying to learn. The first step in reducing mind wandering is to catch yourself doing it.

6. An effective physical learning environment consists of an appropriate place to learn without distractions.

7. An effective mental learning environment consists of a high level of learning self-confidence and an awareness of how you feel.

8. Taking control of your learning environment with specific strategies can help you concentrate better.

Answer the following questions based on the information you learned in this chapter.

1. What are learning influences? Which ones influence your learning the most?

2. What is the relationship between mind wandering and concentration?

3. What are some typical causes of mind wandering for you?

4. How is mind wandering both a good and bad influence on learning?

5. Name at least six things present in an effective learning environment.

6. Name at least six things present in an ineffective learning environment.

7. Which lack of concentration habit(s), if any, are you guilty of possessing (for example, watching TV or answering the phone while studying)?

8. Of the many suggestions in this chapter for concentrating better, which ones are the most useful for you?

9. On a scale of 1 to 10, with 1 being low and 10 being high, how would you rate your level of learning self-confidence? What can you do to make it even higher?

10. Going back to Ajit in the chapter scenario on page 54, what might you suggest he do to be able to concentrate better? How does your answer compare with your opinion when you started working on this chapter?

Case 1

Ellen was trying to complete an important project report for her new boss by the end of the day. Seated by an open window, she could hear children playing in the nearby school yard. The day was warm, a breeze ruffled her report papers, and her thoughts wandered to her upcoming vacation. Visions of swimming and playing on the beach with her son occupied her mind. Suddenly she realized that she had written only two sentences about the project. It was her first project report for this boss, and she wanted it to be perfect. Unfortunately, her last boss had done nothing but criticize her past reports. "I'll never get through this," she thought miserably as she looked out the window.

1.   Suggest four actions Ellen might take to reduce the distractions she is experiencing.

2.   What else could Ellen do to complete her report successfully?

Case 2

Bill was handy with cars. Many in the neighborhood would come to him on weekends with car problems. They knew he'd drop everything to help. When Bill was promoted to a new job, he began working at home in a virtual office. The job started out well, and Bill enjoyed the work environment. But soon his neighbors started calling him during his workday. As usual, Bill dropped everything to help. After a few months, Bill's boss complained about his work. "You're way behind in your customer calls, and when I try to call you, you're never there," said his boss.

1.   What would you advise Bill to do to improve his ability to concentrate on his work without alienating his friends and neighbors?

2.   What office work habits might Bill bring into his new virtual office that would improve his effectiveness?

4CHAPTER

It is Friday morning, and Juanita isn't thinking about the weekend. She is thinking about Monday, the day of her internship interview at a company she would like to work for. She realizes that the more she knows about the company, the better her chances for being hired will be.

Though this interview has been scheduled for two weeks, she hasn't found the time to do any background research.

To make matters even worse, she's in her cousin's wedding this weekend. Tonight is the rehearsal dinner, and tomorrow is the wedding. On Sunday, she's expected to spend time with family and out-of-town guests. If she's lucky and not too exhausted, she may have a few hours Sunday evening to surf the Internet for more information about the company. Unfortunately, she doesn't have enough time to call the company and request the annual report and other background information.

What could Juanita have done to be better prepared for her interview?

In This Chapter

Chapter Goals

After studying and working with the information in this chapter, you should be able to:

♦ Gain awareness of how you currently spend your time.

♦ Identify several short-term and long-term goals.

♦ Recognize how much time you need for learning.

♦ Use a calendar to schedule deadlines and social events.

♦ Use a weekly schedule to plan projects and daily responsibilities.

♦ Define procrastination and identify several ways to over-come it.

♦ Explain the importance of setting goals and planning rewards.

♦ Begin applying the information in this chapter to effectively manage your time and reach your goals.

> "It takes time to save time."
>
> —Alec McKenzie
> Popular time management specialist

How many hours are there in a day? The answer for most people is "not enough." No matter how hard you try, you simply cannot get more than 24 hours out of a day.

Between school, family, and work responsibilities, each day seems to be filled with things to do. Yet you may not have set aside time for yourself or for learning. If you are a student involved in athletics, you must schedule practice and workout time in addition to class and study time. If you are a working mother or father, you must juggle your job and family responsibilities with learning and study time.

Many people who wish for more time don't realize that they are the only ones who can create it. If you take a good look at how you currently spend each 24 hours, you may find ways to make better use of your time.

"Work smarter, not harder" is one of the important ideas expressed throughout this book. Being smart about how you use your time is probably the most important step you can take toward making your learning, and life in general, easier.

In this chapter, you will (1) identify how your time is spent, (2) recognize how much time you really need, and (3) learn helpful tips and suggestions for planning your time.

Do you know where your time goes?

SELF-CHECK

The following self-evaluation will give you an idea of how familiar, or unfamiliar, you are with some of the topics and terms discussed in this chapter. After reading each statement, circle the letter Y, S, or N to indicate the answer that is most appropriate for you. Answer honestly; rate yourself at the end, then complete the information for Chapter 4 in Appendix A.

Y = yes; frequently	S = sometimes	N = no; never

1. I know what is important to me.		Y	S	N
2. I make time for those things I feel are most important.		Y	S	N
3. I know how I spend my time.		Y	S	N
4. I know that learning requires time and repetition.		Y	S	N
5. I keep and follow a monthly calendar.		Y	S	N
6. I keep and follow a weekly planner.		Y	S	N
7. I plan ahead for project due dates and future events (writing projects, tests, presentations).		Y	S	N
8. I set goals for myself.		Y	S	N
9. I reward myself when I reach a goal.		Y	S	N
10. I know what procrastination is and how it affects my ability to manage my time.		Y	S	N

Rate Yourself:

Number of Ys	_____	x	100	=	_____		
Number of Ss	_____	x	50	=	_____		
Number of Ns	_____	x	0	=	_____	**Total**	_____

4.1 WHAT IS MOST IMPORTANT TO YOU?

If you know what is important to you today, tomorrow, or five years from now, you can budget your time wisely in order to meet your goals. Right now you probably make time for the most important activities and for the ones over which you have little or no control, such as a boss' request to meet a deadline. Being more active, conscious, and mindful about how you use your time will enable you to do those things that are truly most important to you.

So what IS important to you? What are your goals? Do you desire academic success? Do you wish to be a good mother or father or daughter or son? Do you want to be active in your community? Do you want to be a first-rate nurse, electrician, or landscaper?

A **goal** is something you want to have, want to do, or hope to be. Goals may be short term or long term. A **short-term goal** is usually considered something you want to achieve within the next six months to a year. Examples include buying a new car, deciding on a major course of study, learning a new computer program, and planning a surprise party.

A **long-term goal** is usually something that takes longer than six months to a year to achieve. Examples include getting a college degree, becoming a medical assistant, and planning a wedding. Research shows that people who think about their goals tend to reach more of them than people who don't think about their goals. And individuals who take the time to write them down almost always reach their goals. Let's test this theory and get you to start writing your goals. (After all, you do want success, yes?)

> " The indispensable first step to getting the things you want out of life is this: decide what you want. "
>
> —Ben Stein
> Contemporary author

On the first five blank lines below, list some of your short-term goals. On the next five lines, list some of your long-term goals. Be as realistic as possible. For example, if you say that one of your short-term goals is to earn a million dollars, you may find this goal unrealistic or difficult to achieve. If you find it difficult to come up with five, write at least one. You are being limited to five goals because working toward even one goal takes a lot of time and energy. Return to this list several times in the next day or two, and add to or clarify the goals as you think about what is truly important to you.

Identifying Short-Term Goals

Example: I want to plan my spring vacation.

1. _____
2. _____
3. _____
4. _____
5. _____

Identifying Long-Term Goals

Example: I want to get a college degree.

1. _____
2. _____
3. _____
4. _____
5. _____

> " Review your priorities; ask yourself the question, "What's the best use of my time right now? "
>
> —Alan Lakein
> Time management author

ACTIVITY 2

Identifying your goals is the first step toward managing your time. The second step requires planning and taking action in order to achieve the goals. For each of your goals listed in Activity 1, write the actions you believe you need to take in order to achieve them. Be as specific as possible. Use the following examples as a model. Notice the detailed actions. Writing specific actions will help you reach your goals sooner.

Sample Short-Term Goals Action List

Example: To plan my spring vacation, I need to:

1. Know who's coming with me.

2. Decide where we want to go.

3. Decide how much money is needed.

4. Look on the Internet for travel deals.

5. Check my wardrobe.

6. Schedule my work projects and family events around my time away.

Sample Long-Term Goals Action List

Example: To get a college degree, I need to:

1. Research colleges with programs I am interested in.

2. Choose and apply to several colleges.

3. Secure loan(s).

4. Find and work with an academic advisor.

5. Do well in my classes.

6. Manage my time well.

Short-Term Goals Action List

1. _____

_____

2. _____

_____

3. _____

_____

4. _____

_____

5. _____

_____

6. _____

_____

Long-Term Goals Action List

1. _____

_____

2. _____

_____

3. _____

_____

4. _____

_____

5. _____

_____

6. _____

_____

Success Skills

Knowing what is important to you helps you plan your time according to *your* needs, not someone else's. Becoming aware of how you spend your time presently is the next step to planning how to spend your time in the future.

There are basically two ways to spend time: productively and unproductively. Spending **productive time** is when you are engaged in some activity that gets you closer to your goal(s). If learning a new computer program is one of your goals, then spending time at your computer trying out the program is a productive use of your time. If you intend to keep a clean house, then doing dishes and vacuuming is a good use of your time.

On the other hand, spending **unproductive time** is when you are not engaged in an activity that carries you toward your goal(s). Spending time at your computer aimlessly surfing the Web will not help you learn the new program and is an unproductive use of your time. (But surfing the Web for a project or for the answer to a question is a productive use of your time.) If you decide to watch TV or read the paper instead of cleaning the house, you are using your time unproductively. (However, if your intent is to relax, then reading the paper or watching TV is a good use of your time.)

In the end, what is considered productive or unproductive depends entirely upon your goals and intentions.

Achieving a balance between time spent on productive versus unproductive activities is a daily challenge. We all know how easy it is to ignore an alarm clock, get up when we want, and do only what we please all day. But reality dictates that we go to work or school and take care of our families. Becoming aware of what you do and how it relates to your goals is a productive step in reaching your goals and getting what you want out of life.

Checkpoint 4.1

1. What is a goal?

2. What are some of your goals?

3. What makes your goals realistic (reachable)?

4.2 WHERE DOES YOUR TIME GO?

Where does your time go? Actually, it doesn't go anywhere. Just like money, you spend it. You have 24 hours to spend each day, and each day you spend it in different ways.

Keeping a **Daily Activity Log**, a list of the activities you do from the time you get up until you go to sleep (Figure 4-1), is a simple way to see how you spend your time. It is also a good way to plan a daily schedule.

Figure 4-1   Sample Daily Activity Log

DAILY ACTIVITY LOG

Time	Activity	Time	Activity
6:00 a.m.	Get up and shower	4:00	Class
6:30	Eat breakfast	4:30	Commute home
7:00	Commute to work	5:00	Watch TV
7:30	"	5:30	Make dinner
8:00	Work	6:00	Eat dinner
8:30	"	6:30	Clean up
9:00	"	7:00	Phone calls
9:30	"	7:30	Fix window
10:00	"	8:00	Check e-mail
10:30	"	8:30	Read newspaper
11:00	"	9:00	Study
11:30	"	9:30	"
12:00 p.m.	Lunch / Go to class	10:00	Read in bed/Get snack
12:30	Class	10:30	"
1:00	"	11:00	Watch TV
1:30	"	11:30	Go to sleep
2:00	"	12:00 a.m.	
2:30	"	12:30	
3:00	Class	1:00	
3:30	"	1:30	

Success Skills

To get an accurate account of how you spend your time, complete the Daily Activity Log. Record every activity you do during the day. Be specific about your activities and the amount of time required for each. Use the log in Figure 4-1 as an example.

Daily Activity Log

6:00 a.m. _____	4:00 _____
6:30 _____	4:30 _____
7:00 _____	5:00 _____
7:30 _____	5:30 _____
8:00 _____	6:00 _____
8:30 _____	6:30 _____
9:00 _____	7:00 _____
9:30 _____	7:30 _____
10:00 _____	8:00 _____
10:30 _____	8:30 _____
11:00 _____	9:00 _____
11:30 _____	9:30 _____
12:00 p.m. _____	10:00 _____
12:30 _____	10:30 _____
1:00 _____	11:00 _____
1:30 _____	11:30 _____
2:00 _____	12:00 a.m. _____
2:30 _____	12:30 _____
3:00 _____	1:00 _____
3:30 _____	1:30 _____

A **Weekly Activity Log** is similar to a Daily
Activity Log, except that it shows your activities
for a full week.

Figure 4-2   Sample Weekly Activity Log

Time	Monday	Tuesday	Wednesday	Thursday	Friday	Saturday	Sunday
6:00 a.m.	Get up and shower	→			→		
6:30	Eat breakfast	→			→		
7	Commute to work	→			→		
7:30	"	→			→		
8	Work	→			→		
8:30	"	→			→		
9	"	→			→	Get up Read paper	Get up Read paper
9:30	"	→			→	"	"
10	"	→			→	Mow lawn	Check e-mail
10:30	"	→			→	"	Bake cookies
11	"	→			→	Shower	"
11:30	"	→			→	Grocery Shop	Brunch with Bob
12:00 p.m.	Lunch Go to class	Lunch	Lunch Go to class	Lunch	Lunch Go to class	"	"
12:30	Class	Work	Class	Work	Class	Unload groceries	"
1	"	"	"	"	"	Laundry	"
1:30	"	"	"	"	"	"	Study
2	"	"	"	"	"	Check e-mail	"
2:30	Get coffee	"	Get coffee	"	Get coffee	Surf Web	"
3	Class	Work	Class	Work	Class	Surf Web	Study

Success Skills

Figure 4-2 continued   Sample Weekly Activity Log

Time	Monday	Tuesday	Wednesday	Thursday	Friday	Saturday	Sunday
3:30	"	"	"	"	"	Nap	"
4	"	Go to gym	"	Go to gym	"	Study	"
4:30	Commute home	Workout and shower	Library research	Workout and shower	Meet Becca for dinner	"	"
5	Watch TV	"	"	"	"	"	Workout and shower
5:30	Make dinner	Commute home	Commute home	Commute home	"	"	"
6	Eat dinner	Watch TV	Make dinner	Vollyball	"	Phone calls	Watch TV
6:30	Clean Up	Make dinner	Dinner	"	Go to movies	Meet Julia for dinner	"
7	Phone calls	Dinner	Clean up Phone calls	Go home Dinner	"	"	Get pizza
7:30	Fix window	Clean up	Phone calls	"	"	"	Dinner
8	Check e-mail	Phone calls	Study	Phone calls	"	John's party	Phone calls
8:30	Read newspaper	"	"	Watch TV	"	"	"
9	Study	Read newspaper	"	"	"	"	Study
9:30	"	Study	"	"	"	"	"
10	Read in bed Get snack	Watch TV	"	Study	Out for ice cream	"	Watch TV
10:30	"	"	Take bath"	"	"	"	"
11	Watch TV	"	Watch TV	"	Go home Watch TV	"	"
11:30	Go to sleep	Go to sleep	Go to sleep	Go to sleep	Go to sleep	"	Go to sleep
12:00						"	
12:30 a.m.						"	
1						"	
1:30						Go to sleep	

ACTIVITY 4

To get an accurate account of how you spend your time, complete the Weekly Activity Log. Record every activity you do during the next seven days. Be specific about your activities and the amount of time required for each. Use the log in Figure 4-2 as an example.

Weekly Activity Log For the Week of_____

Time	Monday	Tuesday	Wednesday	Thursday	Friday	Saturday	Sunday
6:00 a.m.							
6:30							
7							
7:30							
8							
8:30							
9							
9:30							
10							
10:30							
11							
11:30							
12:00 p.m.							
12:30							
1							
1:30							
2							
2:30							

Success Skills

3						
3:30						
4						
4:30						
5						
5:30						
6						
6:30						
7						
7:30						
8						
8:30						
9						
9:30						
10						
10:30						
11						
11:30						
12:00 a.m.						
12:30						
1:00						

ACTIVITY 5

Once you complete the Weekly Activity Log in Activity 4, answer the following questions. Use a calculator, if needed.

How much time did you spend in the following ways?	Weekly Total	Average Number of Hours per Day
sleeping	_____	_____
eating and grooming	_____	_____
commuting	_____	_____
attending classes	_____	_____
studying, reading, or learning	_____	_____
working at a job	_____	_____
writing and responding to e-mail—outside of work	_____	_____
surfing the Internet—outside of work	_____	_____
exercising or participating in sports or leisure activities	_____	_____
socializing with friends	_____	_____
watching TV	_____	_____
not accounted for—don't know	_____	_____
other ways you spent your time	_____	_____

Comparing these answers to your goals, how well are you spending your time? Are you generally productive in your nonschool and work hours? Or do you waste time with nonproductive activities?

Your Weekly Activity Log and your goals list are useful tools for identifying how you spend your time. You can use this knowledge to make better use of the time you have.

Checkpoint 4.2

1. What is a weekly activity log?

2. What did you learn from yours?

3. How might you spend your time differently?

4.3 HOW MUCH TIME DO YOU NEED?

How much time do you need? Probably more than you currently have. For the purpose of this section, you will concentrate on how much time students spend in class and studying for school-related projects. *If you are presently not taking any classes, you will still find this information valuable.*

As a general rule, the amount of study time a student needs is based on the number of hours he or she attends class each week. For every hour you spend in a classroom, you should set aside at least an equal number of hours for doing homework, reviewing, practicing, or studying. For example, if you are in class for six hours a week, then you should allocate at least six hours of study time. If you require more time to learn (perhaps because you are not using effective or efficient learning strategies), you may need two hours of study time for each class hour. If you have a light amount of homework or are efficient at getting it done, you will find yourself with unexpected free time.

Individuals taking training for work can adapt this information to meet their training schedule. For example, you may be taking a two-day computer training course, not a semester-long program. If so, you will need at least two more days of study time, which is usually broken up over several weeks for you to review, practice, and study the new concepts.

Taking the total number of hours per week you are in class (see Activity 6), look at your Weekly Activity Log and see if you scheduled at least an equal number of hours for homework and study time. If you did, good for you! If not, start looking for ways to make room in your schedule for more homework and study time. If you find you don't need the extra study time, you'll have more free time. Just remember that any new learning requires additional time outside the classroom. Repeated exposure to and experience with the subject matter will solidify your knowledge.

> I was taught very early that I would have to depend entirely upon myself, that my future lay in my own hands.
>
> —Darius Ogden Mills
> American educator

ACTIVITY 6

How many hours are you in class per week? You can use your Weekly Activity Log and the following equation to figure it out. An example has been completed based on a computer course that meets one and a half hours a day, three times a week.

Subject	Class hours per Day		Meetings per Week		Hours per Week
Computers	$1\frac{1}{2}$	X	3	=	$4\frac{1}{2}$
		X		=	
		X		=	
		X		=	
		X		=	
		X		=	
		X		=	
		X		=	
		X		=	
		X		=	

Total Hours per Week _____

Checkpoint 4.3

1. Why is scheduling enough time important for learning?

2. What did you discover about how much time you need for learning?

3. What can you do to ensure sufficient learning time?

> Concentrate on the essentials. . . you will then be accomplishing the greatest results with the effort expended.
>
> —R. Alec MacKenzie
>   Time management specialist

Success Skills

4.4 PLANNING YOUR TIME

Adding school into your life means that you will spend time going to class and doing homework. But it also means that you will have to study for exams, do research, create projects, and write essays and papers.

The best way to plan everything you have to do and want to do is to use a calendar. Calendars are meant for nonroutine events, such as appointments, meetings, sporting events, social events, birthdays, and deadlines. They are not meant for small project details. A weekly or daily project planner is more appropriate for these activities.

Most people keep one of three common calendar systems: an academic calendar (used primarily by students), a monthly calendar (used by many individuals including businesspeople and families), and a palmtop calendar (used mostly by businesspeople). This section discusses different time management options. Decide which one or ones work best for you.

Using An Academic Calendar

An **academic calendar** is made up of monthly calendars, typically from September to August. It is meant to be used by individuals taking school or training courses. Whether your school runs on a quarterly, trimester, semester, or yearly schedule, an academic calendar is flexible enough to accommodate everyone.

An academic calendar shows an overview of large assignments, papers, projects, and other requirements due on a certain date. It acts as an engagement book for important school and personal activities for a school term or year.

To set up an academic calendar, it helps to have a **syllabus** (plural: syllabi), or schedule of assignments, from the instructor of each class you take. These are usually handed out the first week of classes. If the instructor does not have a syllabus, you can still complete an academic calendar using what you already know and making changes or additions as time goes on.

Once you have your syllabus, follow the steps in Activity 7 to complete an academic calendar. You may use Figure 4.3 as an example. Use a dark pencil or erasable pen so you can easily make changes. If assignments or dates change, you can easily make changes.

> " Plan your work for today and every day, then work your plan. "
>
> —Dr. Norman Vincent Peale
> Self-help author

Figure 4–3   Sample Academic Calendar

Date	Monday	Tuesday	Wednesday	Thursday	Friday	Saturday	Sunday
Sept. 7 - 13	Labor Day	Classes begin					
Sept. 14 - 20							
Sept. 21 - 27			Trigonometry quiz			Julie & Jack's wedding	Family dinner
Sept. 28 - Oct. 4					Electronics quiz		
Oct. 5 - 11							
Oct. 12 - 18	Columbus Day - no classes					Eric Clapton concert	
Oct. 19 - 25			Trigonometry Mid-term		Electronics Mid-term		
Oct. 26 - Nov. 1	Blue print reading quiz						
Nov. 2 - 8				Motor control demo			
Nov. 9 - 15	Veterans Day		Trigonometry quiz				
Nov. 16 - 22		Nursing project due			To Philadelphia	Philadelphia	Philadelphia
Nov. 23 - 29			Last day of classes	Thanksgiving break	Thanksgiving break	Thanksgiving break	Thanksgiving break
Nov. 30 - Dec. 6	Electronics final		Trigonometry final		School ends		

Complete your school calendar for the current term by following the instructions given in the steps below.

Step 1: Identify the beginning and end of the term. Label the "Week" column in either of two ways. You may list the number of the term week (for example, 1, 2, 3) or the dates of the week (for example, Sept. 7-13).

Week column of term calendar

Week
1
2
3

or

Week
Sept. 7-13
Sept. 14-21
Sept. 22-27

Step 2: Fill in all school holidays and important school events.

Step 3: From the information provided on your syllabus, fill in important dates for tests, quizzes, research papers, and projects. (Daily assignments should not be written on this form; they will be included on the weekly project planner explained in the next section.)

Step 4: Write the dates of any important social events you already know about, such as family get-togethers, parties, and concerts.

Date	Monday	Tuesday	Wednesday	Thursday	Friday	Saturday	Sunday
Sept. 7 - 13							
Sept. 14 - 20							
Sept. 21 - 27							
Sept. 28 - Oct. 4							
Oct. 5 - 11							
Oct. 12 - 18							
Oct. 19 - 25							
Oct. 26 - Nov. 1							
Nov. 2 - 8							
Nov. 9 - 15							
Nov. 16 - 22							
Nov. 23 - 29							
Nov. 30 - Dec. 6							

Success Skills

You can use your academic calendar to make out a schedule for completing papers and projects. Typically, you need a lot of time to complete papers and projects. For example, if today is Tuesday and you have a paper due six weeks from today, you can plan each of the steps you must do to complete the assignment.

Week 1:	By Friday	Decide on a topic
Week 2:	Tuesday	Start research
Week 3:	Tuesday	Continue research
	Thursday	Continue research
Week 4:	Tuesday	Write outline of paper
Week 5:	Tuesday	Write first draft
Week 6:	Sunday	Revise draft
	Tuesday	Hand in paper

Take a look at your academic calendar. See if, as the term progresses, you can add to or change any of the information you have written. The key is to rely on your academic calendar for all of your planning needs.

Now that you have a calendar for keeping track of school-related dates and social events, you still need a way to keep track of daily assignments and responsibilities.

Using a Weekly Project Planner

A **weekly project planner** allows you keep track of your assignments in more detail. It contains a to-do list specific to one day. It looks like a calendar but is divided into 5, one-day periods with plenty of space to write.

For students, using a weekly project planner is an effective way to keep track of assignments and plan study time according to the school calendar. When you were in grade school, you might have carried a small notepad to write your assignments in. Or you might have written them inside your notebooks or textbooks. Now that you are older, you should have one place to keep track of all your study demands.

One blank weekly project planner is shown in Activity 8. Since this page represents one week in a term, you will need to make enough copies of this form to equal the number of weeks in your term. For example, if your term consists of 12 weeks of classes, you will need 12 copies. Many people, other than students, also use a weekly project planner. The planner might look somewhat different, however. It, too, will consist of seven days with space to write notes. Businesspeople find this an effective way to prepare for a meeting.

If Ms. Gregory is running an important meeting on Monday, October 15, she might write a reminder in her weekly project planner on Wednesday, October 10, to begin her preparation. If you are a parent who is responsible for bringing the class snack on Tuesday, January 22, you might write a note in your weekly project planner on Sunday, January 20, to remind you to go shopping or to plan time for baking. See Figure 4-4 as an example. Use Activity 8 to complete your personal weekly project planner.

Figure 4–4   Sample Weekly Project Planner

Project Planner for Week No. __5__

Subject (hardest to easiest)	Physics	Mechanical Drawing	Computer Programming	English Composition	
MON. _Oct. 5_	p. 62—Evans problems 1-4 Write complete solutions	Work on machine spec	No class	For Wed. — Write a one-page essay on my career goals	
TUES. _Oct. 6_	p. 71—Evans problems 6-12 Write complete solutions	Make corrections to spec	Read Chap. 3 "How to Read Error Messages" Do ques. @ end of chapter	Work on essay due tomorrow	
WED. _Oct. 7_ Lisa's b'day	No class	Finalize spec to hand in tomorrow	Go to lab and test program Keep journal of error msgs.	p. 36-40 Read Warriner's p. 41-42 Do exer. A, B, & D	
THURS. _Oct. 8_	Review for quiz tomorrow	Begin wire drawing due Wed. next week	Go to lab and revise steps 6-24	No class	
FRI. _Oct. 9_ 2 p.m. Dr. appt.	p. 76—Evans problems 1-3 Write complete solutions	No class Continue wire drawing	Read Chap. 4 "If/When commands" Do 20 ques. @ end of chapter	No homework	

Focus on Ethics

As the bookkeeper in a small family-run business, you are in charge of printing the paychecks every Friday. Your boss is away today and not returning until Monday. In the past, your boss has given you permission to write his signature on letters and other business documents. You and the other employees desperately need your paychecks this week. Without express approval from your boss, should you sign his name to the checks? How could this situation have been avoided?

WEB LINK

Many Internet sites now offer free web-based calendars on which you can record your personal schedule. Look at one or two of the following web calendars to find a calendar with features useful for you. You can also do a web search using the key word *free web calendar*.

When.com: **http://www.when.com/**

Yahoo: Calendar   **http://calendar.yahoo.com**

Excite Planner   **http://calendar.excite.com**

ACTIVITY 8

Develop a weekly project planner for yourself by following the steps below and completing the blank planner on page 96. Refer to the previous discussion as needed.

Step 1: Before you can use your weekly project planner, you need to set up all of the daily and weekly information for the term. This is done once, at the beginning of the term. At the top left of the schedule, where it says "Project Planner for Week No. __", you can fill in the blank in two ways—either by using the week number (for example, 1 through 12, if 12 is the number of weeks in your term) or by writing in the actual dates (for example, Sept. 7-13 or Sept. 14-20).

Step 2: In the boxes labeled MON _____, TUES. _____, and so on, fill in the weekly dates (such as MON. Sept. 7, TUES. Sept. 8, and so on). This schedule runs Monday through Friday, but you can adapt it if you are taking weekend courses.

Step 3: List the subjects you are taking, from the hardest, or most challenging, to the easiest, or least challenging, going across the top line of the planner. This is done so that you will pay attention to your hardest subject first. When doing homework, most students put off doing the hardest subject for last, when they are either too tired or just not willing to spend the time with it. *However, if you do your hardest subject first, you will have a much better chance of succeeding in that class.* If you are only taking one or two classes, you can create a modified version of the planner by covering up or eliminating several of the vertical lines so the boxes can be enlarged.

Step 4: Using your school calendar to assist you, bring forward to the weekly project planner all important information, such as tests, paper and project deadlines, and school holidays. As the semester progresses, you can make changes to the planner. How you note the due dates of your assignments is up to you.

Step 5: Carry both the weekly project planner and the academic calendar with you at all times, either in a folder with pockets or in a three-ring binder. When you are given a new assignment or if a date or an assignment changes, you can make changes to your planners easily. Most of all, make the planner work for you.

Project Planner for Week No._____

Subject (Hardest to easiest)					
MON. _____					
TUES. _____					
WED. _____					
THURS. _____					
FRI. _____					

Using a Monthly Calendar

In today's hectic world of doing more and doing it faster, people are turning to **monthly calendars** to help keep them on track. (Office supply stores have a variety of shapes and sizes from which to choose.) Working people use a monthly calendar to make and keep appointments. Some also use them to plan for long-term work projects. Parents and guardians track their children's appointments, lessons, and sports and social events, as well as their own activities. If you are a student, you could combine the concept of an academic calendar with a monthly calendar. If you plan to use a monthly calendar, keep in mind that it is not meant to serve as a to-do list.

Using a Palmtop Calendar

A **palmtop calendar** is one of the most popular electronic handheld organizers available. It contains a daily calendar, an appointment scheduler, a location for a to-do list and memos, and an address book. Many business professionals like palmtop calendars, and software companies have added capabilities to make them more powerful.

With a palmtop system, you see only one day's scheduled activities at a time. This is similar to using a Daily Activity Log (see "Where Does Your Time Go?") as your time planner. Palmtop calendars are great for planning day-to-day details, but they do not provide the user with a full view of a month or a week. Some people prefer just the daily view, while others prefer to have the benefit of the bigger picture to better plan their time.

Try out different calendar systems to determine which one works best for you.

Checkpoint 4.4

1. Which calendar system is best for you? Why?

2. For what purpose might you use a weekly project planner?

3. For what purpose might you use a daily log?

4.5 FINDING TIME

What you have been doing up to this point is figuring out how you actually spend your time and then discovering ways to keep track of it by using an academic calendar, weekly project planner, monthly calendar, or palmtop calendar. What you haven't done yet is learn how to plan your schedule so you can do everything you need to do and still have time left for things you want to do.

There are three ways to make sure you have more time in a day. *The first and most important way to gain more time is to plan it!* It's like getting in a car and going somewhere. You need to know where you are going and have a plan to get there. Without a plan, you will waste your time and take longer to get to your destination—if you get there at all!

A second way to gain more time in a day is to do more in less time. You are discovering in this book how to learn more efficiently, which includes how to study effectively in less time. Using active learning strategies will help you gain more time. This can be as simple as doubling up on activities. For example, if you have three errands, you might try to combine them instead of doing one at time, making one round-trip instead of three. If you commute on a bus or train or carpool, you can study during your ride. At lunch, you can review notes. Use your imagination as to how you can get more done in less time.

Yet a third way to gain more time is to use short periods of otherwise wasted time. Activities such as commuting or taking an over-long lunch can be time wasters, but they can be used for dual purposes. For example, businesspeople often combine meetings with meals. On your Daily or Weekly Activity Logs, see if you can locate any wasted, unproductive time that could be turned into unwasted, productive time. Do you have a free half-hour between classes where you can either socialize with friends or study? If your education is important to you, you might choose to spend that time studying. Do you watch a lot of television, spend an excessive amount of time in aimless computer play, or talk frequently on the phone?

This time might be better used by reducing your television and computer time and limiting your phone time. It's always a good idea to carry some of your reading material or project work with you—you never know when you will have to wait in line or in someone's office. If each day you find an extra 20 minutes, in one week you will have an extra two hours and twenty minutes!

To assure your learning success, ask "How can I do more in less time or use time that is otherwise wasted?" Write your thoughts below.

_____

_____

_____

_____

_____

_____

_____

_____

_____

_____

_____

Sometimes even the best-planned schedules must change because of unplanned events. When this happens and you must make a choice regarding what to do, ask yourself, "What is the best use of my time *right now*?" Your answer will make sense based on the things that are truly important to you. Consider this scenario:

Cousin Sheila comes into town unexpectedly and wants to take you to dinner. You have planned to spend several hours on a project that is due the next day. What will you do?

If completing the project on time is important to you, you might tactfully thank your cousin, explain your situation, and offer to meet with her for ice cream after you have completed your work.

Working with a partner, discuss the following scenarios. What would you do in each of the following situations?

Situation No. 1

It's 6:30 p.m. on a Monday night. You have a test on Wednesday that you want to study for tonight between 6:30 and 7:15 p.m. After that, you are scheduled to go to a community meeting that will not be over until at least 10:00 p.m. Your friend calls you on the phone to chat—nothing very important, just a conversation. What do you do?

_____

_____

_____

_____

_____

Situation No. 2

It's 8:00 p.m. on a Sunday night. You have an oral presentation due on Tuesday. You have already done your research, but you still need several hours to prepare for the presentation. Because of work and other family commitments, you have no other time before Tuesday to complete this assignment. Your spouse needs your immediate help moving furniture in the basement and can't do it without you. What do you do?

_____

_____

_____

_____

_____

Procrastination and Other Time Wasters

Procrastination means putting off doing something unpleasant or burdensome until a future time. Most people, unfortunately, are excellent procrastinators. They put work off until the last minute and cram to get it done, hoping not to do a slipshod job. The reality is that only a few people can cram well and do a good job. The others just *think* they can. (See Chapter 5 for more about cramming for exams.)

With a partner or on your own, list some reasons why people put things off until a future time. Then discuss what can happen as a result of procrastinating.

_____

_____

_____

_____

_____

_____

_____

Top Reasons for Procrastinating

✓ An assignment or project is too big or overwhelming.
✓ The assignment is unpleasant.
✓ Fear of the assignment takes over, such as having to get up in front of people to make a presentation.

If you put off an assignment too long, you may not get it done on time; you may not end up doing a quality job; or you may not complete it at all. You may also be embarrassed and frustrated if someone discovers you are behind in your work. Remember, things do not get any easier when they are put off!

So how can you reduce procrastination? Since procrastination means doing nothing, simply doing something is the way to overcome it. Here are some actions to consider:

1. *Start small.* If you take your big assignment and break it down into smaller pieces, you will be able to break through your procrastination. It's like trying to eat a pizza whole; you can't do it. But you can eat it one bite at a time. For example, when studying for an exam, study a little each day instead of all at once; the job won't seem as large.

2. *Realize how miserable you'll feel until the work is done.* If you don't want that annoying feeling hanging over you, remind yourself how

good it will feel to be finished with the assignment. Then get started!

3. *Tell yourself you are wasting time.* You are wasting time if you are not working on your project. If time is valuable to you, why waste it?

4. *Be accountable to someone else.* If you set a deadline with someone, you will be less likely to break it. For example, tell your friends you can't meet them until after you finish your research. Then, get to work.

5 *Add variety.* If you do not enjoy working on a certain subject, try creative learning methods such as using flash cards or studying with a friend. Or alternate the unpleasant work with more pleasant work.

6. *Promise yourself a reward.* When you finish doing your work, give yourself a reward.

Study Goals and Rewards

Doing activities according to the top priority sometimes means that you can't do what you want to do at the moment. Studying may be the last thing you prefer to do. Perhaps you would rather watch television, surf the Web, or go out with friends. But if you want to do well in your classes, you must find time to study.

How often do you feel like studying? If you wait until you feel like it, you might never open a book! So how do you motivate yourself to study when you are tired? or when you have other commitments?

By setting a learning goal and rewarding yourself for reaching the goal, learning will become easier. You will also have a higher level of concentration because you are determined to complete the work on time.

A **learning goal** means completing your projects and assignments in a reasonable time frame. A **reward** is something you give yourself in return for your effort. For example, suppose you are a nursing student who has to read a chapter in the nursing handbook and then write a patient report. You also need to review your medicine interactions for a quiz the following day. In your estimation, these tasks should take you no more than an hour and a half. If you begin doing your work at 6:30 p.m., your learning goal should be to complete the work by 8:00 p.m.

At 8:00 p.m., when the work is completed, you can reward yourself with a non-work-related activity, such as watching television, eating a special snack, or reading a favorite magazine. By deciding on your reward ahead of time, you will be motivated to finish your work as quickly as possible, leaving you with more time to do whatever you want. This is one of the best ways to work smarter, not harder.

The next time you sit down to study, think about setting a learning goal and then rewarding yourself upon its completion. This way you will be less tempted to interrupt your learning time, thereby getting your work done efficiently.

Success Skills

Different people enjoy different rewards. How would you reward yourself for reaching a learning goal? Make a list.

_____   _____

_____   _____

_____   _____

_____   _____

_____   _____

_____   _____

_____   _____

Additional Ways to Master Your Time

What follows is a list of more ways you can use to master your time. See if any of them are useful to you.

1. *Prepare for the morning the evening before.* Put out your clothes, make lunches, pack your books.

2. *Get up 15 minutes earlier in the morning.* Use the time to plan your day, review your assignments, or catch up on the news.

3. *Don't rely on your memory.* Write your assignments, appointments, and due dates on a calendar.

4. *Schedule a realistic day.* Avoid planning for every minute. Leave extra time in your day for getting to appointments and studying.

5. *Leave room in your day for the unexpected.* This will allow you to do what you need to do, regardless of what happens. If the unexpected never happens, you will have more time for yourself.

6. *Do one thing at a time.* If you try to do two things at once, you become inefficient. Concentrate on the here and now.

7. *Let things slide from time to time.* The world will not come to an end if you do your laundry on Sunday instead of Saturday.

8. *Learn to say "No!"* Say no to social activities or invitations when you don't have the time or energy.

9. *Get enough sleep.* When you are well rested, you are more capable of handling anything that comes your way.

10. *Learn to relax.* Take deep breaths, stretch, or exercise to relieve tension and stress.

ACTIVITY 13

What special methods are helpful when you need to control your time? List five ways you master time.

1. _____

   _____

2. _____

   _____

3. _____

   _____

4. _____

   _____

5. _____

   _____

Checkpoint 4.5

1. What is procrastination?

2. What is a learning goal?

3. Why is it important to reward yourself for reaching a learning goal?

Key Terms and Concepts

academic calendar	monthly calendar	short-term goal
Daily Activity Log	palmtop calendar	syllabus
goals	productive time	unproductive time
learning goal	procrastination	Weekly Activity Log
long-term goal	rewards	weekly project planner

Success Skills

Chapter Summary

1. Every day has 24 hours, no more, no less. To spend your time productively means you must work toward a goal. To spend your time unproductively means you are engaged in an activity that is not working toward a goal.

2. Knowing what is important to you and having short-term and long-term goals will help you make wise choices about how you spend your time.

3. Students should plan at least one hour of study time per week for every hour in class.

4. There are three common systems: academic, monthly and palmtop. An academic calendar helps you keep track of school-related dates and social events. A monthly calendar helps you track appointments, family activities, meetings, and birthdays. A palmtop calendar is best for planning one day at a time.

5. A weekly project planner will help you keep track of your daily responsibilities and assignments.

6. There are three things you can do to have more time in a day: plan the day, do more in less time, and use short periods of otherwise wasted time.

7. Procrastination means putting off doing something unpleasant or burdensome until a future time. Ways of overcoming procrastination include starting with small actions, adding variety to the task, and promising yourself a reward upon completing the task.

8. Setting a learning goal means planning to do a certain amount of work in a given time. When you have achieved your goal, give yourself a reward in return for your effort. Setting learning goals and planning for rewards can help you save time and make learning rewarding.

Smart Tip

According to R. Alec MacKenzie, a time management guru, for every minute you plan, you save two minutes in execution. For example, if you take 15 minutes at the end of each day to plan the following day, you would then save 30 minutes that next day because of the forethought and planning. How might this affect your life?

Review

Based on the information you learned in this chapter, answer the following questions using your own words and thoughts.

1. Why is learning how to manage your time important?

2. Why is knowing your goals important?

3. For what purpose can a Daily Activity Log be used?

4. For what purpose can a Weekly Activity Log be used?

5. Describe the three calendar systems.

6. Describe a weekly project planner.

7. What is procrastination, and what can you do to reduce it?

8. Describe how setting learning goals and then rewarding yourself for reaching them can help make studying easier.

9. Which of the time management formats explained in this chapter do you find most useful and why?

10. As a result of working through this chapter, what are you going to do to better manage your time?

Success Skills

Case 1

"I get further behind every day," Jack complained to his brother. "I work in the morning, have classes all afternoon, and when I get home at night, I have a million things to do around the yard just to keep up. I'm exhausted." When his brother asked how Jack spent his time, Jack answered vaguely that he had to do "everything" himself and his chores took a lot of time. "Just cutting the grass takes hours," he said. Jack mentioned that he and a friend were sharing a lawn mower and garden tools and that he often had to wait for his friend to get home from work before he could borrow the equipment. While he waited, he watched TV, even though he didn't like anything that was on.

1. How might Jack avoid wasting time while waiting for his friend to get home from work?

2. What could Jack learn by keeping a Daily Activity Log that would help him better manage his time?

Case 2

Russell wanted to leave a message for his coworker friend, Linda, but was surprised when she answered her phone. "We were supposed to meet 15 minutes ago," he said impatiently. "I forgot. I'm sorry," apologized Linda. "I'll be there in a minute." When Linda arrived five minutes later, Russell reminded her that she had also forgotten several department meetings and that when she did attend, she was usually late. Linda explained, "I don't have a good memory for dates and times." She added that she didn't like team meetings and wouldn't attend when she had other things to do. "And I'm behind in my work right now. I think my project deadline is coming up soon."

1. How might Linda use her time more effectively? Brainstorm four or five ideas that might help Linda meet her time commitments.

2. Would you recommend that Linda use a Daily Activity Log or a Weekly Activity Log? Which one would work best for her? What would be the benefits?

Today is Saturday and all Keyshawn can think about is his upcoming English Literature test first thing Tuesday morning. He has read only half of the assignment and still has a lot of work left to finish.

Between his work and school schedule and his lack of interest in the reading materials, he keeps putting off the assignments, secretly hoping they will just go away.

"If only I didn't have to take this English requirement, if the stories were more interesting, if only I had more time," Keyshawn laments.

Keyshawn is scheduled to work all weekend at his retail job in the mall, and he has a date Saturday night. The earliest he can start any reading is Sunday evening. He estimates he might get through a quarter of the remaining material before he falls asleep.

He mentally schedules time to do more reading during his lunch at work on Saturday and Sunday and then again on Monday after class. "Oh, no," he remembers, "I also have math homework and a science lab due Monday."

What can Keyshawn do to feel more confident and prepared for his upcoming test?

Chapter Goals

After studying and working with the information in this chapter, you should be able to:

♦ Identify five main success factors for taking tests.
♦ Explain how to prepare for a test.
♦ Distinguish between memorizing and learning.
♦ Identify the strategies that are needed for successful learning.
♦ Describe and begin using devices for increasing memory recall.
♦ Explain why learning from mistakes is the most important success factor.
♦ Incorporate at least three new success factors into your learning habits.

In This Chapter

Studying and taking tests are probably not new activities for you. You have been doing both for years. They are among the most important activities that students face while in school and for getting into college. Increasingly, test taking is becoming common for working people, too.

Many certified professionals (such as teachers, nurses, insurance agents, financial planners, lawyers, and accountants) are required to obtain a certain number of continuing education units (**CEUs**) per year in order to keep their certifications. Some CEUs are obtained by attending classes, while others can be fulfilled by taking proficiency tests.

People must pass tests in many careers in order to advance in their professions. Firefighters and police officers take tests to be promoted. Insurance agents may take tests on policies before being allowed to sell them. Computer specialists sometimes take tests on hardware and software products so they can be certified in selling or servicing them. As long as knowledge is evaluated traditionally through tests, studying and test taking will remain a necessary activity for anyone who wants to be successful in school or in a career.

In order to guarantee consistent testing success, you first need to be an effective learner in addition to being an effective test taker. An effective learner studies smart, not hard.

In this chapter, you will take a close look at your own study habits and strategies. (Chapter 10 will look at test-taking strategies.) You will read about some strategies you may already practice and others you may want to start. Your goal for this chapter is to find at least three ways you can increase your testing success. Once you find the strategies most useful for you, you can be successful each time you take a test.

To guarantee success at test taking, a student needs to be both an effective learner and an effective test taker. What factors do you think make a student an effective learner?

SELF-CHECK

The following self-evaluation will give you an idea of how familiar, or unfamiliar, you are with some of the topics and terms discussed in this chapter. After reading each statement, circle the letter Y, S, or N to indicate the answer that is most appropriate for you. Answer honestly; rate yourself at the end, then complete the information for Chapter 5 in Appendix A.

Y = yes; frequently   S = sometimes   N = no; never

1.	Before the day of a test, I know what material will be covered.	Y	S	N
2.	Before the day of a test, I know what type of test will be given (multiple choice, essay, and so on).	Y	S	N
3.	I eat healthy foods, get enough sleep, and exercise regularly.	Y	S	N
4.	I know the difference between memorizing and learning.	Y	S	N
5.	I avoid cramming for tests.	Y	S	N
6.	I do the most difficult and challenging work first.	Y	S	N
7.	I study for a test a little each day for several days or weeks before the testing date.	Y	S	N
8.	I am good at predicting test questions from my notes and reading material.	Y	S	N
9.	When learning new information, I use memory devices.	Y	S	N
10.	I learn from my testing mistakes and take action to prevent them in the future.	Y	S	N

Rate Yourself:

Number of Ys	_____	x	100	=	_____
Number of Ss	_____	x	50	=	_____
Number of Ns	_____	x	0	=	_____ Total_____

5.1 WHAT IS A TESTING SUCCESS FACTOR?

A **testing success factor** is something that contributes to a successful test result. Since you want the end product of your studying efforts to be learning as well as success on a test, you need to be aware of the key testing success factors. Over the years, you have probably learned some of the testing success factors, but others may be new to you.

As you work through the rest of this chapter, note how many factors are familiar to you and how many are new to you. Keep in mind that being familiar with an idea doesn't mean you use it. So look for familiar ideas you would like to start using now.

ACTIVITY I

Think about all of your previous testing experiences. Create a list of factors that helped you perform well. A few examples: "I studied with a friend," "I got a good night's sleep," and "I studied ahead of time." Work individually at first. Then with two or three classmates, try to identify the most important factors.

_____

_____

_____

_____

_____

_____

_____

_____

_____

_____

5.2 BEING PREPARED

If you think about it, every day of your life is a test. Just like an academic test, how well or how poorly your day goes depends on how well or how poorly you prepared for it. Each student needs to prepare for a test in his or her own way; however, there are several common factors that can ensure testing success.

ACTIVITY 2

Read through the following situation. Then write your responses to the questions that follow. You may work alone or in a group.

Scott wakes up one morning, climbs into the shower, and turns on the water. He then realizes he's out of soap. He steps out of the warm shower into the chilly air, dripping water across the floor while he gets a bar of soap from the cabinet. When he finishes the shower, he realizes that he forgot to bring a towel into the bathroom. He trails water in the hallway as he rummages through the closet for a towel. After his shower, Scott looks for his lucky sweater, then remembers it is in the laundry. Though he is disappointed, he eventually finds something else to wear and gets dressed. He decides to eat a bowl of cereal before leaving for the day but finds he is out of milk. Then he spends 10 minutes searching for his bus pass. Finally, he gets to the bus stop—just in time to see the 8:00 bus driving away.

1. Were any of the events in this situation successful? If so, what were they?

   _____

   _____

2. Which events were not very successful?

   _____

   _____

3. What does "being successful" mean to you?

   _____

   _____

4. What are the factors necessary for Scott's success in the future?

   _____

   _____

This situation is a simple, yet powerful, example of how lack of preparation leads to inefficiency and poor results. It also illustrates how preparation can ensure efficiency and good results.

Success Skills

Being prepared is an important success factor for doing well, especially for taking tests. List what you think a student has to have or do in order to be prepared to take a test. Think about what has worked for you. You can add these ideas to the list of testing success factors you created in Activity 1.

_____

_____

_____

_____

_____

_____

_____

Do Your Assignments on Time

Why do you think completing assignments when they are due is important for effective learning? What can happen if you do not complete an assignment on time?

Most instructors base their assignments on what they will be discussing in class on a given day. So, if you read the pages you are assigned for the day they are due, you will better understand the day's lecture. If you don't complete an assignment when it is due, not only will you be at a disadvantage in the class, but you will have twice as much work to do for the following class. Some students get so far behind that they never complete all of their assignments. What can you do to make sure you complete your assignments on time?

If you are a student taking classes, then you have a set schedule for reading or studying. It can be found on your syllabus.

If you are a working person and studying independently for an exam, you typically have no predetermined schedule. Without a schedule, you may try to do all the studying close to your exam date, which is not an effective way to learn. Consider setting your own deadlines. This will encourage you to break the material up into smaller pieces, helping to make the learning permanent. You will have enough time to get help in problem areas, and you will lower your stress level.

Successful students read and take notes on their text assignments before the assignments are discussed in class. What advantage do you think this gives them?

Take Good Notes

Chapter 6 contains all the information you need about effective notetaking. Quickly review that information now.

1. Why is taking good notes a factor in being successful on tests?

   _____

   _____

2. What should your notes include for effective studying?

   _____

   _____

Know What Material to Study

This may sound simple, but all too often students do not ask what material they should study and find out too late that they studied the wrong information. The easiest and most accurate way to learn what will be covered on a test is to ask your instructor. (If you are studying independently, read the testing guidelines of your study material.) Even if your syllabus tells you that Chapters 6 through 10 will be covered, your instructor may decide to test you only on Chapters 6 through 9 or decide to include Chapter 11. If this happens and you are not aware of the change, you will be studying more or less than is needed. Though studying more is better than less, neither is an effective use of your time.

Know What Kind of Test Will Be Given

Before renting a movie from a video store, don't you want to know what the movie is about? Before going to a concert, don't you want to know what kind of music you will hear? Before taking a test, wouldn't you like to know what kind of test will be given? Because knowledge can be tested many different ways, you should know *how* you will be responsible for the information you study. Here are some of the most common types of tests. Most can be taken on paper or on a computer screen. (For specific information about test taking on a computer, see Chapter 10).

> Forewarned, forearmed, to be prepared is half the victory.
>
> —Cervantes
> 16th century Spanish novelist

Types of Tests

Objective Tests
    Multiple choice
    True-false
    Matching
    Fill-in-the-blank

Subjective Tests
    Short answer
    Essay

Performance Tests
    Hands-on
    Project

How you study should depend on the type of test you will take. One type of test is an **objective test.** Objective tests require correct answers and include multiple-choice, matching, true-false, and fill-in-the-blank questions.

Another type of test is the **subjective test;** it includes short-answer and essay questions. These tests are set up to prove not only whether you know the correct answer, but also what your opinion is and how you communicate your ideas on paper. The last type of test is a **performance test.** Performance tests measure how well you can execute, or perform, a certain task or activity.

When studying for a multiple-choice, true-false, or matching test, you need to become familiar with the specific information from your class or textbook reading. Your task is to identify the correct answer, not come up with the answer yourself.

When you prepare for a fill-in-the-blank test, you need to learn and effectively recall small pieces of information as they appear in context. This means you must know small details.

For short-answer and essay tests, you need to learn and remember specific information, have a complete understanding of the material, and be able to explain the ideas clearly. A good working knowledge of the content-area vocabulary is necessary as well. These tests require the most amount of study because they ask for the greatest amount of knowledge.

Application of knowledge, which is the point of a performance test, is the true test of understanding. In a computer class, for example, you may be asked to create a letter in perfect form and then print two copies. In order to perform this activity, you must learn how to create the letter and then practice doing it. You are not asked specific questions; rather you are tested on your ability to apply the knowledge.

Frequently instructors give tests that include several types of questions, so you may need to prepare for more than one. For example, to get your driver's license, you need to take an objective test (usually multiple choice) and a performance test (actually driving the car under an instructor's supervision).

ACTIVITY 4

With the information you just read about the different types of tests and how you are responsible for them, how would you prepare and study for each of the tests listed below? Be specific.

Multiple Choice _____
_____
_____

True-False _____
_____
_____

Matching _____
_____
_____

Fill-in-the-Blank _____
_____
_____

Short Answer _____
_____
_____

Essay _____
_____
_____

Hands-on _____
_____
_____

Project _____
_____
_____

Success Skills

Optimize Your Health

Being prepared physically for a test is just as important as being prepared mentally. Optimizing your health means paying attention to your eating, sleeping, and exercise habits and taking good care of yourself. After all, if you are not well nourished, well rested, and in good shape, your brain isn't either.

Opinions vary about the makeup of a healthy diet. Basically, a diet low in refined sugar products (cookies, cakes, candy) and carbohydrates (bread, pasta) and high in protein (chicken, fish, yogurt) and fruits and vegetables is a good base for most people. When you plan to study, it is a good idea to eat protein foods and vegetables and to avoid heavy carbohydrates and sugars.

Regarding sleep requirements, research suggests that the average person needs seven to nine hours of sleep per night. Are you aware of how much sleep your body needs? A consistent deficit of sleep can cause memory loss, forgetfulness, and lack of focus. Higher incidents of car accidents have also been attributed to lack of sleep.

Regular exercise can take many forms these days. A brisk 20-minute walk three times per week is a good beginning exercise routine for busy people. Adding movement into your day whenever possible helps too. For example, take the stairs instead of the elevator, park your car at the end of the parking lot, or walk a message over to a coworker instead of calling or e-mailing.

In addition to your eating, sleeping, and exercise habits, it is wise to visit a doctor both on an as-needed basis and a regular basis. If you suffer from physical discomfort, such as back pain or headaches, seek medical help. Persistent pain will interfere with your ability to learn. You also might consider getting an eye exam or a hearing test, especially if you haven't had an examination for several years. Many stores that sell eyeglasses have an optician who can perform eye exams, while hearing tests can be performed at a doctor's office. Since your eyes and ears are valuable learning tools, it is wise to keep them both tuned up.

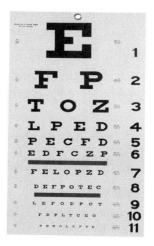

 healthy learner is a physically and mentally prepared learner. When was the last time you had a checkup?

Checkpoint 5.2

1. What does "being prepared" mean for a student?

2. Name and describe the three types of tests.

3. Think about your eating, sleeping, and exercise habits. What might you want to do differently to optimize your health?

5.3 AVOIDING CRAMMING

Cramming refers to trying to memorize a lot of information in a very short period of time. Millions of students cram for their exams every term.

Cramming is an ineffective way to study because it occurs under stressful conditions.

When you are stressed, you don't think as well or retain information as easily. In addition, most facts memorized during a cramming session disappear quickly, which defeats the purpose of studying.

ACTIVITY 5

Respond to the following questions, basing your answers on your personal experience. (You have probably crammed for a test sometime in your school career.) You may work alone or with another person.

1. What are some reasons for cramming? _____

_____

2. What typically happens when you cram? _____

_____

3. Why might cramming not be an effective means for learning? _____

_____

Smart Tip

According to Tony Buzan, author of *Use Both Sides of Your Brain*, if you are not interested in using the information you just memorized, you will forget nearly 80 percent of the detailed information within 24 to 48 hours.

Memorizing versus Learning

When you say you are planning to study, do you distinguish between *memorizing a list* of vocabulary and *learning a list* of vocabulary? Do you know that there is a difference between memorizing and learning?

Memorizing means trying to commit information to memory by rote, or mechanical repetition. Memorizing is the result of trying to remember a lot of information in a short period of time. For tests, you memorize lists, vocabulary terms, people's names, events, formulas, dates, facts, and other information.

Memorizing is *not* learning. It is using information for a short period of time, say, for identifying correct answers on multiple-choice, true-false, or matching tests. If you try to memorize information for a fill-in-the-blank, short-answer, or essay test, you will have a difficult time responding accurately to the questions. Since these tests require you to recall information *and* to understand and communicate that information, they are not suited for memorization. Many students get by, but rarely do very well, memorizing for tests.

Memorizing is an inefficient way to learn; if you want to use information sometime in the future, you will have to study it again. Has this ever happened to you? You memorized information for a test at the beginning of the term and found at the end of the term that you had to study most of it all over again.

Learning is much more than memorizing. It is acquiring knowledge through systematic, methodical study (or in simpler terms, by frequent review). In order to learn, you must keep the information over a long period of time. The information you study becomes part of your valuable background knowledge. If the object of getting an education is to understand and learn for use in the future, then why memorize?

In order to learn new information, two factors are needed: time and repetition. Figure 5-1 describes the levels of short-term memory and long-term memory. Levels 1 and 2 are a part of your short-term memory, while levels 3 and 4 are a part of your long-term memory.

Level 1

Level 1 is your shortest short-term memory. It is good for only approximately five to eight

Frequent review over a period of time helps you learn, not just memorize. Are you a memorizer or a learner?

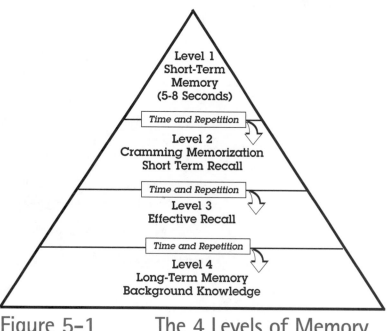

Figure 5–1   The 4 Levels of Memory

seconds. This is where you process information, such as writing a new phone number or reading an unfamiliar address on an envelope. Later in the same day, if someone asks you for the phone number or address, you are unable to recall it without looking at the piece of paper. The expression "in one ear and out the other" has been traced to this behavior.

Level 2

Level 2 is your cramming, or memorization, level. This is where  you try to cram a lot of information into your head by mechanical repetition for slightly longer retention. Since time and repetition are the two key factors in going from short-term to long-term memory, this repetition is an active process, but not the most effective way of achieving long-term memory.

Level 3

Level 3 is your **effective recall** level. This is where you can recall, or remember, studied information in a variety of ways. Effective recall

demands that you have a solid understanding of the information and that you can apply it in the area you are studying. At this level, you can identify the information and talk or write intelligently on the subject.

To be able to recall information effectively, (1) be active in your learning and (2) review frequently. For example, while in class, if you listen and hear what the instructor says, take good notes, and ask and answer questions, you will begin to understand the information. If while reading, you read actively and take notes, you will begin to understand the material instead of just memorizing it. Reviewing any material you have read will reinforce what you already know. In summary, if you are active in your learning and review your information frequently, you will cross the time-and-repetition boundary from short-term memory to long-term memory.

Level 4

Level 4 is your long-term memory, where learning is permanently stored. This is also called your **background knowledge**. To get from effective recall to this learned level, you must continue to learn actively and to review frequently. The more time and repetition you give the information, the longer it will stay in your memory.

Checkpoint 5.3

1. After reading this section, have your thoughts changed about cramming? Explain.

2. When might you use cramming? Why?

3. What can you do to avoid cramming?

5.4 LEARNING ACTIVELY

You have already learned and hopefully begun to use some active learning strategies. Read through the following strategies, looking for more ways to learn by doing.

Create an Effective Learning Environment

Do you remember Chapter 3? The entire chapter was devoted to creating an effective learning environment. Without looking back, complete the following statements:

1. An effective learning environment includes

   _____

   _____

2. An effective learning environment is important because

   _____

   _____

3. I can create an effective learning environment by

   _____

   _____

If you have difficulty completing these statements, review Chapter 3.

Find a Study Buddy

When you are learning, either in a classroom situation or on your own, it is common to doubt yourself: "Did I write what I needed?" "What is meant by that?" "Am I studying the right things for this test?" By working with another person on the same material, you can gauge your level of understanding, compare notes and ideas, and possibly teach the other person something as you learn from that person too.

It's best to find a study buddy whom you like and whose work habits are similar to yours. Begin working together early in the learning process. If you wait until test time, you might find the person is not as helpful as you originally thought, which wastes your preparation time.

Though socializing is a benefit of working with others, it can also be a hindrance to getting serious work done. Together with your study buddy, come up with a few working guidelines. You might allow the first 10 minutes of each work session for socializing, then start to study. Decide how often to take breaks and how long they will be. If the workload is to be split, decide who will do what by when. Without guidelines, you might socialize more than study!

The acronym TEAM stands for <u>T</u>ogether <u>E</u>veryone <u>A</u>chieves <u>M</u>ore. By working effectively with others, everyone can win.

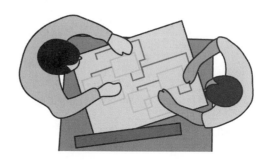

Have a Study Order

Active learning is easier when you have a step-by-step approach for learning the information. The order is determined by importance and difficulty first, then by your level of fatigue.

Though the guidelines for study order given below are somewhat flexible, use your common sense in applying them to your personal study style.

1. **Work on Hardest First.** If you save the hardest studying for last, you may become tired and stressed. You're looking forward to being done, and studying will become more difficult.

2. **Do Reading Before Writing.** Reading takes more mental concentration than writing, so it is wise to read early in your day or work session. If the assignment is long, break the material into small sections, and read some in between other work.

3. **Study First and Last.** Since repetition and time are the keys to long-term memory, studying before you get into new material and again after you finish new material will help you learn better and faster. Doing so also breaks up a big chunk of information into smaller pieces.

ACTIVITY 6

List the recommended study order for the assignment below. Pretend that math is your hardest subject. In addition, state your reasons for picking the order you did. Notice that five blanks are provided in the Order-of-Study column, and only four assignments are shown in the Assignment column. One of the assignments needs to be repeated.

Assignment	Order of Study
1. Write a one-page essay on ways to build background knowledge.	1. _____
2. Read Chapter 12 in Psychology.	2. _____
3. Study for Electrical Design test in three days.	3. _____
4. Do ten math problems on pages 54-57.	4. _____
	5. _____

Reasons for the order I chose:

_____

_____

_____

_____

_____

Plan Your Study Time and Breaks

All of the information you have learned in this chapter will be wasted if you do not plan enough study time before a test. Chapter 4 presented a great deal of information on managing and planning your time. Now is a good time to review the information if you do not remember how to manage your time or if you have not begun using a time planner.

Planning study breaks helps you to learn. Research shows that you remember the first and last pieces of information you study better than the information in the middle. For this reason, you should take frequent breaks in between multiple short study sessions. A short study session could be 15 minutes or half an hour. Choosing 15-minute study sessions doesn't mean you only study 15 minutes every hour. It means you have three to four sessions per hour with a few minutes' break between each session. If you choose 30-minute sessions, you should study for 30 minutes, take a break of about 5

minutes, and begin another 30-minute study session. The only time you should not stop for a break is when you are totally involved and concentrating on what you are doing. Here, taking a break would negatively affect your learning.

Since short study sessions are recommended, using the free time you may have found between daily activities or classes will allow you to get some of your work done earlier in the day. The later you plan your study sessions, the harder it is to concentrate and learn because you are naturally more tired at the end of a day than at the beginning.

When you have finished your studying for the day, reward yourself. It could be a call to a friend, a hot bath, an ice cream cone, or a little extra sleep. After all, you have just worked hard and deserve to be rewarded!

ACTIVITY 7

One problem you may encounter when taking short breaks is that they can become much longer than you had planned. It is easy to become distracted and sidetracked.

1. Brainstorm a list of things you can do in a two-minute break, a five-minute break, and a ten-minute break. Use your imagination.

   _____

   _____

   _____

   _____

   _____

   _____

   _____

   _____

   _____

   _____

2. What are some things that you should avoid doing because they will distract you for longer than ten minutes?

   _____

   _____

   _____

   _____

   _____

   _____

   _____

   _____

   _____

   _____

   _____

Success Skills

Remember to Use Memory Devices

Tests measure your working memory and knowledge base. To help yourself remember, you can use several **memory devices** to recall the information you need to study. After all the devices have been explained and examples given, you will then be challenged to use them.

Try a positive attitude

In order to remember anything, you first have to want to remember! While remembering every-thing may not be realistic, as a learner who takes tests, you need to remember a lot of informa-tion. By approaching your learning in a positive way, you will find studying easier. Honestly convince yourself that you really want to remember what you are about to study. Block out all other thoughts, and focus on the information. Know that by doing this, your mind will be open and ready to accept the information you feed it.

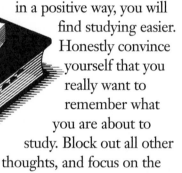

Try recitation using your own words

You will learn more when you reinforce your learning in as many ways as possible. You can reinforce your learning through hearing, writing, reading, reviewing, and reciting.

By the time you study for a test, you may have already heard the instructor present the information, written your notes, read the assignments, and reviewed your notes. The last reinforcement is recitation, or repeating aloud the information you are studying from memory.

Many people try to memorize exactly what an instructor or a dictionary says without giving any thought to what it means. A better use of your learning time is to first understand what you are studying, put the concepts into your own words, and then recite them.

Read the following text-book glossary definition of the marketing term *elastic demand*.

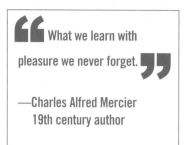

Glossary Definition

Elastic demand—Demand for a product that increases or decreases dramatically when the price changes.

The definition itself is not easy to understand, let alone remember. Using your imagination and your own words, you can come up with an easier-to-remember definition of elastic demand.

Your Own Words

Elastic demand—Changing demand due to price changes.

The words *elastic* and *demand* may also hold some other meanings for you, helping to anchor the information in your mind. Now that the information is in your own words, ask yourself a question: "What is elastic demand?" Without looking at your notes, repeat the definition aloud from memory. If you have trouble remembering it, review again until the answer comes easily for you or until you find an even easier way to remember the definition!

ACTIVITY 8

Put the following information in your own words. The first two are defined terms; the last two are informational paragraphs.

1. Fluorescent lights: Tubelike bulbs that are used for general illumination purposes. The major advantage is moderate price.

   _____

   _____

2. Bank cards: Third-party credit cards, such as VISA™ and MasterCard™. Individual banks issue cards to consumers who, when they use the credit cards for purchases, owe the amount charged to the bank.

   _____

   _____

3. Electronic retailing: Has arrived in many forms, affects all retailers. Electronic retailing provides consumers with the convenience of at-home shopping through computer catalogs and TV shopping channels, which are constantly updating their merchandise. Consumers can examine product information and make purchases from their homes.

   _____

   _____

   _____

   _____

   _____

4. What is marketing? Marketing means identifying the need for goods or services, developing products or services to meet the needs, communicating the benefits to people or organizations needing the goods or services, and distributing the goods or services to the proper markets. The American Marketing Association provides us with a more formal definition. Marketing is the process of planning and executing the conception, pricing, promotion, and distribution of ideas, goods, and services to create exchanges that satisfy personal and organizational objectives. To a businessperson, marketing means having the right product at the right place at the right time at the right price and at a profit. Sony® identified the need for a personal stereo, developed a product to meet the need, informed consumers about the product, and distributed it. Many of the people who need the Walkman® are now able to enjoy it.

   _____

   _____

   _____

   _____

   _____

Success Skills

Try acronyms

Acronyms are words or names formed from the first letters or groups of letters in a phrase. Acronyms help you remember because they organize information according to the way you need or want to learn it. When you study for a test, be creative and make up your own acronyms. Read the list of acronyms shown in Figure 5-2 below. Some may be familiar to you; others may not.

Try mnemonic sentences, rhymes, or jingles

Mnemonic sentences are similar to acronyms; they help you organize your ideas. But, instead of creating a word, you make up a sentence. Creating a rhyme or song jingle can make the information even easier to remember. The more creative, even sillier, the sentence, the easier it is to remember. Take, for example, the nine planets listed in order according to their distance from the sun:

Mercury Venus Earth Mars Jupiter Saturn Uranus Neptune Pluto

The first letters of these words are: M V E M J S U N P.

The acronym, it would be difficult to remember; but if you create a sentence using the letters in order, you will remember the sequence better. For example:

My Very Educated Mother Just Served Us Nine Pizzas

When learning to read music, you use a popular mnemonic sentence that represents the lines of the music staff: EGBDF (starting at the bottom).

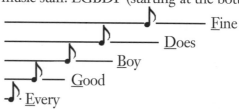

<table>
<tr><td colspan="2">## Figure 5–2   Sample Acronyms</td></tr>
<tr><th>Word or Term</th><th>Acronym</th></tr>
<tr><td>RAdio Detecting And Ranging</td><td>RADAR</td></tr>
<tr><td>TeleVision</td><td>TV</td></tr>
<tr><td>The colors of the rainbow:
    Red, Orange, Yellow, Green, Blue, Indigo, Violet</td><td>ROY G. BIV</td></tr>
<tr><td>American Telephone & Telegraph</td><td>AT&T</td></tr>
<tr><td>Collect On Delivery</td><td>COD</td></tr>
<tr><td>Light Amplification by Simulated Emission of Radiation</td><td>LASER</td></tr>
<tr><td>Accounting term refers to warehouse inventory:
    Last In, First Out</td><td>LIFO</td></tr>
<tr><td>   First In, First Out</td><td>FIFO</td></tr>
<tr><td>Financial documents being signed by two people:
    Joint Tenancy With Rights Of Survivorship</td><td>JTWROS</td></tr>
</table>

Try linking ideas

Your memory will work better if you associate, or link, related ideas. Also, remembering information in a meaningful order is easier than remembering information in a random order. Isn't ABCDEFG easier to remember than FBAGDEC?

For instance, in science class you might need to learn the parts of a flower. The parts of a flower are:

stigma, anther, pistil, sepal, stamen, petal

You could rearrange the parts in alphabetical order for easier remembering:

anther, petal, pistil, sepal, stamen, stigma

You could create an acronym:

appsss

You could create a mnemonic sentence with order of the acronym:

A purple pansy shared sunflower's sunshine.

You could create a mnemonic sentence in its original order:

Susan and Pam sent Sam presents.

Try visualization

Visualization refers to creating or recalling mental pictures related to what you are learning. Have you ever tried to remember something while taking a test and visualized the page the information was on? This is your visual memory at work.

Using the parts of the flower example, you can draw your own picture of the flower and work on remembering the picture and its parts. When you take a test, your visual memory will help you to recall the information.

Smart Tip

Approximately 90 percent of your memory is stored visually in pictures so trying to visualize what you want to remember is a powerful study tool.

Success Skills

Now it's your turn to be creative. Below is a list of miscellaneous facts and information. Using the memory devices discussed in this chapter, how would you go about remembering the information. You can work individually or in a group.

1. The Great Lakes (listed in no special order):

   Ontario, Michigan, Huron, Erie, Superior

   _____

   _____

2. The six parts of soil:

   air, humus, mineral salts, water, bacteria, rock particles

   _____

   _____

3. Three ways to reduce rabies:

   a. Immunize more dogs and cats   b. Enforce leash laws   c. Educate the public about the dangers of rabies

   _____

   _____

   _____

4. Ways to improve listening:

   a. Listen for the speaker's main ideas   c. Watch for nonverbal signals

   b. Listen for specific details   d. Take notes

   _____

   _____

   _____

5. Where retail consumers make purchases:

   a. Department stores   d. Web sites   g. Supermarkets

   b. TV shopping channels   e. Superstores   h. Warehouse clubs

   c. Specialty stores   f. Discount department stores   i. Catalog sales

   _____

   _____

   _____

   _____

Checkpoint 5.4

1. What does "learning actively" mean?
2. Which of the suggestions in this section are you familiar with?
3. Which of the suggestions in this section are new to you?

Focus on Ethics

You are cramming for a big test and decide to take a study break to go to the grocery store for some necessities. The store is extremely crowded, and your trip takes much longer than planned. It's getting late, and you are in a rush to get back to your studying. As you are loading your groceries into your car, you realize you forgot to pay for the large bag of dog food at the bottom of the cart. Going back in to pay for it will mean another wait in a very long line. What can you do? How could you have avoided this situation?:

WEB LINK

www.academictips.org

A general site for getting more study tips. Worth a look around!

www.premiumhealth.com/memory/

Online tutorials and activities for improving memory.

www.ucc.vt.edu/stdyhlp.html

This Virginia Tech site has some of the most comprehensive study information available on the Web.

5.5 ANTICIPATING TEST QUESTIONS

As a an active learner, you will get better at discovering what your instructors think is important. (See Chapter 6 for ways to identify personality clues and verbal clues.) If you can become a champion of what your instructors are most interested in and can impress them with your knowledge of the subject, then you will have prepared well.

Learning to predict test questions based on your notes, from both classes and reading assignments, will enhance testing success. (Refer to Chapters 6 and 7 for information about predicting test questions using the recall column and margin notes.)

ACTIVITY 10

Look at your notes from a class you recently attended. Using your experience as a student with this instructor, come up with five possible test questions. Make sure your notes have the answers.

1. _____

   _____

2. _____

   _____

3. _____

   _____

4. _____

   _____

5. _____

   _____

Checkpoint 5.5

1. How can you know what is important to your instructor?

2. How can you predict test questions from your notes?

3. How can you predict test questions from your reading material? (See Chapter 7 for clues.)

5.6 LEARNING FROM YOUR MISTAKES

Let's look at approximately how many tests a college student takes in order to earn a two-year degree, and adapt the information to your own situation. Sixteen courses must be completed for a two-year degree. For each course, a minimum of two tests per class (a midterm and a final) are usually given. This equals a minimum of 32 tests in two years.

16 courses × 2 tests per course = 32 tests

For a four-year degree, expect twice as many tests, or 64.

If you a take a test each week or at the end of every chapter or section you study, the number of tests increases greatly.

Since test taking is so important to your overall success in earning a degree, how can you ensure greater success on each one?

Review Returned Tests

Some instructors do not return tests, but others do. If you don't get your test back, ask your instructor for an appointment to review it. If the test is returned, examine it carefully. Look first at where you succeeded, and think about what you did to achieve that success. Then look at the areas where you need to improve, and commit yourself to doing better the next time. Did you read the directions carefully? Did you study the important handouts? Were your notes helpful in studying? Did you read all of the assignments you were tested on? Whatever you did, or did not do, find a way to improve the next time you take a test.

Figure Out What Worked and What Didn't

When you decide upon the improvements you want to make, realize you may not be 100 percent successful the first time. You may need to change, to add or subtract something you are doing to refine your testing knowledge. If at first you don't succeed, use a different approach and try again. This is another way to improve your scores.

Be Honest with Yourself

Say you spent three hours at the library preparing for a test. In that three-hour time frame, a friend dropped by to chat, and you took a 30-minute coffee break. You also decided that while you were at the library you would check out the music collection. Of the three hours you were at the library, how much of it was quality study time—a little more than two hours at most? Being honest with yourself means saying you spent two hours studying, not three. An hour of quality study time can make a difference in your results.

One way to discover areas to improve upon is to use the Success Factors Checklist on page 133. For every test, use this checklist as a reminder of what you must do for your studying to be successful and as a means of tracking your study activities.

> **"** The greatest accomplishment is not in never falling, but in rising again after you fall. **"**
>
> —Vince Lombardi
> Former professional football coach and Hall of Famer

Ask for Help

Being a successful student means getting help from others from time to time. If you are having trouble with the subject matter, ask your instructor or another qualified person for help. Ideally, requests for help should be arranged long before the day of the test. Fellow learners are a good resource for help, especially if they can be relied upon as effective study partners.

If you would like help with your writing skills or extra help with a certain class, look into your school's learning skills center, counseling center, tutoring center, or related campus location. Help may also be found online. By doing an effective search, you might find handouts or even a virtual tutor who can help you.

Successful students recognize they need help and actively seek it out. Have you ever needed help with one of your subjects? If so, were you willing to ask for that help? Who did you go to, and what did that help do for you?

Checkpoint 5.6

1. Describe the four ways you can learn from your mistakes.

2. To whom or where do you go when you need help?

3. Which success factors are you strongest and weakest in?

Key Terms and Concepts

acronyms

background knowledge

cramming

CEUs

effective recall

learning

memorizing

memory devices

mnemonic sentences

objective tests

performance tests

subjective tests

testing success factors

Chapter Summary

1. The five success factors for taking any test are being prepared, avoiding cramming, learning actively, anticipating test questions, and learning from mistakes.

2. Being prepared is one of the most important qualities of a test taker. Being prepared means doing assignments on time, taking good notes, knowing what material to study, knowing what kind of test will be given, and optimizing your health.

3. Memorizing is *not* learning. Memorizing is trying to commit information to memory by mindless repetition. Learning means acquiring knowledge through systematic, methodical study.

4. Being an active learner makes studying easier and ensures better results. This includes creating an effective learning environment, finding a study buddy, having a study order, planning study time and breaks, and remembering to use memory devices.

5. In order to remember, you can try six memory devices: wanting to remember, reciting using your own words, using acronyms, using mnemonic sentences, linking ideas, and visualizing.

6. Making mistakes is the best way to learn, provided you learn from your mistakes.

Success Factors Checklist

For every test, use the following checklist as a reminder of the factors for successful studying. The checklist can also be used as a means of tracking your study activities. If you find areas you have not checked or would like to improve for your next test, place an asterisk (*) next to the items, and make your own plan of improvement.

Course Name_____   Date of Test_____

Being Prepared

I prepared for this test by:

- ❏ doing my assignments on time.
- ❏ taking good notes.
- ❏ knowing what material to study. (List what you need to study.)

    _____

- ❏ knowing what kind of test it will be. (Write it below.)

    _____

- ❏ optimizing my health.
- ❏ other ways. _____

Avoiding Cramming

I avoided cramming for my test by:

- ❏ reviewing a little each day before a test.
- ❏ other ways. _____

Learning Actively

I actively learned the information for this test by:

- ❏ creating an effective learning environment.
- ❏ finding a study buddy.
- ❏ having an effective study order.
- ❏ planning my study time and breaks.
- ❏ remembering to use memory devices.
- ❏ other ways. _____

Anticipating Test Questions

I anticipated test questions by:

- ❏ paying attention to my instructors personality and verbal clues (if applicable).
- ❏ using effective highlighting and margin notes from my reading assignments.
- ❏ other ways. _____

Learning from Mistakes

I learn from mistakes by:

- ❏ reviewing returned tests.
- ❏ figuring out what worked and what didn't.
- ❏ being honest with myself.
- ❏ asking for help.
- ❏ other ways. _____

Review

Based on the information you learned in this chapter, answer the following questions using your own words.

1. What do you think "studying smart" means?

2. Being prepared for a test means a lot of things. What does it mean for you? (Think about the classes you are taking now or plan to take in the future.)

3. What is the difference between memorizing and learning?

4. How can you learn instead of memorize?

5. Learning actively means a lot of things. What does it mean for you?

6 a. Of the memory devices discussed in this chapter, which ones were you already familiar with?

   b. Which memory devices are you going to try during your next study session?

   c. Which memory devices don't you like and why?

7. Learning from your mistakes is the best way to learn. Write about a mistake you made as a student and what you did or should have done to learn from it.

8. Of the three types of tests discussed in this chapter, which are easier for you? more difficult? Why?

9. If you were taking a self-study course where you were responsible for all your learning, which success factors would work best? Which wouldn't apply?

10. Now that you have learned about the testing success factors, look back at the list you created in Activity 1 and compare. What are the most important things you learned?

Case 1

Barbara showed Art, a new employee, how to review customer order forms. Art, who didn't ask any questions, just nodded his head as she gave instructions. Barbara left him five forms to complete and returned to her office. Although Art couldn't remember exactly what Barbara had told him to do, he started reading one of the order forms. Getting confused by the terms used, Art tried reviewing another order form. He read through all five order forms and realized he was confused. Finally, he told Barbara he was having a problem. "Your instructions weren't very clear," he said. "I guess I need you to review a couple of these forms with me again before I can do them by myself."

1. What could Art have done while Barbara was instructing him that would have helped him learn what he needed to know? What study strategies would be useful in learning a new job?

2. What could Barbara have done during or following her instruction that would have improved Art's ability to review the customer order forms? How could she have helped Art learn faster?

Case 2

Steve volunteered to help at the local swimming pool as a summer lifeguard. To become certified, he had to attend classes over several weeks, pass a written test, and demonstrate his ability to do certain maneuvers in the water in order to rescue people. Steve wanted to be prepared for any emergency, so he studied the safety material seriously. He read through his assignments before each class, asked the instructors questions, wrote their responses, and reviewed the comments he received from the instructors on the weekly quizzes. Despite his hard work, the night before the written test, Steve was nervous about doing well.

1. Steve used some effective study techniques. What were they? What other techniques might he have used during the classes?

2. What would you recommend Steve do the night before the written test? What would help him be prepared to do his best on the test?

Jessica is a freshman at a local community college. Like many other students, she works full-time during the day and goes to school at night. Someday she hopes to be a social worker or psychologist. So it makes sense that one of the first classes she signs up to take is Psychology 101. The class meets one evening a week for three hours in a lecture hall that holds 100 students. Jessica brings one pen and several pieces of notebook paper in a folder labeled "Psych 101" to the first class. She also brings a tape recorder because her cousin suggested she listen to the lecture afterward to make sure she got all the information. She sits down in one of the back rows of the hall, sets up the tape recorder, and gets ready to listen.

The professor starts by reviewing the syllabus and distributing handouts about the night's lecture. The notes are organized well in outline form and seem to include most of what is being discussed. Jessica decides to just sit back and listen. She figures she already has most of the notes on the handout, and her tape recorder will get the rest.

If Jessica continues this way for the entire term, what problems may result?

Chapter Goals

After studying and working with the information in this chapter, you should be able to:

♦ Identify THE reason for taking notes.
♦ Summarize effective note-taking habits.
♦ Identify and list action clues of instructors.
♦ Identify and list verbal clues of instructors.
♦ Explain how to take notes and learn using the Cornell Method of Note Taking.
♦ Describe how to take notes and learn with Mind Mapping®.

In This Chapter

6.1 Why Take Notes?

6.2 Preparing to Take Notes

6.3 Taking Notes from Instructors

6.4 How to Take Notes

How many times have you written a list of things to do? or a shopping list for the grocery store? or a telephone message for someone? Believe it or not, these common activities are note-taking activities. Writing notes on paper is an effective yet simple means of remembering important information.

Taking good notes is extremely important to your success as a learner and a worker. For students, the content of classroom lectures often becomes the content of exams. For independent learners, taking notes from reading material is an important strategy for building knowledge. (See Chapter 7 for information about taking notes from reading material.) Workers need to take notes about meetings, projects, and other work activities.

Taking good notes is like making a photo of what happens on a particular day. Without notes, you lose the picture of the class or meeting, and studying becomes more difficult.

Throughout this chapter, remember that no two learners take notes in exactly the same way. Your notes—whatever way you choose to take them—must be useful and complete enough for you to learn easily. The key is to adapt the information provided in this chapter to your own style of learning and note taking.

What methods do you use to capture the key concepts from speakers?

Effective note takers are more successful learners than non-note takers. Are you an effective note taker?

SELF-CHECK

The following self-evaluation will give you an idea of how familiar, or unfamiliar, you are with some of the topics and terms discussed in this chapter. After reading each statement, circle the letter Y, S, or N to indicate the answer that is most appropriate for you. Answer honestly; rate yourself at the end, then complete the information for Chapter 6 in Appendix A.

Y = yes; frequently   S = sometimes   N = no; never

1.	I come prepared to meetings and classes with the tools for note taking.	Y	S	N
2.	I can pick out the important information from a lecture or meeting to take notes on.	Y	S	N
3.	I take notes from others using key words, not full sentences.	Y	S	N
4.	I abbreviate often when I take notes.	Y	S	N
5.	I frequently use my own words when taking notes.	Y	S	N
6.	At work, I have occasion to take some form of notes while on the phone.	Y	S	N
7.	I know at least four effective note taking habits.	Y	S	N
8.	I am aware of personality clues of speakers.	Y	S	N
9.	I am aware of verbal clues of speakers.	Y	S	N
10.	My class or meeting notes are easy to study and learn from.	Y	S	N

Rate Yourself:

Number of Ys	_____	x	100	=	_____		
Number of Ss	_____	x	50	=	_____		
Number of Ns	_____	x	0	=	_____	**Total** _____

6.1 WHY TAKE NOTES FROM PEOPLE?

Taking notes in your classes or meetings is a way to organize and remember what is discussed. When you can't take notes, learning is passive instead of active.

More learning takes place when you use a variety of ways to reinforce the information you are trying to learn. The circumstances dictate which of the following strategies will be most helpful in reinforcing your learning. Whether you are taking notes from a speaker or from written material or for a test or for a meeting, you decide on the proper strategy.

1. Hear the information.
2. Write it down.
3. See it either on paper or in your mind's eye.
4. Draw a picture of it.
5. Outline it.
6. Summarize it.
7. Discuss it with others.
8. Review it.

ACTIVITY I

Think about the times you took notes in a class or meeting and the times you didn't. Discuss the pros and cons of each strategy with a partner or small group. Document your thoughts in the columns below.

PROS	CONS
_____	_____
_____	_____
_____	_____
_____	_____
_____	_____

Imagine you are in a class or a meeting without a pen or notepaper. All you are able to do is listen. Would you concentrate on what was being said, or would your mind wander? Why do you think that is so? Now imagine you have a pen and notepaper in front of you and are taking notes. Why might you concentrate more this way?

_____
_____
_____
_____
_____
_____
_____

The most important reason to take notes in any situation is to improve your concentration. If you are a student in a classroom or business professional in a meeting room, the more you concentrate, the more successful you will be at understanding the information you are hearing. Writing down your version of what you see, hear, or read (an active learning skill) is the best way to increase your concentration.

Having notes *to review and study* will save you review time, help you learn more, and improve your test scores. Notes will also help you organize the information and establish main ideas. They will help you *retain the information longer* and will serve as a visual reminder of what was said.

Throughout the rest of this chapter note taking refers to good, useful note taking strategies. The first step is to be prepared to take notes.

Checkpoint 6.1

1. Without looking back, list five ways you can reinforce your learning.

2. What is the most important reason for taking notes from people?

3. What are some other reasons for taking notes?

Smart Tip

We remember:

10 percent of what we read.
20 percent of what we hear.
30 percent of what we see.
50 percent of what we see and hear.
70 percent of what we discuss with others.
80 percent of what we personally experience.
95 percent of what we teach each other.

—William Glasser, educational reformist

6.2 PREPARING TO TAKE NOTES

You have been taking notes for years in your own way. Your way may be very effective, or it may be comfortable but ineffective. As you read through the next sections, try to identify your note-taking habits. More importantly, look for new ways to make your note taking more effective.

The Tools for Note Taking

Before you can take good notes, it helps to be prepared. You need the appropriate tools.

Three-ring binder

A useful tool for note taking in a class is a three-ring binder notebook. In contrast to a spiral notebook, the three-ring binder:

♦ Allows you to remove or add extra pages or handouts while maintaining the order of your notes.

♦ Allows you to lend some pages of your notes without lending the whole notebook.

♦ Provides protection with its plastic cover, especially during wet weather.

♦ May be used more than once.

♦ Helps keep your notes organized.

8 1/2" × 11" lined paper

Smaller paper may be all right for taking notes in business meetings but generally, you need longer size paper to hold more information.

Summary paper

Summary paper is used for the Cornell Method of Note Taking discussed on page 151. It is not the same as regular notebook paper. Instead of having a 1-inch margin on the left, summary paper has a 3-inch left margin. Figure 6-1 is an illustration of summary paper. You can make this paper yourself by taking lined notebook paper and using a pen to mark off a 3-inch margin. You can also purchase summary paper through most college bookstores or special order it from office supply stores. (Summary paper is called 3-inch Law Margin Rule.)

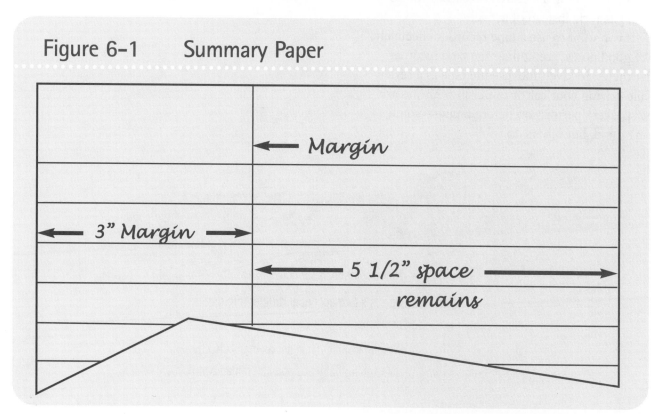

Figure 6-1   Summary Paper

Plain white paper

For the Mind Mapping note-taking method discussed on page 156, you will use unlined white paper, preferably three-hole punched.

Erasable pen or dark pencil

For correcting mistakes and making changes or additions, you will want to use an erasable pen or dark pencil. These provide flexibility to your note taking.

A tape recorder

When used appropriately, a tape recorder can support your note-taking efforts but not replace them. If you use a tape recorder in a class or meeting and don't take notes, you will be forced to listen to the entire lecture afterward to review the information. If the tape is of poor quality (which is often the case because the speaker moves away from the tape recorder) or the batteries run out or your tape runs out you won't have anything to review. Recording a lecture also causes you to listen passively instead of actively.

If you want to use a tape recorder effectively, take good notes, pretending the tape recorder isn't there. To save time, use the tape as a review while driving your car or exercising. Always ask the speaker's permission before taping—some don't mind, but others do.

Before moving on to the next section, create a few pieces of summary paper (3-inch left margin rule). Have an erasable pen or pencil handy.

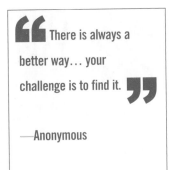

Effective Note Taking Habits

Some effective note-taking habits are easy to use. They are bulleted here but explained more thoroughly in Appendix B.

♦ Pre-view related readings before a class or meeting.
♦ Start each day with a fresh piece of paper.
♦ Write on only one side of the paper.
♦ Date and title every page.
♦ Write in the shortest form possible.
♦ Use abbreviations.
♦ Use key words.
♦ Use your own words.

> ## Checkpoint 6.2
>
> 1. Name some tools for note taking.
> 2. How is summary paper different from other notepaper?
> 3. Without looking back, list as many effective note-taking habits as you can remember.

Success Skills

6.3 TAKING NOTES FROM INSTRUCTORS

Though this section focuses on taking notes from instructors, you can learn a great deal about how to take notes from anyone in any situation, such as meetings or phone conversations. If you watch and listen carefully to speakers, their actions and words will help you quickly identify the important information.

As a classroom student, taking good notes from an instructor can only improve your chances of doing well; however, many students face the problem of not knowing what information is worth writing in note form. Some try to write everything. That's not practical or really possible.

Being an effective note taker means being an active and skilled observer and listener. Finding and writing the appropriate information is easy, once you learn how to watch and listen effectively. There is no right or wrong information, only too much or too little.

ACTIVITY 2

Think about some of the teachers you have had in the past. What did they do or say to let you know that what they were discussing was important enough to write down? Discuss this with a partner or in a group, and write your ideas in the space below.

_____

_____

_____

_____

_____

_____

_____

_____

_____

_____

_____

_____

_____

_____

_____

Six Instructor Personality Clues

Almost everything an instructor says is important. You can identify specific actions an instructor takes to alert you that the information is particularly important and should be written in note form.

1. **They tell you it's important.** Instructors may say, "This will be on the test" or "You need to know this." Unfortunately, they don't always make it this obvious.

2. **They repeat information.** If you listen carefully, you may hear your instructors repeat information. This is their way of telling you that the information is important enough to write down. An instructor will use repetition when discussing a new vocabulary term, an important name or date, or a difficult concept.

3. **They write information on the board or overhead.** Do you think you will take good notes by only including what an instructor writes on the board? Many students believe these are the only notes they need. Typically, though, what instructors write on the board is information that supports their lectures. It does not usually represent all of the important information. As a result, learn to use the notes on the board as supplemental information.

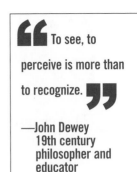

4. **They change their voice and facial expressions.** Because your instructors are human, their voices and facial expressions change when they describe something exciting or of interest to them. Think about your instructors and what they do when they are enthusiastic about a subject. Do their voices get louder or softer? Do they speak faster or slower? Do their faces and eyes "light up"? Do their eyes stare with more intensity than usual? Do their faces become flushed with color? Some instructors actually get so excited about their topic that they perspire and breathe heavily!

    If any of these changes occur, pay close attention to what the instructor is saying and take notes. If your instructor is excited about something or finds an idea interesting, chances are you will see it again, most likely on a test.

5. **They pause.** When an instructor stops speaking for a few moments, it is to give you time to write what he or she just said. Pay attention so you can use this pause in the lecture to capture the material in your notes. If you are not listening or you're daydreaming, then the quiet in the room will capture your attention. Other students will be furiously writing, while you will be wondering what you just missed. If this happens, use the active learning technique of asking your instructor to repeat what he or she just said.

> " To see, to perceive is more than to recognize. "
>
> —John Dewey
> 19th century philosopher and educator

6. **They use handouts.** Many instructors provide handouts related to the topic being discussed in class. These handouts are important, so you should make a note to review them while you are studying. (A simple note will suffice: "Review handout of mgmt. styles— 9/16 class," for example.)

ACTIVITY 3

In one of your next classes or meetings, try to identify the speaker's action clues. What does the speaker do to tell you something is important? Write your thoughts in the space below.

_____

_____

_____

_____

_____

_____

_____

Six Instructor Verbal Clues

What follows are descriptions of common verbal clues that tell you the information is important and to take notes. You will probably encounter this same information on a test. How an instructor or other speaker delivers information and what he or she says provide you with clues.

Definitions

When an instructor teaches a new topic, chances are that terms go with the topic. For example, let's say the topic is automation. Automation is defined by your instructor as "mechanical tools that do a job with less human effort." Your instructor gives you an example of a computer.

Your notes could look similar to this:

Automation = mechanical tools that do job w/ less human effort (e.g., a computer)

The pattern is *new word, definition, example or concept.*

Description

Continuing with the automation topic, the instructor might describe in more detail what is meant by automation:

"Automation makes work more efficient. When an assistant makes a mistake on a typewritten letter, the whole letter had to be retyped. With word-processing software on a computer, the assistant only has to make necessary changes on the screen and reprint the document. This saves time and increases the amount of work that can be done in a day."

Your notes could resemble these:

computer > efficient than typewriter, saves time & ↑ amt. of work in day.

The pattern is *description of the term and list of its qualities.*

Compare and contrast

Comparing is used to look at things that are similar; **contrasting** is used to look at things that are different. Continuing with the technology example, suppose your instructor says, "There are obvious similarities between a typewriter and a computer. They both have keys that produce typed information, they both are found in offices, and they both are commonly used by office workers. But this is where the similarities end. Computers produce information much faster than typewriters. Their 'brains,' called memory, are programmed to do many more functions than a typewriter and to save the information for future use."

Your notes need to reflect these similarities and differences because they are fair game for a test. You could expect this instructor to ask, "What are some similarities and differences between a typewriter and a computer?" or "Compare and contrast the typewriter and the computer." You could write your notes many ways, but they should answer the question "How are the two items alike and how are they different?"

One good example is as follows:

Typewriter vs. Computer

Similarities

♦ *keys produce typed info*
♦ *found in offices*
♦ *used by office workers*

Differences

♦ *Comp's faster*
♦ *Comp's have a memory for programming*
♦ *Comp's save info for future*

These notes are written in an informal outline that is explained in more detail in the next section of this chapter.

Chronological order

Chronological order is the same as time order and step-by-step order. In class discussion on automation, the instructor may tell you the date the typewriter was invented and then continue giving dates that coincide with the development of automation and computers. Your notes should accurately document the dates and what happened.

1867 = 1st manual typewriter

1956 = 1st electronic typewriter

1964 = 1st word-processing computer

Your instructor could tell you step-by-step how to turn on a computer. Your notes should include all the steps of the process.

How to turn on a computer:

Step No. 1—Turn on hard drive. Wait 5 seconds

Step No. 2—Turn on monitor

Step No. 3—Turn on printer

Classification

Classification means what class, group, or category a subject falls into. For example, a  college student in the first year of study is in the freshman class. In the second year, he or she is in the sophomore class, and so on. Computers belong in the category of automation. Almost every concept you learn belongs to a class, group, or category of information. Your notes should answer the question "To which class, group, or category does this information belong?"

Cause and effect

When something happens (the **cause**) a result occurs (the **effect**). If you don't turn the lights off when you leave a room (the cause), your electric bill will increase (the effect). If you don't put gas in your car (the cause), eventually it will stop running (the effect). If you try to mix water with oil (the cause), they will separate (the effect).

ACTIVITY 4

In your next few classes or meetings, listen carefully for all types of verbal clues. Write them down. Use the space below to classify the clues according to those described in the previous section.

_____

_____

_____

_____

_____

_____

_____

_____

Predicting Test Questions

If you listen attentively, observe the instructor's behavior, and take notes based on the instructor's actions and verbal clues, you have useful information for an upcoming test. By paying attention to what the instructor thinks is important, you will be able to predict test questions and know which areas to focus on during your review time. In the next section, you will learn how to use summary paper for predicting test questions and studying for tests.

Checkpoint 6.3

1. What are the six action clues to observe when taking notes from an instructor?

2. What are the six verbal clues to identify?

3. How can you become good at predicting test questions?

Focus on Ethics

You work in an accounting firm where your job is to order and keep track of the office supplies. You have a relaxed policy, and employees are permitted to take whatever supplies they need for their work. You have noticed that one employee, a single mother who is also a part-time college student, is taking more pens and notepads than usual. Is this important issue? What should be done? Would your answer change if the employee had been taking computer disks and printer cartridges. Why or why not?

WEB LINK

www.dartmouth.edu/~acskills/no_frames/learning_enhancement .html#guides

This site provides learning strategies, note taking tips, and helpful information.

www.utexas.edu/student/lsc/handouts/1415.html

This site provides a system for effective listening and note taking.

6.4 HOW TO TAKE NOTES

Notice that up to this point, you have not been instructed in any specific note-taking method. Rather, you have learned what all good note takers do. Now you will be given more information on the method to use when, taking your notes. *Remember that you are to use and adapt the information to your own style of learning and note taking.*

Before writing down anything, it is helpful to know if the speaker's lecture style is sequential or random. If the speaker is sequential, he or she may follow an outline, which means that taking organized and logical notes will be fairly easy. If the speaker is random, keeping organized, logical notes will be more of a challenge. (For more information on identifying teaching styles, see Chapter 2.)

Sequential learners and random learners need to be able to take good notes from both styles of speakers. Two recommended methods are described below. The first method, the Cornell Method of Note Taking, will probably be favored by a sequential learner, while the second method, Mind Mapping will probably be favored by the random learner. Both types of learners can benefit from knowing both methods and using the one best suited to the style of the speaker.

The Cornell Method of Note Taking

The Cornell Method is a unique note-taking format that has proven to be highly effective by college students for over 50 years. Many businesspeople also use this method for taking notes in meetings and for general business use.

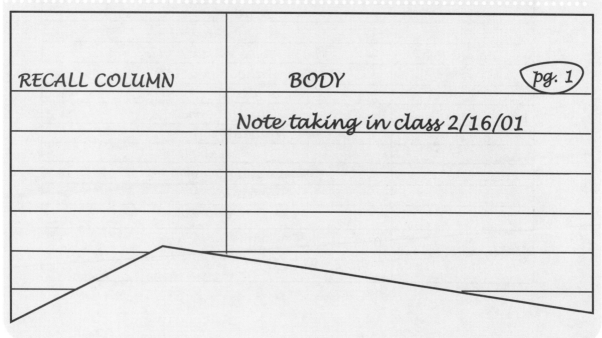

Figure 6–2   Labeling the Parts of the Summary Paper

RECALL COLUMN	BODY	pg. 1
	Note taking in class 2/16/01	

The Cornell Method was developed by Walter Pauk, a professor at Cornell University in the early 1950s. Many students were not performing well on their exams, even though they were attending classes and completing their assignments. Professor Pauk found that students were lacking effective method for taking notes.

Look at Figure 6-2. Notice the labels that have been added to indicate the parts of the summary paper: "**body**" on the right side of the margin and "**recall column**" on the left. Each of these two columns is used in a specific way.

The body

The **body**, or the right-hand side of the margin, is where you write the bulk of your notes. These notes be in an informal outline that organizes your thoughts on the page. Outlines are easy to study and quickly let you know which ideas are more important than others. An informal outline is shown in Figure 6-3.

Learning to take notes in informal outlines becomes easier with practice. Notice that:

- The most important ideas are closer to the margin.
- The supporting ideas and details are indented and farther away.
- Indenting too much will cause you to run out of space.
- You can indicate new details by using numbers and letters or symbols such as the dash.

Figure 6-3   An Informal Outline

Informal Outline	=	Organizes thoughts
They look like		_Themes, Topics, or Main Idea_
		-supporting idea or info.
		-detail
		-example
OR numbered →		Theme, Topic, or Main Idea
		1. Supporting idea or info.
		a. detail
		example
		b. detail
		example
		2. Supporting idea or info.
		a. detail
		example

Success Skills

- Keeping similar items lined up makes your notes easy to read. (If all of your notes were lined up next to the margin, you would have difficulty deciding which ideas were more important than others.)
- Skipping lines between main ideas gives you the flexibility to add to or change your notes.

In Appendix B, you will find a note-taking activity to give you practice at creating your own informal outlines.

The recall column

The recall column is the most important part of the Cornell Method. This left-hand column is used for information you want to recall, or remember, and is based on the notes you took on the right side. Information in the recall column can be a simple word (a vocabulary word), a name, or a date. The information can also be a mathematical formula or the number of details you want to remember. *One of the best uses of the recall column is to make up questions*

Figure 6-4   Notes Using the Recall Column

	NOTE TAKING IN CLASS 2/2/01
(vocabulary term) Lectures	=ideas & concepts presented by an instructor
	—will forget unless written
(Question format) What are the 5 things to do in class	What to do:
	1) Concentrate on lecture
	2.) Develop good note-taking system
	—informal outline
	3) Pick out important pts.
	—listen 4 key terms
	4) Learn to write in short forms
	5) Review notes ASAP to fill in & refresh memory.
(Restatement) 3 Reasons for taking good notes	<u>Reasons for taking good notes</u>
	—help U pay attention
	—help U remember
	—help U organize ideas
(Title) Prevent Mind Wandering	Ways to Prevent Mind Wandering
	—Choose sear <u>in front</u> of room.
	—Avoid friends
(5)	—Keep thoughts on what tchr. saying
	—be an active listener
	—take notes

about your notes from the right side of the page to help you predict what may be on a test.

Look at the notes in Figure 6-4. Imagine you are the student who took these notes and you have an upcoming test on them. Look specifically at the recall column and the notes in the body directly across from it. These notes demonstrate four examples of how the recall column can be used.

1. **Vocabulary Terms** The first example begins with the word Lectures. This is a *vocabulary term* to know for your test, so it is set apart in the recall column.

2. **Question Format** A question, created to reflect the information in the body of your notes, is a good tool for knowing what to study for a test. Based on the notes you took, would it be fair for the instructor to ask on a test, "What are five things you can do in class to take good notes?" If you can answer this question while you are studying, then you will be able to answer it on a test.

3. **Restatement** Restating means rephrasing what is in the body of your notes, such as "three reasons for taking good notes." If you can remember all three reasons while you study, then answering them on a test will be easy.

4. **Creating a title**

   You base a title on the notes in the body and write it in the recall column. The circled number 5 under this title indicates that you have five things to remember about preventing mind wandering, according to your instructor's lecture.

The recall column is usually filled in after class, preferably the day of the class or, at the latest, the day after. This is so you don't forget what happened in class. It is quite challenging to fill in the recall column while you are in class because taking notes in the body requires most of your time and concentration.

You can, however, learn to take using the recall column for information such as a name, date, or event on a topic. If you are taking notes on anything that needs to be defined, you can immediately place the word on the left side and define it on the right. You can put topics that are being described on the left and their descriptions on the right. You can write topics that are being compared and contrasted on the left and identify how they are alike or not alike on the right. You can write a math formula on the left and the actual calculation on the right. And instead of writing topics and other main ideas in the body of your notes, you can use the recall column (so you don't have to take time later).

Success Skills

Before completing your recall column, add missing information and cross out the unimportant information, in the body of your notes. Then look at your notes and decide what word, question, restatement, or title you need to put in your recall column that will help you remember to summarize what is important on the page.

Using the recall column makes studying easy. It is an active way of reviewing your notes and making studying more effective. Practice this by covering up the body of your notes with a blank piece of paper. Begin testing yourself based on the information you wrote in the recall column. You can recite the information aloud or write it on blank paper to compare to your actual notes. Another way to ensure that you understand the notes is to place a blank paper over your recall column and test yourself on the information written there. Think of the recall column as a flash card, giving you an active way to review your notes. The goal is to recall all of the information accurately. Keep working at this skill until you master the information.

Using the recall column means you should never have to rewrite your notes again. Even if your notes are messy, you can neaten them by using the recall column to organize and clarify.

ACTIVITY 5

Locate some notes you recently took in a class, in a meeting, or from reading material. Tape them on top of the body section (right side) of a piece of summary paper. You should now have a blank 3-inch margin on the left and your notes out to the right. Fill in the recall column as best you can using the ideas presented above and your own creativity. Remember, you don't want to rewrite your notes; only include as much as you need to "recall" the information. What other information might you put in a recall column?

_____

_____

_____

_____

_____

_____

_____

_____

_____

_____

_____

Mind Mapping

Mind Mapping is a creative way to take notes that organizes ideas through visual patterns and pictures. For some people, worrying about an outline while taking notes interferes with their ability to focus on the information from the speaker. Mind Mapping allows flexibility for jotting down the information you need.

When you first look at a Mind Map, the information doesn't seem to be organized at all. Looking closer, you will see that it is very organized with a natural association of ideas in clusters or groups. Each cluster of ideas creates a visual picture, which helps you remember the ideas better.

To create a Mind Map, start in the center of a piece of unlined paper with the main idea or topic, and branch the supporting ideas and details in various directions, as shown in Figure 6-5.

If you are a sequential learner in a random instructor's class, Mind Mapping will help you get the ideas of the instructor down on paper without worrying about the proper order. Because there is little order in the random instructor's lecture anyway, it is best not to try to put order into the lecture during class. Try jotting your thoughts down in Mind Map form, and then make an outline from the mapped notes as a later review. Using summary paper makes it easy to add the outline.

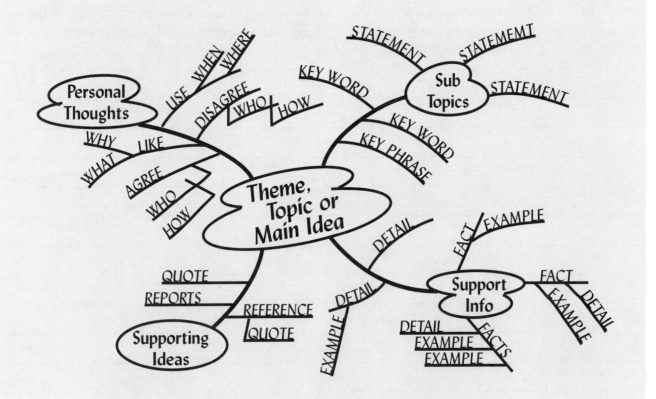

Figure 6-5   The Creation of a Mind Map

The extra step of restructuring your notes into a more sequential order is a good review, essential for learning success. By taking notes in Mind Map form, you will also be better able to see the "big picture," the connections, and the relationships—all tested later by the random instructor.

If you are a random learner in a sequential instructor's class, Mind Mapping will ensure that you get all the details and facts into your notes during a lecture. When you, as a random learner, review your notes, you can add more details to the map, color code the main ideas, and number items in terms of importance. You can outline the information if you wish.

Look at Figures 6-6 and 6-7. These particular Mind Maps contain all the key ideas that were discussed in Chapter 2 about identifying teaching styles. Figure 6-6 is a sequential approach to Mind Mapping, while Figure 6-7 is a more random approach. Though the styles look different, they are both Mind Maps.

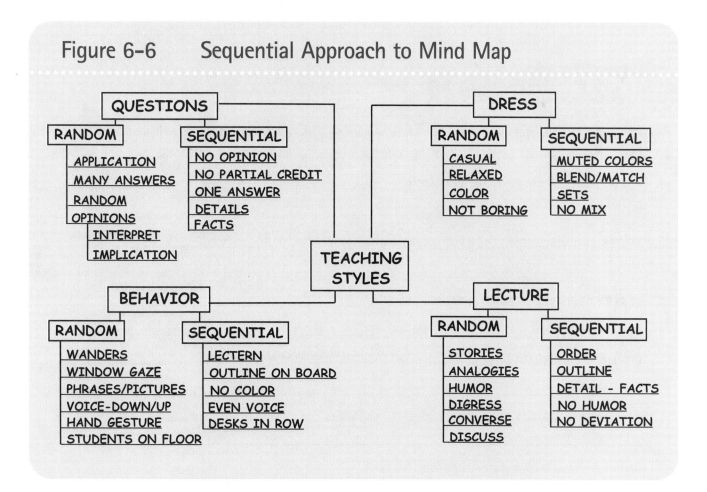

Figure 6-6   Sequential Approach to Mind Map

Figure 6-7   Random Approach to Mind Map

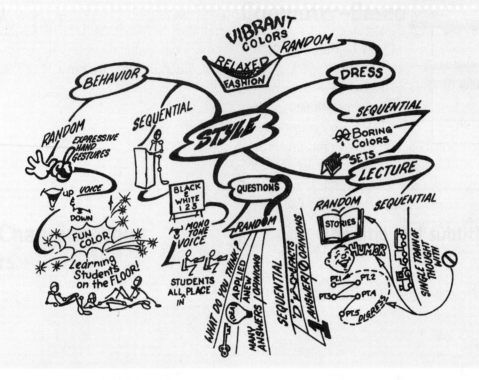

ACTIVITY 6

Follow the flow of ideas in Figure 6-6 and 6-7 by connecting one idea to the next. Compare these notes to the information you read in Chapter 2, remembering the different styles of the random and sequential instructor. Then answer the following questions.

1. What did you notice about about the Mind Map? _____

    _____

2. Could an informal outline be created from one map? If so, how would you do it? _____

    _____

3. Are all the main ideas and details contained on the map? _____

4. How are the main ideas separated from one another? _____

5. Why are small words (such as *of, at, the, a, when*) and other unimportant words omitted? _____

    _____

6. Why is it easy to determine relationships, connections, similarities, and differences about the information in the map?

    _____

7. Why is it important to leave white space around the map? _____

    _____

Success Skills

In Figure 6-7, the added pictures will also help your memory. This is because we remember pictures better than words. If you enjoy doodling, you may find the Mind Map method an outlet for what you do naturally.

Adding different print sizes, shapes, and colors to your Mind Map is an easy and fun way to review your notes. This personalization will improve later recall of the information. If you have notes in an outline, you can create a Mind Map from your outline as a study tool. When you finish creating your Mind Maps, you can hang them in your learning area, as you would a picture. The more you look at something, the more you learn.

By choosing and working effectively with a note-taking method that fits your learning style, you will possess a valuable tool for your learning success. Using the other methods will also help you succeed with instructors whose styles are different from yours. The most important thing to remember about note taking is to use whatever method works best for you.

> **"** Learning is what most adults will do for a living in the 21st century. **"**
>
> —Sydney Joseph Perelman American humorist and essayist

Checkpoint 6.4

1. Describe the Cornell Method of Note Taking.

2. Describe Mind Mapping.

3. Which method of note taking would a sequential learner prefer? Which method of note taking would a random learner prefer? Why?

Key Terms and Concepts

body (of summary paper)
cause
chronological order
classification

compare
contrast
effect

mind mapping
recall column (of summary paper)
summary paper

Chapter Summary

1. Of the many reasons to take notes, the most important is to improve your concentration.

2. Getting prepared to take notes includes having the appropriate tools for the job. Without the proper tools, the job cannot be done well.

3. Effective note-taking habits lead to good notes. This includes using abbreviations, key words, and your own words.

4. Watching a speaker for action clues and listening for verbal clues will provide information about what is important enough to take notes on and what may be on a test.

5. The Cornell Method of Note Taking is an effective method for taking sequential notes. Learning to use the recall column helps in organizing your thoughts and gives you a tool to study from.

6. Mind Mapping is an effective method for taking random notes. It is a creative way to organize ideas through visual patterns and pictures.

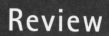

Based on the information you learned in this chapter, answer the following questions using your own words.

1. In your view what are the most important reasons for you to take notes in your classes?

2. What tools do you need to take good notes and why?

3. What are some effective note-taking habits? Write as many as you can remember.

4. What are some personality clues that your instructors use in class? What do you think they mean?

5. What are some verbal clues that your instructors use? What do you think they mean?

6. Of the two methods recommended in this chapter, is there one that you think will work better for you? Why or why not?

7. If you are a sequential learner in a random instructor's class, what would you suggest in order to take good notes?

8. If you are a random learner in a sequential instructor's class, what would you suggest in order to take good notes?

9. In a business meeting which note-taking method might you use?

10. From everything you read about and learned in this chapter, what pieces of information are the most valuable to you and why?

Case 1

Marshall sat taking notes in the third department meeting in a month. A complex new project had been outlined at the first meeting. Broad action plans and timelines had been discussed at the second meeting. This third meeting covered specific tasks and job assignments, information that was critical to Marshall's work. Returning to his office, Marshall tossed his folder full of notes onto his desk. The folder popped open, spilling the many scraps of paper he had used during each meeting. Picking up the papers, Marshall groaned, "How am I ever going to figure out what order these should be in?" As he sorted through the various-sized papers, he saw that, in some cases, he had only written part of the information given, and he recalled that as he wrote exactly what a speaker was saying, he frequently got behind and missed information that followed.

1. What advice would you give Marshall to help him make his note taking more effective?

2. Would you recommend the Cornell Method or Mind Mapping note taking technique to Marshall? Why? What are the advantages of this technique?

Case 2

Bob and Rochelle went to hear a well-known speaker whose topic was highly interesting to both of them, "Careers in the 21st Century." Each planned to take notes; Bob had a notebook, and Rochelle brought a 3x5 assignment pad. At the end of the speech, Bob was enthusiastic, mentioning several key points the speaker had made. In contrast, Rochelle felt she had gotten little out of the lecture, although she had taken a lot of notes and filled up many cards. "How did you understand so much of what she said?" Rochelle asked Bob with frustration. "I paid attention to the speaker's clues and followed her outline," replied Bob. "It seemed pretty obvious to me."

1. What are some of the specific clues Bob might have noticed the speaker using to identify important information?

2. Bob also mentioned that he used a recall column during the lecture. How, specifically, might Bob have used a recall column?

Ashley and Jordan are study partners in their Business Law class. However, when it comes to reading assignments, they are very different. Ashley finds the reading tedious, especially the 60-page chapters the instructor assigns each week. The night before a reading assignment is due, she settles into her cozy couch and spends four hours highlighting, while fighting sleepiness. When she's called on during class discussions the next day, she doesn't remember much of what she read. She also has to reread in preparation for exams.

Jordan, on the other hand, previews the chapters and breaks them down into manageable sections. He reads one section a night and takes notes at his kitchen table. Sometimes he highlights key words; but, mostly, he uses summary paper to document the important information. He keeps a running list of new vocabulary terms in the back of his notebook. During class discussions, he backs up his points with details from the reading. When it comes time for a test, he reviews his notes and rarely has to re-read the text.

What makes Jordan's study habits effective and efficient? Why are Ashley's study habits ineffective and inefficient?

In This Chapter

Chapter Goals

After studying and working with the information in this chapter, you should be able to:

♦ Discuss the importance of reading actively.
♦ Define highlighting and explain the most effective way to use it.
♦ Distinguish between two types of margin notes and explain how to use them.
♦ Describe full notes and discuss when to use them.
♦ Begin to use effective note-taking skills.

Taking notes from reading material helps your concentration, but it requires time. If you take notes on every school or work-related reading, you will be wasting your time. If, however, your purpose for taking notes is to use them for a class discussion or a test or a work-related task, such as a meeting or presentation, taking notes is a good use of your time. (When your purpose for reading is pleasure, taking notes is not necessary.) Any time you are reading new or unfamiliar information, the best way to understand and learn from it is to spend the extra time taking notes.

Read through the following information about the Active Learning Staircase. You will learn about notetaking options that will enhance your reading and note-taking abilities.

What methods do you use to capture the key concepts and information from your reading?

Taking notes from reading materials is an effective way to learn about a subject.

SELF-CHECK

The following self-evaluation will give you an idea of how familiar, or unfamiliar, you are with some of the topics and terms discussed in this chapter. After reading each statement, circle the letter Y, S, or N to indicate the answer that is most appropriate for you. Answer honestly; and rate yourself at the end; then complete the information for Chapter 7 in Appendix A.

Y = yes; frequently   S = sometimes   N = no; never

1.	The notes I take from my reading are easy to study and learn from.	Y	S	N
2.	When reading material that I need to learn or refer to later, I usually take some form of notes.	Y	S	N
3.	I know how to study without a lot of rereading.	Y	S	N
4.	I take notes from reading using key words, not full sentences.	Y	S	N
5.	I mark areas I don't understand in my text so I can ask questions about them.	Y	S	N
6.	I know how to use a highlighter effectively.	Y	S	N
7.	I know how to create margin notes.	Y	S	N
8.	I can locate the important information from reading material and take effective notes from it.	Y	S	N
9.	I use note taking as an active way to concentrate and learn when I read.	Y	S	N
10.	I learn more when I take effective notes.	Y	S	N

Rate Yourself:

Number of Ys	_____	x	100	=	_____	
Number of Ss	_____	x	50	=	_____	
Number of Ns	_____	x	0	=	_____	**Total_____**

7.1 JUST READING VERSUS ACTIVE READING

On the Active Learning Staircase in Figure 7-1 **just reading** is the most passive learning method. This is when you read from the beginning to the end of material without pre-viewing (see Chapter 8 to review pre-viewing) or taking notes. With this type of reading, your mind wanders frequently, and you lose your concentration easily. Though most people use this method occasionally, it is ineffective because the reader comprehends and retains only 10 percent over a three-day period. The loss continues over time.

Reading Actively

Reading actively is much more than "just reading." Active reading occurs when you use some or all of the following reading efficiency tools.

1. Pre-viewing the chapter—to gain background knowledge (Discussed in Chapter 8.)

2. Reading key words—to read faster and concentrate more (Discussed in Chapter 9.)

3. Reading phrases—to read faster and concentrate more (Discussed in Chapter 9.)

4. Reading with a pacer—to read faster and concentrate more (Discussed in Chapter 9.)

5. Adjusting your reading speed—to reduce wasted time (Discussed in Chapter 9.)

By reading actively, you reduce mind wandering while learning at the same time. This active reading method results in 50 percent (or more) comprehension and retention lasting over a three-day period.

When you add other active note-taking strategies (such as highlighting, writing margin notes, and taking full notes) you climb even higher on the staircase. Reading actively with effective note taking is a powerful learning combination!

Figure 7-1
Learning Staircase for Note Taking

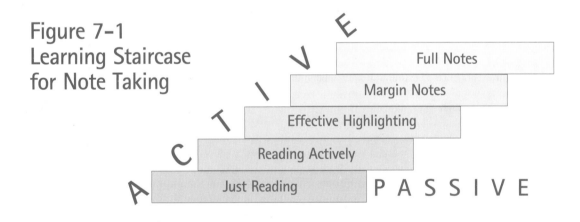

Full Notes

Margin Notes

Effective Highlighting

Reading Actively

Just Reading

A C T I V E

P A S S I V E

Checkpoint 7.1

1. What does "just reading" mean?

2. What does "reading actively" mean?

3. Why do you think you get better comprehension and retention by reading actively?

7.2 EFFECTIVE HIGHLIGHTING

Highlighting means using a colored marker to underline the important information in reading material. Highlighting helps you become a more active learner because you focus on locating the most important information. It leaves less time and energy for mind wandering.

Passive learners often highlight also, but their method is ineffective. They highlight too much information, often wasting their time highlighting whole paragraphs and pages. When it comes time to study for a test or review for a meeting, they lose more time because they have to reread everything they highlighted. Some use a fancy color-coding system that requires them to remember what color they used for what reason.

When a passive learner highlights a paragraph, he or she is saying, "This is important information, but I am too lazy to learn it now. I'll come back to it and read it again at another time." Active learners highlight less and try to understand as much as possible while they are reading. This avoids wasting time later having to reread.

Effective highlighting means:

1. *Reading a complete paragraph or section before highlighting anything.* This keeps you from highlighting too much. When you read material for the first time, everything may seem important because the information is new and unfamiliar. If you are patient and finish reading the paragraph or section, you will have a better understanding of how the ideas are related and what important ideas to highlight.

2. *Never highlighting more than a few words or a phrase at a time.* Within an important paragraph, you will find key words and phrases, vocabulary terms, a name, an event, a dollar amount, a date, or other information that should be highlighted. Learning to highlight less can lead to more learning.

3. *Deciding what is most important.* Keep in mind that what is important to one person may not be important to another. If you are worried that you did not highlight the "right" information, remember that *there is no right or wrong information to highlight, only too much or too little.*

Effective highlighting, coupled with reading actively, again results in 50 percent or more comprehension and retention lasting over a three-day period. How much more information you understand and remember depends upon how effective your highlighting methods are.

> "Nothing takes root in mind when there is no balance between doing and receiving."
>
> —John Dewey
> 19th century philosopher and educator

Professor Claude Olney, the author of the study skills program "Where There's a Will, There's an A," said, "Ineffective highlighting postpones learning." What do you think he means by this statement?

_____

_____

_____

_____

_____

_____

Figure 7-2   Brian's Highlighting Example

Ergonomics ["ergon" (work) + "nomos" (natural laws)] is the science of work. Specifically, it is the science that addresses people's performance and well-being in relation to their job tasks, their equipment, and their environment. The key to understanding the true value and role of ergonomics is knowing that an organization's most important resource is people. Therefore, anything that contributes to the performance, health and well-being, and commitment of the workforce is important to both the employer and the employee.

ERGONOMICS IN THE OFFICE ENVIRONMENT

As you might expect, ergonomics has become increasingly important in automated office environments where more and more workers are using computers as a tool for completing job tasks. Recently, several important organizations have endorsed ergonomics as a means of meeting the needs of workers in automated offices. For example, ergonomics has been endorsed as a solution to the problems of desktop computer users by the Occupational Health and Safety Administration (OSHA), the American Medical Association (AMA), and the World Health Organization (WHO).

In a 1987 directive, OSHA made ergonomics and ergonomic training a priority. OSHA states, ". . . the most fundamental strategy is to promote workplace education and awareness programs aimed at the maintenance of musculoskeletal health and the prevention of injuries." In addition, the OSHA model curriculum now includes ergonomics as one area to be included in a course of study on both the graduate and undergraduate levels.

Source: Joyce, Marilyn. *Ergonomics: Humanizing the Automated Office.* © 1989 South-Western, a division of Thomson Learning, Inc.

Figure 7-3   Carol's Highlighting Example

Ergonomics ["ergon" (work) + "nomos" (natural laws)] is the science of work. Specifically, it is the science that addresses people's performance and well-being in relation to their job tasks, their equipment, and their environment. The key to understanding the true value and role of ergonomics is knowing that an organization's most important resource is people. Therefore, anything that contributes to the performance, health and well-being, and commitment of the workforce is important to both the employer and the employee.

ERGONOMICS IN THE OFFICE ENVIRONMENT

As you might expect, ergonomics has become increasingly important in automated office environments where more and more workers are using computers as a tool for completing job tasks. Recently, several important organizations have endorsed ergonomics as a means of meeting the needs of workers in automated offices. For example, ergonomics has been endorsed as a solution to the problems of desktop computer users by the Occupational Health and Safety Administration (OSHA), the American Medical Association (AMA), and the World Health Organization (WHO).

In a 1987 directive, OSHA made ergonomics and ergonomic training a priority. OSHA states, "...the most fundamental strategy is to promote workplace education and awareness programs aimed at the maintenance of musculoskeletal health and the prevention of injuries." In addition, the OSHA model curriculum now includes ergonomics as one area to be included in a course of study on both the graduate and undergraduate levels.

Source: Joyce, Marilyn. *Ergonomics: Humanizing the Automated Office.* © 1989 South-Western, a division of Thomson Learning, Inc.

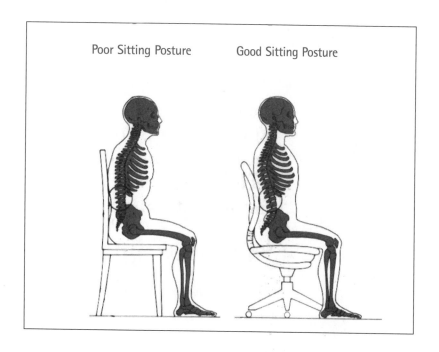

Poor Sitting Posture   Good Sitting Posture

Look over Figure 7-2 and Figure 7-3, examples of Brian's and Carol's use of a highlighter. Who will spend more time learning? Who will spend less time? Why?

_____

_____

_____

_____

_____

_____

_____

_____

Smart Tip

If you are a college student who buys your textbooks for the term, avoid purchasing used books that contain highlighting. The highlighting makes reading difficult and interferes with your ability to take notes and use fresh highlights. Though this means you may have to buy a new book, the money is an investment in active learning. After all, how do you know the former owner knew what material to highlight?

Checkpoint 7.2

1. How do passive learners use a highlighter?

2. How do active learners use a highlighter?

3. How can effective highlighting save you learning time?

7.3 CREATING MARGIN NOTES

Margin notes are yet another step up the Active Learning Staircase. **Margin notes** are either summary notes or questions you create in the margin of your material. The notes are used just like the recall column in the Cornell Method of Note Taking.

Creating margin notes is an active form of note taking because you are forced to locate (or concentrate on finding) the important information. When it comes time to review, you will spend most of your time studying from the margin notes. As a result, you will have less information to reread as well as an effective, time-saving method for review.

Margin notes are most effective if you:

1. *Read a complete paragraph or section before writing anything.* Everything you read seems important when the material is new or unfamiliar. If you are patient and finish reading a paragraph or section, you will have a better understanding of how ideas are related and what material is most important to summarize.

2. *Decide what is most important.* In some paragraphs, you may think everything is important. In others, none of the information may seem important. Remember, *there is no right or wrong information for margin notes, only too much or too little.*

3. *Use your own words, key words, and abbreviations.* Margin space is limited, so writing less is more effective. Creating and writing a title in the margin for a paragraph or section helps you identify the main idea you want to capture. Other markings that can be added to margin notes include:

- Placing a question mark (?) in the margin next to information you do not understand (so you can remind yourself to find the answer).
- Placing an asterisk (*) next to very important information.

Can you think of any others?

Writing margin notes, as with other methods of active reading, takes time but adds to your ability to comprehend and retain 50 percent or more of the material lasting over three days. How much more depends upon the effectiveness of your methods.

Look at Figure 7-4, Sandy's summary-in-the-margin notes, and Figure 7-5, Kate's question-in-the-margin notes. These are two different ways to use the margin for notes.

WEB LINK

Visit these web sites for online study skills guides and tips for getting the most from your reading.

http://www.mtsu.edu/~studskl/Txtbook.html

http://www.brunel.ac.uk/~mastmmg/ssguide/sshome.html

Summary-in-the-Margin Notes

A **summary** is a brief statement or restatement of main points. It is a shortened version of what you consider important in the text you are reading.

In the first paragraph of Sandy's text, you will see three separate summaries in the margin. The information in each one could possibly show up on a test. The first summary indicates a definition to remember. A bracket surrounds the definition in case Sandy needs to quickly review it. *Using a bracket is a simple and time-saving form of highlighting.*

The second summary indicates another important idea and is written in Sandy's own abbreviated language. Sandy does not think the third note is as important as the others, but she expects to may be tested on it. Notice that the numbering indicates each of the ideas she wants to recall. This type of numbering is effective when you need to remember a series of related ideas.

Figure 7-4   Sandy's Summary-in-the-Margin Notes

Margin notes	Text
DEF. ERGONOMICS PEOPLE = ORGANIZNS MOST IMP. ASSET 3 IMP. CONTRIBUTIONS TO EMPLOYERS & EMPLOYEES	Ergonomics ["ergon" (work) + "nomos" (natural laws)] is the science of work. Specifically, it is the science that addresses people's performance and well-being in relation to their job tasks, their equipment, and their environment. The key to understanding the true value and role of ergonomics is knowing that an organization's most important resource is people. Therefore, anything that contributes to the performance, health and well-being, and commitment of the workforce is important to both the employer and the employee.

ERGONOMICS IN THE OFFICE ENVIRONMENT

ERGON ↗ IMPORTANT — COMPUTERS
3 ORGANIZATIONS ENDORSE ERGON. AS WAY TO MEET OFFICE WORKERS' NEEDS

As you might expect, ergonomics has become increasingly important in automated office environments where more and more workers are using computers as a tool for completing job tasks. Recently, several important organizations have endorsed ergonomics as a means of meeting the needs of workers in automated offices. For example, ergonomics has been endorsed as a solution to the problems of desktop computer users by the Occupational Health and Safety Administration (OSHA), the American Medical Association (AMA), and the World Health Organization (WHO).

1987 OSHA DIRECTIVE

In a 1987 directive, OSHA made ergonomics and ergonomic training a priority. OSHA states, ". . . the most fundamental strategy is to promote workplace education and awareness programs aimed at the maintenance of musculoskeletal health and the prevention of injuries." In addition, the OSHA model curriculum now includes ergonomics as one area to be included in a course of study on both the graduate and undergraduate levels.

Source: Joyce, Marilyn. *Ergonomics: Humanizing the Automated Office.* © 1989 South-Western, a division of Thomson Learning, Inc.

Success Skills

Question-in-the-Margin Notes

In the margin of Kate's text, you will find questions. She prefers to summarize important ideas as questions, similar to what she might find on a test. The answer to each question is easily found by rereading the text next to the question. Notice that she uses her own form of abbreviation. She indicates exactly how many things she needs to recall when a question can be answered in more than one way ("What is imp. to both employer and employee?" 3).

Figure 7–5   Kate's Questions-in-the-Margin Notes

WHAT IS ERGONOMICS?

WHAT IS AN ORGANIZATION'S MOST IMP. RESOURCE?

WHAT IS IMP. TO BOTH EMPLOYER AND EMPLOYEE?
③

WHY IS ERGO. INCREASINGLY IMPORTANT?

WHAT ORGANIZATIONS ENDORSED ERGON...?
③

WHAT HAPPENED IN 1987? BY WHOM?

WHAT WAS SAID?

Ergonomics ["ergon" (work) + "nomos" (natural laws)] is the science of work. Specifically, it is the science that addresses people's performance and well-being in relation to their job tasks, their equipment, and their environment. The key to understanding the true value and role of ergonomics is knowing that an organization's most important resource is people. Therefore, anything that contributes to the performance, ① health and ② well-being, and ③ commitment of the workforce is important to both the employer and the employee.

ERGONOMICS IN THE OFFICE ENVIRONMENT

As you might expect, ergonomics has become increasingly important in automated office environments where more and more workers are using computers as a tool for completing job tasks. Recently, several important organizations have endorsed ergonomics as a means of meeting the needs of workers in automated offices. For example, ergonomics has been endorsed as a solution to the problems of desktop computer users by the ① Occupational Health and Safety Administration (OSHA), the ② American Medical Association (AMA), and the ③ World Health Organization (WHO).

In a 1987 directive, OSHA made ergonomics and ergonomic training a priority. OSHA states, ". . .the most fundamental strategy is to promote workplace education and awareness programs aimed at the maintenance of musculoskeletal health and the prevention of injuries." In addition, the OSHA model curriculum now includes ergonomics as one area to be included in a course of study on both the graduate and undergraduate levels.

Source: Joyce, Marilyn. *Ergonomics: Humanizing the Automated Office.* © 1989 South-Western, a division of Thomson Learning, Inc.

Combining Margin Notes and Effective Highlighting

By combining effective highlighting and margin notes, you can quickly identify important ideas and reinforce others. Several highlighted words or phrases in addition to margin notes provides good review material. Do not waste time becoming preoccupied with the mechanics of combining the two methods.

Studying With Margin Notes

Margin notes, either summary form or questions, force you to:

♦ Concentrate on what you are reading.

♦ Focus on what is really important.

♦ Reduce your study time when you review.

Imagine it is now time to review the reading in Figure 7-4 or Figure 7-5 in preparation for a test. Cover the text with a blank piece of paper while you review the summaries or questions. Test yourself to see how much you know and what information you need to review. You can use the paper covering the text to write your responses on, or you can say the answers aloud. When you finish reviewing, remove the paper and check yourself. If you are having trouble recalling a certain piece of information, place your own reference mark next to it and review the material again. Turn to Appendix B for practice on becoming an active note taker.

Checkpoint 7.3

1. What are margin notes?

2. What are two suggested ways to create margin notes?

3. How can you best learn with margin notes?

7.4 TAKING FULL NOTES

Full notes are the top step on the Active Learning Staircase. They are also the most time-consuming. You need to know how to take full notes when learning technical or difficult material. *Using a combination of effective highlighting and margin notes will be sufficient for most of your non-fiction reading.*

Full notes means taking all your notes on summary paper instead of highlighting the textbook. For full notes, you must re-create the author's outline in the recall column on the left side margin and fill in the important details in the body of notes on the right side margin. (For more information on how to find the author's outline, see pre-viewing in Chapter 8.) Full notes can also be taken in the form of a mind map using unlined paper.

Taking full notes along with reading actively, results in 75 percent or more comprehension and retention lasting over three days. How much more depends upon the effectiveness of your methods.

Look at the text in Figure 7-5. Each paragraph contains many important facts and useful information. Understanding and thoroughly learning the information is important for doing well on a test. Though effective highlighting and margin notes may be enough in some situations, full notes become a more effective study tool for difficult material like this.

Success Skills

Figure 7-6 Text Samples for Using Full Notes

WHAT CIVIL LITIGATION IS

Civil litigation is the process of resolving private disputes through the court system. Unless the parties are able to resolve their dispute, the litigation process usually results in a trial, or hearing, where the parties present their evidence to a judge or jury. The judge or jury then decides the dispute. Before this happens, however, a great deal of investigation, research, and preparation takes place. Although most of this occurs outside of the courtroom, it is an important part of the litigation process. Litigation attorneys and their assistants often spend considerable time gathering and analyzing the facts as well as researching the law. Formal legal documents must be prepared and filed with the court, witnesses must be interviewed, and other evidence must be identified and located.

Civil Law v. Criminal Law

Not all disputes that end in litigation are civil in nature, for our court system handles both civil and criminal cases. However, the litigation procedures for civil cases vary considerably from the litigation procedures employed in a criminal case. Being able to distinguish a civil case from a criminal one is therefore very important.

The rules of civil litigation, sometimes referred to as **civil procedure**, apply only if a civil law is involved. **Civil laws** are those that deal with private disputes between parties. If a lawsuit results, it is between the disputing parties. The parties may be individuals, organizations, or governmental entities. Civil law includes such areas as contracts, real estate, commercial and business transactions, and torts (civil wrongs or injuries not stemming from a contract). A typical civil case is illustrated by the following situation. While shopping at Dave's Department Store, Kirkland trips on torn carpeting, seriously injuring himself. The carpeting had been torn for several weeks, but the store had ignored the condition. Kirkland requests that the department store pay for his injuries, but the store refuses. Kirkland could sue the department store, asking the court to force the store to pay for his medical bills, for his lost wages, and for any pain and suffering he may have experienced. The basis for such a lawsuit is found in the law of torts, in particular, negligence. The procedures and rules that would govern that lawsuit are known as the rules of civil procedure or civil litigation.

Criminal law, on the other hand, deals with acts that are offenses against society as a whole, and includes such acts as murder, robbery, and drunk driving. If a criminal action results, it is usually between the government and the accused. The procedures and rules that apply when an individual is accused of committing a crime are known as the rules of **criminal procedure**. To a large extent, the Bill of Rights found in the U.S. Constitution governs the rules of criminal procedure. In a criminal case the defendant enjoys various rights, such as the right not to testify against himself. The defendant also has the right to a court-appointed counsel if he or she is indigent, and is entitled to speedy trial, all rights found in the Constitution. None of these rights exist in civil cases.

Source: Kerley, Peggy, et al. *Civil Litigation for the Paralegal.* © 2000 Delmar Publishers Inc.

Figure 7-7   Jim's Samples Using Full Notes

pp 3-22	_What Civil litigation is 4/6/01_
Civil Litigation =	resolving private disputes thru court system
trial or hearing =	parties present evidence to judge or jury
litigation attys & assts. =	gather & analyze facts/research law
	- legal doc's prep'd & filed
	- witnesses interviewed
	- other evidence identified & located
Civil law vs. Criminal law	
Civil Procedure =	rules of civil Litigation
Civil Laws =	laws dealing w/prin disputes btw parties
	- contracts
	- real estate
	- com'l & bus. transactions
torts	- torts (= civil wrongs)
	- negligence
Criminal law =	offense against society
	- murder
	- robbery
	- drunk driving
	- disputes btw gov't & accused
criminal procedure =	rules that apply when someone is accused of a crime.
Bill of Rights =	governs criminal procedures
defendant's rights =	1) to not testify against himself
3	2) has right to court appointed counsel
	3) entitled to speedy trial

Read the notes in Figure 7-6, Jim's notes using summary paper. Think about or discuss with your classmates the following questions. Write your answers below.

1. What is your first impression of Jim's notes? _____

2. What do you notice about them? _____

3. Do you think Jim learned better by creating full notes? Explain your answer._____

4. Would he have learned as much using another method of note taking? _____

   Explain._____

5. Do you think his time was well spent? Why or why not?

   _____

   _____

6. When it comes time to study for your test, which would you rather have: the full text or the notes? Why?

   _____

   _____

If you would like to learn how to take full notes, begin by using reading material required for school or work. This will be the best use of your time and active learning energy. Turn to Appendix B for a practice activity in taking full notes.

Checkpoint 7.4

1. What are full notes?

2. Why is summary paper ideal for full notes?

3. Though full notes are the most time-consuming note taking method, how does this method save you time ultimately?

7.5 ABOUT FICTION NOTE TAKING

Taking notes from fiction material, such as a novel or another piece of literature, requires a few special considerations. Effective highlighting and making notes in the margin are useful. However, since there is no author outline as with a textbook or other nonfiction material, taking full notes from fiction is challenging.

While there is no one best way to take notes from fiction, here are some good ideas:

♦ Keep track of the characters, as this is the most challenging part of any story. You can designate a piece of paper or a large index card to each character. As he or she is introduced in the story, write the name at the top. Write descriptions about the characters, including their relationship to others, examples of what they say, examples of what they do, examples of what other characters say about them, and examples of what the author says about them.

♦ Identify and take notes about the basic elements of fiction. These are the elements you can expect to find in every short story, novel, or play:

- Title – *a clue pointing you towards the theme of the story*
- Setting – *a time and place*
- Point of View – *spoken either in the first person (a character serves as the narrator) or third person (a narrator outside the story)*
- Conflict (part of the plot) – *problems that change the belief system or lives of characters involved*
- Climax and Resolution (part of the plot) – *the moment in the story when the character makes a decision that leads to the ultimate resolution of the conflict*

Checkpoint 7.5

1. Why might you want to take notes from fiction?

2. What might your fiction notes include?

3. How might you study with your fiction notes?

Key Terms and Concepts

effective highlighting	just reading	reading actively
full notes	margin notes	summary

Chapter Summary

1. Learning how to take effective notes from reading material will increase your concentration while reading, save review time, and make your learning more active.

2. Just reading is the most passive and ineffective way to read and learn. Reading actively focuses you and results in better comprehension and retention.

3. Highlighting only key words and phrases is more effective than highlighting whole paragraphs and pages.

4. Creating either summary-in-the margin or question-in-the-margin notes increases your concentration while reading, saves you time when reviewing, and forces you to predict test questions at the same time.

5. Taking full notes is for technical or difficult material that is new to you and which you need to learn in detail.

6. You can take notes from fiction by tracking the characters and paying attention to the basic elements of fiction.

Review

Based on the information you learned in this chapter, answer the following questions using your own words.

1. Describe the Active Learning Staircase as it relates to learning from reading materials.

2. When should notes be taken from reading materials?

3. How do you decide which note taking method to use?

4. What does reading actively mean? How does it affect your learning?

5. What is the most effective way to use a highlighter?

6. What are the most effective ways to create margin notes?

7. When is taking full notes a good idea? How can full notes help?

8. Why is it important to avoid rereading from your textbooks?

9. In your view, what are the most important reasons to take notes from reading materials? Why?

10. From everything you read and learned in this chapter, what pieces of information are the most valuable to you and why?

Case 1

Linda's goal was a Certificate in Supervision and she studied hard to achieve it. During lunch one day, she read several lengthy articles she had downloaded from the Internet. She knew she would be tested in a week, and she wanted to make a good grade. On the train home later, Linda struggled to recall what she had read. When she returned home, she sat down and started rereading the articles from the beginning. Disheartened, she felt she had wasted her lunchtime.

1. For Linda to read actively instead of passively, what should she do?

2. How might taking notes have helped Linda use her study time more effectively?

Case 2

Connor was not doing well in his electronics course. He read the highly technical course materials diligently; however, his weekly test results had not been good. His friend Brenda had done well on the most recent test, and Connor asked her what she had done to improve. "I found that highlighting the text wasn't enough for difficult material like this," Brenda told him. Brenda said she was using additional note taking techniques including margin and full notes. Since Conner's new job depended on him getting a good grade, he was anxious to improve on his next test.

1. Describe for Connor's benefit the basic structure of full notes. How should he organize his notes so that they are easy to review for his next test?

2. Compare the benefits of margin notes to full notes. What would be the advantage of one over the other in this case?

C H A P T E R

8

Kayla is taking a course in American history and has been assigned several chapters of reading. This assignment piles up with the assignments from her other three classes.

When she is assigned reading, Kayla opens the book to the first page and reads word for word until the end. Her mind frequently wanders. Because she's distracted, she sometimes stops reading to call a friend or watch a TV show.

When she gets back to the assignment, she has to reread quite a bit of material to remember where she left off. When she finally finishes, she is happy. However, she has only the slightest idea of what she just read and hopes she won't have to answer any detailed questions in class or on a test. When it's time to review for a test, she has to reread most of the chapter because she doesn't remember what it was about. Sometimes, because of time limitations, she doesn't review all the material.

What do you think is the problem with Kayla's way of reading?

Chapter Goals

After studying and working with the information in this chapter, you should be able to:

♦ Identify what active readers know and do.

♦ Distinguish between nonfiction and fiction reading.

♦ Explain the importance of identifying your reading purpose and responsibility before you begin.

♦ Describe the procedure for pre-viewing a nonfiction book.

♦ Describe the procedure for pre-viewing a nonfiction chapter or article.

♦ Understand the role background knowledge plays in reading and learning.

♦ Identify and describe 5 approaches to dealing with unfamiliar words.

In This Chapter

8.1 What Active Readers Know and Do

8.2 Pre-viewing

8.3 Building Vocabulary

Reading and understanding factual nonfiction material may be one of the most challenging learning tasks you experience—for several reasons. The first and most important is that you are working with inadequate reading skills learned in elementary school. Second, there is so much available to read both on paper and on screen, for school, work, and pleasure. Third, finding time to read in today's busy world is challenging and, lastly, knowledge and one's ability to gain it has become a necessity in the working world.

Reading is a necessary lifelong skill. You must read in school to participate in classroom discussions and to complete homework assignments, quizzes, and tests. You must read at work to gain knowledge, learn a new skill, understand information, participate in informal

discussions, and grow in a career. You may read for pleasure, or to become a healthier person or a better parent, friend, or spouse.

This chapter will focus on (1) a reading skill called pre-viewing that can be used with all of your nonfiction reading, (2) methods to build vocabulary, and (3) ways to use your background knowledge to learn new words easily.

What is your reading workload like? How do you manage it?

Success Skills

SELF-CHECK

The following self-evaluation will give you an idea of how familiar, or unfamiliar, you are with some of the topics and terms discussed in this chapter. After reading each statement, circle the letter Y, S, or N to indicate the answer that is most appropriate for you. Answer honestly; rate yourself at the end, then complete the information for Chapter 8 in Appendix A.

	Y = yes; frequently	S = sometimes	N = no; never		

1.	I understand what active readers know and do.	Y	S	N
2.	I know the difference between nonfiction and fiction material.	Y	S	N
3.	I am aware of my purpose and responsibility before I read.	Y	S	N
4.	I know how to pre-view a nonfiction book or magazine.	Y	S	N
5.	I know how to pre-view a nonfiction chapter or article.	Y	S	N
6.	When I come across a word I don't know, I use context clues to understand its meaning.	Y	S	N
7.	When I come across a word I don't know, I use prefixes, roots, and suffixes to identify its meaning.	Y	S	N
8.	When I come across a word I don't know, I use a dictionary effectively.	Y	S	N
9.	I have a system for tracking new words.	Y	S	N
10.	I can manage my reading workload.	Y	S	N

Rate Yourself:

Number of Ys	_____	x	100	=	_____
Number of Ss	_____	x	50	=	_____
Number of Ns	_____	x	0	=	_____ Total_____

8.1 WHAT ACTIVE READERS KNOW AND DO

The first step to becoming an **active reader** is to know what active readers understand and do. Read the qualities of a passive reader and an active reader in Figure 8.1.

Many differences exist between passive and active readers. **Passive readers** like Kayla don't take an active role in their learning.

Figure 8–1   Qualities of Passive and Active Readers

Passive	Active
1. Unaware of purpose and responsibility before reading	1. Aware of purpose and responsibility before reading
2. Cannot identify where the main ideas are located	2. Knows where the main ideas are located
3. Understands poorly	3. Understands well
4. Allows mind to wander frequently	4. Allows mind to wander rarely
5. Reads slowly most of the time	5. Reads rapidly, especially on familiar material
6. Does not vary reading speed	6. Uses different reading speeds for different purposes
7. Has a limited vocabulary	7. Has a wide vocabulary
8. Reads the same kind of material repeatedly	8. Reads diverse materials
9. Cannot identify the writer's outline (nonfiction)	9. Can identify the writer's outline (nonfiction)
10. Does not evaluate what is read	10. Evaluates what is read
11. Rarely takes notes	11. Takes good notes when the situation justifies doing so
12. Has a limited background of general knowledge and experience	12. Has a broad background of general knowledge and experience
13. Reads seldom and dislikes it	13. Reads often and enjoys it

Here again is a list of qualities of passive and active readers. Notice that the traits in the two columns are opposites. Place a check mark next to the quality that best describes you. If you believe you are in between the qualities (meaning you possess some of both), place a check mark in the middle.

Passive Reader Qualities	In Between	Active Reader Qualities
❏ Unaware of purpose and responsibility before reading	❏	❏ Aware of purpose and responsibility before reading
❏ Cannot identify where the main ideas are located	❏	❏ Knows where the main ideas are located
❏ Understands poorly	❏	❏ Understands well
❏ Mind wanders frequently	❏	❏ Mind wanders occasionally
❏ Reads slowly most of the time	❏	❏ Reads rapidly, especially on familiar material
❏ Does not vary reading speed	❏	❏ Uses different reading speeds for different purposes
❏ Has a limited vocabulary	❏	❏ Has a wide vocabulary
❏ Reads the same types of material repeatedly	❏	❏ Reads diverse materials
❏ Cannot identify the writer's outline (non-fiction)	❏	❏ Can identify the writer's outline (nonfiction)
❏ Does not evaluate what is read	❏	❏ Evaluates what is read
❏ Rarely takes notes	❏	❏ Takes good notes when the situation justifies it
❏ Has a limited background of general knowledge and experience	❏	❏ Has a broad background of general knowledge and experience
❏ Reads seldom and dislikes it	❏	❏ Reads often and enjoys it

After you have worked with this chapter and Chapter 9, *Survival Reading Skills*, you will be asked to return to this list and reevaluate your reading qualities.

In this chapter and in Chapter 9, you will learn how to become an active reader. It helps to be able to identify nonfiction and fiction reading material. The first steps are to identify fiction and nonfiction reading material and know your purpose and responsibility for reading.

The Difference Between Nonfiction and Fiction

Nonfiction reading material is factual in nature. Textbooks, how-to books, encyclopedias, and most magazine articles are examples of factual material. Nonfiction contains information on many topics and is the most challenging to comprehend. The information in this chapter will concentrate on reading nonfiction, since most school- and work-related learning requires reading factual material.

Fiction reading is imaginative in nature and is composed of invented ideas. Novels, short stories, and some magazine articles are examples of fiction. Fiction reading is easier than non-fiction because it generally centers on one topic or story. The challenge of fiction reading is following the story line and being able to interpret its meaning. (See Chapter 7 for ideas on how to take notes from fiction material.) Figure 8.2 lists several examples of nonfiction and fiction.

Figure 8-2   Examples of Nonfiction and Fiction Reading

Nonfiction

Textbooks

♦ *Design Guidelines for Desktop Publishing*
  —Roberta Mantus

♦ *Retail Buying: From Staples to Fashions to Fads*
  —Richard Clodfelter

Magazines

♦ *Time*

♦ *Rolling Stone*

Newspapers

♦ *The New York Times*

♦ *The Wall Street Journal*

Fiction

Novels

♦ *A Portrait of the Artist As a Young Man*
  —James Joyce

♦ *One Hundred Years of Solitude*
  —Gabriel Garcia Marquez

Short Story Collections

♦ *Heat: And Other Stories*
  —Joyce Carol Oates

♦ *Enormous Changes at the Last Minute*
  —Grace Paley

Poetry

♦ *Earthlight*
  —Andre Breton

♦ *Shaker, Why Don't You Sing*
  —Maya Angelou

Think about the books, magazines, and other materials you are currently reading. Which are nonfiction and which are fiction? What do you find challenging about each?

_____

_____

_____

_____

_____

_____

_____

_____

_____

_____

Finding Your Purpose and Reading Responsibility

In Chapter 1, knowing your purpose and responsibility for learning was presented as a way to become actively involved with all learning tasks. In this chapter, it is specific to reading.

Your **reading purpose** is the reason *why* you are reading. It might also be considered your intent for reading. The purposes can be as simple as "because I want to read for my own information" or as challenging as "My instructor assigned the reading, and I will be responsible for understanding it."

Your **reading responsibility** refers to the ways you are accountable for the information. Reading responsibilities include (1) becoming familiar with the information for a class discussion or for a meeting, (2) being able to perform well on a quiz or test based on the information, (3) answering another person's questions or (4) incorporating the information into your knowledge for future use.

Each responsibility requires a different amount of reading and study time. For example, if your reading task is to prepare for a class discussion, you do not need to spend a lot of time studying the information in depth—you need only be familiar with it. If your task is to write a report based on what you read, then you should read more closely, take notes, and think about how the material relates to your report.

Without knowing your purpose or your reading responsibility, you are a passive reader who wastes time and has no direction. By knowing your purpose and reading responsibility, you become an active reader who is efficient with time and proceeds in the proper direction.

Chapter 8: Reading Comprehension Skills

ACTIVITY 3

Think about several reading tasks you must complete or have recently completed. Write a description for each one.

    a. Identify your reading purpose (the reason why you are reading).

    b. Identify your reading responsibility (what you need to do as a result of your reading).

    c. Identify other purposes and responsibilities.

Reading Task 1   *Read a section of a software manual.*

  a.   *Learn how to use new software.*

  b.   *Use the software to do work tasks.*

  c.   *Advance my career.*

Reading Task 2 _____

  a. _____

  b. _____

  c. _____

Reading Task 3 _____

  a. _____

  b. _____

  c. _____

Reading Task 4 _____

  a. _____

  b. _____

  c. _____

Checkpoint 8.1

1. What are some differences between passive and active readers?

2. What is the difference between nonfiction and fiction material?

3. Why is it important to have a reading purpose and responsibility?

Success Skills

8.2 PRE-VIEWING

Consider possible answers to the following questions:

- ♦ Why do football players watch films of their opponents' games *before* facing them?
- ♦ Why do people ask for directions or look at maps *before* traveling? How else do they find directions?
- ♦ Why do people read film reviews in the newspaper *before* going to movies? How else can they get this information?

The first question responds to the need for *preparing a plan of attack*. Football teams must create a strategy of attack against their opponents, which they can do more easily if they know the strategies their opponents have used in previous games. This gives them a competitive edge on the playing field.

The second question speaks to the need *for mapping out a direction*. Without directions, people get lost, frustrated, and detoured from their destinations. On the other hand, with directions, people are able to get where they want to go and can reach their destinations in a reasonable amount of time.

The third question responds to the need for *using time effectively*. If you blindly select a movie, not knowing whether it is a horror, a comedy, an action-adventure, or another type of film, you may end up wasting your time and money by watching something you don't like. A little preparation can make the time you spend at the movies worthwhile and enjoyable.

How does this relate to reading? When approaching reading, most people are passive, like Kayla. They don't establish a plan of attack or map a direction, so they waste time by reading from the first word to the last. Active readers, on the other hand, prepare a plan of attack, map out a direction, and create a course of action for using their time wisely.

> " There are those who travel and those who are going somewhere. They are different and yet they are the same. The most successful is the one who knows where he is going. "
>
> —Mark Caine
> Contemporary author

Looking at a road map before leaving on a trip makes a journey enjoyable, comfortable, and relaxing. Without the map, the same journey could be unpleasant, frustrating, and time-consuming. What preparation can you make before reading?

Pre-viewing is one of the best strategies for becoming an active reader. **Pre-viewing** means examining nonfiction material to discover the writer's outline before reading in detail. The outline gives clues to the content.

By pre-viewing, you learn how the material is organized, what the main ideas are, and what and where content will be covered. Pre-viewing is an important tool for understanding all nonfiction reading tasks. (For information about pre-viewing fiction, see Appendix C.)

The most serious drawback of pre-viewing, commonly mentioned by beginning pre-viewers, is that it takes more time than just reading from beginning to end. At first, pre-viewing may take ten minutes for a ten-page chapter or article. However, once you know what to look for and are skilled at finding the information quickly, it should take less than five minutes.

The benefits of taking time to pre-view before reading are as follows:

1. It builds background knowledge for easier learning.

2. It helps to transfer new information into long-term memory because you will have seen the material more than once.

3. It helps you to be active in your reading by having a plan of attack and a mapped direction.

It takes time to save time, and the time you spend pre-viewing is well spent toward learning.

Pre-viewing a Nonfiction Book

Pre-viewing a nonfiction book, such as a computer manual, school textbook, or how-to book, is easy once you know what to look for. This pre-view process should be done once, the first time you pick up a new book, before you start reading, to familiarize yourself with the material. It's like getting acquainted with a new friend.

Pre-viewing a nonfiction book is accomplished by briefly focusing on each of the following elements.

The title and subtitle

The title of a nonfiction book tells you the topic, or the main idea. For example, a text entitled *Automotive Electronics* tells you that the book contains information about the electronic workings of a car. However, the text may not provide information about changing a car's oil or tires. A subtitle gives you more information. For instance, *Automotive Electronics: An Advanced Course* suggests that the basics will not be discussed and that more difficult topics will be emphasized.

The author

Chances are that you will have never heard of a book's author. So why even look at the name? Because the qualifications of the author or authors are important. Is he or she a specialist on the topic? Does the person have any college degrees or related work experience on the topic?

This information can be found on a book's title page (for example, Dr. John Jones, Ph.D., Professor of Auto Mechanics at Abernathy College), on a page entitled "About the Author," or sometimes at the end of the book. (See page x of this book for information about the author of this book.)

The copyright date

A text's copyright date is found on the left-hand page, immediately before or immediately after the title page, and is usually located next to the symbol ©. The copyright date, sometimes referred to as the publishing date, tells you how recent or how old the information is. For example, if you are taking a computer course and the book you are assigned is three years old, you know that developments in the field over the last three years will not be covered. A book with more than one copyright date has been revised or updated or is popular enough to have been reprinted. If 33 percent or more of a book has been revised, reworded, or rewritten, the title will indicate this by identifying the edition (2d edition, 3d edition, and so on).

The preface

The preface of a textbook is usually found after the table of contents. The preface may also be referred to as the foreword or introduction. It may tell you why the author wrote the book and what you need to know about how the book is organized.

The table of contents

Nonfiction books are written in outline form. The table of contents is the outline of the text. By reviewing the table of contents, you can better understand the strategy the author used in writing the book, learn what will be covered, and discover what direction the author intends for communicating the information to the reader. Most textbook outlines are divided into *units* or *parts*, which show the general topics, then divided again into *chapters*, which indicate more specific areas of discussion.

> " Almost all men are intelligent; it's the method they lack. "
>
> —F. W. Nichol
> Business educator

The appendix, index, glossary, and bibliography

The *appendix*, *index*, *glossary*, and *bibliography*, usually found at the back of a book, provide additional information. By pre-viewing them, you will know what resources are available to you. Too many people do not realize that a valuable learning tool is right in their own hand.

An appendix contains supplementary information that further explains a subject in the text. It might also contain an answer key to questions.

An index is an alphabetical listing of names, places, and topics and the numbers of the pages on which they are mentioned or discussed. The index is helpful when searching for specific information, especially when researching a specific topic.

A glossary is a list of terms with accompanying definitions. In a book entitled *Computer Basics*, the glossary would list the jargon, or specialized vocabulary terms, relating to computers. Though a regular dictionary may contain the same vocabulary terms, the textbook glossary will give practical definitions for use in your course.

A bibliography describes what reading resources the author used in writing the book. You can use the bibliography to do further research on a specific topic.

ACTIVITY 4

Locate a nonfiction textbook, preferably one you have not seen before. Answer the following questions.

1. What is the title of the textbook? What does the title suggest about the content? _____

_____

2. What is the subtitle of the text, if any? What additional information does it provide about the book's content? _____

_____

3. What can you learn about the author(s) of your text? _____

_____

4. What is the copyright date of the text? What does it tell you about the book? _____

_____

5. What is the edition of the text? _____

_____

6. Read the preface of the text. What information does it give you? _____

_____

7. Review the table of contents. How is the author's outline presented to you? Does it give the structure of your book? _____

_____

_____

8. Does the text have an appendix, an index, a glossary, or a bibliography? _____

_____

9. How would this information be helpful to your learning? _____

_____

_____

Success Skills

Figure 8-3 is a quick-reference worksheet you can copy and use for pre-viewing a nonfiction book. It is meant to remind you of what to examine in a book. After locating the information in several different books, you will probably be able to pre-view a book without using the worksheet.

Place a check mark in the blank before each item once you have pre-viewed it in a book. After each item, write any related information you believe is appropriate or important. As you become used to pre-viewing nonfiction books, keep this list as a reminder tool.

Figure 8-3   A Quick-Reference Worksheet

Previewing A Nonfiction Book

_____Title: _____

_____Author(s): _____

_____Copyright Date: _____

_____Preface or Introduction: _____

_____Table of Contents: _____

_____ Units or Sections: _____

_____ Chapters: _____

_____Appendix: _____

_____Index: _____

_____Glossary: _____

_____Bibliography: _____

_____Other Comments: _____

_____

_____

Focus on Ethics

You work part-time answering the phone in a pharmacy. One day, a customer calls with a question regarding the proper dosage of a medication—something you've never heard of with a long, complex name. You don't want to appear ignorant, so you don't ask the customer for the correct spelling. Instead, you write a message for the pharmacist, taking a guess at the name of the medication. Unknowingly, you write the name of another medication with a very similar name. Why might this be a problem? How could it have been prevented?

Pre-viewing a Nonfiction Chapter or Article

Once you have pre-viewed a complete nonfiction book or magazine article, you are ready to pre-view a single chapter or section. This will provide you with detailed information you need to prepare a plan of attack, map out your direction, and create a course of action for using your time wisely.

Pre-viewing a chapter or an article is accomplished by briefly focusing on each of the following elements.

The title

The title of a chapter or an article tells you the topic or main idea. A title alone may not describe the specifics, but it will give you a general idea of the subject matter.

Headings and subheadings

Headings and subheadings provide you with more specific information about the chapter as well as an outline of the information. Publishers usually indicate headings and subheadings by printing them on separate lines or in slightly larger print than the rest of the text. Figure 8-4 illustrates headings and subheadings in more detail.

Figure 8-4   Headings and Subheadings

This is a → **FACTORS AFFECTING MERCHANDISE** heading **ASSORTMENTS**

When planning merchandise assortments, you will want to provide a variety of merchandise that is best suited for your customers' needs and consistent with your store's image. As you develop the assortment plan, there are several key factors that must be considered. They include: (1) type of merchandise carried, (2) store policies, and (3) variety of merchandise available.

This is a → **Type of Merchandise**
subheading

The type of merchandise your store or department carries will affect your assortment planning. There are many methods used to categorize merchandise, and each one requires the development of a different type of assortment plan. Merchandise can be divided as fashion or basic (staple) merchandise or classified as convenience or specialty goods.

This is a → **Fashion or basic merchandise**
subheading
to the above
subheading

Merchandise can be grouped into two broad classifications—fashion or basic (staple) merchandise. Fashion merchandise has high demand over a relatively short period of time, usually a season. Appeal for fashion merchandise is limited, which causes customer demand to end abruptly. In order to maximize sales, fashion buyers must quickly identify "best sellers" in their merchandise assortments and place reorders immediately. As the selling season progresses, few or no reorders should be placed. Consumer demand could end quickly, leaving you in an overstocked position, and then even substantial markdowns may not move unwanted merchandise.

Source: Clodfelter, Richard. *Retail Buying: From Staples to Fashions to Fads.* © 1993 Delmar Publishers Inc.

Success Skills

The length of reading

The length of a chapter or an article is important because it suggests how much time you can expect to spend reading. If the material is long, you may want to break the reading up into smaller, more manageable sections. This helps you take more control over your reading time.

Introductory paragraphs

Introductory paragraphs are the first several paragraphs of the material. They are, in effect, the start of your reading journey. These paragraphs give you an overview of what is ahead. Some chapters include an outline on the first page. If your chapter has one, look it over because it will tell you what material will be discussed.

Topic sentences

Topic sentences in nonfiction material are almost always found in the first sentence of every paragraph. A topic sentence provides you with the main idea of a paragraph. Though there may be more than one topic sentence in a paragraph, you need to pre-view only the first sentence. By looking at the topic sentences before beginning to read, you will know specifically what information will be presented and in what order.

When pre-viewing topic sentences, be careful not to read every sentence in the paragraph. Until you become accustomed to pre-viewing, you will tend to read passively from the first word to the last. Here, you are asked to read actively, look only for topic sentences, and follow the author's train of thought.

> **"** Knowledge is of two kinds. We know a subject or we know where we can find it. **"**
>
> —Samuel Johnson
> 18th century author

Summary paragraphs

Summary, or concluding, paragraphs are found at the end of the chapter or article. They tell you, in effect, where your journey will end and summarize where you have been. Some books make this easy for you by including a subheading called a summary or a conclusion at the end of a chapter.

ACTIVITY 5

Locate a nonfiction chapter or article, preferably one you have not seen before. Find the information requested below, and answer the questions.

1. List the title, headings, and subheadings, in order, of your chapter or article.

   _____

   _____

   _____

2. Count and note the number of pages. Then estimate how long it will take you to read the chapter or article. What did you find?

   _____

   _____

   _____

3. Pre-view the introductory paragraphs of your chapter or article. What material do you expect to read about?

   _____

   _____

   _____

4. Pre-view the topic sentences of every paragraph. If the chapter or article is long, work with one section (or approximately ten pages). What kinds of specific information do the topic sentences tell you to expect to read about?

   _____

   _____

   _____

5. Pre-view the summary or concluding paragraphs of your chapter. What other information do they suggest?

   _____

   _____

   _____

At this point, you have established the outline of the chapter and uncovered how the writer has sequenced his or her thoughts. Knowing this is useful in pre-viewing as well as in taking notes. (See Chapter 7.) In addition to the organization of the chapter, there are other pieces of information that can help you uncover clues to what will be discussed.

Boldface and italicized print

Boldface and *italicized print* are other ways that publishers indicate something is important, such as a new vocabulary term, a person's name, a date, or an event. **Boldface** words, **dark print like this**, usually indicate a new vocabulary term, while *italicized* words, *slanted printing like this*, usually mean something important.

If your material has many boldface or italicized words or includes a list of key terms, you should create a way to become familiar with them before you read. Some people keep a running vocabulary list with definitions, while others use flash cards. Either method will help you become familiar with the new vocabulary and read with greater understanding.

Margin notes and footnotes

Margin notes and footnotes are additional ways publishers indicate that something is important. **Margin notes** usually point out an important idea the author wants you to understand. They may also contain additional information related to the subject. Margin notes are located in the blank space outside the printed text on a page.

Footnotes are explanatory comments or reference notes that relate to a specific piece of information on a page. They are found either at the bottom of the page, at the end of a chapter, or at the end of a book. Footnotes are indicated with numbers. For example, if the author wants to provide more information about osmosis[12], you would

BOLDFACE
Boldface
Italicized
Italicized

look for footnote number 12. Review footnotes before you begin reading to learn whether you need the information to better understand the text. Noting this before reading will facilitate your learning, make your reading easier, and help you make the best use of your time.

> " A young person, to achieve, must first get out of his mind any notion either of the ease or rapidity of success. Nothing ever just happens in this world. "
>
> —Edward William Bok
> 20th century author and editor

Illustrations and captions

The saying "a picture is worth a thousand words" is a good reason to pre-view illustrations and captions. Illustrations include any photos, figures, graphs, tables, or cartoons. Captions provide information above, below, or alongside the illustration to explain its content or purpose. Publishers provide illustrations and captions to help the reader better understand the material being presented.

End-of-chapter questions

The questions at the end of the chapter of a textbook are useful for students. Though some students feel they are cheating when they look ahead, these questions are vital for establishing your purpose in learning the material and in fulfilling your reading responsibility. They tell you what the author wants you to learn from the chapter and offer a way to check your understanding of the material. By pre-viewing them, you will know what you should examine while you are reading, and you will be better prepared to answer the questions quickly and effectively. These questions are also fair game on a test.

Many different types of questions and information requests are used in an end-of-chapter review. A vocabulary or key term list provides new vocabulary for the chapter. A review or **d**iscussion section asks questions about the information presented in the chapter.

Sometimes you will be asked to discuss your answers either on paper or with another classmate. By answering all the questions, you will have a clearer understanding of the material. Activities or projects are a way to learn first-hand about the information discussed in the chapter. They are active ways to apply the new information to the real world.

ACTIVITY 6

Using the same chapter or article from Activity 5, find the information requested below, and answer the questions.

1. Look for boldface and italicized words. Make a list of any that you don't know; then find the meaning of each one.

   _____

   _____

   _____

2. Look for margin notes and footnotes. Read any important information provided in the margins, and observe where the footnotes are located. What do you see?

   _____

   _____

   _____

3. Look at the illustrations and captions. What do they say about what you will be reading?

   _____

   _____

   _____

4. Review the questions at the end of your chapter (for textbooks only). How many different types of questions are asked? Which type seems the easiest? most difficult? Which are most time-consuming to answer?

   _____

   _____

   _____

At this point, you have spent time becoming familiar with your reading and have gained valuable background knowledge that will make the reading easier. Are you able to read familiar material faster with better comprehension than unfamiliar material?

Figure 8-5 is a quick-reference worksheet you can copy and use for pre-viewing a chapter or an article. It is meant to remind you of what to observe that will enhance your understanding of the material. After locating the information several times, you will probably be able to pre-view without using the worksheet.

Place a check mark in the blank before each item once you have pre-viewed it in a chapter or an article. After each item, fill in the information requested with any related information you believe is appropriate or important. Once you feel comfortable with pre-viewing, keep this list as a reminder tool.

Figure 8-5   A Quick-Reference Worksheet

Pre-viewing a Chapter or an Article

The Reading: _____

_____Purpose: _____

_____Reading Responsibility:_____

_____Chapter Title: _____

_____Headings and Subheadings: _____

_____Length of Material: _____

_____Expected Reading Time: _____

_____Introductory Paragraphs: _____

_____Topic Sentences: _____

_____Summary or Concluding Paragraphs: _____

_____Boldface and Italicized Print: _____

_____Margin Notes and Footnotes: _____

_____Illustrations and Captions: _____

_____End-of-Chapter Questions: _____

Chapter 8: Reading Comprehension Skills

You should now be able to read actively because you know how to prepare a plan of attack, map out a direction, and create a course of action for using your time wisely. Since all nonfiction material is similar in structure, you can approach any reading with confidence and assurance. (For information about pre-viewing fiction, see Appendix C.)

A note about pre-viewing and writing

Since your job as a nonfiction reader is to find the writer's main ideas, you have a responsibility to make those ideas easy to find when you write. This job will be easier if (1) you create an outline before you write and (2) you pre-view your writing *after* you write by focusing on the first sentences of paragraphs.

Checkpoint 8.2

1. In your own words, what does pre-viewing mean?

2. What are some benefits of pre-viewing?

3. What are some drawbacks, if any, to pre-viewing?

WEB LINK

www.dictionary.com

This site is a guide to dictionaries and reference materials found on the Web.

http://wordsmith.org/awad

This web page offers an e-mail subscription to A Word A Day.

www.utexas.edu/student/lsc/handouts/330.html

This site is from the University of Texas at Austin. It offers more tips for improving your vocabulary.

8.3 BUILDING VOCABULARY

The easiest way to understand what you read is to develop a broad vocabulary. No matter what your reading strategy is, without adequate vocabulary your reading task will be more difficult. Think for a moment about the following questions:

1. Do words have meaning?

2. Are words given meaning depending upon the way they are used?

If you believe both statements are true, you are right. Every word has a specific meaning, and words change their meaning depending upon how they are used. So how can you ever learn all of the meanings of words? The two things you can do are (1) recognize your word choices and (2) realize that many words have more than one meaning.

The ways for building vocabulary include (1) looking for context clues, (2) using word structures, (3) skipping words (only at certain times), (4) using a dictionary, and (5) asking someone.

Though each way of building vocabulary will be discussed, the ones introduced first are those that encourage you to use the dictionary you already have—your brain. *If you can figure out word meanings on your own, you will build your vocabulary more quickly and easily.*

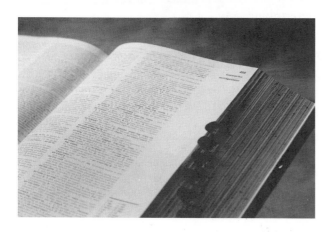

Using Background Knowledge

Learning new vocabulary is easiest when you start with your own **background knowledge**. Background knowledge is what you already know based on your previous experiences and learning.

Since you already know many words, you can use them to increase the size of your vocabulary. If, for example, you know how to change the oil in your car, you have some background knowledge in the way a car functions. If you were taking a course in automotive repair, this information would be useful in learning more about a car's workings. Without knowing how to change a car's oil or anything about the engine, your job of learning would be more challenging.

The following strategies use your background knowledge to build vocabulary.

Looking for context clues

Gaining a good understanding of what you are reading without wasting time can be accomplished by using context clues. **Context clues** are the words surrounding the unknown word. They give hints to the meaning of the vocabulary word. Many times you will be able to predict or guess the meaning of the word by using these clues. Since getting an exact dictionary definition is not always necessary and sometimes not possible, you can develop a working definition that is good enough to help you understand the passage you are reading.

> " Learning is not compulsory but neither is survival. "
>
> —W. Edward Deming
> 20th century statistician

ACTIVITY 7

In the following sentences, use context clues to predict the meaning of each word in italics.

1. Though the weather was not in their favor, the research team members were *optimistic* that their mission would be successful.

   _____

   _____

2. In the concert hall, the enthusiastic fans *congregated* around the band like bees around honey.

   _____

   _____

3. The telephone company helped the assistant save space on her desk by *consolidating* the four telephone lines into one.

   _____

   _____

4. After listening to the *interminable* speeches, the graduates were tired and anxious to leave the heat of the auditorium.

   _____

   _____

Though always helpful, context clues may not be enough to help you guess the meaning of the unknown word. For example, mononucleosis is commonly found among young people who work hard and do not eat well or get enough sleep.

In a sentence that uses a complex word like *mononucleosis*, figuring out the definition through context is not possible using word structures. The option described below for learning vocabulary will be more helpful.

Using word structures

Word structures are the parts of words called prefixes, roots, and suffixes. A **root word** is the basic part of a word that conveys the word's foundation or origin. The other two parts are added to a root, and each of them changes the word meaning. A **prefix** is the portion of the word added to the beginning, and a **suffix** is the portion of the word added at the end. Each of these parts is a link to a chain of meaning.

If you learn to identify the meaning of one or more parts of a word, you will be able to closely predict the meaning of a word.

The word *mononucleosis*, in the previous example, is made up of a prefix, a root, and a suffix. With this information, you could determine that the meaning of mononucleosis is "the condition of one cell." (See Figure 8-6.)

Figure 8-6 Word Structures

Type of Word Structure	Word	Meaning of Word Structure
prefix	mono	one
root	nucle(us)	cell
suffix	osis	condition of

A single word part can be found in many words. A list of other words that contain the word *mono* follows. Notice how the meaning of mono—one—is present in all the definitions in Figure 8-7.

Figure 8-7 Word Structures Example

Example	Definition
monorail	**one** rail
monograph	a writing about **one** thing
monochrome	involving **one** color
monomania	concentration on **one** idea or thought
monopoly	**one** seller of a product or service
monocular	involving **one** eye
monogamy	marriage to **one** person at a time
monologue	a talk by **one** speaker
monomial	a mathematical expression consisting of **one** term
monoplane	an airplane with **one** set of wings
monosyllabic	describing a word with **one** syllable
monotony	doing **one** thing over and over again

ACTIVITY 8

Using the prefixes, root words, suffixes and their meanings provided below, create new words that use the same word structures. Also provide the meanings of the words you create. You can work individually or with a partner.

Prefix	Meaning	Examples
bi	two	binocular = involving **two** eyes
		_____
in	not	inseparable = **not** able to be pulled apart
		_____
re	again, back	reconstruct = to build **again**
		_____

Root Word	Meaning	Word and Its Meaning
bio	life	microbiology = study of small **living** things
		_____
dem	people	epidemic = affecting a lot of **people** (such as a disease)
		_____
graph	writing	monograph = a **writing** about one thing
		_____
nov	new	renovate = to make **new** again
		_____
thermo	heat	thermostat = a device that measures **heat**
		_____

Suffix	Meaning	Word and Its Meaning
able	capable of	portable = **capable of** being carried
		_____
ation	the act of	collation = **the act of** putting things together
		_____
ous	full of	religious = **full of** belief in religion
		_____

Success Skills

These are just a few of the common prefixes, roots, and suffixes you can learn. In Appendix D, you will find more words to study. Trying working with a few at a time. Every word part you recognize is another valuable addition to your background knowledge.

Skipping words

Skipping an unfamiliar word is not the best way to build your vocabulary. However, it is an effective way to avoid wasting time while still understanding most of what you've read. The trick is to make sure you understand enough.

Read the following two paragraphs. Of the two, which contains an italicized word that you think could be skipped, and which one contains a word that needs to be defined?

Paragraph One:

A scanned photograph can be *cropped* using desktop publishing software, which makes *cropping* electronically a relatively simple procedure. If you must *crop* a photograph by hand, never draw *crop* marks directly on the photograph.

Paragraph Two:

Illness has always been a part of the human condition. Care has been given according to the *folkways* and beliefs of society. Care also depends on the knowledge and kinds of treatments available.

In the first paragraph, the word *crop* appears several times and describes a concept that would be lost if you did not know what the word *crop* meant. *Cropping* means trimming a photograph to make it smaller.

In the second paragraph, the word *folkways* serves as a descriptive word that doesn't carry a lot of importance to the meaning of the sentence. *Folkways* are the traditional patterns of life common to people. In this case, you might not take the time to figure out the word in paragraph two, but you would determine the meaning of the word in paragraph one.

You may decide that skipping a word would not greatly affect your understanding. If that is the case, then don't spend time trying to determine the meaning of the word. But if you don't understand what you are reading because you don't know a word, you should try to figure out its meaning.

Using a Dictionary

Using a dictionary is a common way to find out the meaning of an unfamiliar word if you cannot determine its meaning otherwise. Keep a dictionary nearby during your study sessions so it is handy to use.

Using a dictionary can be a time-consuming process. Imagine you come across an unfamiliar word when reading. If you can figure out the word by using your brain as a dictionary (context clues or word structures), you will be able to continue your reading quickly. If you cannot figure out the word on your own, you'll have to use the dictionary, a process

> " If you want to make good use of your time, you've got to know what's most important and then give it all you've got. "
>
> —Lee Iacocca
> Former CEO of Chrysler

that will take longer.

To use a dictionary, you will stop reading, find a dictionary, return to your reading to locate the unfamiliar word again, determine how it is spelled, and look it up in the dictionary by flipping pages until you locate the word. If the word has more than one meaning, you will look at each meaning and decide which one best fits the context of your reading. Once you identify the correct meaning of the word, you will close the dictionary, locate the place where you stopped reading, and reread a few lines to remember what the material was about. This process takes much longer than using context clues and word structures.

The other problem with using a dictionary is that you may not remember the word a week or a month later without looking it up again. You don't always remember new things the first time you come across them. This is why using a dictionary as the only way to find the meaning of unfamiliar words is a less effective way of learning.

Remembering words through the use of repetition or frequent review is helpful. Smart dictionary users write an unfamiliar word on a piece of paper (Figure 8-8) or an index card (Figure 8-9). The word is on one side; the meaning on the other. This allows you to review the words repeatedly without wasting time looking them up more than once. They then become part of your background knowledge for use in the future.

Figure 8-8   Using Notebook Paper for Learning New Vocabulary

	Chapter 7 p. 91-97	Wind and the Landscape
○		
	Erosion=	A wearing away of land due to wind or waves—it happens over time
	Dunes=	Sand deposited by wind in the form of hills or ridges
	Transverse dunes=	Long, wavelike ridges-found on beaches
	Parabolic dunes=	Contain a blowout in the center with high-ridge sides
	Barchan dunes=	Crescent-shaped dunes
	Waves=	Formed by wind blowing over water
○	Wave period=	Time required for a wave to go the distance of one wave length
	Tsunamis=	Waves created by earthquakes very large and destructive length

Success Skills

Figure 8-9   Using Index Cards for Learning New Vocabulary

The front of the card has the word spelled out clearly and correctly.

> *HYPOTHETICAL*

The back of the card has the definition in your own words.

> *SOMETHING IMAGINED OR PRETENDED*

Types of dictionaries

There are several types of dictionaries. An **unabridged dictionary** is the most complete because it includes all words and definitions. An **abridged dictionary** is a shorter version of an unabridged dictionary. It is smaller in size because words are omitted. However, an abridged dictionary is useful for finding the meaning of most vocabulary. Abridged dictionaries are popular because they are easy to carry and store. Many dictionary publishers also sell a pocket or vest dictionary which is convenient for school or work.

A **thesaurus** is a type of dictionary that contains only synonyms and antonyms. **Synonyms** are words that are similar in meaning; **antonyms** are words that are opposite in meaning. A thesaurus is useful for expanding your background knowledge and for writing essays and reports. Figure 8-10 shows entries taken from *The Merriam-Webster Thesaurus*.

Figure 8-10   Thesaurus Example

Word	Meaning	Synonym	Antonym
danger	the state of being exposed to injury, pain, or loss risk	hazard, jeopardy, peril	security
silence	absence of sound or noise	noiselessness, quiet, quietness, quietude, soundlessness, still, stillness	din, uproar, noise

Another type of dictionary is a walking dictionary. This is not a book but a person (such as a relative, an instructor, or a friend) you ask to help you figure out a word you don't understand.

Before asking a walking dictionary the meaning of a word, you should try to figure the meaning out on your own. The person you ask can save you time and energy, but he or she cannot help you remember the word when you come across it again, which is another good reason to write down new words on notebook paper or index cards.

Vocabulary of Your Trade

Every trade has vocabulary unique to its subject matter. Your job as a learner is to master and use this vocabulary while speaking and writing. You learn the needed terms from an instructor's lecture, nonfiction books, related projects, and experiences. In nonfiction books, the terms are easy to locate because they are often printed in italics or boldface. There may also be a vocabulary list at the beginning or end of a chapter. In addition, some books have a glossary, a specialized dictionary, at the back to help you find the meaning of a word.

Create your own glossary

If vocabulary in a chapter is unfamiliar to you, you will find learning the words easier if you write the words and their definitions on notepaper or on index cards *before* you read. This provides valuable background knowledge that helps you understand the information you read. You will also see a word and its meaning several times by the time you complete a chapter. And you will have an instant review tool to use when studying for a quiz or test.

Use word structures

Using what you know about prefixes, roots, and suffixes will be very useful in learning specialized terms. For example, if you were taking a medical course or a science course, the following word structures would be used often. Note how the meaning of the word part relates to the meaning of the word.

anti- = against

> **anti**coagulant = prevents the formation of blood clots
>
> **anti**septic = prevents growth of germs
>
> **anti**body = prevents infections

cardio(a)- = heart

> **cardio**logy = the study of the heart
>
> tachy**cardia** = a rapid heartbeat
>
> myo**cardial** infarction = a heart attack

-ectomy = to take out; to remove

> hyster**ectomy** = to remove the uterus
>
> tonsill**ectomy** = to take out the tonsils
>
> laryng**ectomy** = to remove the larynx, or voice box

-itis = inflammation of; swelling

> tendon**itis** = inflammation of the tendons
>
> phleb**itis** = swelling of the lining of the veins
>
> bronch**itis** = inflammation of the windpipe

If you were taking paralegal studies or a government course, the following word structures would be common. Note how the meaning of the word part relates to the meaning of the word.

appel- = to appeal to; to ask for help

appellant = a person bringing an appeal

appellee = a person who is against an appeal

appellate jurisdiction = the power of a court to appeal a trial court's actions

jur- = to judge; having to do with justice; to swear

jurisdiction = the power of a court to judge a particular case

jury = a group of people who judge a court case

juror = a person on a jury

jurisprudence = a body of laws; having to do with law

Now you see that every subject has a unique vocabulary. Learning the new terms is easier when you apply the information provided in this chapter.

Checkpoint 8.3

1. Why is knowing a large number of words important?

2. What are the easiest ways to learn new words?

3. Why is it important to develop a broad vocabulary?

Key Terms and Concepts

abridged dictionary

active reader

antonym

background knowledge

context clues

fiction

footnotes

margin notes

nonfiction

passive reader

prefix

pre-viewing

reading purpose

reading responsibility

root word

suffix

synonym

thesaurus

unabridged dictionary

Chapter Summary

1. Becoming an active learner means becoming an active reader. Active readers develop a plan of attack, map out a direction, and create a course of action for using their time wisely. Having a reading purpose and responsibility is an active beginning for any reading assignment.

2. Nonfiction material is factual in nature, while fiction is made up, or imaginative. Academic textbooks are nonfiction.

3. Pre-viewing is examining material before reading it to discover clues to its contents.

4. You should pre-view a nonfiction book before you begin reading the book for the first time to familiarize yourself with the material.

5. Pre-viewing a nonfiction chapter or article allows you to determine the author's outline and other important information related to the topic. Pre-viewing also provides background knowledge about what you will be learning.

6. Your background knowledge is what you already know based on your previous experiences and learning. The more background knowledge you have, the easier it is to discover word definitions using the dictionary you were born with—your brain.

7. Looking for context clues and using word structures are two ways to build vocabulary using background knowledge.

8. Skipping unfamiliar words is not the best way to build your vocabulary. You can, however, skip an unfamiliar word when you believe your understanding won't be greatly affected.

9. Use a dictionary to learn the meanings of unfamiliar words. The best time to use a dictionary is when you cannot figure out a word meaning using your background knowledge.

10. There are four types of dictionaries: unabridged, abridged, thesaurus, and walking.

11. Keeping track of your vocabulary by writing any new word and its definition on notebook paper or index cards is useful.

12. Learning the vocabulary of your trade is easier if you create your own glossary and use word structures.

Success Skills

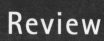
Based on the information you learned in this chapter, answer the following questions using your own words.

1. What is pre-viewing? Why is pre-viewing important?

2. When pre-viewing a nonfiction book, what do you look for?

3. When pre-viewing a nonfiction chapter or article, what do you look for?

4. What do you think the differences in learning are between someone who pre-views and someone who doesn't?

5. What is background knowledge? How does it influence your ability to learn new vocabulary?

6. What does background knowledge have to do with learning in general?

7. What is the relationship between pre-viewing and background knowledge?

8. What are some ways to figure out the meaning of an unknown word? Describe at least three.

9. What would you recommend another learner do to build his or her vocabulary?

10. What are the most important things you learned from this chapter?

Case 1

Ralph told a friend about a book he just finished reading. "It was really great," he said enthusiastically. "It had some terrific ideas." When his friend asked him for more details, Ralph found himself at a loss for words. He reached for the book and opened it. "Here," he said pointing to a paragraph, "it says, 'cryptic slogans that to a Western manager sound fatuous are in fact highly effective tools for creating new erudition. Managers everywhere recognize the serendipitous quality of innovation and Eastern managers manage that serendipity'." His friend looked bewildered, and Ralph realized vocabulary that made sense to him had little meaning for his friend.

1. What approach could Ralph take to break down the unfamiliar words for his friend and make the meaning clear?

2. As Ralph tried to explain the reading, he realized he wasn't sure of some of the words. What could Ralph do to improve his understanding and ability to use these words confidently and accurately?

Case 2

When Marjorie's community group asked her to run the next meeting, she knew she needed some guidelines to make it an effective session. At her local library she located six books on how to conduct meetings and took them all to a reading table. She felt overwhelmed when she looked at the stack of books in front of her. Which one or two of the books would be most useful, she wondered. She nervously looked at her watch thinking about all the other things she needed to do, knowing she didn't have time to read all six books.

1. Based on her time constraints, what "plan of attack" would you suggest to Marjorie to help her organize how she will examine the six books?

2. What information would be most important for Marjorie to look at in each book so she can choose the one or two books that will be most useful to her?

Kim, a customer service representative for an insurance company moans, "Oh, no. I'm running out of time again. I can't believe I let this happen."

"What's the matter now?" asks Rosita, a coworker who sits beside her.

"I'm so backed up on my reading, it's ridiculous!" says Kim. "Between all the meetings, people dropping by my office, the e-mail that beeps constantly, and the phone that keeps ringing, I can't get any work done. Our department's policies are being revamped, and I'm supposed to read the proposed changes before every meeting. Sometimes there are 30 to 60 pages!

I really hate being unprepared for these meetings, but I usually can't get the policy changes read in time."

"Aren't you also taking a night class?" asked Rosita.

"Yeah, an English Lit course. You should see the pile of reading I have for that course too! How am I ever going to get it all done?"

Do you have any suggestions that might help Kim manage her reading workload?

In This Chapter

Chapter Goals

After studying and working with the information in this chapter, you should be able to:

♦ Explain the unlearning to relearn concept.

♦ Identify the main reason to read faster.

♦ Describe THE tools for reading faster.

♦ Identify the three factors that determine your reading speed.

♦ Identify the reading gears and qualities of a flexible reader.

♦ Describe the similarities and differences between skimming and scanning.

♦ Begin using the recommended tools on your own daily reading.

Speed-reading courses, which became popular in the early 1950s, are now in demand more than ever for several reasons. First, people want to do more in less time. Reading has typically been a time-consuming task that seems to take forever—especially for those who want to learn from printed material.

Second, there seems to be an information explosion. Information is produced and processed faster today than ever before due to computers and other high technology advances. When someone comes up with a new idea or way of doing something, it often ends up being published on the Internet or in magazines, newspapers, or books. According to the American Booksellers Association of America, there were more than 180,000 new titles added to *Books in Print* in 1998 alone! This figure is up from 50,000 in 1991. This does not include magazines, newspapers, junk mail, and other forms of printed and electronic information! Because the Internet is so easy to use, a massive amount of information is added every day.

Third, reading faster with good comprehension enables students and professionals to keep current in their fields and to advance in their careers. Reading is an important tool for those who want to be successful.

In Chapter 8, you learned how to pre-view both a nonfiction book and a nonfiction chapter. Pre-viewing helps you read faster because you become familiar with the material first. In this chapter, you will learn other tools to help you read faster. You will also learn to read efficiently, which is as important as reading quickly.

Today's information explosion makes increasing your reading speed essential. What have you learned that can help you read faster and more effectively?

Success Skills

SELF-CHECK

The following self-evaluation will give you an idea of how familiar, or unfamiliar, you are with some of the topics and terms discussed in this chapter. After reading each statement, circle the letter Y, S, or N to indicate the answer that is most appropriate for you. Answer honestly and rate yourself at the end; then complete the information for Chapter 9 in Appendix A.

Y = yes; frequently   S = sometimes   N = no; never

1. I can handle my reading workload with ease.   Y   S   N

2. I know how to effectively increase my reading speed.   Y   S   N

3. I know how to locate and read key words.   Y   S   N

4. I know how to locate and read in phrases.   Y   S   N

5 I know how to use my hands or a white card to help me increase my reading speed.   Y   S   N

6. I know how to adjust my reading speed according to my purpose and background knowledge.   Y   S   N

7. I know the difference between skimming and scanning.   Y   S   N

8. I know how to skim effectively.   Y   S   N

9. I can scan accurately.   Y   S   N

10. I know that reading everything all the time is not an efficient use of my time.   Y   S   N

Rate Yourself:	Number of Ys	_____	x	100	=	_____	
	Number of Ss	_____	x	50	=	_____	
	Number of Ns	_____	x	0	=	_____	Total_____

9.1 THE READING GEARS

Unskilled passive readers are like a one-speed vehicle. They read their favorite magazine and a textbook at the same speed. Skilled flexible readers are like a multispeed vehicle. They change speeds according to the type of material, their purpose, and their background knowledge.

When you hear the term speed reading, you probably imagine someone reading very fast. Actually, speed readers vary their rates. They know when to speed up and when to slow down.

There are basically *three reading gears*, or speeds, that a reader can use. (See Figure 9.1.) *Low gear* ranges from about 100 words per minute (wpm) to 300 wpm and is used for word-for-word reading, as in studying, proofreading, or committing information to memory. First gear is also used for material that is difficult or about which you have little or no background knowledge. In low gear, you look for a high level of comprehension, somewhere around 80 to 90 percent.

If you read everything in *low gear*, you are definitely a passive reader. Chances are you talk while you are reading—either physically moving your lips or hearing your voice reading every word. Talking to yourself while reading slows you down, tires your eyes, and hinders comprehension. It causes your eyes to stop on every word instead of allowing you to focus on the more important words or thought units. Reading key words or phrases and using pacers, described next in this chapter, will help you avoid reading everything in low gear.

Figure 9-1   The Reading Gears

Reading Gear	Type of Reading	Reading Speed in Words-per-Minute	Percent of Comprehension
LOW	Difficult material Studying Notetaking Unfamiliar material	100-300	High (80%+)
MIDDLE	Everyday reading Magazines Newspapers Somewhat familiar material	300-600	Average (70%)
HIGH	All kinds of material Skimming Scanning Familiar material	600-1000	Lower (50%+)

Success Skills

Middle gear ranges from 300 wpm to 600 wpm. Reading in the middle gear is appropriate for everyday reading, such as newspapers and magazines, and for somewhat familiar material. Having some background knowledge helps too. In middle gear, you should have a comprehension ranging from 70 to 90 percent. You also cover more material in a given period of time.

High gear should be almost twice as fast as middle gear, or from about 600 wpm to 1,000 wpm. Reading in high gear is appropriate for skimming and previewing, where you don't read everything but still accomplish your purpose. In high gear, your level of comprehension may be lower or higher than middle gear, depending on your background knowledge.

Scanning is also a high-gear speed, but because you look only for a piece of specific information, the speed can go even higher than 1,000 wpm. With scanning, accurately finding what you are seeking means 100 percent comprehension. Both skimming and scanning are described in more detail later in this chapter.

At times, a major speed shift, up or down, needs to occur because the material changes from familiar to unfamiliar or because you change your concentration level. Before reading, it is a good idea to decide which gears might be appropriate for your reading purpose. This will keep you on track.

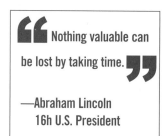

"Nothing valuable can be lost by taking time."

—Abraham Lincoln
16h U.S. President

Identify which gear might be appropriate for the following reading. Is one gear enough or could more than one gear be used?

Type of Reading	Purpose	Background Knowledge	Gear
Newspaper	To be knowledgeable about current events	Varies	*Middle to High*
Magazine	To build my background knowledge	Varies	_____
Textbook	To read an assigned chapter	Some	_____
Web site	To research Albert Einstein	None	_____
Instructions	To replace an oil filter	Some	_____
Manual	To locate a specific topic	Little	_____
Instructions	To format a computer disk	None	_____
Fiction book	To relax and enjoy	None	_____

Checkpoint 9.1

1. What are the reading gears?

2. What helps you decide what speed you might read?

3. What do you think happens to comprehension when you increase reading speed?

9.2 LEARNING TO READ MORE IN LESS TIME

Learning to read faster is a skill that is developed over a period of time. Since most people learn to read in the first grade—around age six—subtract six years from your current age; the result is the number of years you have been developing your reading habits. If you change your reading habits now, you may feel uncomfortable because you are taking a new approach. But by practicing the new habits, you will become comfortable with them and attain better reading skills. *This is called unlearning to relearn.*

Unlearning to Relearn

Unlearning to relearn can happen only after you have already learned how to do something. In this case, you have already learned to read. In order to improve your reading, you first need to unlearn how you have been reading, then relearn it.

Let's take the example of a car with an automatic shift versus a car with a manual shift. Suppose you become an excellent driver using an automatic car. You are both comfortable and capable behind the wheel. However, the first time you try to drive a stick shift, you have trouble working the clutch, stall out in the middle of intersections, and grind the gears. You do not feel comfortable or capable. This is what unlearning can feel like.

At this point in driving, you might want to give up, thinking that you are no good at driving a stick shift. On the other hand, if driving a stick shift is necessary or important enough, continued practice will help you learn how to drive the car. Relearning the skill takes time and energy. Relearning means finding what works for you while making some mistakes along the way. With a little practice, you can master the stick shift and once again become an excellent driver.

> " Learning isn't a means to an end; it is an end in itself. "
>
> —Robert Heinlein
> 20th century science fiction writer

ACTIVITY 2

Discuss with a partner or group what other skills might require unlearning to relearn. Write your thoughts below.

_____

_____

_____

_____

_____

_____

_____

_____

_____

_____

Chapter 9: Survival Reading Skills

While you are reading this chapter, try using some of the recommended tools to increase your reading speed. Keep in mind that feeling uncomfortable is a sign of breaking an old habit and creating a new one. The key is to keep using the new tools until they work for you. Not all of the tools work equally well for everyone, but by giving them a try you will find the ones that work best for you.

THE Reason to Read Faster

You have already learned some of the reasons why reading faster is important. However, *the* main reason—concentration—has not been discussed yet. What do you think the relationship is between reading faster and your ability to concentrate? To read faster, you have to concentrate!

Speeding up forces you to focus on an activity. Compare reading faster to walking down a street. When you walk down a street, you can window shop, chew gum, talk with a friend, daydream, kick a rock, and so on. Now if you were to run down the street, which of these activities could you still do well?

This example shows that you cannot do as many things when you run as when you walk. The same is true for reading. When you speed up, you are forced to focus and concentrate, which reduces your ability to daydream. By concentrating on the reading, you understand better what you are reading, learn more from everything you read, and finish your reading in a shorter amount of time. Does this sound like something you'd like to do? Read on!

Checkpoint 9.2

1. How might reading faster help you learn better?

2. What is meant by "unlearning to relearn"?

3. How does the speed of reading affect concentration?

9.3 HOW TO INCREASE YOUR READING SPEED

Remember that just reading, or beginning with the first word and stopping with the last, is the most passive learning activity. When you add pre-viewing to your reading habits (Chapter 8), you become more active.

The next three strategies for reading actively include (1) reading key words and phrases, (2) using a pacer, and (3) adjusting your speed. These strategies will help you read more efficiently.

The ability to read faster depends on a natural human visual feature called peripheral vision. Your **peripheral vision** is the distance you are able to see on your left and right while staring straight ahead.

When you look at a page, you cannot see a wide distance. What you do see is your eye span. Your **eye span** is how much information you see at a time when you look down at a page. Reading faster can be accomplished by working with your peripheral vision to increase your eye span. There are three simple tools you can use to increase your eye span to read faster: reading key words, reading phrases, and using pacers.

ACTIVITY 3

Stare straight ahead at a point on a wall or at an object. Extend both arms in front of you with your fingertips pointing up. Still staring at the point, spread your arms out and back to each side while still seeing your hands. When your hands disappear from sight, bring them back in a little. Once you have found the farthest point your hands can spread without disappearing, look at how far apart they are. This is the range of your peripheral vision. If your vision, for whatever reason, is mostly from one eye, you probably will still have peripheral vision ability from that eye. How wide is your peripheral vision?

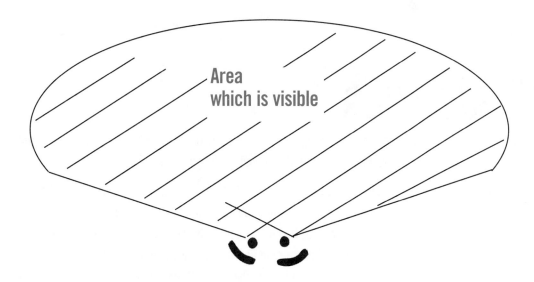

Area which is visible

Reading Key Words

Key words are the big important words in text. They are *usually* more than three letters long and carry the most meaning in a sentence. For example, most people read the following 13-word sentence word for word:

When you pick up a book, the world is literally at your fingertips.

However, by looking for and stopping your eyes only on the more important words, you can still understand the text while saving time. Read only the words in bold below:

When you **pick** up a **book,** the **world** is **literally** at your **fingertips.**

Now look at the words that are not in bold. Are you familiar with them? Have you seen them thousands of times? Are they as important as the words in bold?

When reading only key words, understand that you are *not skipping* the other words. You are simply spreading your peripheral vision to increase your eye span to see both the key words and the nonkey words at the same time.

Now is the time to remember the unlearn-to-relearn idea. Learning to read key words is probably very different for you. If you feel uncomfortable, that's good! This is the first step toward relearning. With a little practice, you will feel more comfortable and find that you are reading quicker than before with the same or better understanding.

The paragraph in Activity 4 contains 117 words; 68 were identified as the key words. Think about it: If you can learn to read and understand a 117-word paragraph by reading only 68 key words, what will that do to your reading time? What will it naturally do to the word-for-word talking in your head?

ACTIVITY 4

Read only the key words indicated in boldface in the following paragraph. Try to spread your peripheral vision to see both the nonbold face and boldface words. Can you understand the text without reading every word?

One of the **characteristics** of the **modern world** is the **ease** and **degree** of **travel. Historically, people** have **always traveled,** but **much** of that **travel** was **not** for **pleasure. While** the **terms** travel and **tourism** are **often** used **interchangeably** and the **terms** may **appear synonymous,** in the **past, travel** was **generally undertaken** for **financial, military,** or **business reasons, while** tourism was **travel** for the **sake** of **recreation** and for the **enjoyment** of **new** and **different places** and **people. While people** have **always traveled** to **some extent** for the **thrill** of **travel** or **curiosity** about other **places, mass tourism** is a **modern phenomenon. Until** the **last few decades, only** a **select few** were **able** to **travel** for **tourism.**

Use the following paragraphs to practice finding key words. Do not read each sentence first to figure out which words are more important to the meaning of the sentence; this will waste your time. Instead, as you read, quickly underline the bigger words. They will generally be three letters or more, so your eyes will naturally stop on them. After you are done, reread the paragraph to see if your key words make sense. Change your underlines as needed. The first sentences are completed for you. There are no right or wrong key words as long as they make sense to you. (If you want more practice underlining key words, you can use newspapers, magazines, and nonfiction books. Try reading key words on a few pages in this book. Keep in mind that reading key words is only one tool for increasing your reading speed.)

Paragraph 1

<u>Once</u> <u>in</u> <u>a</u> <u>while,</u> you may <u>think</u> that a <u>store</u> or <u>company</u> you are <u>dealing</u> <u>with</u> has <u>made</u> a <u>mistake</u>. The store or company could also give you some other reason to make a complaint. Maybe you bought something and were told you would receive it in a few weeks. After months go by and you still do not have the item, you receive damaged goods that you want to take back. Getting big businesses to take care of complaints is sometimes hard. Have faith; there are ways to register a complaint so that it will be handled.

Paragraph 2

<u>There</u> <u>is</u> <u>strong</u> <u>evidence</u> to <u>suggest</u> that the <u>use</u> of <u>standardized</u> <u>tests</u> which <u>assess</u> <u>abilities</u>, <u>personalities,</u> and <u>integrity</u>, are a <u>valuable</u> <u>screening</u> <u>tool</u> in the <u>preemployment</u> <u>process</u>. While initially companies and selection experts were hesitant about the use of these tools, many hospitality organizations now use testing as a regular component in the selection process. We predict that testing will become both more sophisticated and more widely used in our industry.

Note: Once you have begun to master the key word idea, *avoid using your pen to underline because it will slow you down.*

Reading Phrases

Most passive and unskilled readers read one word at a time, which is inefficient and time-consuming. As you learned in the last section, not all words are equally important. Reading key words allows you to get the information you need without reading word for word. Read the following paragraph, and notice that each phrase, or thought, is indicated between slash marks.

Doctors have found/ that many people/ spend many hours/ in sleep/ for which/ there is/ no physical need./ When these habits/ are changed/ and these people/ try to do with less,/ they often find/ no difference/ in health/ or efficiency./ You might experiment/ with reducing your sleep time/ by half an hour./ Give yourself/ a few days/ to get adjusted/ to the new pattern./ If you are/ as effective/ as you were before,/ you will gain/ the equivalent/ of a week/ of Sundays/ in the course/ of a year./

Reading phrases is a way to make reading more effective. A **phrase** is a group of words that expresses a thought. If you can learn to read in thoughts instead of word for word, you will understand better what is written and be able to read faster.

The term **column width** pertains to how wide or narrow the printed text is on a page. Newspapers and magazines are typically printed with narrow columns. Educational material is printed with both wide and narrow columns as illustrated in Figure 9-2. Reading in key words works very well with all kinds of columns, but reading phrases works well only when reading wide-column material. Because with phrasing you want to put words together, narrow columns

ACTIVITY 6

Look for phrases, or groups of words that form a thought, in the paragraphs below. Do not read each sentence first to figure out the phrases; this will waste your time. Instead, quickly place a slash mark as you read where you believe one thought ends and another begins. Then reread the paragraph to see if your phrases make sense. Change the slash marks as needed. The first sentences are completed for you. There is no right or wrong length to a phrase, as long as it makes sense to you. (If you want more practice with phrasing, you can use newspapers, magazines, and nonfiction books.)

Paragraph 1

Once in a while,/ you may think/ that a store/ or company/ you are dealing with/ has made a mistake./ The store or company could also give you some other reason to make a complaint. Maybe you bought something and were told you would receive it in a few weeks. After months go by and you still do not have the item, you receive damaged goods that you want to take back. Getting big businesses to take care of complaints is sometimes hard. Have faith; there are ways to register a complaint so that it will be handled.

Paragraph 2

There is strong evidence/ to suggest/ that the use of standardized tests,/ which assess abilities,/ personalities,/ and integrity,/ are a valuable screening tool/ in the preemployment process./ While initially companies and selection experts were hesitant about the use of these tools, many hospitality organizations now use testing as a regular component in the selection process. We predict that testing will become both more sophisticated and more widely used in our industry.

Note: Once you have begun to master the phrasing idea, *avoid using your pen to make slash marks because it will slow you down.*

Figure 9-2   Multiple Column Widths on the Same Page

The Case Continues

In the chicken carry-out business a situation similar to the McDonald story occurred. In 1955, the Kentucky Fried Chicken franchise chain was begun by 66-year-old Colonel Harland Sanders. In 1964 John Y. Brown, later the governor of Kentucky, purchased the organization, and in 1974 he sold the operation to the giant distiller Heublein. Although Colonel Sanders was no longer a company official, he was retained by Heublein as a $200,000-a-year public relations figure. In contrast, when the McDonald brothers closed their deal with Ray Kroc, they completely dropped out of sight. What is the rest of the story regarding why the McDonalds never became spokespeople for the mammoth fast-food chain bearing their name?

Early in their negotiations, there was a personality clash between the reserved New England-reared McDonald brothers and the flashy Chicago salesman, Ray Kroc. When Kroc built his first restaurant in Des Plaines, Illinois, he discovered that in order to store potatoes, he needed to modify the building plan and construct a basement. For legal reasons, he required written documentation from the McDonald brothers to alter the restaurant. Although Kroc made the alteration, the brothers refused to furnish him with the required written statement. Kroc confided to his friends that the McDonalds acted as though they wanted him to fail.

In another incident, after the McDonalds agreed to sell their organization to Kroc, they insisted at the last minute on keeping their original restaurant in San Bernardino. Kroc wanted this profitable outlet in order to generate necessary cash for the growing franchise chain. Kroc became extremely angry and disillusioned with the McDonalds when they would not budge from their position. Eventually, Kroc opened a restaurant directly across the street from the original one, and because he owned the McDonald name, the brothers were forced to rename their operation "The Big M." Kroc was greatly elated when he finally ran the brothers' restaurant out of business. Now you can understand why the McDonalds never became spokespersons for the worldwide restaurant organization that bears their name.

Sources: Adapted from Robert Johnson, "McDonald's Combines a Dead Man's Advice with Lively Strategy," *The Wall Street Journal*, December 18, 1987, pp. 1, 13; Ray Kroc with Robert Anderson, *Grinding It Out* (Chicago, Henry Regnery Company, 1977), pp. 69, 70, 115, 116; and "The Burger that Conquered the Country," *Time*, September 17, 1973, pp. 86, 87.

Nationalism is a political/economic attitude that encourages the development of stronger domestic industries, which results in greater self-sufficiency within the country.

Nationalism is a political/economic attitude that encourages the development of stronger domestic industries, and this results in greater self-sufficiency within the country. International events will probably cause nationalism to remain an important factor in overseas marketing activities. All countries seek a favorable balance of trade. This means that they want to export more goods than they import. Domestically produced goods are being heavily promoted in the United States for that reason. The labor union's national TV advertising campaign makes the point with the memorable "Look for the Union Label" song and other commercials featuring Bob Hope and other celebrities displaying "Made-in-the-U.S.A." labels.

Demographic Forces

Demography is the study of population characteristics, such as age, birthrate, education, geography, number of households, income, occupation, race, and the mix of women and men.

Demography is the study of population characteristics, such as age, birthrate, education, geography, number of households, income, occupation, race, and the mix of women and men. Astute marketers look

Using Pacers

You may have been told not to use your hands when reading, or you may have never tried using your hands to improve your reading. The key to using your hands effectively when reading is knowing the right way to do it.

Pacers can be either your hands or a white card that helps you keep your place while reading. They force you to move your eyes down the page faster. Learning how to use pacers correctly is important because these tools, when used incorrectly, will slow you down.

Pacer as a place keeper

Many readers have a hard time tracking their eyes from the end of one line to the beginning of the next. If you miss the next line, you have trouble understanding the author's ideas. You also waste your time because you have to go back to find your place. Reading wide-column material is especially challenging because the return distance from the end of one line to the beginning of the next is long. If you can use your hands or a white card to keep your place, you will be able to understand your reading material better; the ideas will flow more smoothly. You will also save time because you won't lose your place.

Pacer as an eye mover

Pacers are also used to force the eyes to move forward faster, especially when you are tired or bored. If you are reading facing a window or an aisle and a person walks by, your eyes naturally follow the person for a moment. This is because *the eyes naturally follow movement*. If you can create movement on your page, your eyes will move faster down the page.

Pacer rules

To use a pacer correctly, try following these two important rules:

1. Keep the pacer moving downward, *not* across.

2. Do not stop or go back.

While using pacers may be challenging at first, these two guidelines will help you learn how to use pacing tools well.

The pacers

The following activity describes five different pacers to try. You may not like all of them, but you should find at least one you are comfortable using.

> **" If you only care enough for a result, you will almost certainly attain it. "**
>
> —William James
>   Harvard psychologist and philosopher

WEB LINK

www.stepware.com

Download a 30-day free trial version of Ace Reader software. It helps you develop efficient eye movements and provides you with ways to test your reading speed and comprehension.

http://sas.calpoly.edu/asc/ssl/personal.reading.imprvmnt.html

More guidance and suggestions for tracking your reading progress can be found at this site.

Read each pacer description and study the accompanying figure. Then reading either this book or some other material, try using the pacer on several paragraphs. Keep the pacer rules in mind.

1. The Center Pull Method

   The Center Pull Method is done by placing the index finger of either your right or left hand under the first line of the text in the center of the column. While your eyes read from left to right, your finger pulls your eyes down the page. (This works best with narrow columns.)

2. The Left Pull Method

   The Left Pull Method is similar to the Center Pull Method. Place your index finger on the left margin or the beginning of the line. Your finger pulls your eyes down the page while keeping your place. This works well with all material.

3. The Two-Finger Pull Method

   The Two-Finger Pull Method uses the index fingers of both hands. Place your left index finger on the left margin or the beginning of the line, and place your right index finger at the end of the same line. While your eyes move from left to right, your hands should move down with your eyes. Your fingertips should be on the same line as your eyes most of the time. (This works well with all material, especially wide columns.)

4. The Thumb or Pen Push Method

   The Thumb or Pen Push Method works from the top down. Place your thumb or a closed pen above the words you want to read. Start your thumb or pen moving down, and try to read fast enough to keep your thumb or pen moving. This works well with narrow columns.

5. The White Card Method

For the White Card Method, use a blank white card or piece of paper. *The card should be equal in length to the size of the column you are reading.* A blank 3" x 5" index card can be used for both narrow and wide columns depending on which edge of the card you use. You can tape two cards together for very wide columns.

While you can place a card above or below the line of text, the most effective method is above the line. If you place the card *below* the line, it is easy to regress, or to go back over material you just read. The card also covers the text you are about to read. This is like placing a wall between you and the upcoming words. On the other hand, placing the card above the line covers what you have already read, which avoids regression. It also leaves exposed the words you are about to read. So to use the card effectively, place it <u>on top</u> of the words you have read, and leave exposed the words you are going to read. Start moving the card down the page.

Combining Your Reading Tools

You now have three new tools to help you read faster. They are (1) keys words, (2) phrases, and (3) pacers. When you read faster, you increase your concentration. More concentration means more comprehension.

As you practice your reading tools, you may find, as do others, that combining them is very powerful. For example, reading key words with a pacer, reading phrases with a pacer, or reading a combination of key words and phrases are extremely helpful techniques in increasing your reading speed. Remember that whatever you do, the key is to use a tool or tools that help you read actively, not passively.

Now that you have begun to use tools to increase your reading speed, you are ready to experiment with the exercises in Appendix E. Please turn to those pages now.

Checkpoint 9.3

1. Describe the three tools for increasing reading speed.

2. When might you use them?

3. Why should you use them?

9.4 SKIMMING AND SCANNING

Skimming and scanning are two very different strategies for reading faster. They are each used for different purposes, and they are not meant to be used all the time. They are at the fast end of the speed range, while studying is at the slow end.

People who know how to skim and scan are flexible readers. They read according to their purpose and get the information they need quickly without wasting time. They do *not* read everything which is what increases their reading speed. Their skill lies in knowing what specific information to read and which method to use.

What Is Skimming?

Skimming is one of the tools you can use to read more in less time. **Skimming** refers to looking only for the general or main ideas. With skimming, your overall understanding is reduced because you don't read everything. You read only what is important to your purpose. Fortunately, you have some background knowledge in skimming, though you may not realize it. In Chapter 8, you learned about a form of skimming called pre-viewing.

There are a few differences between skimming and pre-viewing. Pre-viewing occurs before the actual reading process and requires you to search only for the main ideas in the writer's outline.

Skimming, on the other hand, takes place while reading and allows you to look for details in addition to the main ideas.

How to skim

To skim, read at a fast speed, but do not read everything. *What you read is more important than what you leave out.* So what material do you read and what material do you leave out?

Let's say you are researching a long chapter or a web site. By reading the first few paragraphs in detail, you will get a good idea of what information will be discussed. Once you know where the reading is headed, you can begin to read only the first sentence of each paragraph. Also called **topic sentence**s, they give you the main idea of the paragraph. If you do not get the main idea in the topic sentence or if the paragraph greatly interests you, then you may want to skim more.

At the end of each topic sentence, your eyes should jump through the rest of the paragraph, looking for important pieces of information, such as names, dates, or events. Continue to read only topic sentences, jumping down through the rest of the paragraphs, until you are near the end. Since the last few paragraphs may contain a conclusion or summary, you should stop skimming there and read in detail.

> " The true art of memory is the art of attention. "
>
> —Samual Johnson
> 18th century author

Remember that your overall comprehension will be lower than if you read in detail. If while skimming, you feel you grasped the main ideas, then you are skimming correctly.

Figure 9-3 provides an example for you to practice. This passage also provides an introduction to "scanning", which will be covered later in this chapter. While skimming the material, your eyes should move quickly down the page. Read Figure 9-3 by putting the words together and ignoring the blank spots, being very aware of where your eyes are going and how they are moving and feeling.

Figure 9-3   Passage for Skimming Practice

Step 1: Read the title

The title of a book, article, or other document usually gives you the first clue to the content. It gives you the *big picture*. For example, if your boss hands you a document called "Organizing a Quality Control Program," you can see from the title what the report is about. The text of the document will support or explain how to organize a quality control program. Look at the sample article on the preceding pages. The title "The Computer System" describes the content.

Step 2: Read headings and subheadings

To get a *quick overview* of a long document and learn more about the contents, scan the text, stopping to read the headings and subheadings. Look at the headings, in bold type, in the sample article. Note how Hardware, Peripherals, and Software relate to the contents. Then note how the subheadings Central Processing Unit, Keyboard, Monitor, Printer, Modem, Disk Drives, Business Software, Home Office Software, and Personal Software tell you more about what is under each heading.

Step 3: Scan your way to information

To learn more about *the contents* of a document and to help you identify the information you might need, scan each paragraph. First, read the topic sentence for the main idea. The main idea is the one sentence that covers the subject of the entire paragraph and tells you who or what the paragraph is about. After reading the topic sentence, scan the rest of the paragraph. Underline or highlight important words, sentences, or passages.

You can also use scanning to find certain kinds of information quickly. Scan when you look up a word in a dictionary or a topic in an encyclopedia or when you check the arrival and departure times of trains or buses on a schedule. Scan memos, reports, e-mail messages, and other business documents to determine whether you need to read more closely. Sometimes documents that land on your desk are not relevant to you, and they can go right into the wastebasket or recycling bin after a quick scan.

Say you're looking for your friend Jessica Heller's name in the telephone book. Your purpose is to find the name without worrying about the surrounding information.

Knowing this, you probably don't start with the first page of the telephone book and go through all the A's and B's, C's, D's, and so on. Instead, you turn to the bold headings in the H section. You locate He, then scan the list until you find the name Heller. You find this information quickly because you are looking for something specific. The same idea applies when reading for any specific information.

Success Skills

When to skim

Because skimming is done at a fast speed with less-than-normal comprehension, you should not skim all the time. There are many times, however, when skimming is useful.

Suppose you are taking a presentation skills class and have to deliver an oral report in a few days about the first automobiles ever made. You locate six books and four newspaper articles about this topic. (Chapter 12 will provide information on how to do this.) Because you must be ready soon, you do not have time to read each word, but you need a large quantity of solid information.

Skimming will help you locate the information quickly while making sure you use your time wisely. It will also increase the amount of usable material you obtain for your research.

Suppose you have an exam in a few days. You need to review the material you learned, but you don't want to reread everything. By skimming, you can quickly locate the information you haven't mastered yet and study only *that* material.

While reading, ask yourself the following questions to help you decide whether to skim. If you answer yes to any of these, then skimming is a useful tool.

♦ Do I have a lot to read and only a small amount of time?

♦ Is a pre-view or re-view enough?

♦ Do I already know something about this?

♦ Can any of the material be skipped?

If you have sufficient background knowledge or believe you don't need the information, then skip it! That's right—do not read it at all! Believe it or not, skipping material may sometimes be the best use of your time. Just because someone wrote something doesn't mean you have to read it. *If you pick and choose carefully what you skim and skip, you will be pleasantly surprised at the large amount of information you can get through in a short period of time.*

Now that you have learned how and when to skim, you are ready to experiment with the skimming exercises in Appendix E. Please turn there now.

Smart Tip

Researchers report that most Internet users do not read web sites. Rather, they skim them first, looking for general information; then they scan them, looking for specific information related to their search. This illustrates how effective skimming is a useful strategy for finding what you want quickly.

ACTIVITY 8

Respond to the following questions about how skimming might be helpful to you.

1. How can skimming help your reading speed?_____

_____

2. How can it satisfy your reading purpose?_____

_____

3. How can it help with your educational reading material?_____

_____

4. How can it help with your career?_____

_____

5. How can it help with research?_____

_____

6. How can it help when you read newspapers or magazines?_____

_____

7. What other ways do you think skimming might be helpful to you?_____

_____

What Is Scanning?

Scanning is another useful tool for reading in high gear. Unlike skimming, when **scanning,** you look only for a specific fact or piece of information without reading everything. You scan when you look for your favorite show listed in the television guide, for your friend's phone number in a telephone directory, and for the definition of a word in a dictionary. For scanning to be successful, you must be able to comprehend what you read so you can locate the specific information you need. Scanning also allows you to find details and other information in a hurry.

How to scan

Because you already scan many different types of material in your daily life, learning more details

about scanning will be easy. Establishing your purpose, locating the appropriate material, and knowing how the information is arranged *before* you start scanning is essential.

If you need to find the meaning of a word, using a dictionary is the most appropriate tool to accomplish this purpose. To look up the word *loquacious*, you should immediately look for it under the L section. Starting from A at the beginning of the dictionary would be a huge waste of time. (*Loquacious* means "very talkative," by the way!)

In daily life, you have many reasons to look for specific information. What specific information do you currently need or expect to need in the future? What sources will you use to find it? Identify where you would find the information listed below. In the first column, add a few more types of information you might need.

Information I Need	Where to look for it
The meaning of an unknown word	*In a dictionary*
What courses to take	*In the school catalog*
The time a television show is aired	
Information on Gandhi	
The zip code for Cary, SC	
The day of the week for Christmas this year	
How to print labels on the computer	
The population of South Africa	
The capital of Utah	

The material you scan is typically arranged in the following ways: alphabetically, chronologically, nonalphabetically, by category, or textually. **Alphabetical** information is arranged in order from A to Z, while **chronological** information is arranged in numerical order. Information can be also be arranged in **nonalphabetical** order, such as a television listing, or by **category**, as in an auto parts catalog. Sometimes information is located within the written paragraphs of text, also known as a **textual s**ense, as in an encyclopedia entry.

ACTIVITY 10

Look at the types of reading material listed on the left. How do you think text is arranged in each? Write the words <u>Alphabetical</u>, <u>Chronological</u>, <u>Nonalphabetical</u>, <u>by</u> <u>Category</u>, or <u>Textual</u> on the right to identify the arrangement of each type of material.

Type of Material	Arrangement of Material
Dictionary	*Alphabetical*
Television listing	*Nonalphabetical*
Encyclopedia entry	*Textual*
Book index	
History reading passage	
Zip code directory	
Magazine article	
Sports page of the newspaper	
Reference listing in a book	
Newspaper article	
Computer manual	

Learning to use your hands while scanning is very helpful in locating specific information. Do you do anything with your hands to locate a word in a dictionary? to find a meeting time on your calendar? to read a train or bus schedule? Using a pacer is extremely helpful in focusing your attention and keeping your place while scanning a column of material.

Your peripheral vision can also help you scan effectively. When your hand moves down a list of names, you see not only the name your finger is pointing to, but also the names above and below. Let your eyes work for you when searching for information.

Keep the concept of key words in mind while scanning. Your purpose will determine the key words. Suppose you are looking for the time a train leaves from New York City for Washington, D.C. The key words to keep in mind are *from New York City* and to *Washington, D.C.* If you are looking for the cost of a computer printer with the code number *PX-710*, the key word to locate in a list of many printers is *PX-710*.

When to scan

You should scan when your aim is to find specific pieces of information. If you were doing the research for the oral presentation mentioned in the skimming section of this chapter, you could scan the index of books, web sites, and reference materials. You would discover whether they contain any information you want and the pages where the information can be found.

In the past, you probably scanned without knowing you were doing it. Now with the information provided in this section, you can use scanning more frequently. The more you practice, the more effective your scanning will become. Finally, the most important benefit of scanning is its ability to help you become a more flexible reader. Scanning adds another high gear to your reading. Now that you are familiar with the basics for scanning, turn to Appendix E for some practice exercises.

ACTIVITY 11

Scanning is a reading survival skill. Finding specific information quickly and accurately can make your life easier. Respond to the following questions about how scanning might be used in your daily life.

1. How can scanning be used to increase your reading speed?

_____

_____

2. How can it be used to satisfy your reading purpose?

_____

_____

3. How can it be used to help with your classwork and other educational reading?

_____

_____

4. How can it be used for doing research?

_____

_____

5. How can it be used for reading newspapers and magazines?

_____

_____

6. How can scanning be helpful to you in other ways?

_____

_____

Chapter 9: Survival Reading Skills

Permission to not read everything

Because you may be used to reading every word and may be uncomfortable leaving some words out, you need to give yourself permission to overlook some words by skimming, scanning, and skipping material according to your reading purpose. Your permission slip from the author is given below.

Permission Slip

I, _____, am hereby granted permission *not* to read everything. I am also *not* required to remember everything I read. By doing so, I am not cheating. I understand that skimming, scanning, or skipping material may be the best way to accomplish my reading purpose. I understand that just because material has been written, I do not have to read it all. By exercising this right, I will be able to read actively, read more in less time, and still get the information I need without reading it all.

My signature of approval of these methods gives me permission to be a flexible reader now and forever more!

Your signature _____

The author's signature *Abby Mark-Beale*

Checkpoint 9.4

1. What is skimming?
2. What is scanning?
3. When might you skim?
4. When might you scan?

Success Skills

9.5 ADJUSTING YOUR READING SPEED

When driving a car, a person should not drive fast all the time. On an open highway, the driver can go faster. But on city streets, he or she needs to slow down for pedestrians, stop lights, and other cars. A driver needs to change driving speeds according to the conditions of the road.

Similarly, a reader should not read fast all the time. If you always read fast, you may miss important information. If you read slowly all the time, you will daydream more and waste your time. So how fast should you read?

Three Factors for Determining Reading Speed

Your reading speed depends mainly on the following three factors: your *purpose for reading,* the *difficulty of the material,* and your *familiarity with the subject matter or background knowledge.*

Reading speed depends first on your *reading purpose*—why you are reading what you are reading. (In Chapter 8, you were introduced to reading purpose.) Let's say your reading purpose is to get only the main ideas of a nonfiction chapter. In this case, you read fairly quickly, looking for the main ideas while avoiding the details. If your reading purpose is to learn step-by-step how to put a faucet on a sink, you would read more slowly.

Your reading speed also can depend on *how difficult the reading material is.* If you are reading material that contains complex vocabulary or technical information, you need to read more slowly than when the vocabulary is easy and the information is not as technical.

Finally, your *background knowledge*—or what you already know—greatly affects your ability to increase your reading speed. The more you already know about a topic or material, the faster you can read. The less familiar you are with it, the slower you will read. By pre-viewing a chapter, you will be able to increase your reading speed because you are familiar with the chapter contents before you begin reading more thoroughly.

When to Speed Up and When to Slow Down

Since reading one way all the time—either fast or slow—is not efficient, you need to learn when to speed up your reading and when to slow it down.

> " Nothing happens by itself… it will all come your way, once you understand that you have to make it come your way, by your own exertions. "
>
> —Ben Stein
> Lawyer, speechwriter, and contemporary author

Smart Tip

Reading on a computer screen reduces your reading speed by 25 to 30 percent compared to reading on paper. This may be why people have a tendency to print out longer documents on paper to read them. So much for the paperless

While reading an article or a chapter, your reading speed naturally goes up and down depending on how much you daydream, how familiar the material is, and other factors. If you learn to change your reading speed *on purpose*, instead of accidentally, you will complete your reading in an efficient amount of time and with better understanding.

In Chapter 8, you discovered the influences that affect your ability to learn. Briefly review the chapter to help you complete Activity 12. Most of the factors that affect reading affect learning as well.

ACTIVITY 12

Factors that help you speed up your reading are shown in the first column and factors that cause you to slow down your reading are shown in the second column. Working with a partner or small group, list several conditions or influences that help you read faster. Then list in the second column the factors that cause you to slow down. (Important clue: There is usually an opposite relationship between one side and the other.)

Things that help me speed up	Things that cause me to slow down
Reading for main ideas (purpose)	Reading for details (purpose)
Easy vocabulary	Difficult vocabulary
Some background knowledge	Little background knowledge
Preparation for class discussion	Preparation for quiz or test
_____	_____
_____	_____
_____	_____
_____	_____

In Appendix E, you will find one student's list of factors for reading faster and slower. Since readers are different, you may not always agree with this list. What is essential is that you know what affects your ability to speed up or slow down. This is an important quality of an active, efficient reader!

Flexibility Is the Key

Being an active reader means being a flexible reader. **Flexible readers** adjust their reading strategies according to their reading purpose, the difficulty of material, and their background knowledge. In this chapter, you discovered why it is important to adjust your reading speed. You also became aware of the factors that affect reading and speed, and you learned new tools to apply to your reading to increase your speed. This combination of awareness and skill will make you a flexible reader.

Now that you have read about and experienced some active reading tools, go back in Chapter 8 and reevaluate your reading abilities. Summarize your abilities on the lines below. Have any of your qualities changed? Explain your thoughts below.

_____

_____

_____

_____

_____

_____

_____

_____

Checkpoint 9.5

1. Why should you adjust your reading speed?

2. What helps you read faster?

3. What slows you down?

Focus on Ethics

You have been asked on very short notice to report to your company's human resources committee on an article entitled *Technology and High-Income Careers.* You are sure you can skim the material for several important points without reading the entire twenty-page article, though you know your boss expects you to read the entire article. What are your options? Would you handle the situation differently if the article was on manufacturing safety requirements? Why or why not?

Key Terms and Concepts

alphabetical	flexible reader	scanning
category	key words	skimming
chronological	pacers	textual
column width	peripheral vision	topic sentence
eye span	phrases	

Chapter Summary

1. The three basic reading gears are low, middle, and high.

2. Unlearning is uncomfortable but important to improving a skill or habit.

3. Learning to read faster increases your concentration.

4. Reading faster can be accomplished by using peripheral vision to increase your eye span.

5. The three tools for increasing eye span are:
   - Reading key words.
   - Reading phrases.
   - Using pacers.

6. The tools you use to enhance reading speed can depend on the width of the column.

7. The three factors for determining reading speed are:
   - Reading purpose.
   - Difficulty of the material.
   - Background knowledge.

8. Skimming means looking for the general or main ideas. It is similar to previewing and should be used when your purpose is to get an overview of the material. Skimming can help you obtain information quickly without wasting time.

9. Scanning means looking for a piece of specific information, like a topic in an index. Using a pacer and your peripheral vision can help you quickly find what you need.

10. Flexible readers shift their reading gears depending on their purpose and background knowledge.

11. The most important thing about learning to read actively is to figure out what works best for you.

Based on the information you learned in this chapter, answer the following questions using your own words.

1. Why is learning how to read faster important? Give at least three reasons.

2. Why is changing your reading habits difficult? How can you improve your skills?

3. How does your peripheral vision affect the way you read? What can you do to expand your peripheral vision while reading?

4. Why is it helpful to know about the reading gears?

5. What are the similarities and differences between skimming and scanning?

6. What would you tell another learner about how to skim?

7. What would you tell another learner about how to scan?

8. Which of the reading tools do you find most useful? least useful?

9. Going back to Kim on the first page of this chapter, do you have any new suggestions to help her manage her reading load?

10. Why should you learn to adjust your reading speed? What can you do to adjust your reading speed?

Case 1

Jeanne looked at the stack of magazines that had come in the mail during the last three weeks and sighed. She had been so busy that she had looked at only a few of them. They were beginning to pile up and create clutter. She didn't want to throw the magazines out because that seemed a waste of money and she might find some useful information in a few of them. Besides, she enjoyed reading when she had the time. Jeanne felt frustrated. At the very least, she wanted to read the most interesting and helpful articles in each magazine.

1. By raising her normal reading speed, Jeanne might be able to solve her dilemma and read the important articles in each magazine before she feels compelled to throw it away. What techniques for reading faster would you recommend to Jeanne to accomplish her purpose?

2. What factors do you think Jeanne should consider in deciding when to speed up and when to slow down as she reads the various articles? What conditions or influences would help her speed up or cause her to slow down?

Case 2

Pedro's boss asked him to review several lengthy research papers and identify the most important technical information for an upcoming design project. Once Pedro had done this, his next task was to produce a report of the key trends he had uncovered and distribute the report to his coworkers. The success of future design projects depended on Pedro's doing a good job; however, as usual, Pedro's time was limited and he knew he would have to work efficiently to gather the vital information.

1. Pedro's boss had not selected the research papers carefully, so Pedro knew his first task was to determine which papers were relevant to his department. What would be the best "reading gear" for Pedro to use to identify the most important papers? Why would that be the best reading gear for this task?

2. After Pedro has selected the papers he will review in greater detail, which technique would you recommend he use for identifying the key trends: skimming or scanning? Brainstorm some benefits of using the technique you recommend.

For four years, Naoki has worked as an information technology consultant at a large pharmaceutical company. He is good at his job, continues to learn  new skills, and has made some close friends. One day Sidra, a coworker, asks him to attend an important meeting in her place, as she will be out of town on business. Sidra prepares Naoki for the meeting by telling him when and where it will be held. She also gives him a 40-page document that will be discussed and asks him to read it ahead of time, which he dutifully does.

When Naoki arrives at the meeting at the scheduled time, he realizes that although he read the document, he doesn't know what the meeting's objectives are supposed to be or whether he will be called on to present. When the meeting leader asks him to describe the project's pitfalls, he speaks off the top of his head. He feels foolish and shrinks away from any questions. He knows he did not represent Sidra well, and he worries about the aftermath of his performance.

I f you think of Sidra as the instructor and Naoki as the student, what oversights did both make? What could each have done to create a more positive outcome? How does this story relate to test taking?

Chapter Goals

After studying and working with the information in this chapter, you should be able to:

♦ Identify your reactions to test taking.
♦ Determine how your reactions to test taking affect your ability to be successful.
♦ State the "rules" of the test-taking game.
♦ Identify and explain winning strategies for different types of tests.
♦ Explain the difference between paper tests and computer tests.
♦ Use the information in this chapter to improve your testing success.

In This Chapter

Tests are evaluations of what you know and what you can do as a result of this knowing. Students take formal tests to evaluate how much they have learned from classroom or web-based learning. Workers take informal tests when they perform their jobs and share their knowledge with co-workers.

For purposes of this chapter, the term test is generalized to include those formal learning evaluations given for classroom or web-based learning and professional or career-type tests taken for on-the-job training, certifications, and continuing education credits. While reading the chapter, look for similarities and differences between formal and informal tests. Keep in mind that informal tests, like those of the workers, are subjectively evaluated (from one's own view-point) and are purely performance based.

Taking a formal test is like playing a game. The object is to get as many points as possible in the time you are given to play. Throughout this chapter, tests are sometimes referred to as games. The reality is that tests are games and your testing success begins when you look at them this way. How well you do on any test, or game, depends on a combination of your knowledge, preparation, and test-taking ability. In this chapter, you will learn how to put that preparation into play and how to test effectively.

On what occasions do you take tests?

SELF-CHECK

The following self-evaluation will give you an idea of how familiar, or unfamiliar, you are with some of the topics and terms discussed in this chapter. After reading each statement, circle the letter Y, S, or N to indicate the answer that is most appropriate for you. Answer honestly; rate yourself at the end, then complete the information for Chapter 10 in Appendix A.

Y = yes; frequently	S = sometimes	N = no; never

1. I know that a low test grade does not make me a failure.   Y   S   N

2. I realize that it is okay not to know everything on a test.   Y   S   N

3. I follow both written and oral test directions carefully.   Y   S   N

4. Before I begin a test, I pre-view it by looking for the point values.   Y   S   N

5. When previewing my tests, I look for answers to other questions.   Y   S   N

6. I budget my time effectively when I take a test.   Y   S   N

7. On paper tests, I do the easiest questions first and come back later to the harder ones.   Y   S   N

8. I am aware of the differences between computer-based and paper tests.   Y   S   N

9. I review returned tests for topics I need to understand better.   Y   S   N

10. I learn from my testing mistakes.   Y   S   N

Rate Yourself:

Number of Ys	_____	x	100	=	_____	
Number of Ss	_____	x	50	=	_____	
Number of Ns	_____	x	0	=	_____	Total _____

10.1 STRESS, TESTS, AND YOU

Stress and tests seem to go together naturally. Many people feel stress before a formal test, an oral presentation, or another important event where they have to prove what they know or can do. For some people, stress appears as fear and anxiety. For others, it takes the form of excitement and anticipation.

How does test-taking affect you? Are you calm and relaxed or tense and uptight? Are you patient or impatient? How does your body react? Do your muscles tighten? Does your appetite disappear, or do you overeat? Do your sleeping habits change? Is your breathing steady?

Stress is not something that happens, rather it is your body's reaction to something that happened or is about to happen. It can be good or bad. Good stress helps you perform better, even when you feel anxious or scared. It gets your adrenaline flowing, which tells your body and mind to become alert.

Bad stress makes performing well or achieving your goals challenging because of fear and worry. Some medical researchers link an excess of bad stress to increased health problems, such as depression, heart disease, and cancer.

Good stress helps you become motivated and energizes your body, while bad stress demotivates you and zaps your energy. When you hear someone refer to being stressed, he or she is usually referring to bad stress.

When you think about playing softball, volleyball, or a board game, do you experience the same reactions as you do for an academic test? Probably not. Learning how to react to tests as if they are games can reduce your test-taking stress.

> Do not let what you cannot do interfere with what you can do.
>
> —John Wooden
> Former college basketball coach for UCLA

This exercise will help you become aware of your reactions to test taking. Common stress reactions to test taking are described below. Place a check mark on the line next to reactions you experience; then check when the reaction happens to you. Add one or two other reactions you experience in testing situations.

Stress Reactions to Tests	Before,	During, or	After
_____ I feel nervous.	_____	_____	_____
_____ I feel excited.	_____	_____	_____
_____ I feel relieved.	_____	_____	_____
_____ I feel optimistic and make positive comments.	_____	_____	_____
_____ I feel pessimistic and make negative comments.	_____	_____	_____
_____ I usually get a headache.	_____	_____	_____
_____ My neck, back, or shoulders ache.	_____	_____	_____
_____ I usually feel pretty good.	_____	_____	_____
_____ My breathing is rapid and shallow.	_____	_____	_____
_____ My breathing is relaxed and deep.	_____	_____	_____
_____ My heart pounds, and my palms sweat.	_____	_____	_____
_____ I lose my appetite.	_____	_____	_____
_____ I panic.	_____	_____	_____
_____ I have trouble sleeping.	_____	_____	_____
_____ My mind goes blank.	_____	_____	_____
_____ I'm afraid I won't have enough time to finish.	_____	_____	_____
_____ I worry others may are finish before me.	_____	_____	_____
_____ I worry that I've studied the wrong things.	_____	_____	_____
_____ I worry that I have done poorly.	_____	_____	_____
_____ I am confident in my ability to do well.	_____	_____	_____
_____ I am afraid I don't know everything.	_____	_____	_____
_____ I feel stupid.	_____	_____	_____
_____ _____	_____	_____	_____
_____ _____	_____	_____	_____

Think about or discuss in a group which of the above reactions are helpful? Which are hurtful? Why?

Test Results and Self-Worth

Do you think an athlete's self-worth depends on how well he or she plays a game on a specific day? If a baseball player hits the ball one out of three tries, he has a batting average of .333, or 33 percent, and is considered very successful. If he strikes out one day, does that lessen his overall ability?

In some states, students who aspire to be lawyers can take the bar exam an unlimited number of times before striking out. Unfortunately, many students allow one good or poor test grade to influence their self-worth. C or D grades may make them feel less valuable, while a grade of A or B, may increase their self-worth.

Tests are *not* a judge of your self-worth. They are indicators of what you have learned, how well you communicate your knowledge, and what remains to be learned. Doing poorly one day should not affect your overall worth. It means you need to pay close attention to what you are doing or not doing and take action to improve for the next test.

Meeting Expectations

One of the reasons athletes turn professional is because they (and their coaches and fans) have high expectations. When athletes don't perform well in one game, the coaches and fans do not abandon them. They look forward to the next game and hope for improvement.

People in your life also expect you to do well, but they know you will encounter some setbacks. They will not abandon you because of a few unsuccessful attempts.

Let your own expectations motivate you to improve. You are the only one who is responsible for meeting your own expectations. Though others may have expectations of you, what you expect from yourself is more important.

Does one good game make this individual a good baseball player? Does performing poorly on one test make you a poor learner? What determines your self-worth? Do you use your grades as proof of your ability or as a measure of what you have learned and what you still need to learn?

Success Skills

You have expectations of yourself as a learner. Perhaps you aspire to enter a certain career or make more money. What are your expectations. Discuss them with a partner, and summarize them in a short paragraph.

_____
_____
_____
_____
_____
_____
_____

It's All in Your Perspective

Perspective is how you personally view things, based on your background and expectations. In this book, perspective refers to how you view test results and learning. Suppose you are taking a basic electrical wiring course; and on your first test you don't do well, even though you studied for the test. "Not doing well" could mean getting a B or a D, depending on your perspective.

It is important to remember that *one test does not make or break your academic career.* It does not mean that you are destined to do poorly on all your tests. And it does not mean you are a failure. It does mean, however, that you have to look at and recognize what you can do to do better next time.

Respond to the following questions about perspective in testing situations. Try to be specific for each type of learning.

1. On four separate tests, you received the following grades: A-, C+, 83, and 62. How would you react?

_____
_____

2. At your job, you received a less than perfect year-end evaluation. How do you react? What role does your perspective play in your reaction?

_____
_____

3. How can you change your perspective to eliminate stressful reactions to tests?

_____
_____

You Won't Know Everything

Many learners get a sinking feeling of disappointment when they are presented with a question they just cannot answer. It could be on a test, posed from your boss or from some other person in authority. You may go so far as to believe you are a total failure because you didn't know the answer. Of course the more answers you know and can document accurately, the better your test result. But it is unrealistic to think you will know all of the answers all of the time. Therefore, you should *focus on what you do know, not on what you don't know. Accept that you will not know everything.*

Taking Responsibility

When passive learners do poorly, they often blame their instructors for the test. Active learners assume responsibility for their own performance and don't blame someone or something else. Which do you do?

ACTIVITY 4

Think about how you take responsibility for your learning success and testing outcomes. What do you say or do that shows your responsibility? What do you say or do that shows your lack of responsibility? List these below.

How I Take Responsibility	How I Do Not Take Responsibility
1. _____	1. _____
2. _____	2. _____
3. _____	3. _____
4. _____	4. _____
5. _____	5. _____
6. _____	6. _____
7. _____	7. _____
8. _____	8. _____
9. _____	9. _____
10. _____	10. _____
11. _____	11. _____
12. _____	12. _____

Attend to Your Body's Needs

Another important way to reduce your stress is to listen to your body. It constantly gives you signals about its needs. When you are sleep deprived (which could mean getting only six hours of sleep a night instead of seven or eight), your brain doesn't learn as well, and you can't deal with stress as effectively as when you are rested. If you regularly skip meals or consume a lot of sugar, caffeine, or simple carbohydrates, your body and mind will feel sluggish. If you neglect aerobic activity (such as walking, jogging, and swimming), you will feel lethargic. Feed your body with sleep, healthy foods, and exercise, and it will reward you with the resources and energy you need to learn.

> **When I am delivering my very best, that is when I feel successful.**
>
> —Art Fettig
> Contemporary author, president of "Growth Unlimited"

Checkpoint 10.1

1. What is stress?

2. What are some causes of test-taking stress?

3. What can you do to reduce test-taking stress?

10.2 THE TEN RULES OF THE TEST-TAKING GAME

The object of a formal test or a game is to get as many points as possible in the time allowed. In each case, you need to know the rules. While reading the following rules for test taking, place an asterisk (*) next to those you want to remember or review later.

Rule 1
Act As If You Will Succeed

Thought is powerful. When you think negative thoughts, your stress level rises. Your confidence level may drop, which often leads to feelings of failure.

When this happens, think about success. Smile and take deep, slow breaths. Close your eyes, and imagine getting the test back with a good grade written at the top. Try doing this now by thinking about an upcoming test. Do you feel different? (If this short exercise was powerful for you, you may be interested in learning more about the power of visualization. Consult your library or the Internet for more information.)

Rule 2
Arrive Ahead of Time

Being on time or early for a test sets your mind at ease. You will have a better chance of getting your favorite seat, relaxing, and preparing yourself mentally for the game ahead.

Rule 3
Bring the Essential Testing Tools

Don't forget to bring the necessary testing tools along with you, including extra pens, sharpened pencils, erasers, a calculator, dictionary, and other items you may need. You won't need your notes or a textbook unless it is an open-book test. Just a brief outline or flashcards of what you know well will be enough.

Rule 4
Ignore Panic Pushers

Some people become nervous before a test and hit the panic button, afraid they don't know the material. **Panic pushers** are people who ask you questions about the material they are about to be tested on. If you know the answers, you will feel confident; however, if you don't, you may panic and lose your confidence. Instead of talking with a panic pusher before a test, spend your time concentrating on what you know, not on what you don't know.

Rule 5 Pre-view the Playing Field

Before you play any game, it is wise to pre-view the field. The information you find during your preview will help you determine your game-playing strategies. In baseball, players inspect the field looking for wet and slippery spots, and they judge the height of the fence to hit a home run over. Once you have received your test, you should do several things before you begin, as listed on the next page.

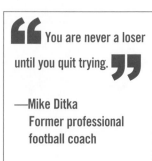

"You are never a loser until you quit trying."

—Mike Ditka
Former professional football coach

♦ **Listen to instructions, and read directions carefully.** Have you ever lost points on a test for not following directions? You may have known the answers to the questions, but you failed to follow the rules of the game. For example, if you see a column of vocabulary words on the left side of a test sheet and definitions on the right side, you might assume that you should match the two columns. However, if the directions said to look for opposite definitions, you would lose points for not following directions.

♦ **Determine the point spread.** Look at the total number of questions and the point of value of each. Decide how much time you can spend on each question and still finish the test on time. Let's say your test is made up of 30 multiple-choice questions and two essays. Each of the multiple-choice questions are worth 2 points for a total of 60 points, and each essay is worth 20 points for a total of 40 points.

30 multiple choice	x	2 points	=	60 points
2 essay	x	20 points	=	40 points
				100 points

The points should add up to 100; if they don't, ask your instructor if you understand the breakdown correctly. Once you figure out the point values, you can budget your time accordingly.

♦ **Budget your time.** If you budget your time and stick to your time limits, you will always complete the test in the amount of time given. If you had 60 minutes to complete the test in the example above, approximately how much time should you spend on each of the multiple-choice questions? How much time, approximately, should you spend on each essay?

Don't worry if others finish before you. Those who leave early don't always get the highest grades.

♦ **Use the test as an information tool.** Be on the lookout for clues that answer other questions. Frequently, instructors will test you on a single topic in more than one way. You may see a topic in a multiple-choice question and again in an essay. Sometimes you can use the terminology from the objective questions for your essays.

Rule 6
Write in the Margin

Before you begin the test, write key terms, formulas, names, dates, and other information in the margin so you won't forget them. (Chapter 13, on writing essays and papers, discusses how to create a map in the margin so you can communicate your ideas in an organized fashion.)

Rule 7
Complete the Easy Questions First

Answering easy questions first helps build your confidence. If you come across a tough question, mark it so you can come back to it later. Avoid spending so much time on a challenging question that you might run out of time to answer the questions you do know.

Rule 8
Know If There Is a Guessing Penalty

Chances are your tests will carry no penalty for guessing. If your time is about to run out and there is no penalty, take a wild guess. On the other hand, if your test carries a penalty for guessing, choose your answers wisely, and leave blank the answers you do not know. If you are unsure whether a test carries a guessing penalty, ask your instructor.

Rule 9
Avoid Changing Your Answers

Have you ever chosen an answer, changed it, and learned later that your first choice was correct? Research indicates that three out of four times your first choice is usually correct; therefore, you should avoid changing an answer unless you are *absolutely sure* the answer is wrong.

Rule 10
Write Clearly and Neatly

If you are handwriting your test (versus using a computer), imagine your instructor reading your writing. Is it easy to read or difficult? Does it look presentable, with the answers in the right places and no words crossed out, or does it look messy? The easier your test is for the instructor to read, the better your chances of getting a higher grade.

If you haven't already placed an asterisk (*) next to those rules you find most important or want to review again later, do so now.

What You Need to Know About Computer-Based Tests

Sometime in your life, if not already, you will probably experience a computer-based test. Stockbrokers, teachers, architects, financial planners, and other professionals are required to take licensing and certification tests on the computer. Students can take certain precollege tests, such as the GREs and GMATs, on a computer, too. Tutorials about how to use the computer are usually provided, so you can take these tests even if you have little or no computer experience.

Though most computer-based tests are multiple choice, the multiple-choice questions can be presented in either a computer-adaptive or linear manner. A computer-adaptive test selects the difficulty of the next question based on your previous answer. This means different test takers answer different questions. Linear questions are preset and given in numerical order. This is the type of test you usually take.

On computer-adaptive tests, you must answer the question the first time you see it. You cannot go back and change your answer. Linear tests allow you to return to the question.

On both types of tests, your score depends on how well you

answer the questions and on the number of questions you answer. So managing your time is key. Makers of these tests suggest you familiarize yourself with the test format by completing the tutorials and sample questions before attempting the tests.

With most computer-based tests, results are provided immediately. However, before you finish, you are given a chance to cancel the test without seeing your score. If you cancel it, you will need to schedule another testing date and pay again. If you ask to see your score, you cannot cancel the test. You must accept the result of your performance.

For more information about computer-based tests, check out the web sites of some of the test makers: www.ets.org (Educational Testing Service) and www.prometric.com (Prometric Testing).

Figure 10-1   Mind Map Review

The information on this map is a general review of the concepts discussed in Chapters 5 and 10. Read the map by following the thoughts and pictures on each of the branches. This will reinforce what you have already read and learned while preparing you for the next section on test-taking strategies.

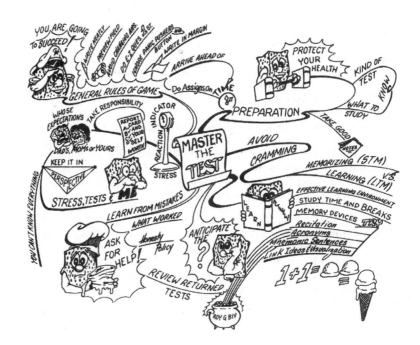

Checkpoint 10.2

1. What are the ten general rules for taking any test?

2. Which rules do you already know and follow?

3. Which rules do you want to remember and use?

10.3 WINNING GAME STRATEGIES

Now that you have read the rules of test taking, it's time to apply winning game strategies to objective tests, subjective tests, and performance tests. Chances are you already know many of the strategies and use them successfully. Your job is to look for the ones that you don't know or use and make them work for you. Some of the strategies will be useful all of the time, while other strategies will be useful only some of the time. By becoming aware of the strategies and putting them into practice, you will quickly find which ones work best for you.

Multiple-Choice Questions

Multiple-choice games are sometimes called **multiple guess**. When you don't know an answer, you actually have to take a wild guess. Taking a wild guess is a popular strategy, but it should be used only when all else fails. On the other hand, learning how to make educated guesses adds to your success. **Educated guesses** are a result of using testing strategies to come up with your answer.

Many strategies can be used to answer multiple-choice questions correctly. Five multiple-choice questions are shown in Figure 10-2. Strategies for answering these questions are shown in 10-3. Read each question; then review the matching strategy that leads you to the correct answer.

Figure 10-2   Sample Multiple-Choice Questions

1. Bears can be found wandering
   a. in the woods.
   b. in parks.
   c. in fields.
   d. in the mountains.
   e. all of the above.

2. Students frequently succeed in test taking because
   a. all tests are easy.
   b. they are usually prepared.
   c. they always do their assignments on time.
   d. they always try hard.

3. Migraine headaches are most commonly caused by
   a. allergic reactions to foods.
   b. lack of sleep.
   c. allergic reactions to medicine.
   d. heredity.

4. The reasons most students give for failing tests include
   a. studying the wrong information.
   b. cramming and being unprepared.
   c. not having enough time to study.
   d. being given unfair tests.

5. All of the following are ingredients of student success except
   a. taking good notes.
   b. studying ahead of time.
   c. learning from mistakes.
   d. cramming for exams.

Success Skills

Figure 10-3   Answering Multiple-Choice Questions

♦ **Look at all possible answers before choosing.**

Question 1 asks you to circle the best answer. Respond to each multiple-choice question with each answer (a, b, c, d, and e) in order to find the best answer.

a. Bears can be found wandering in the woods. Correct

b. Bears can be found wandering in parks. Correct

c. Bears can be found wandering in fields. Correct

d. Bears can be found wandering in the mountains. Correct

e. Bears can be found wandering in woods, parks, fields, and mountains. Correct

All answers to this questions are correct, but e is the best answer. If you answered this question without looking at all the choices, you might have chosen incorrectly.

♦ **Look for key words.**

Can you identify the key word in the solutions to question 2? The key word is *usually*, which is found in answer "b". All the other answers give definite answers, such as *all* and *always*. The only answer that is not definite—*usually*—answers the question best.

♦ **Look for similar answers.**

Many times in multiple-choice questions, you are asked to make a choice between two similar answers. Answers a and c are similar in question 3, which indicates that the answer may be one of them. If you had *no* idea of the answer to this question, looking for similar answers would help you narrow your wild-guess possibilities from a, b, c, and d to a and c. Now you can take an educated guess. The correct response to this question is a. In this example, the strategy worked, but it may not work all the time.

♦ **Know what the question is asking.**

Does the test ask you to write the best answer or the worst answer? Are you looking for similarities or opposites? Is the question asking for a singular or plural answer? In question 4, you are asked to supply more than one reason, as indicated by the word *reasons*. The only answer that gives more than one reason is "b". Though some of the other responses may be a reason, the best answer to the question is "b".

♦ **Answer negatives positively first.**

Many students become confused when a question asks for an exception instead of the best answer. In question 5, if you look first for the answers that *are* important to student success, only the exception remains a choice.

a. Is taking good notes an ingredient to student success? Yes

b. Is studying ahead of time an ingredient to student success? Yes

c. Is learning from mistakes an ingredient to student success? Yes

d. Is cramming for exams an ingredient to student success? No

A few more strategies exist, but instead of reading about them, you can discover them in Activity 5.

ACTIVITY 5

Below is a series of multiple-choice questions. For many of the questions, you will make an educated guess. Use your background knowledge, common sense, and multiple-choice testing strategies. Questions 5 through 11 contain fictitious, or made up, words. Even so, each question has a correct answer. Circle your answer, then explain why you chose it. When you have completed all of the questions, turn to Appendix F for the answers.

1. Dickens' *A Tale of Two Cities* takes place in what two cities?

   a. Glasgow and London   c. Paris and London

   b. New York and Paris   d. Dublin and Edinburgh

   I chose this answer because: _____

2. Italy has been handicapped by all of the following *except*

   a. limited natural resources.   c. a lack of adequate ports.

   b. a shortage of fertile soil.   d. overpopulated farmlands.

   I chose this answer because _____

3. Which of the following is closest in value to 1/3?

   a. 1/4   b. 3/8   c. 3/16   d. 5/16   e. 7/16

   I chose this answer because _____

4. An example of a mismatched relationship is

   a. Chicago and Illinois.   c. Kansas City and Missouri.

   b. Birmingham and Florida.   d. Phoenix and Arizona.

   I chose this answer because _____

5. The purpose of the cluss in furmaling is to remove

   a. cluss-prags.   b. tremalis.   c. cloughs.   d. plumots.

   I chose this answer because _____

6. Trassig is true when

   a. lusp crosses the vom.   c. the belgo frulls.

   b. the viskal flans, if the viskal is donwil or zortil.   d. dissles lisk easily.

   I chose this answer because _____

Success Skills

7. The sigla frequently overfesks the trelsum because

    a. all siglas are melious.

    b. siglas are always votial.

    c. the trelsum is usually tarious.

    d. no tresla are feskable.

    I chose this answer because _____

8. The fribbled breg minters best with an

    a. derst.   b. morst.   c. sortar.   d. ignu.

    I chose this answer because _____

9. Among the conditions for tristal doss are

    a. the spas fropt and the foths tinzed.

    b. the kredges trott with the orots.

    c. few rakobs accept in sluth.

    d. most of the polats are thenced.

    I chose this answer because _____

10. Which of the following (is, are) always present when trossels are being gruven?

    a. rint and yost   b. yost   c. shum and yost   d. yost and plume

    I chose this answer because _____

11. The mintering function of the ignu is most effectively carried out in

    a. a razma tool.

    b. the gorshing stanti.

    c. the fribbled breg.

    d. a frally sush.

    I chose this answer because _____

12. If a test contained a question that you didn't understand or know the answer to, which letter would you pick?

    a.   b.   c.   d.

    I chose this answer because _____

True-False Questions

True-false questions are probably the easiest to answer because you have a 50 percent chance (one in two) of getting the correct answer. In a multiple-choice question, your chances are reduced to 33 percent (one in three), 25 percent (one in four), 20 percent (one in five), or another percentage based on the number of answers. Use the following strategies to obtain better results on true-false tests.

Read each question carefully

By reading each question carefully, you will find key words and terms to help you choose your answer. This is the best strategy for taking true-false tests.

1. *Look for definites and absolutes.* How many things in this world are definite and absolute? Not many. In some true-false questions, certain key words tell you that a definite is being included as part of the answer. Most but not all definite answers are false.

2. *The longer a true-false statement is, the more likely it is to be true.* If all else fails, take a guess. Read the longest answers in Activity 7 and decide whether they are true. You have a 50 percent chance of getting the answer correct.

ACTIVITY 6

Definite key words are listed in the first column. In the second column, write the exception, or nondefinite term, that is related to the key word. Use the examples to help you. Can you think of any others?

Definite/Absolute Terms	Exception Terms
All	Some
Always	Sometimes
Never	_____
Everyone	_____
Nobody	_____
Is/Are	_____
Must	_____
None	_____
Absolutely	_____
_____	_____
_____	_____

Try your luck on the following true-false questions. Place a T for true or F for false in the blank next to each statement. State the reason for your answer. Identify any key words that support your reason. Then discuss your answers with a partner or group.

_____1. All people have similar ways of learning.

Reason for my answer: _____

_____2. The best time to begin reviewing for a test is within 24 hours of the test.

Reason for my answer: _____

_____3. Rote memorization is the most efficient way to learn.

Reason for my answer: _____

_____4. All men are created equal.

Reason for my answer: _____

_____5. Men are usually physically stronger than women.

Reason for my answer: _____

_____6. Some birds do not fly.

Reason for my answer: _____

_____7. College is always harder than high school.

Reason for my answer: _____

_____8. For a job interview, you must wear clean, neatly pressed clothes and look presentable.

Reason for my answer: _____

_____9. Eating oat bran reduces cholesterol.

Reason for my answer: _____

_____10. Most students can benefit from learning active study skills.

Reason for my answer: _____

What have you learned about taking true-false tests?

_____

_____

Matching Tests

A matching test, when used, is usually only part of a test, not an entire test itself. Matching is similar to multiple choice because only the correct response needs to be identified. Matching tests are slightly more challenging than multiple choice because you must locate matching terms or ideas from lists of information. Some instructors ask for the opposite term or idea, so read the directions carefully! When taking a matching test, keep several points in mind.

Understand the format

A matching test is made up of two columns of information. Most often you are asked to match a piece of information in the left column to a piece of information in the right column. Sometimes the format is reversed, and you are asked to match a piece of information on the right with a piece of information on the left. By reading the directions carefully, you will understand the test format.

Count the possible answers

Suppose you are asked to match the information found in two columns. The left column lists 10 vocabulary terms, and the right column lists 12 definitions. It is obvious that two of the definitions on the right do not have a matching term on the left. On some tests, you may need to use the same answer more than once.

Review all possible choices before answering

The better answer may be at the end of the list. You can make a correct judgment only after reading all the answers.

Use the process of elimination

If you answer the easy questions first, cross off the used ones. You will have fewer possibilities, which makes the more difficult terms easier to match. This also saves time by forcing you to look at only the unmarked answers.

Mentally repeat the choices

Mentally say the term on the left; then go down each possible answer on the right, and fill in the best answer. Mentally talking to yourself helps you focus.

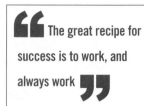

The left column contains a list of terms from this book; the right column contains a list of definitions. Match the terms by placing the correct letter from the right in the blank on the left. (See Appendix F for answers.)

_____ 1. Active learning

_____ 2. Background knowledge

_____ 3. Cornell Method

_____ 4. Critical thinking

_____ 5. Previewing

_____ 6. Passive learning

_____ 7. Mind Map

_____ 8. Mind wandering

_____ 9. Learning influences

_____ 10. Skimming and scanning

A. A reader's road map

B. Note-taking method best used by a random learner

C. What you already know

D. High or fast reading gears

E. Learning like a sponge

F. Note-taking method used effectively by the sequential learner

G. Some things that affect your study concentration

H. Learning like a rock

I. Can only be reduced, not eliminated

J. Listening for instructor clues

K. Thinking about thinking

L. An effective means of time management

Fill-in-the-Blank Tests

Usually, fill-in-the-blank tests are one part of a test, not entire tests themselves. Generally, they ask you to identify the meanings of new words associated with the subject you learned.

Fill-in-the-blanks are more difficult than multiple choice, true-false, or matching because you must think of the answer instead of just identifying it. Several guidelines will help you when responding to fill-in-the-blank tests.

Complete fill-in-the-blank questions last

If your test has several parts, leave fill-in-the-blank questions until last. You may find the answers in the other sections.

Be sure your answer makes sense

If the question asks for more than one item or the verb is plural, the answer is probably plural.

If the question asks for one thing or the verb is singular, your answer is probably singular. If the word *an* appears before the blank, the answer must start with a vowel. Above all, your answer must make sense based on the context in which it is written.

Consider the length of the blank

Usually, a short blank means a short answer. A long blank probably means a long answer or a large word. Two blanks usually mean a two-word answer.

ACTIVITY 9

Try your skill answering the following fill-in-the-blank questions based on information covered so far in this book. If you have trouble with an answer, refer to the chapter identified in parentheses after each statement. (See Appendix F for answers.)

1. An _____ learner is one who takes responsibility for his or her learning and learns from mistakes. (Chapter 1)

2. A _____ learner is one who blames others for his or her learning failures. (Chapter 10)

3. A _____ learner is organized and logical, while a _____ learner is more unorganized and creative. (Chapter 2)

4. _____ means putting off doing something unpleasant or burdensome until a future time. (Chapter 4)

5. The best way to build vocabulary is to use your _____ _____. (Chapter 8)

6. The first two things readers should know before they start to read is their _____ and _____. (Chapter 8)

7. All readers should learn to read faster because it increases their _____. (Chapter 9)

8. In order to read faster, you can read _____, _____, or use_____. (Chapter 9)

9. In The Cornell Method of Note Taking, the _____ of the notes is for your informal outline and the _____ _____ is for key words and questions to study. (Chapter 6)

10. The goal of this book is to help you study _____ not _____. (Chapters 1-13)

Short-Answer Questions

Short-answer questions generally require an answer of only a few sentences. For example, you may be asked to define a vocabulary term or identify a person. Or you may be required to state the reason for an event or provide the date it took place.

To ensure that you answer short-answer questions accurately, look for key words. The key words are listed on the left below, and the answers are listed on the right.

Key Words	Best Answer
Who?	Identify the person.
When?	Provide the date.
Where?	Name the place.
Why?	State the reason or cause.
What?	Explain the event.
How?	Describe the method or reason.

When you are unsure of an answer, take a guess as long as there is no guessing penalty. You may be right or get partial credit.

Essay Tests

Essays are the most challenging types of tests because they require you to understand the material well. Realize that this type of test will require you to put in more study time over a longer period of time. However, doing well on an essay test means you mastered the material and were able to prove that mastery to your instructor.

There are many strategies to keep in mind as you begin the essay part of a test. (Also see Chapter 13 for more ideas.)

Read the directions carefully

Though reading directions is essential in any test taking situation, essay test directions are especially important. The essay directions will tell you:

1. *How many essay questions you need to answer.* Sometimes you will be given a choice of questions to answer, such as three out of five. In this case, make sure to answer only three. If you answer four, chances are that the instructor will count the first three you wrote, not the best three.

2. *How long the essay should be.* Few instructors enjoy reading long essays. Try to come close to the number of words required, while also answering the question to your satisfaction.

3. *How you should budget your time.* The amount of time you allow for answering an essay question depends on how many points the question is worth, the suggested length of the answer, and how quickly you can develop an answer. This is where pre-viewing the test is very helpful.

4. *What type of answer you should give.* Before you answer any essay question, make sure you understand what the question is asking. Avoid giving your opinion unless you are asked for it. Review Figure 10-4 for additional guidance.

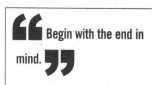

" Begin with the end in mind. "

—Stephen R. Covey
Author of *The 7 Habits of Highly Effective People*

TURN THE PAGE

Figure 10-4   Understanding Essay Directions

Below are some common words and related definitions used in essay-test directions. Learn them now so you can respond appropriately and accurately on tests.

Directions	Meanings	Example Questions
Name	List in 1, 2, 3 order.	*Name* the first five U.S. presidents.
List	Provide the information required.	*List* three ways to improve listening.
Give	Explain.	*Give* two reasons for taking notes.
Discuss	Provide a comprehensive answer.	*Discuss* active learning.
Describe	Illustrate in words.	*Describe* life in the twenty-first century.
Define	Provide a definition.	*Define* previewing.
Identify	Give a brief and correct answer.	*Identify* the parts of a flower.
Explain	Provide clear, complete thoughts.	*Explain* why procrastination is a student's worst enemy.
State	Explain in your own words.	*State* why jobs are not for life anymore.
Compare	Discuss similarities and differences.	*Compare* computers and typewriters.
Contrast	Discuss differences only.	*Contrast* (or distinguish between) computers and typewriters.
Illustrate	Give examples, or draw a picture labeling the parts.	*Illustrate* how to use Mind Mapping.
Criticize	Give evidence on both sides.	*Criticize* the use of force by police in arrests.
Evaluate	Draw conclusions and make judgments.	*Evaluate* the need for affordable day care.
Comment	Write your reaction to the topic; support your opinion with facts or illustrations.	*Comment* on the increase of unemployment in America during the 1930s.

5. *How many components you should discuss.* Some essay questions ask you to respond to more than one question. In the following sample essay question, four responses are required.

    Sample essay question: Students benefit from becoming active learners. *Define* active learner, and *compare* this person to a passive learner. *Discuss* the reasons becoming active in the learning process is important. *Evaluate* your experiences as an active and passive learner.

Write for the intended audience

In the case of a test, your intended audience is your instructor, an individual who knows the subject matter. However, to communicate simply, clearly, and completely, write as though the reader knows nothing about the topic.

Make your paper easy to read

Many students forget that someone has to read their test paper. Follow these guidelines for improving your essays.

- ♦ Write neatly, and use an erasable pen to correct mistakes.
- ♦ Write on the right-hand side of your test booklet, if possible, and leave the left side for making changes and additions.
- ♦ Name, date, and number every loose page.
- ♦ Summarize your answer in the first paragraph. Restate it in your concluding paragraph.
- ♦ Substitute synonyms for words you use frequently to reduce repetition.
- ♦ Use connecting words to make the essay flow. (See Chapter 13.)

Organize your ideas before starting to write

Many students begin writing answers to essay questions without thinking about how their ideas will flow. Since one of the grading criteria for papers is organization, organize your thoughts *before* you begin writing. In Chapter 13, you will learn about idea mapping as a prewriting process for essays and papers. Idea Mapping is a way to create a quick outline of what you want to write. It can be written in the margin to guide you while writing. (Turn to Chapter 13 now if you want to learn more.)

Proofread your answers

Silently reread your answers word for word, pronouncing every word in your head. This will help you catch grammatical mistakes. Also review your answers for misspellings, flow of ideas, and organization.

WEB LINK

Many colleges and universities provide test-taking tips on their web sites. Research the following sites to learn more about test taking.

Essay tests and a checklist for essay tests

www.calpoly.edu/~sas/asc/ael/tests.essay.html

www.utexas.edu/student/lsc/handouts/1446.html

Checklist for essay tests

www.mtsu.edu/~studskl/essay.html

General test taking

www.calpoly.edu/~sas/asc/ael/tests.general.html

Posttest analysis

www.calpoly.edu/~sas/asc/ael/tests.post.test.analysis.html

Objective tests

www.utexas.edu/student/lsc/handouts/1444.html

ACTIVITY 10

Practice taking an essay test by completing the exercise below. Respond to three out of the four items. Each answer should be approximately 100 words.

1. *Define* active learner, and compare an active learner to a passive learner.

   _____

   _____

   _____

2. *Discuss* the reasons why becoming active in the learning process is important.

   _____

   _____

   _____

3. *Evaluate* your experiences as an active and passive learner.

   _____

   _____

   _____

4. For a student to be successful, effective note-taking skills are important. *Describe* two effective note-taking methods.

   _____

   _____

   _____

Performance Tests

Taking a driving test behind the wheel of a car is an example of a performance test. What other types of performance tests have you taken? What types of performance tests do you expect to take in the future?

Performance tests are sometimes combined with written tests, and sometimes they stand alone. They are different from written tests because they require a performance or demonstration. To prepare for a performance test, first study and understand the information you have to demonstrate. Then practice until you are sure you can perform the required task well. For example, suppose you are taking a computer repair course; on a performance test, you are asked to add RAM to a computer. To accomplish this, you need to know how to open the computer, locate the memory chip, place the new chip in its correct slot, and close the computer safely. How would you prepare for this test?

You can probably guess that the most effective way to prepare for a performance test is to study, then practice, practice, practice.

Success Skills

Pretend you are the instructor of a class you are currently taking. Working independently or with others, choose a topic, and create a test worth 100 points. Include at least one section of objective questions and one section of subjective questions. If the content lends itself to a performance test, describe what the learner will be required to do on the test. Once the test is written, decide how you will evaluate the learner's outcome.

_____
_____
_____
_____
_____
_____
_____
_____
_____
_____
_____
_____
_____
_____
_____
_____
_____
_____

Checkpoint 10.3

1. Which type of test do you take most often?

2. Which test strategies work best for you?

3. What new strategies did you learn in this chapter?

Focus on Ethics

Upon returning home after purchasing your textbooks for your psychology class, you realize you were given a copy of the instructor's guide, complete with the bank of tests and their answers. Discuss the benefits and risks of both keeping the guide and taking it back. What is the best choice? Why?

Key Terms and Concepts

bad stress

educated guess

good stress

multiple guess

panic pushers

perspective

stress

Chapter Summary

1. Understanding how you react to tests provides important personal information about how you deal with stress.

2. Taking responsibility for your own learning, keeping grades in perspective, realizing you won't know everything, and taking care of your body's needs are ways to reduce test-taking stress.

3. Taking a test is just like playing a game. The object of the game is to get as many points as possible in the time you are given to play.

4. The rules of the game are the important pieces of information you need to know before a game or test begins. The ten rules are as follows: Act as if you will succeed, arrive ahead of time, bring the essential testing tools, ignore panic pushers, preview the playing field, write in the margin any information you want to remember, complete the easy questions first, know if there is a guessing penalty, avoid changing your answers, and write clearly and neatly.

5. You can use these strategies for every type of test you take. They may not work all the time, but they work most of the time.

Success Skills

Answer the following questions based on the information you learned in this chapter.

1. What is stress? Give an example of good and bad stress.

2. How might your reaction to taking a test affect your ability to be successful?

3. How can you reduce testing stress?

4. What does "preview the playing field" mean?

5. What do think "pretend as if" means in relation to test taking?

6. Of the ten rules for test taking, which ones are easiest to remember?

7. What did you learn about taking objective tests?

8. What did you learn about taking subjective tests?

9. What did you learn about taking performance tests?

10. Using the suggested web links, find at least one more testing rule or strategy not mentioned in this chapter.

Case 1

Teresa hated taking any kind of test. She often had trouble sleeping for several nights before a test, which made her cranky and unpleasant to be around. The day of a test, she usually woke up with a blinding headache. Teresa never ate before a test, even though she knew she needed energy to do well. She said her stomach was tied in knots, and she was afraid eating would make her feel worse. Because of these reactions, Teresa passed up promotional opportunities that required taking qualifying tests, even though friends told her the tests were not difficult.

1. Brainstorm ways Teresa could reduce her test stress. Think of some unique approaches she could take to manage her stress reactions before a test.

2. Which of the "general rules of the game" would be most useful to Teresa when she finally takes a test? Specifically, how would these rules help her manage her stress during a test?

Case 2

Teresa learned some techniques for reducing her stress reactions before a test. As a result, she signed up to take two qualifying tests for a certification. If she performed well, her name would be added to the list of high potentials, people to be considered for promotions. She was very excited and positive about finally making it to this list. Nonetheless, she was worried about the types of questions that she would be asked. When Teresa was given the booklet that contained the test questions, she saw fill-in-the-blank, multiple-choice, and true-false questions.

1. Which type of question should she answer first, second, and last? Why did you choose this order?

2. At the end of Teresa's qualifying test, there was an optional essay question for extra credit. It asked the test taker to evaluate the first three sections of the test. Teresa decided to write an essay in response. What strategies should she keep in mind as she begins her essay? How would these strategies help her earn the extra points she wants?

Angel, who has been a sales representative for a food service company for six years, enjoys the time he spends with his customers. His paycheck covers his family's monthly expenses, but not many extras. He wants more for himself and his family. Unfortunately, he cannot move up until he gets additional education. Last year he returned to school to take classes toward a business degree.

One day the head of the sales department calls him into his office and describes a restructuring of the sales department that provides an opportunity for Angel. Because of his experience and career ambition, Angel is asked to head up a team that will develop a customer response plan. The purpose of the plan is to make the sales department more responsive to outside customers and to departments inside the company.

Angel thinks, "This project could give me good experience and set me up for a promotion. It would also be a great case study for my business classes. But I don't know where to start!"

Have you ever faced an important project and, like Angel, wondered where, when, and how to start? What might he do to get started?

In This Chapter

11.1 What Are Critical and Creative Thinking?

11.2 The Critical Mind

11.3 The Creative Mind

11.4 Improving Life Through Critical and Creative Thinking

Chapter Goals

After studying and working with the information in this chapter, you should be able to:

♦ Define critical thinking and creative thinking.

♦ Describe the differences in critical and creative thinking.

♦ Identify situations requiring critical and creative thinking.

♦ Use a variety of thinking skills for problem solving.

♦ Demonstrate greater confidence in your own thinking processes.

Think about an important purchase you have made, such as a car, a bicycle, an engagement ring, or another big-ticket item. How much time did you spend considering the cost and the best value? Have you ever discussed a problem with a trusted friend, hoping to get good advice? Have you ever had to decide which school to attend or which organization to join?

If your answer to any of these questions is yes, then you have used critical and creative thinking. Thinking critically and creatively is as natural for the mind as movement is for the body. Both are improved with know-how, practice, and good coaching.

This is a know-how, practice, and coaching chapter for improving your critical and creative thinking. By studying the material, you will better understand how you think, and you will gain confidence in your thinking ability. In addition, you will learn to appreciate the importance of effective thinking in today's world.

> " Today, intellectual capital has replaced equipment and muscle power as the most valuable resource for market viability. Intellectual capital is more than research development. It is the brainpower of everyone in the organization. "
>
> —Diane L. Alexander
>   President of MindWorks, Inc.

SELF-CHECK

The following self-evaluation will give you an idea of how familiar, or unfamiliar, you are with some of the topics and terms discussed in this chapter. After reading each statement, circle the letter Y, S, or N to indicate the answer that is most appropriate for you. Answer honestly; rate yourself at the end; then complete the information for Chapter 11 in Appendix A.

Y = yes; frequently	S = sometimes	N = no; never

1. I regularly analyze my thinking process.	Y	S	N
2. I can define critical thinking and creative thinking.	Y	S	N
3. I know what metacognition means.	Y	S	N
4. I know the difference between divergent and convergent thinking.	Y	S	N
5. I know at least four guidelines for critical thinking.	Y	S	N
6. I can identify common thinking errors in advertising and political speeches.	Y	S	N
7. I can recognize the difference between facts and opinions.	Y	S	N
8. I take time to use thinking skills when I solve problems.	Y	S	N
9. I know the four rules of brainstorming.	Y	S	N
10. I realize that know-how and practice can improve thinking.	Y	S	N

Rate Yourself:

Number of Ys	_____	x	100	=	_____	
Number of Ss	_____	x	50	=	_____	
Number of Ns	_____	x	0	=	_____	Total _____

Chapter 11: Using Your Critical and Creative Mind

11.1 WHAT ARE CRITICAL AND CREATIVE THINKING?

The use of critical and creative thinking skills is an important part of learning and living. In the past, most work was done by hand, and individuals followed their boss's instructions. Today more and more employers look for workers with good thinking skills. People work in teams; they use highly technical equipment such as computers, robots, and communications links; and they often make decisions that were assigned to supervisors only a few years ago.

This new workplace requires brainpower; that is, employees who have skills in critical and creative thinking—people who can decide what needs to be done and create ways to do it. When you use critical and creative thinking, you *think* about your thinking. This is called **metacognition**.

Critical and creative thinking are similar yet different. The following explanations will help you understand the difference.

1. **Critical thinking** means *thinking about thinking in order to decide what to believe and how to behave.*

2. **Creative thinking** means *thinking about thinking in order to bring something new into existence, such as an idea, an event, or an object.*

Both types of thinking ask you to stop, reflect, and plan before you act. When you use *critical thinking*, you think about things that *already* exist, and you wonder how to react to them. For example, when a doctor decides which critically ill heart-transplant patient should get an available heart, he or she uses critical thinking. When you *think creatively*, you think about the need for something that *doesn't yet exist*! Inventors are a good example of people who use creative thinking.

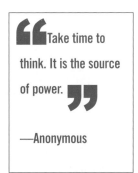
" Take time to think. It is the source of power. "

—Anonymous

Common Characteristics of Critical and Creative Thinking

Critical and creative thinking share five attributes. Knowing these common characteristics will be helpful.

1. Both critical and creative thinking are processes (ways of doing things) that are used to solve problems.

2. Both critical and creative thinking are time consuming.

3. Both critical and creative thinking aim for solutions or outcomes.

4. Both critical and creative thinking can be improved through knowledge, practice, and coaching.

5. Critical and creative thinking work together for effective problem solving.

Angel, at the beginning of this chapter, has to develop a plan to make the sales department more responsive to customers and other departments. The plan has to be created, which requires *creative thinking*. To create the plan, Angel must learn what policies already exist in the sales department, gain information about customers, and identify ways to help other departments. In creating the plan, he must consider how to work with what already exists. That is *critical thinking*.

Angel's case shows how critical and creative thinking work together for effective problem solving (Attribute 5). Take a few minutes to write your thoughts below about the other four attributes as they relate to Angel's problem.

1. In what ways is the project a process? _____
   _____

2. In what ways will the project be time-consuming? _____
   _____

3. What are some possible products or outcomes of the project? _____
   _____

4. What skills might improve Angel's ability to do the project? _____
   _____

Now think about tasks in your own life that require critical thinking and creative thinking. List two tasks below; then analyze each to determine when you would use critical thinking and when you would use creative thinking. Examples of tasks include planning your course of study, writing a paper, giving a party, and organizing a sales campaign.

Task 1: _____

1. Processes—What do you have to do? _____

2. Time—How much time do you estimate it will take? _____

3. Products—What are some possible outcomes? _____

4. Skills—What skills are needed? _____

5. Critical Thinking—Which aspect is critical thinking?
   (Hint: decision-making) _____

6. Creative Thinking—Which aspect is creative thinking?
   (Hint: being open to possibilities) _____

Task 2: _____

1. Processes—What do you have to do? _____

2. Time—How much time do you estimate it will take? _____

3. Products—What are some possible outcomes? _____

4. Skills—What skills are needed?_____

5. Critical Thinking—Which aspect is critical thinking?
   (Hint: decision making) _____

6. Creative Thinking—Which aspect is creative thinking?
   (Hint: being open to possibilities) _____

Thinking Takes Time

As you can see from Angel's and your own examples, thinking is a time-consuming process that involves doing something. Effective thinking often takes time, yet you are used to things happening quickly in life. Because technology allows the events of everyday life to move at a fast pace, you usually get fast results. Stopping to think can feel dull and boring.

Metacognition can help you here. When you are involved in tasks requiring critical and creative thinking and you get feelings of "too slow," "boring," and "too much trouble," use these feelings as signals that you need to slow down. Be metacognitive, and tell yourself that your reactions are normal but out of place when you need to solve a complex problem or reach a difficult decision.

> " We are what we think. All that we are arises with our thoughts. With our thoughts we make the world. "
>
> —Buddha
>   Indian religious leader

Smart Tip

"Thinking about thinking" was given the term *metacognition* in 1979 by John Flavell, a former professor of psychology at Stanford. The term comes from *meta*, which means "beyond" and *cognition*, which means "thinking." The regular use of metacognition will improve your thinking.

Checkpoint 11.1

1. Create your own definition of critical thinking.

2. Create your own definition of creative thinking.

3. In what ways are critical and creative thinking similar? In what ways are they different?

11.2 THE CRITICAL MIND

Critical thinking focuses on the here and now. When you think critically, you concern yourself with what you think is happening and how you will deal with a given situation. How you behave depends on your beliefs. Critical thinking concerns beliefs and behaviors.

Beliefs are interpretations, evaluations, conclusions, and predictions you consider to be true. If you believe that women are not mechanically inclined, you may not think a woman can change a car's spark plus. If you have failed mathematics in the past, you may have mistakingly concluded that you can't do math.

Your beliefs guide your behaviors. The physical and mental skills you've acquired, such as driving a car or reciting the multiplication tables, were influenced by your belief that they were important. The only behaviors not influenced by beliefs are those that are automatic (that is, bodily functions and reflexes).

ACTIVITY 2

Write possible behaviors related to the beliefs listed below. Add a few beliefs and behaviors of your own to the list.

Belief	Possible Behaviors
1. I'm not a great golfer. I doubt I'll ever do better than John.	_____
2. I'm a good cook.	_____
3. I don't understand what's going on, so I must be stupid.	_____
4. I've worked hard for my money, so I can spend it however I want.	_____
5. Living in the north is too cold for me.	_____
6. _____	_____
7. _____	_____

Prioritize the following behaviors (or situations) you may experience, with 1 being very important and 5 being unimportant. List your beliefs that will guide each behavior.

Behavior (Situation)	Priority	My Belief
1. Making a career change	_____	_____
2. Deciding what to wear to a dinner in my honor	1	*If I change jobs, I'll make more money. I might be happier.*
3. Organizing my collection of photographs	_____	_____
4. Selecting a mate	_____	_____
5. Attending a school reunion	_____	_____
6. Deciding how to vote	_____	_____

Why and When to Think Critically

You need critical thinking to help you solve problems or make decisions that are important to you. Many common behaviors, such as bathing and eating, don't require daily critical thinking. You perform them based on previously established beliefs.

Being in new situations calls for critical thinking. Seeing new products, hearing dramatic news stories, and experiencing personal or work problems all require you to decide what you believe.

You trust your instructors because they are experts in their fields. You trust the references libraries have to offer because libraries must meet professional standards for selecting and purchasing their books. When you read, however, you must decide whether to believe the author.

♦ Is the author of a book a recognized authority on the subject?
♦ Are the author's credentials cited?
♦ Is the work of other experts referenced in the material?

When you research on the Internet, you ultimately decide what to believe because information sources are unknown. (See Chapter 12 for more information.)

How Do You Think Critically?

While you can't be sure critical thinking will provide correct answers, you can avoid obvious mistakes in thinking. First, metacognate.

When you have a problem to solve or a decision to make, think about your thinking. Sleep on it, count to ten, or use some other method to give yourself time to think. You need to be able to calm your brain because many situations requiring critical thinking are emotionally upsetting. The part of the brain that thinks critically does not function at its best under stress, time pressure, or emotional shock.

The following six guidelines can help you develop your critical-thinking ability. They were adapted by Louise Loomis from material written by Anita Harnadeck.

1. Be open-minded about new ideas.

2. Know when you need more information.

3. Be aware that different people have different ideas about the meanings of words, expressions, gestures, etc.

4. Know the difference between something that must be true and something that might be true.

5. Separate emotional and logical thinking.

6. Develop your vocabulary in order to understand others and to make yourself understood.

By using these six guidelines, you can increase your self-esteem because you will feel mentally competent in many situations. The guidelines will be helpful for:

♦ Identifying situations that can be improved by critical thinking.
♦ Developing conscious attention to your thinking (metacognition).
♦ Increasing your confidence about your thinking.
♦ Avoiding harmful gossip and futile arguments.

Review the descriptions of the six critical-thinking guidelines given below. Discuss them with your coworkers or classmates, and relate them to examples from real life. Answer the questions that follow each guideline.

1. Be open-minded to new ideas.

   The world is changing rapidly, and a lot of ideas are floating around. It is important to become open-minded in order to survive. While resistance to new ideas is natural, being open-minded takes practice.

   Learning is the continuous exposure to new ideas by breaking old habits and ways of thought. What new ideas or information have you learned recently? _____

   _____

   _____

2. Know when you need more information.

   Do you ever feel incompetent or inadequate? Chances are you just need more information. Calmly say to yourself, "I need more information!" Locate the background knowledge you need, and eliminate the negative self-talk.

   When was the last time something didn't make sense to you? How did you feel? What did you do? What will you do in the future?_____

   _____

   _____

3. Be aware that different people have different ideas about the meanings of words, gestures, expressions, and other communication signals.

   This guideline is also known as "diff'rent strokes for diff'rent folks." It's easy to get angry when others see things differently from you. Just be open-minded to new ideas, count to ten, and hear the speaker out. This is a heavy-duty metacognitive guideline. Use it to avoid unpleasantness, fights, and violence.

   a. Think of a time when someone disagreed with you. What happened? How did you feel? What did you do? _____

   _____

   _____

   b. Think of a time when you were with people who dressed or acted differently from you: What happened? How did you feel? What did you do? _____ _____

   _____

   _____

   c. How can Guideline 3 help you deal with other people? _____

   _____

   _____

4. Know the difference between something that must be true and something that might be true.

This helps you separate facts (must be's) from opinions (might be's). This is a useful technique for dealing with rumor, gossip, and the Internet. When someone makes a statement, ask yourself if the statement is a fact (must be) or an opinion (might be), and look for evidence to support or refute the statement.

Which of the following statements are "must be's" (facts), and which are "might be's" (opinions)?

a. Albany is the capital of New York State. _____

b. New York City should be the capital. _____

c. Newton is a great scientist because he discovered the law of gravity. _____

d. The woman standing next to me in line must be upset about the wait because she looks angry. _____

e. My friend is always late when we meet; I must not be important to him. _____

5. Separate emotional and logical thinking.

Recent research about the brain has revealed that people have emotional responses to all situations in their lives. Good critical thinking invites you to combine emotions and logic to make decisions and solve problems. Acknowledging and managing feelings is called "emotional intelligence" and is commonly talked about in schools and the workplace.

Guideline 5 suggests that you constantly collect both logical and emotional information in situations that require critical thinking. For example, your logic may tell you that the red shirt is a better buy than the blue one. But if you don't like the red shirt (an emotional response), purchasing it will be a waste of time and money and a source of regret if you never wear it.

If you are in school, you may receive some grades that make you unhappy. While you use your logic to evaluate your mistakes and make plans to improve your work, you might find that supportive friends and family help you express your feelings and recover from your disappointment.

What are your emotional and logical thoughts about the following situations?

	Emotional	Logical
Writing a long paper or document	_____	_____
Preparing for an oral presentation	_____	_____
Making plans for a vacation	_____	_____
Telling your boss about a mistake you made	_____	_____

6. Develop your vocabulary in order to understand others and make yourself understood.

Chapter 8 discusses how to build vocabulary. Use its tips and guidelines to enjoy the power of a large vocabulary. Your reading and learning will be easier and faster. The brain loves words. Feed it!

How do you keep track of new words? _____

_____

_____

Mistakes in Critical Thinking

So many mistakes in critical thinking are made by people that numerous books have been written about the topic. Though you will make mistakes on your own, the actions and words of other people often contribute to your mistakes. By being aware of how others influence your thinking process, you will be able to judge situations more clearly and come to better decisions. Some of the most common mistakes in thinking are described in the following paragraphs.

Mistakes in thinking are called **fallacies**. They distract you from making decisions based on critical thinking. Several fallacies are described below.

Peer pressure

Peer pressure causes you to go along with the crowd in order to be accepted or popular.

Example: "Ling and I are skipping class tonight to go to the hockey game. Aren't you coming with us?"

Horse laugh

Horse laugh refers to making fun of someone or something when you disagree. This fallacy is best communicated by one's tone of voice or body language.

Example: Wallie is talking to a co-worker, and the coworker says, "*You* are doing *that* project?"

Two wrongs make a right

This refers to returning an insult with an insult.

Example: "My coworker invited everyone to her party but me, so I'm not going to help with her project."

Hasty generalization

This refers to making a decision too quickly.

Example: "I know I just met him, but I don't like him" or "I tried playing tennis once, and I'm not going to try it again."

Name calling

Name calling substitutes a personal insult for a direct response.

Example: Joe says, "Being metacognitive about studying is a great help." Pat responds, "That's a typical nerd statement if I ever heard one."

Scare tactics, appeals to pity, and apple polishing

These fallacies all focus on emotional thinking and ignore logic.

Scare Tactics Example: "We, the membership committee of the Sigma Club, see in your application that you've been very active with the student newspaper. Did you know that our club president was kicked off *your* paper's editorial board last year?"

Appeal to Pity Example: "Professor Amato, please let me hand in my paper tomorrow. I had to take care of my grandmother last night. When I finally started typing, I ran out of paper, and it was too late to buy any. If you accept my paper late, I'll be able to stay off probation."

Apple Polishing Example: "Hamid, please let me photocopy your notes to study for the exam. Your handwriting is so much neater than mine, and you always get more out of Professor Smith's lectures than I do."

False dilemma

People use a false dilemma to make you think there are only two choices in a situation—the one they favor and an unappealing alternative.

> *Example*: The statement "Strong men watch wrestling on TV, so what's the matter with you?" is intended to make you think you aren't strong if you don't enjoy professional wrestling. Actually, one has little to do with the other; there are many ways to be strong. People often combine peer pressure, mentioned earlier, with the false dilemma tactic.

Slippery slope

People tend to use slippery slope thinking in situations involving change. Claims are made that the change will lead to many more changes and that the end result will be bad.

> *Example*: "If we let you have two excused absences, then you'll want three. Before we know it, all of our absentee standards will have disappeared."

Begging the question

This is also known as "circular reasoning." The same statement gets repeated with different words, but nothing is added to the meaning. This is very popular in advertisements.

> *Example*: "Athletes need a good, healthy diet. Therefore, it's important to pay attention to what you eat if you want to perform well in sports."

Straw person

Have you ever had someone disagree with you by changing your statement? The changed statement is the "straw person." Notice how the brother changed the one time clean-up request in the following example to a daily one.

> *Example*: You ask your brother to help you clean the bathroom. He says he can't clean it every day. It's too much work and a waste of time.

Testimonial

Using someone of status to convince others of the "right" thing to do is one of the most common fallacies used in advertising and political campaigns.

> *Example*: Famous people (prestige identification) or people just like you (ordinary people) tell you how great something is: "Buy it!" "Vote for it!"

Smart Tip

Critical-thinking guidelines for using the Internet:

- Ask your librarian for reliable reference sources.
- Look for reference sources on the web sites of libraries in major metropolitan areas, such as Boston (www.bpl.org), New York (www.nypl.org), Chicago (www.chipublib.org), and Philadelphia (www.library.phila.gov).
- Consider the source of the web site for reliability and point of view, such as government (.gov), a company (.com), an educational institution (.edu), or an organization (.org).
- Check on the credentials of the web site's author. Is the person a recognized, authentic expert?

Review the examples of the thinking mistakes listed below. Match each fallacy with its example by placing the correct letter on the answer line. (Answers are given in Appendix F.)

Fallacy

_____ 1. Two wrongs make a right

_____ 2. Hasty generalization

_____ 3. Peer pressure

_____ 4. Apple polishing

_____ 5. Horse laugh

_____ 6. Scare tactics

_____ 7. Slippery slope

_____ 8. Begging the question

_____ 9. Straw person

_____ 10. Name calling

Example

a. One look at that woman's clothes, and I knew we had nothing in common.

b. I'd like to have you on my committee. You're always on time, you have lots of ideas, and you are great on the phone.

c. José, tell me how to do this assignment. I need to get a good grade. If you help, I won't tell your girlfriend I saw you out with Susannah.

d. After Anita ruined my dress and made no effort to replace it, I had no problem borrowing her cashmere sweater without asking her permission.

e. I don't know if we should admit anyone under 25 to this club. The next thing you know, they'll be running everything their way and older people will all quit.

f. Recycling in this town? You've got to be kidding. What a joke.

g. Antonio says that regular planning helps him keep on top of his studies. That's too much work for me. I can't be bothered jotting things down every five minutes.

h. You don't have a laptop computer? Everyone I know owns one.

i. That's just like a freshman to ask the way to the bookstore.

j. Keeping an up-to-date assignment book helps you remember your assignments. You won't forget your homework if you write your assignments all in the same place.

Point of View

The fallacies you've been learning are frequently used by people who want to persuade you to believe or do something. They have a particular point of view, and their message to you is tilted to favor that point of view. That tilt is called **bias**. Two common groups of persuaders in American society are politicians and advertisers. Politicians want you to vote for them. Advertisers want you to buy their products or support their cause.

In order to be influenced, a persuader only shows you a part of the picture (that's the bias) or a point of view he or she thinks you will like. Presenting part of a picture is called **card stacking**. The persuader only shows you the cards he or she has chosen instead of the full deck.

Several of the critical-thinking guidelines can help you with bias. *Know when you need more information* (Guideline 2) is something to keep in mind when you suspect the persuader is stacking the cards. *Separate emotional and logical thinking* (Guideline 5) when you sense that the persuader is appealing to your emotions —greed, fear, pity—and is omitting a logical approach. *Know the difference between something that must be true and something that might be true* (Guideline 4) when the persuader is making statements that are not backed by any proof. *Build up your vocabulary* (Guideline

6) when the persuader uses unfamiliar words and terms.

Looking for points of view is a critical-thinking strategy. While it is easy to believe people who share your point of view, *remember to be open-minded to new ideas* (Guideline 1). Consider using other points of view and accepting people who have them.

Points of view connect with what you believe is important in life. Because what's important carries feelings, part of your critical thinking is always connected to your feelings. Your brain has emotional and logical responses. A careful thinker notices how feelings are involved in problem solving and decision making.

Most sources of information have points of view. This book, for example, is biased in favor of studying and learning. The author values learning and believes that education is important and that everyone can learn how to learn.

> " Brainpower and creativity are the currency of today's Knowledge Age. "
>
> —Diane L. Alexander, President MindWorks, Inc.

1. Describe the point of view of a person who would not want to use this book.

   _____

   _____

   _____

2. Describe the points of view of someone who pierces parts of his or her body and someone who does not.

   _____

   _____

   _____

3. Describe the points of view of an employee who feels he or she deserves a raise and the boss who disagrees.

   _____

   _____

   _____

Checkpoint 11.2

1. In what situations might you think critically?

2. List as many of the six guidelines for critical thinking as you can remember.

3. Describe at least three fallacies, and explain their role in critical thinking.

11.3 THE CREATIVE MIND

As you might recall from earlier in this chapter, creative thinking means "thinking about thinking in order to bring something new into existence." This new thing can be an idea, a plan, an event, an object, a book, a play, a research paper, or a process. It's important to know that:

♦ You are a natural creative thinker because creative thinking is part of being human.
♦ You can improve your creative thinking by learning about it.
♦ You don't have to be artistic to be a creative thinker.

There are lots of ways to think creatively, and you will learn some of them in this section.

WHY AND WHEN YOU NEED CREATIVE THINKING

You use creative thinking when you need choices for solving a specific problem. Several situations requiring creative thinking are listed.

♦ When something you care about isn't working out the way you want
Example: You haven't found enough reference material for your research paper.

♦ When you want to think of ways to deal with bad situations
Example: You have a flat tire on your way to class.

♦ When you want to change the way you are doing something
Example: You are chair of an important committee, and the meetings are too long, are poorly attended, and are inefficient.

Creative thinking and critical thinking are similar. You use them in daily life to assist in problem solving and decision making. Critical thinking leads to creative thinking, and creative thinking leads to critical thinking. For example, your critical thinking tells you that you need to study more to get better grades. Your creative thinking comes up with ideas for increasing your study time. Then your critical thinking selects the best ideas. Finally, your fear of failure drives you to do the necessary work.

ACTIVITY 6

Many common daily activities that engage you in creative thinking are listed below. Describe why they require creative thinking. Can you list more?

Driving in heavy traffic _____

Deciding what to cook or eat for dinner _____

Allocating time for studying and reading _____

Responding to criticism _____

Playing a strategic game such as chess or checkers _____

_____

_____

Success Skills

How Do You Think Creatively?

You can do creative thinking alone or with others. In either case, your goal is to bring something new into existence, such as an idea, an event, a plan, an object, or a process. Creative thinking consists of five stages. Knowing about these stages can help you improve your creative thinking.

Stage 1

Insight—Insight occurs when you realize you need to think creatively about some-thing in your life that isn't working right. You want or need to do something about it. Insight can come from within ("My study skills need improvement") or from outside ("My sociology paper is due next week.").

Stage 2

Preparation—Preparation refers to naming or identifying your specific problem and gathering information. Preparation time varies based on available resources.

Stage 3

Incubation—Incubation is the mulling-things-over stage. For example, you may have researched a paper or project and are now thinking about how to organize all the information and present the topic. What are its main ideas? What important points should be included? What can be omitted?

For scientists, incubation is a period of puzzling over the meaning of new evidence gathered during the preparation stage that doesn't fit previous explanations.

Incubation time varies from a few minutes or days to many years in some instances. "Sleep on it" is an incubation term. Often when you wake up, you have a solution or an inspiration.

Stage 4

Inspiration —Inspiration often comes in a quick flash of knowing. Suddenly you "see" a way to solve your problem. It's frequently called the "Aha!" experience. Your inspiration makes you feel good because you realize you can solve your problem.

Inspiration doesn't produce a sociology paper, nor does it complete a work project. Instead, inspiration tells you how to approach the paper (what the theme will be, what you should include, and the sequence

Smart Tip

Famous scholars are awarded sabbaticals and grants for time and support while they study and complete research in preparation for writing a book or carrying out a project. Often this is the only way they can do the preparation part of their creative work.

Chapter 11: Using Your Critical and Creative Mind

sequence of thought) and how to proceed on your project (calling those who can help, getting the boss's support, researching additional information). The next step, actualization, actually gets the paper written and the project completed.

Stage 5

Actualization —Actualization is the heavy-duty work that makes your inspiration a reality. It can be very time-consuming and is often accomplished in long intensive hours of continuous work called massed practice. You get all your research together and work through the process. In school, writing marathons are often called "all-nighters." At work, getting a project realized means hours of overtime.

ACTIVITY 7

Below are examples of the stages in the creative process as they relate to writing a paper. Read each example and write in the name of the stage it represents.

1. _____ You're stuck. You have found a lot of information about American women in World War II, but you can't decide which aspect to focus on.

2. _____ Your sociology instructor has assigned a paper on World War II. You realize you want to write about American women in World War II because you've heard about them from your grandmother.

3. _____ You've got it! Your grandmother was a WAC (Women's Army Corps). You're going to write about women in the Army in World War II. You'll use anecdotes and other materials from your grandmother in addition to information from library and Internet research.

4. _____ You are gathering information for a paper about the role of American women in World War II.

5. _____ Now the process of writing the paper has begun. You select information from your original research, determine what additional information you need, and organize your findings into an outline. You also assemble a bibliography.

Success Skills

Divergent and Convergent Thinking

Both convergent and divergent thinking are necessary for real-life problem solving and decision making. **Divergent thinking**, mostly related to creative thinking, is thinking aimed at finding many possible answers. **Convergent thinking**, mostly related to critical thinking, looks for correct answers or guides us toward selecting from many possible answers.

The answer to the question "What work did American women do during World War II?" requires divergent thinking, while the answers to "What does WAC stand for?" and "Which aspect of American women shall I write about?" require convergent thinking.

In Chapter 2, you identified your learning style as leaning toward either sequential or random learning. A preference toward random learning generally means you find strength and comfort in divergent thinking (more creative), while a preference toward sequential learning generally means you find strength and comfort in convergent thinking (more critical). Since everyone possesses qualities of both types of learners, everyone is able to think both creatively and critically.

ACTIVITY 8

Write six questions that require divergent thinking and six that require convergent thinking.

Divergent Thinking Questions

1. _____
2. _____
3. _____
4. _____
5. _____
6. _____

Convergent Thinking Questions

1. _____
2. _____
3. _____
4. _____
5. _____
6. _____

Chapter 11: Using Your Critical and Creative Mind

The Brainstorming Process

Brainstorming, one of the oldest and most widely used divergent thinking skills, is an open-minded process to come up with as many ideas as possible on a topic as quickly as possible. Many people enjoy brainstorming and often do it just for fun.

Brainstorming's inventor, Alex Osborn, is one of the great names in the field of creativity and creative thinking. He and J. Guilford, creator of the concepts of divergent and convergent thinking, are considered founding fathers in this field.

Many people are familiar with the term brainstorming but don't really know how to do it correctly. You can do brainstorming alone or with others. Both ways can be productive if you follow the guidelines and establish the proper environment. Here are four guidelines for brainstorming:

1. *Defer any kind of judgment.*
   This is the most important guideline. When coming up with possible ideas, don't judge them for value. Doing so slows things down and inhibits the production of ideas. Let the ideas flow.

2. *Aim for quantity, not quality.*
   Try to get at least 20 ideas. The first few ideas will be the most familiar. Pressure to produce more ideas forces new ways of thinking, which is what you're after.

3. *Accept wacky ideas.*
   These ideas often open the way to new insights and lead to practical adaptations.

4. *Piggyback.*
   Build on your own and others' ideas. This is not copying. If an idea comes up twice, make no comment. Just record it. The person you presented it to may be on a train of thought that will lead to new ideas.

Establishing the right environment for brainstorming is just as important as following the guidelines. Here are some tips:

♦ Review the four guidelines before starting.
♦ Set an established time and place.
♦ Plan to brainstorm for 15 to 30 minutes.
♦ Set up groups of no more than seven so everyone can talk. Permit no interruptions and no socializing.
♦ Work rapidly, with one participant recording the ideas. (Note: This person can also receive ideas from people after the session.)
♦ Set up the room so people can sit comfortably in circles.
♦ Value the process, and thank participants for their help.
♦ Report later to participants on the outcomes of the brainstorming session.

> " You see things and you ask, "Why?" But I dream things that never were and ask, Why not? "
>
> —George Bernard Shaw
> Author and playwright

Focus on Ethics

You ordered one bookcase from an online store. The store's delivery company called you to arrange delivery. It arrived on time; you put it together and are using it. A week later, to your surprise, the delivery company is calling again to arrange delivery of your bookcase. What should you do?

To practice brainstorming, follow the instructions in each section below. If possible, work with a group, following the tips described on the previous page. Otherwise, write your own brainstorming ideas.

1. Warm up by naming ten things that:

   are green.

   _____ _____ _____ _____ _____

   _____ _____ _____ _____ _____

   have wheels.

   _____ _____ _____ _____ _____

   _____ _____ _____ _____ _____

   have push buttons.

   _____ _____ _____ _____ _____

   _____ _____ _____ _____ _____

2. Now list ten uses for:

   a paper clip.

   _____ _____ _____ _____ _____

   _____ _____ _____ _____ _____

   a plastic bag.

   _____ _____ _____ _____ _____

   _____ _____ _____ _____ _____

   an aluminum pie plate.

   _____ _____ _____ _____ _____

   _____ _____ _____ _____ _____

3. List as many ways as possible to use:

   a stack of wire coat hangers.

   _____ _____ _____ _____ _____

   _____ _____ _____ _____ _____

   _____ _____ _____ _____ _____

   _____ _____ _____ _____ _____

   _____ _____ _____ _____ _____

   _____ _____ _____ _____ _____

   a paper clip.

   _____ _____ _____ _____ _____

   _____ _____ _____ _____ _____

   _____ _____ _____ _____ _____

   _____ _____ _____ _____ _____

   _____ _____ _____ _____ _____

Smart Tip

Alex Osborn invented brainstorming in 1948. In the 1950s, Osborn and his colleagues were busy using brainstorming with companies such as General Motors, DuPont, and General Electric. Brainstorming is still widely used today. You can brainstorm any time you need a lot of ideas to help you come up with a new approach to some situation.

ACTIVITY 10

Using the four brainstorming guidelines, practice brainstorming ideas for the following real-life problem. Write down your brainstorming ideas.

Wilhemina is in Angel's Organizational Development class at business school. Team projects are a feature of this course. One evening, Wilhemina approaches Angel to discuss a problem she has with a person on her project team. The person has skipped many meetings, has not shown any progress on his part of the project, and can't be reached by telephone. The project is worth 25 percent of Wilhemina's grade and is due in two weeks. What should she do?

_____

_____

_____

_____

_____

_____

Checkpoint 11.3

1. What is creative thinking?

2. What are the five stages in the creative-thinking process?

3. What are the four guidelines for brainstorming?

11.4 IMPROVING LIFE THROUGH CRITICAL AND CREATIVE THINKING

All of the thinking skills you've learned and practiced in this chapter can improve your life by helping you solve problems, make decisions, and get things done. Here are a few ways to apply the information to improve the quality of your thinking and your life.

1. Be metacognitive in difficult situations.
2. Use the guidelines for critical thinking.
3. Avoid mistakes in thinking.
4. Find reliable resources on the Internet.
5. Honor the stages of the creative process.
6. Brainstorm.
7. Give yourself time to think.

The 20-Minute Problem-Solving Model

Now it's time to put the thinking skills to good use with a model of Creative Problem Solving. You may get some inspirational solutions and come up with a satisfactory result. Though you can use this model by yourself, it is easier to learn the process by working with one or two other people. One person identifies a problem and the others help solve it. Follow these steps:

Step 1

Describe the problem to the other people for five minutes. Say everything you can about the problem. Remember the 5Ws and H: Who? What? When? Where? Why? and How? What led to the problem? What are the consequences? What are your feelings? What are the feelings of others? If you run out of things to say, start repeating things you said before. Just keep talking for five minutes. Let the others listen and take notes.

Step 2

Allow the others to ask you questions for five minutes; then answer their questions. Some suggested questions: What do you really want? Is this a new problem? If the problem occurred before, how did you and others react? How has it worked out?

Step 3

In the group, brainstorm ideas for solutions for five minutes. One of the other two participants records the ideas for you.

Step 4

Select the ideas that seem best to you. If you want, you can ask the others for suggestions, but you don't have to. If you don't ask them, they are not allowed to volunteer their ideas. As a group, develop a plan of action.

People are always amazed at what they can accomplish with this 20-minute creative problem-solving process. The most difficult part is the first five minutes. It's often hard for the problem owner to talk for five minutes and for the listeners to stay quiet! But it keeps everyone focused, and no time is wasted on socializing.

Checkpoint 11.4

1. What are the seven thinking skills that improve your life?

2. Describe the 20-minute Creative Problem-Solving Model.

3. Why is it important to spend time identifying a problem?

WEB LINK

www.brain.com

This site has dozens of articles about the brain, including articles on creativity, memory, and IQ intelligence. It also offers a range of online timed tests on intelligence, mental performance, memory, emotional state, and more.

www.coun.uvic.ca/learn/crit.html

This web site contains more information on the critical-thinking guidelines.

Key Terms and Concepts

appeals to pity

apple polishing

begging the question

beliefs

bias

brainstorming

card stacking

creative thinking

critical thinking

convergent thinking

divergent thinking

fallacies

false dilemma

hasty generalization

horse laugh

metacognition

name calling

peer pressure

scare tactics

slippery slope

straw person

testimonial

two wrongs make a right

Chapter Summary

1. Critical and creative thinking are important because they help you with the decision-making and problem-solving tasks of your life.

2. Critical and creative thinking skills are important because they slow you down when you need to solve a difficult problem or make a difficult decision. When you slow down, your brain is more at ease and can do its best work for you.

3. You need to use critical and creative thinking for success in school and at home. In addition, you need these skills in your career because today's workplace requires people who are effective thinkers and effective problem solvers.

4. When you are mindful of your thinking (metacognitive), you can improve the quality of your thinking.

5. Critical thinking asks you to stop and think, especially when you need to make important decisions. Not necessarily believing everything you read and hear, using the guidelines for critical thinking, and being aware of fallacies and points of view can help you think clearly and effectively.

6. Creative thinking goes through five stages: insight, preparation, incubation, inspiration and actualization.

7. Divergent thinking asks you to find choices for solving problems, while convergent thinking asks you to make a decision from the choices.

8. Brainstorming is an open-minded process of coming up with many ideas on a topic as quickly as possible. The four brainstorming guidelines lead you through the process.

9. You can use the 20-minute Creative Problem-Solving Model to help you solve problems.

Review

Based on the information you learned in this chapter, use your own words to answer the following questions.

1. In your own words, what is critical thinking?

2. What are beliefs, and how are they important to critical thinking?

3. What is the relationship between metacognition and critical thinking?

4. Why is point of view important?

5. Describe a situation where you did some critical thinking.

6. Describe a situation where you did some creative thinking.

7. Give several examples of mistakes in thinking you have seen or heard.

8. When might you use brainstorming? List at least four situations.

9. Explain how creative and critical thinking can improve your life.

10. What have you learned from this chapter?

Case 1

Ted wanted to buy his best friend, Charlie, a really nice birthday gift, but he didn't have a great deal of money to spend. The first items he considered, a computer and an audio sound system, were way over his budget, even though he knew Charlie would appreciate them. "Charlie loves entertainment and electronic gadgets," Ted thought. "How can I come up with a good gift that meets one or both of those interests and still falls within my budget?"

1. Using your creative thinking, brainstorm 20 ways Ted can solve his dilemma. (One solution, for example, is looking for items at tag sales.)

2. Choose one interesting idea from your list that might lead to a good solution. Develop your idea so that Ted can use it to find an appropriate gift. Add details and specifics, such as skimming local newspapers for tag sales.

Case 2

Ted found a store that carried a large variety of items he knew Charlie would like. Many of the items were reasonably priced. As he looked at an electronic game that was within his budget, a salesperson approached him. "That's not very good quality," she said pointing to the game. "We have several better ones over here." The salesperson rattled off some technical terms about the better, more expensive items. Ted didn't understand the terms, but they sounded impressive. The salesperson finally added that one item (the most expensive) was the most popular, the best quality, and would make the nicest gift.

1. Using your critical thinking, what can you recommend Ted do to make a wise decision about his purchase?

2. How might Ted compare the different items to make his decision? What criteria should he use to make the best choice?

Michael, a college student, works part-time at a music store in the center of his small town. In the past year, store traffic has fallen off. Even the local college crowd has thinned out. The shop's owner, Art, worries about losing the store if

business continues to drop.

One afternoon, when no one is in the shop, Michael and Art talk about how to attract more business.

"Michael, why do you think the kids stopped coming in? Are my prices too high?" asks Art.

"It's not your prices; it's where you're located." Michael tells him.

"What do you mean? This store has been here for 35 years! It's been doing fine until now," said Art.

"What I mean is, your store is not located where everyone can easily shop. People of all ages now do much of their shopping on the World Wide Web. I know you've been resisting e-commerce, but you're missing out. The Web is the first place many people look to buy merchandise. Your competition is no longer local; it's global."

Since Art wants to keep his business alive, he decides to investigate selling music on the Web.

What does Michael mean when he says, "Your competition is no longer local; it is global"?

Chapter Goals

After studying and working with the information in this chapter, you should be able to:

♦ Describe the World Wide Web.
♦ Differentiate between a search engine and a directory.
♦ Use search features of the Web.
♦ Refine searches to locate exact information.
♦ Compare results from different services.
♦ Download text and pictures and understand copyright restrictions.
♦ Validate and evaluate web sources.
♦ Understand the challenges and risks of gathering information from the Web.

In This Chapter

By the late 1990s, practically every piece of information ever written was placed in some location on the World Wide Web. This means that all the information you might have looked for in a library is now available to you anywhere there's a computer with an Internet connection —on your desk at work or at home, and even in hotels and airports when you travel.

The main problem is: all the information in the world is an overwhelming amount of information. Finding the one piece of information you want in this giant pile is an art. To complicate things further, the tools for searching the Web change constantly. While this chapter was being written, two popular services closed down, and two new ones became available.

Using the Web is a key intellectual skill for now and the future. Consider this: you can use the Web to read Homer's *Odyssey* in Greek; trade stocks; find a job as an accountant anywhere in the world; compare car prices; get the latest news, weather, and entertainment; or locate a long-lost relative. The Web is a powerful research and information tool that is here to stay.

> " Almost over night, the Internet's gone from a technical wonder to a business must. "
>
> —Bill Schrader
> CEO of PSINet

The Internet has transformed the way we communicate and receive information.

SELF-CHECK

The following self-evaluation will give you an idea of how familiar, or unfamiliar, you are with some of the topics and terms discussed in this chapter. After reading each statement, circle the letter Y, S, or N to indicate the answer that is most appropriate for you. Answer honestly and rate yourself at the end; then complete the information for Chapter X in Appendix A.

Y = yes; frequently   S = sometimes   N = no; never

1. I understand what the World Wide Web is and what kind of information can be located on it.   Y   S   N

2. I know the difference between a search engine and a directory.   Y   S   N

3. I know how to use the basic search features of the Web.   Y   S   N

4. I know how to refine searches to locate exact information.   Y   S   N

5. I am able to analyze and compare the search results from different web services.   Y   S   N

6. I understand the copyright restrictions of downloading text and images from web sites.   Y   S   N

7. I know how to evaluate the validity of web sources.   Y   S   N

8. I know how to look for a job on the Web.   Y   S   N

9. I know how to create an educational report using web site sources.   Y   S   N

10. I feel confident that I know how to find information on the Web.   Y   S   N

Rate Yourself: Number of Ys   _____   x   100   =   _____

                            Number of Ss   _____   x   50   =   _____

                            Number of Ns   _____   x   0   =   _____   Total_____

12.1 WHAT IS THE INTERNET?

In the early 1970s, the U.S. Department of Defense commissioned a study on computer technology. The goal of the study was to develop a more secure computer-to-computer communication system, and from the study, the Internet was born. A communication system was developed that would allow information to be sent along a complex network of electronic paths. If one path or computer system was destroyed or unavailable, the information could still continue to travel along alternate paths to reach its intended destination. For two decades, this early Internet was used mainly by the military, universities, and scientists who were conducting research.

The **Internet** today is an international electronic network that is composed of thousands of smaller networks, including governmental, commercial, and educational networks. The Internet has been standardized to allow large computer networks to interconnect and communicate with one another. It has also evolved to allow users to post information on computers that others can visit—the first Internet sites.

Accessing information over the Internet has become much simpler due to the innovations of scientists such as Dr. Tim Berners-Lee. He came up with an easier way to navigate the Internet by enabling users to move from document to document by clicking highlighted words or phrases, known as **hyperlinks**. From this innovation, attractive graphics and mouse technology have been developed to provide a transmission mechanism for accessing information. Many users now use this mechanism, known as the **World Wide Web,** to access the information on the Internet. The World Wide Web, or the Web, is a huge system of linked resources that contain hyperlinks to other resources, or web sites.

Today, everything from cars to pizza is sold on the Internet. More than $1 billion a year is spent by people who buy goods online. About a hundred million people worldwide access the Internet, or "surf," for business and pleasure. The Internet contains millions of web sites—everything from major corporations and media outlets to second-grade classrooms and skateboarders' conventions. The Internet and the Web have transformed the ways we run businesses, conduct research, communicate, buy and sell products, and receive information.

> " The Web today is a medium for communication between people, using computers as a largely invisible part of the infrastructure. "
>
> —Dr. Tim Berners-Lee
> Developer of the World Wide Web

Getting Connected

Two main things are needed to access information on the Web: (1) an **Internet Service Provider** (ISP), a company through which you access the Internet on a paid subscription basis, and (2) a Web **browser**, a software program that is used to view Web pages (such as Netscape and Internet Explorer). You can also subscribe to online services such as America Online, Prodigy, or CompuServe. To send messages and transfer files over the Internet, you also must have an

e-mail program and a file transfer program. Most ISPs and online services provide these programs, as well.

To access a single page of information, or web site, you must know that site's unique address. That address, known as the **URL**, or **Uniform Resource Locator,** can be keyed into Address or Location box in your browser software. For instance, if you wanted to visit the web site for the publisher of this textbook, you would need to know the URL www.swep.com.

Search Engines and Subject Directories

Once you are connected to the Internet, you will have access to millions of pages of information, so you can't possibly know all the URLs. Search engines and subject directories are programs that allow you to search quickly for the information you need and link to the web sites that contain that information.

A **search engine** is a computer program that recognizes keywords that users enter to locate specific web pages. A search engine checks the complete text of each web page for the keyword or words. When you use a search engine, you are not searching the entire Internet—you are searching the pages in a particular database. There are thousands of search engines. Some popular ones are:

Alta Vista	www.altavista.com
Google	www.google.com
FAST	www.fast.no
Northern Light	www.northernlight.com
GoTo	www.goto.com
Ask Jeeves	www.ask.com
Excite	www.excite.com

A **subject directory**, or **web directory**, is a database of hand-chosen sites that have been reviewed and selected by people rather than by a computer program. The sites are organized into subject categories such as the Arts, Science, Entertainment, Reference, News, Government, and Business. Many directories also contain a search engine. Some popular subject directories are:

Yahoo!	www.yahoo.com
Google	www.google.com
Hot Bot	www.hotbot.lycos.com
LookSmart	www.looksmart.com
Lycos	www.lycos.com

Tim works for Super Appliance, Inc. At 4:45 pm on a Friday afternoon his boss says, "We need to check out the market for espresso makers. Get me a report by Monday morning!" Is Tim's weekend ruined, or is there an Internet shortcut?

1. Enter the search term "espresso makers" in your favorite search engine. What are the first five web sites listed?

_____

_____

_____

_____

_____

2. Visit these web sites. What information do they contain that could help Tim compile a report for his boss in very little time?

_____

_____

_____

_____

3. How could Tim have gathered this information before he had access to the Internet?

_____

_____

_____

_____

Checkpoint 12.1

1. Where and when did the Internet begin?
2. What is the difference between a search engine and a directory?
3. How can the Web be helpful to you?

12.2 WHAT'S ON THE WEB?

For this chapter, we'll assume you have a computer that can connect to the Internet. The following section provides a series of web search activities and step-by-step explanations. You can learn from them just by reading, but they will be more beneficial if you try them on a computer.

In Search of People

Would you like to find information about someone? The Web can help you. To prove that the Web can supply nearly all the information you want, try a search. In the web address space near the top of your browser window, type http://people.yahoo.com/

This takes you to a special section of Yahoo!, one of the Web's biggest directories, where you'll find subdirectories that resemble telephone books. This Yahoo! site contains a huge e-mail directory and a complete national set of telephone books. As an experiment, enter your own name and information in the blank boxes and click the search button.

If you've successfully managed to maintain your privacy and there are no search results, try typing the name of a relative or friend (who you know has e-mail) in the e-mail directory. Was the address shown?

In Search of Literature

The Web is not just for news and computing—you can also find extensive academic and library materials online. To check this out, try another search service, Google. In your browser's address space, type http://www.google.com/

You'll then see the nice, clean Google web site, with a space for keying your search terms. For this search, type "William Shakespeare" in the space. You don't need to use quotes or capital letters. Click on Google Search, and you should see a page of web links with different literature resources. If you click through the links, you'll find several that will let you download the entire text of Shakespeare's plays.

Because Shakespeare's plays were written long ago, they are no longer protected by copyright laws, so the full texts are available online. If you try to search for the works of more contemporary authors, you may find that you'll have to pay a fee to download the work or order it from an online bookstore.

Web Factoid

Dr. Tim Berners-Lee, the English scientist, actually invented the World Wide Web in the early 1990s. It expanded rapidly around 1995, going from a handful of commercial (.com) sites to millions in a matter of a few years.

In Search of Reference Materials

Most public and university libraries maintain a database of their contents. They let you look through online references and specify books to be held for you. This can be done from your home, school, or work computer.

One library database example is the online resource for the University of California at Berkeley (www.lib.berkeley.edu). If you examine the site, you will see that everything from the card catalog to dictionaries is now available online. If you visit your local library, you will likely find a guide to using the local and national library database services.

Locate a local library online by doing a key word search in your preferred search engine. If you can't find it, phone the library and ask for the URL. You should be able to search the database for materials from all your state's libraries. You may need to enter your library card ID information to access some information like indexes to articles or magazines or Facts-On-File, a weekly news service that summarizes current events. Each library develops its own web site, so links to other sites and services to users will vary among libraries. Be aware that many libraries offer homework help online too.

To find a college library, all you need is the college's URL, which is an address with the ".edu" extension for education, as in www.harvard.edu. On the home page for the college, there's always a link for the library system. Just click it and you're on your way.

In Search of Graphics

If you've spent much time on the Web, you have noticed that pictures are as prominent as words and numbers. Graphics such as charts, tables, drawings, and photographs can be **downloaded** from the Internet, that is, saved onto your computer, for use for nonprofit educational purposes. For instance, if you needed a picture of Van Gogh's famous painting, Starry Night, for use in a report for your Art History class, you could get it from the Web. Using Google again, try typing in the following word string in the Google search query space:

starry night van gogh

One of the first links on the list will be:

The Vincent van Gogh Gallery
(www.vangoghgallery.com),

where you will immediately see the painting Starry Night on the first page.

How you download the picture depends on your browser and computer system. On a PC, click the right mouse button and you'll get the options Save Picture As (Internet Explorer) or Save Image As (Netscape Navigator). On a Macintosh computer, click in the middle of the picture and you'll see a pop-up menu with an option to Save Image. With both systems, you will then be asked where you want to save the image and what you want to name it. When you select these, you'll see a dialog box asking where you want to store the image. Select the folder or location where you want to save the file on your computer. You can then insert the picture into a Word file or other document. Note that this Van Gogh site sells posters and also invites you to download images for your own use.

In Search of a Job

The Web has extensive resources for gathering job search and career readiness information. While almost every newspaper now has its job classified ad section online, the big Web job services have national want-ad directories. Four services you should look into are:

- www.monster.com
- www.careermosaic.com
- www.hotjobs.com
- www.ajb.dni.us (America's Job Bank)

Many personnel services report job offers to all the big online job banks at the same time, so you will find duplication between services. You can also check out the web site of your local newspaper.

Suppose that you received an accounting degree in Texas and find yourself homesick for Nashville. A good place to start looking for a job is Monster.com, which asks you for job type and geographic restrictions. A few seconds of searching will bring up a large list of accounting positions in Nashville, most of which will accept your resume by e-mail.

Note that all the big services give resume advice, and you would be wise to take it. At most big firms, resumes are scanned electronically, matching keywords to a list. If you want your resume ever to be seen by a human, follow the Web services' tips for preparing it.

Web Factoid

The first browser that could gracefully handle pictures was called Mosaic. It was developed at the University of Illinois in 1994. Some believe it was responsible for the explosion of the Web.

In Search of Money

One of the most practical uses of the Web—one used by millions of people non-stop every day—is to locate stock market quotes. For a simple source of stock market quotes, type http://finance.yahoo.com in your browser's address space.

For example, to locate the stock price for Microsoft, type MSFT (the company's ticker symbol) in the space at the top of the Yahoo Finance window. In the pull-down menu to the right of the Get Quotes button, select Chart. Now click on Get Quotes.

You'll see detailed financial information and charts including price histories, and links to relevant news stories. Note that if you click the option for "historical quotes," you get a web page with the chart data in a table and the option to "download spreadsheet format." You can put all this data in a spreadsheet on your own computer. (No wonder serious investors have embraced the Web as an information resource.)

ACTIVITY 2

Use the Web to locate answers to the following questions. Write the answer to the question and the URL of the web site where you found it.

1. When was poet Langston Hughes born?

   _____

2. Find a good picture of an armadillo and download it.

   _____

3. What were Verizon's earnings for first Quarter 2001?

   _____

4. Where is Saipan?

   _____

5. How many job openings in Administrative and Support Services are currently available in Cleveland, Ohio?

   _____

6. What is E-Trade's (www.etrade.com) price for a 100-share purchase of a $30 stock?

   _____

7. Search for the same keywords on at least two different engines. List some pages that each one provides, and describe the similarities and differences in the two lists.

   _____

Focus on Ethics

You are the supervisor of several employees. You suspect that at least one person is abusing company policy by using e-mail for personal use during work hours. You know that, by law, you have the right to read the employees' e-mail. What will you do?

WEB LINK

Access the following web sites to learn how to use the Internet to its fullest potential.

www.CNETHelp.com

www.Webmonkey.com

www.learnthenet.com/english

If you are a beginner, you might want to visit one of the following sites for more information and background on the Internet and World Wide Web:

www.about-the-web.com

www.refdesk.com/factbeg.html

Checkpoint 12.2

1. Name five categories of information that can be found on the Web.

2. When downloading images from the Internet, what are the restrictions?

3. What types of information can typically be found on online job banks?

12.3 SEARCH TECHNIQUES

The problem with the Web as an information resource is its sheer size. If, for example, you perform a search on Google using "help" as the query term, you'll get about 97 million links. No matter what kind of help you need, not all of these 97 million links are going to be useful to you. So for effective searching, you need a way to narrow your search.

Narrowing the Search: Adding Terms

For example, suppose you need help using the Outlining function in Microsoft Word. At the Google home page, use the Advanced Search option, which takes you to a page with several options for including or excluding different terms in your search query. For starters, try the Google Advanced Search using the terms "help Microsoft Word outline" for the query. (Do not type the quotes.) Adding these terms reduces the search results from 97 million links to about 75 thousand, which is promising. By changing the query terms to "help Microsoft Word outlining" the search results are reduced to about 11 thousand links. The first ten links contain a few that actually offer help on using the Outlining function in Microsoft Word.

Most search services offer some form of Advanced Search option, but they all make provisions for adding terms to the search. "Adding terms" means that the page being searched must have ALL the terms listed in the query. That is, the search finds pages with "help" AND "Microsoft" AND "Word" AND

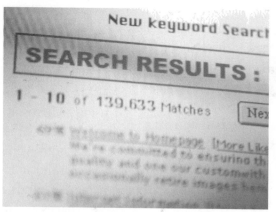

"outlining" on the same page. Some services, without telling you, take the terms in your search query and connect them with OR, which broadens the search instead of narrowing it.

To make sure that you're narrowing the search, nearly every search service lets you input your query as "+help +Microsoft +word +outlining." (Do not enter the quotes.)

If you tried this exact search, called a **Boolean** (or logical) search, on the service www.altavista.com, several of the first ten links would give you the information you need. This demonstrates the amazing power of the Web to pull exactly the information you want from a massive amount of information. It can be done quickly if you know a bit about search design.

Narrowing the Search: Subtracting Terms

As you might expect, wherever you can add terms, you can also subtract them. In the Google search service, the Advanced Search page gives you the choice of specifying terms to exclude, so that the search won't return any page with the excluded terms.

Suppose you are interested in the migration and feeding habits of Baltimore orioles (birds). The problem facing you is that the Baltimore Orioles baseball team and their ardent fans have posted tens of thousands of high-traffic Web sites. So to improve your chances of finding what you want on Google, try this for a search query in the Advanced Search page:

Include **Baltimore orioles bird**
Exclude **baseball team**

Although the team still pops up in the results (some pages about the baseball team don't contain baseball or team), the first link that appears is a page about orioles that is sponsored by bird-watchers.

Once again, there's an equivalent operation with most other search services, using a minus sign instead of a plus. On the search service www.altavista.com, the query

+Baltimore +orioles +bird –baseball –team

turns up a nice assortment of bird sites, including the official oriole site near the top of the list of links.

You should be aware that all search services have their own methods of ranking web sites, and they usually differ. If you conduct searches on four different engines: Google, Alta Vista, Excite, and HotBot with the same search query terms, it's very unlikely that the first ten links will be the same on each service. Note also that even if the service gives you just a tiny space for typing your query, you can still type in the whole query—pluses, minuses, and all, and the space will scroll to accommodate you. Some search services show more understanding than others. The oriole search on HotBot turns up a page of bird links with no baseball.

You can often simplify searches by using quotes. In the earlier example, you could use +"Microsoft Word" as a search term, instead of using +Microsoft and +Word. The quotes make the search engine look for the expression "Microsoft Word," instead of looking for "Microsoft" and "Word" separately. If your name is Rhonda Smith and you want to find Web pages about yourself, you'll want to search on "Rhonda Smith," otherwise the search will find every page with "Rhonda" or "Smith". That's a lot of pages, most of which won't interest you.

Web Factoid

As of June 2000, the biggest search services have indexed more than a billion Web pages.

Success Skills

If you find all this business about plus and minus and quotes baffling, you might want to try your luck on the search service Ask Jeeves at www.askjeeves.com. This service lets you ask an ordinary English-language question. Often, it finds just what you're looking for, but sometimes it produces strange results that arise from the ambiguities of your question. It's worth a look, though, because it can also find pages that a straight logical search might miss.

> With so much information now online, it is exceptionally easy to simply dive in and drown.
>
> —Alfred Glossbrenner, Author

ACTIVITY 3

Suppose you're buying a car and doing all the research over the Internet. You need to decide which car to buy, based on safety, performance, fuel efficiency, and price. You also want to research auto loans for the best deal and get some tips for bargaining with the car dealer. Try to find two sites for each kind of information you need. Indicate what terms you used to refine your search.

Topic	Search Terms	URLs
General performance		
Safety		
Fuel efficiency		
Price		
Auto loans, percentage		
Dealing with car salesperson		
Other		

Use your Internet searching skills to answer the questions in this chart. Identify the search engine you select, the keywords you use, and the amount of time it takes to find each answer.

Question	Search Engine	Keywords	Time
In what year did South Dakota become a state?			
What is the population of Denver?			
Which horse won the 1984 Kentucky Derby?			
What is the average temperature of San Diego?			
What is the seating capacity of Yale University'sfootball stadium?			
Who are the three highest-paid movie actresses?			
Who is Steven Jobs?			

Checkpoint 12.3

Try these Web searches using on your favorite search engine. Use logical terms to refine each search.

1. Jeffersons +television +Manhattan

2. Jeffersons –television +Monticello

3. Charleston – West Virginia + beaches

4. Charleston +West Virginia + Capital

In each case, what kind of links are you ruling in and out with the logical terms?

12.4 USING SEARCH RESULTS

Often, at school and at work, you are asked to produce reports of various types. How would you obtain information from the Web for a report?

Assume you are assigned to do a report on the famous Internet retailer Amazon.com. Your task is to investigate the question: Has this firm, despite expanding sales, ever shown a profit? As a starting point, locate information on your favorite search engine by typing in the terms

+Amazon +profitability

What links did you find? Fortunately for you, this search turns up page after page of links to articles about Amazon's financial health. Now all you have to do is look through the information, evaluate it, and blend it into your report. For simplicity, assume your report is being written in Microsoft Word.

Text by Section

The simplest way to extract some text from a Web page is to select it by a click-drag as you would do in a word processing document and select Copy from the Edit menu of your browser. Then in your word processing document, find a place for the text and select Paste from the Edit menu.

The only problem with this method is that the text you selected might have some unwanted formatting attached to it. The block of text

might contain carriage returns making each line a half-page wide. To use the material you'll have to edit it one line at a time. That can be very time-consuming. The following alternative is better.

Text by Page

Another tactic for adding web information to your document is to save the whole web page as a separate file. All common browsers allow this choice under the File menu. You can typically Save As Web Page or Save As Text.

When you open the Web page in Microsoft Word, you will see a fairly close representation of the page as it appeared in the browser. But now when you select and copy text, and paste that text into a Word document, the lines are set to the page width automatically. If you're going to be clipping quotes from a dozen different sources, this simplifies things greatly.

Using Images

To dress up your Amazon report, you may want to include a chart of its stock performance. Go to finance.yahoo.com, and search in the Get Quotes space on AMZN (the stock ticker symbol for Amazon) using Chart from the pull-down menu to the right of the query space. Scroll down the page in your browser until you see the chart. Select and save the image.

Smart Tip

The expression "surfing the Net" perfectly captures the idea of skimming across an ocean of information. Once you catch an e-wave, you can ride it as far as you want. The phrase was originally "surfing the Internet." Jean Armour Polly coined it in 1992.

Then use the word processor's Insert command to place the image in your report. It will take you only a few minutes to include a picture of Amazon.com president, Jeff Bezos, or a copy of the Amazon logo, using the same method.

Note that all this work is fine for nonprofit or educational purposes, but if you were preparing a document for publication in a magazine, the copyright rules apply: get permission for everything from the original source. Much material on the Web is taken from print sources (*Business Week Online* is based, naturally enough, on *Business Week*), so reference the print original wherever possible. Even though the content of web sites changes rapidly, you should always cite the web page as a source when you use web material in your own reports. Most style manuals such as APA and MLA include the proper format for citing a web site as a source in a bibliography or footnote.

ACTIVITY 5

1. Prepare a short report on nylon. Turn in the report to your instructor.

   Who discovered nylon?

   What year was it discovered?

   What is the chemical structure of nylon? Include a picture in your report.

2. Prepare a detailed plan and a written travel itinerary for a trip to Washington D.C. Be sure to include the following information. Turn in the report to your instructor.

   Round-trip flight information (include airlines, flight numbers, times, airports, costs)

   Metro transportation (include schedule, fares, and maps)

   Hotels near the Capitol (include address, phone number, prices)

   Meal information (include a variety of restaurant information, price ranges, locations)

Checkpoint 12.4

1. What is the best method for copying a small section of text from a web site?

2. What is the best method for copying an entire web page?

3. When is it appropriate to cite a web page as a source in a bibliography?

Success Skills

12.5 EVALUATING WEB SITES

Despite the amazing benefits to online research, there are risks for online users to avoid. It is important to evaluate the sites you find. Unlike printed documents such as textbooks and magazines, which are professionally written and checked for accuracy, documents on the Internet may be posted by anyone. No one is required to make sure they are correct. You may not know whether a seventh grader or a national expert has written the site you visit. Consequently, you must learn to assess any source you find.

The Web may house thousands of valuable research and sales sites, but it is also home to a good deal of inaccurate and potentially-dangerous information. Hate groups recruit new members online. Con artists have created fake charity sites to swindle people out of thousands of dollars. Chat room rumors have spread inaccurate information about a company's stock resulting in a significant change in the stock value. In one highly-publicized mistake, well-known journalist Pierre Salinger wrote that TWA flight 800 had been shot down by a Navy missile. Because of Salinger's reputation as an ethical journalist, many people believed his incredible accusations. However, his claims were quickly discredited when it came to light that the source of his information had been a web site run by an unreliable conspiracy monger. It's a good idea to approach every site you visit with a bit of skepticism.

Evaluate web sites based on the following four criteria:

♦ Credibility—The name of the author or the source of the information is included. The web site presents all sides of an issue. Spelling and grammar are accurate.

♦ Accuracy—Conclusions are based on facts and logic, not emotional appeal. Opposing views are presented fairly and correctly. A current date indicates that the web site has been updated and kept current.

♦ Reasonableness—Language and tone are moderate and professional, not judgmental or emotional. The site does not make exaggerations or generalizations. The content is objective and unbiased.

♦ Support—The sources of the material are identified. Sources of graphics and statistics are labeled. Links to other web sites make it possible to verify information or obtain further information on the subject.

For documenting Internet research, you can document resources in a variety of ways. See Appendix G for some guidelines from the Andrew Mellon Library.

ACTIVITY 6

Use the following questions to evaluate at least two web sites on the same subject. Explain your answers with details and examples from the site.

Web Site 1 _____   **Web Site 2** _____

1. Who is the creator of this site? What are the writer's credentials? Can these credentials be checked? Who is funding the site?

   _____   _____

   _____   _____

   _____   _____

2. What makes this a credible source?

   _____   _____

   _____   _____

   _____   _____

3. Does this source have a bias?

   _____   _____

   _____   _____

   _____   _____

4. Is the site affiliated with a reputable organization? Have other reliable sources referred to or linked you to this site?

   _____   _____

   _____   _____

   _____   _____

5. Is the information accurate? How do you know?

   _____   _____

   _____   _____

   _____   _____

6. When was the site last updated? Is this information current?

   _____   _____

   _____   _____

   _____   _____

Success Skills

Web Site 1	Web Site 2

7. Are there multiple perspectives for the topic? What are they?

8. What sources—experts, scientific studies, statistics, and so on—does the site use? Can any of this be verified? Does the site credit its sources or list where its information was obtained?

9. Is information professionally and accurately written, with very few grammar and spelling errors?

10. Are there a variety of external links that supplement the information given in the site? Are these links well maintained, and are they helpful and insightful?

11. Is this site easy to navigate? What features make it user friendly?

12. Is this site visually appealing? Do the visual features enhance the site's information or are they just decorations?

The Reality of the Web

With about one afternoon's training, you can learn how to post information on the Web yourself. So can anyone else, whether they are recognized authorities on a subject or disreputable sources. Validating Web information by comparing multiple sources and referring to established sources is, therefore, an important part of Web use.

ACTIVITY 7

1. Perform a search on the words "face on Mars." Notice that even the fairly respectable scientific site www.space.com has quite a few "face on Mars" pages to drive traffic to the site. How many pages were listed? Are there reputable sources on the subject?

   _____

   _____

2. Locate an example of a health scare or product scare that was circulated via e-mail or web posting. (Some examples are shampoo, anti-perspirant, sunscreen, and artificial sweetener warnings). Are the warnings valid? How do you know? How difficult is it to find information on the Internet that contradicts the health warnings?

   _____

   _____

   _____

   _____

3. Conduct a search on the term "Lockerbie." Look through the links and select what you feel is the least promising conspiracy theory about the crash of Pan Am Flight 103 in 1988. On what information did you base your decision?

   _____

   _____

   _____

   _____

Success Skills

Advantages of the Web

Major cultural and technological changes always tend to make people worry. And the Internet has been blamed for all kinds of problems: from eyestrain to anti-social behavior. On balance, however, it seems clear that the Internet offers far more benefits than risks:

♦ The Internet is an interactive and comprehensive source of information combining text, images, and sound in a way no other medium can.

♦ The Internet fosters computer literacy and technology skills—important skills for the 21st century.

♦ The Internet develops problem-solving skills by requiring users to think logically and critically about content and search methods.

♦ The Internet makes it easy to find information that once was obscure and difficult to locate.

♦ The Internet is versatile and convenient— open 24 hours a day and accessible from most locations.

Key Terms and Concepts

Boolean search	Internet	URL
browser	ISP	World Wide Web
download	search engine	
hyperlink	subject directory	

Chapter Summary

1. Using the World Wide Web is a key intellectual skill for home, school, and work.

2. The Web started as a U.S. Department of Defense project in the 1970's.

3. The Web contains an astonishing amount of information, from phone numbers to stock prices to literature.

4. With a little practice, you can learn how to use search services on the Web to find the information you want.

5. Narrowing your web search requires the effective use of keywords, quotes, and plus and minus signs.

6. With a computer, you can search a library's online database from any location.

7. Text and pictures found on the web can be downloaded to your own hard drive for use in other programs, but you must always document your sources.

8. Learning to evaluate web sites requires some skepticism and the ability to ask and answer important questions. You should compare information from several Web sources, since there is no overall authority supervising Web content.

Review

Based on the information you learned in this chapter, use your own words to answer the following questions.

1 In your opinion, why should you learn how to use the Web?

2. What is the basic difference between a search engine and a directory?

3. What type(s) of information might you look for on the Web?

4. When looking for general information on a topic, would you add terms or subtract them? Why?

5. When looking for specific information on a topic, would you add terms or subtract them? Why?

6. How can you use the information on the Web for a report or project?

7. How do you capture an illustration for a report or project?

8. Why is it a good idea to evaluate web sites?

9. What other ways might the Web help you personally, academically, or professionally?

10. What have you learned from this chapter?

Success Skills

Case 1

Maria needed to buy a car. She had never done this before and she was concerned she would not get a good quality car at a fair price. Her friend Paul had spent a lot of money on a brand new car and still got a "lemon" which took him a lot of time to get fixed. Maria's new job meant she had to have a reliable car, one she could deliver large packages in, and one with good gas mileage. She also wanted a car with a sporty look. She knew before she made this important decision, that she would have to find a lot of useful information about cars, features, and costs.

1. Recommend where Maria should search for information on cars, their features (including mileage, storage space, and other factors.), and costs.

2. After Maria has gathered the information, how should she evaluate and use what she has found out in order to buy a car that meets her needs?

Case 2

Vacation time was coming up in a month and Eric wanted to go some place new and different. Sitting on his kitchen table were some brochures about the Caribbean. As he thumbed through them, he realized they had great photos but not much detailed information about the various locations shown. Some travel packages included airfare; others did not state whether it was included or not. Also there were different price levels for each travel package but no clear explanations about what exactly was covered. Eric realized he needed more detailed information in order to have the vacation he wanted.

1. Name five or six sources of travel information Eric should research before making his vacation plans.

2. Eric went to a travel agent who gave him brochures with more details. These showed what each travel package cost, dates available, number of days, and specifically what was included for meals and hotels. How should Eric deal with the information in these brochures to make it helpful?

Brendan has worked for ten years in a company that manufactures athletic equipment. Recently, the company was sold, and Brendan's new boss asked him to prepare a report to be presented at the next meeting of the company's Board of Directors in two weeks. The report needs to describe the duties of each person in Brendan's department, including Brendan himself, and the reasons to keep the department intact rather than consolidating or laying off the employees.

Because he has been the department supervisor for four years, Brendan feels confident he can describe the department's functions and its benefits in a way that convinces the Board to keep all the employees. He sees no need to do any research and waits until the day before the Board meeting to write his report.

If you were an employee in Brendan's department, would you think he has done his best to write a report that will save your job?

What else might he have done in preparation for writing the report?

Chapter Goals

After studying and working with the information in this chapter, you should be able to:

♦ Describe the importance of writing.
♦ Identify the types of materials people write.
♦ Describe the writing process for essays, papers, and reports.
♦ Use the 5Ws and H to create an organized outline.
♦ Write effective e-mails.
♦ View writing as an important part of life.

In This Chapter

Learning how to effectively communicate on paper IS an important part of the world you live and function in, the jobs or careers you choose, and the people with whom you interact. Learning to effectively communicate in this real world means that you are not only able to be heard, but also to be understood.

Perhaps up until now, you haven't done a lot of writing. You may not have confidence in your writing ability or maybe you just don't know how to get started. This chapter provides information that will help you become a better writer. In it, you will learn how to approach your writing tasks.

Do you feel intimidated or overwhelmed with the idea of having to write a college entrance essay, a detailed report for your boss at work, or a complaint letter to a store that delivers the wrong item? This is a feeling shared by many others; but if you reflect on it, it's the thinking that is intimidating. Actually doing it is empowering.

Getting started is probably the most challenging part of any writing task. This chapter will provide strategies for getting started and a writing process to follow that will make getting started easier.

This one chapter does not contain all you need to know about writing. Many books are devoted to the topic, and courses are designed to help you develop your writing fully. But the chapter will certainly give you the tools you need for writing short essays, longer papers, and reports and e-mails. In the bibliography located at the back of this book, you will find other resources for improving your writing. In addition, a school or local library may have several other books in their collection for you to research and reference.

> " The great struggle for a writer is to learn to write as he would talk. "
>
> —Lincoln Steffens
> Early twentieth-century editor and author

Writing is something that you use every day of your life. What writing activities are required in your world?

SELF-CHECK

The following self-evaluation will give you an idea of how familiar, or unfamiliar, you are with some of the topics and terms discussed in this chapter. After reading each statement, circle the letter Y, S, or N to indicate the answer that is most appropriate for you. Answer honestly, and rate yourself at the end; then complete the information for Chapter 13 in Appendix A.

	Y = yes; frequently	S = sometimes	N = no; never

1.	I know that writing is an important part of school, work, and personal life.	Y	S	N
2.	I understand that good writing follows a process.	Y	S	N
3.	I schedule time ahead for my longer writing projects.	Y	S	N
4.	I know how to use the Internet for research.	Y	S	N
5.	I know how to decide on a topic.	Y	S	N
6.	I know how to write a good thesis statement.	Y	S	N
7.	I can create an organized outline for my writing by using the mapping process.	Y	S	N
8.	I can describe the three parts of most written communication.	Y	S	N
9.	I know how to effectively present the final draft of my writing.	Y	S	N
10.	I know how to write effective e-mail.	Y	S	N

Rate Yourself:

Number of Ys	_____	x	100	=	_____
Number of Ss	_____	x	50	=	_____
Number of Ns	_____	x	0	=	_____ Total _____

13.1 WRITING FOR SCHOOL, WORK, AND PERSONAL LIFE

Communicating your thoughts effectively on paper or talking on paper is very important to your success in school, at work, and in your personal life. When you write essays and papers for an academic assignment, you are learning how to effectively talk on paper. These writing activities are the training ground for writing tasks in the workplace and for personal use. Developing this ability enables you to communicate your thoughts and ideas more easily, both on paper and orally.

Since writing is such an important part of life, it is essential that you learn how to write well. Though this chapter focuses primarily on writing essays, papers, reports, and e-mails, you will learn many valuable strategies that can be applied to all types of writing tasks.

> " A pen is the tongue of the mind. "
>
> —Miguel Cervantes
> Author of *Don Quixote*

Figure 13-1   Types of Writing

In the working world, writing is essential for doing a job. Here is a partial listing of the types of workplace writing:

✓ e-mail	✓ meeting minutes	✓ reports
✓ letters of recommendation	✓ job applications	✓ diaries/journals
✓ letters of complaint	✓ lab reports	✓ policies/procedures
✓ letters of inquiry	✓ technical reports	✓ newsletters
✓ phone messages	✓ directions	✓ resumes
✓ customer service logs	✓ instruction manuals	✓ service reports
✓ advertisements	✓ financial statements	✓ product reviews
✓ magazine articles	✓ research reports	✓ progress reports
✓ annual reports	✓ job descriptions	✓ press releases
✓ cover letters	✓ memos	✓ speeches

Writing is often needed in your personal life. A partial list of personal writing follows:

✓ mortgage documents	✓ notes to your child's teacher	✓ bank loan solicitation
✓ billing questions	✓ credit card applications	✓ complaint letters
✓ personal letters	✓ e-mail	✓ job hunting cover letters

ACTIVITY I

Think about people you may know who do the jobs listed in the left column. In the right column, list some of the writing activities these people do. You may use the lists in Figure 13-1 for reference.

Profession	Writing Activities
Nurse	*Medical chart updates, patient reports*
Business professional	*e-mails, memos, letters, reports, meeting minutes, presentations*
Electrician	
Secretary	
Auto mechanic	
Teacher	
Job seeker	
Parent	
Computer technician	
Police officer	
Lawyer	
Building contractor	
Entrepreneur	
Pharmacist	
Doctor	
News reporter	
Salesperson	
Travel agent	
Other	

Checkpoint 13.1

1. What is the primary purpose of writing?
2. At what writing activities are you already skilled?
3. What writing activities would you like to do better?

Success Skills

13.2 WRITING ESSAYS, PAPERS, AND REPORTS

Writing a good short essay or longer research paper or report involves following a **writing process,** or series of related steps. Doctors follow a process when they operate on a patient, and mechanics follow a process when they repair a car. Travel agents follow a process when arranging vacations for their clients, and event planners follow a process when setting up special events and parties. A process is not just one action but a series of steps or procedures that enables these individuals to do their jobs. By understanding that writing is also a process, you will be better equipped to handle any writing task.

Eight detailed steps in the writing process follow. Lengthy research papers and reports will require all eight steps, while shorter essays, papers, or letters will require only a few steps.

Before completing any of the activities in the eight steps of the writing process you should pre-view each step before reading them in detail. (See Chapter 8 for more information on pre-viewing.) This will help you understand how each step flows into the next and leads to a quality piece of writing. The eight steps are shown in Figure 13-2.

Step 1 Creating Time to Write

Creating time for writing is the first step in the writing process. While any process, especially writing, takes time, the length of time depends on the task. If you are asked to write an essay in class, you have to complete it in the time allowed, but if you are asked to write a one- or two-page report for your boss, you may have several days to prepare it. If you are asked to write a five- to ten-page research paper, you might need to schedule six to eight weeks for the task.

Working on a research paper for six to eight weeks does not mean that you write for six to eight weeks; it means you work on the paper a little at a time over a six- to eight-week period. Planning for this in advance ensures that you still have enough time for both the paper and your other responsibilities.

Figure 13-2   Eight Steps of the Writing Process

Step 1:   Creating Time to Write

Step 2:   Deciding on a Topic

Step 3:   Doing Research

Step 4:   Creating a Thesis Statement

Step 5:   Creating an Outline

Step 6:   Writing the Rough Draft

Step 7:   Revising the Rough Draft

Step 8:   Creating the Final Draft

Effective writing occurs step by step over a period of time, not all at once. Even for essay tests and letters, you need time to create an outline, do the actual writing, and revise and edit. Research papers and long reports require more development, such as a thesis statement, research, a rough draft and a final draft.

The following guide will help you schedule the writing of a lengthy research paper. Since this is only a guide, you can adjust the time frame according to your task. It is always wise to plan a little extra time, just in case unexpected events get in the way. (See Chapter 4 on Learning Time Management for more information on scheduling time for papers.)

Decide on a topic (may include some research)	1 week
Research time	2 weeks
Creating a thesis statement and outline	1 week
Writing your first draft	2 weeks
Revision	1 week
Final draft	1 week

Follow the writing process for longer papers and reports shown in Figure 13-3. Notice that some of the more time-consuming tasks are repeated several times instead of being shown as a one-time activity. By breaking the steps into shorter time frames, you can fit them into your daily life while also providing quality time, not just quantity time to your writing project. The break you schedule between each writing activity allows you to think so that you bring a fresh perspective to your process when you do the next activity.

Step 2 Deciding on a Topic

After you schedule your time, you must decide on a **topic**, if you don't already have one, such as global warming, gardening, pollution, music, or some other subject. Some topics can be covered in only a few paragraphs, while others require many pages.

If you are given the topic, obviously, you must write about that topic. If you make the choice, you may become overwhelmed by the

Figure 13-3   The Writing Process for Longer Papers and Reports

options. The best topic is one that interests you, so that the time and effort you put into it will be more satisfying.

You can use the Internet, encyclopedia indexes, and tables of contents to look for possible topics. Others can also help you settle on an appropriate topic. If you are writing for a class, it is always wise to get your instructor's approval of a topic before spending time on research.

The following is a list of considerations when choosing a topic:

♦ Does it interest you? If so, then use it; if not, don't.

♦ Is there enough information to write the appropriate amount of material?

♦ Is the subject very new? (If so, you may have trouble finding enough research material.)

♦ Is there *too much* information available? Can you narrow the topic and still report on it effectively?

For the purpose of practicing this writing process, choose a topic. You can use one that has been assigned by an instructor or boss or one you just want to know more about. Review the previous recommendations before you make your final decision, then write your topic below.

My topic is: _____

Step 3 Doing Research

Doing research means locating usable information about the topic or learning about something you want to know. If you have not already read through Chapter 12 on Finding Information on the Web, do so now. It provides you with information about how to use the Internet for research. Your local or school library is also a great source for information. Ask the librarian to help you locate the best material on your topic.

Step 4 Creating a Thesis Statement

A *topic* is what you study, while a **thesis** is the main point of your writing or the conclusion you draw from what you learn. Creating a thesis statement narrows your topic down so you can focus on one issue surrounding the topic.

A **thesis statement** is a summary of your thesis. *Every essay and research paper must have a thesis statement because it tells the reader what you are going to prove. Though business reports generally do not require thesis statements, a statement may add to the effectiveness of your writing.*

Creating a thesis statement requires a two-step process. First, you must identify the issues that surround your subject. Then you must state your position on the **issue**—the unresolved question. Your **position** is your point of view on an issue.

Topic	Issue
Global warming	♦ whether global warming is a threat to people and the environment
	♦ whether global warming should be stopped
	♦ whether global warming is caused by industrial pollution

Albert Einstein
- ♦ whether Albert Einstein's childhood affected his view of the world
- ♦ whether religion played a role in Albert's upbringing
- ♦ whether Albert was influenced by Germany at the turn of the century

Gardening
- ♦ whether planting too early in the year affects plant height
- ♦ whether gardening is therapeutic
- ♦ whether gardens can help the quality of the earth's air

ACTIVITY 2

Try to come up with issue statements for the topics listed below. Remember to include the topic you listed earlier in this chapter.

Topic	Possible Issues
Pollution	
Music	
the Internet	
School uniforms	
Your topic	

Success Skills

Identifying your position

Now that you have identified several issues, you can begin to identify your position. By identifying your position, you create a statement that you will argue in your writing. Your position, or point of view on an issue, can also be considered a thesis statement.

Topic	Possible Thesis Statements
Global warming	Global warming is a threat to people and the environment.
Albert Einstein	Albert Einstein's childhood affected his views on the world.
Gardening	Planting a garden can improve the earth's air quality.

Note that a thesis statement does not give any explanation or reason why you think the way you do. Your explanation will be found in your writing.

ACTIVITY 3

Try to come up with thesis statements based on the issues you listed in Activity 2. Remember to include the topic you listed earlier in this chapter. Though you will come up with a thesis statement before you write, you may change it as you develop additional ideas. This is all right as long as your paper or essay proves your position.

Topic	Thesis Statements
Pollution	_____
Music	_____
the Internet	_____
School uniforms	_____
Your topic	_____

Step 5 Creating an Outline

Now it is time to organize your thoughts and information. By the time you get to this step, you will have already written some material. If you researched a long report, you should have plenty of information. If you are writing a short essay or letter, your writing process may start at this step.

Organized writing aids the writer in understanding what is being said and receives a higher grade than unorganized writing. If your writing is unorganized or confusing, readers will have a difficult time understanding your thoughts. If, on the other hand, your writing is organized and flows smoothly from one idea to the next, you will have succeeded in communicating your thoughts effectively. Organizing your thoughts is easily accomplished by using a pre-writing process called mapping.

Mapping is a pre-writing process that helps you organize your thoughts and information on paper and results in an informal outline. The informal outline is a writer's road map—the same one you follow for pre-viewing. (See Chapter 8 for more information on pre-viewing.) It is similar but not the same as the note taking method of Mind Mapping® (see Chapter 6).

1. **Set-Up**. Mapping begins when you draw a circle or cloud shape in the middle of a blank piece of paper and write the thesis statement inside it. You proceed by drawing about ten lines coming out from the circle. The picture will look similar to a spider. See Figure 13-4 for the global warming example.

2. **Brainstorm with 5W's and H.** Once you have written your thesis statement, it is time to brainstorm questions. **Brainstorming,** which is described in more detail in Chapter 3, is a random, unorganized thought-generating process that results in new ideas. For writing, brainstorming is guided by using the same 5Ws and H also introduced in Chapter 3. To refresh your memory the **5Ws and H** are: Who, What, When, Where, Why and How.

Write each of the 5W's and H across the top left of your sheet of paper with the thesis statement in the middle.

Using the global warming example from Figure 13-4, the questions in Figure 13-5 can be generated from the 5Ws and H and written on the paper. There are no rules to follow for how often or which of the 5Ws and H you use.

Though your paper or essay may not answer all of these questions, you are beginning to think actively and creatively about the paper's contents and organization before you write.

3. **Organizing the Outline**. You now have many good questions about the thesis statement, but they are not organized. To organize them, first review all of the questions. Then decide which question your reader should learn about first. On a separate blank piece of summary paper, write your first choice question in the recall column. Place a check mark √ next to this question

Figure 13-4   Beginning the Mapping Process

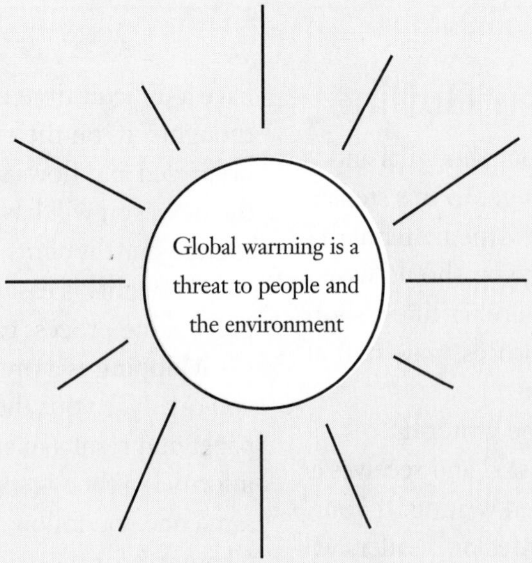

Global warming is a threat to people and the environment

Figure 13-5   Mapping: Brainstorming with the 5W's and H Example

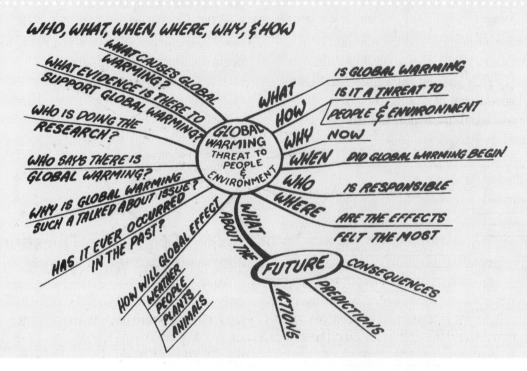

on your brainstorm sheet indicating that the question has been used. Then continue evaluating your questions to decide which question would make the most sense for the reader to read about next. *Leave at least five blank spaces between each question.* If you see a question that does not relate well to the thesis, cross it off your brainstorm sheet. If you think a question should be reworded or added, then do so.

Figure 13-6 is one suggested way of organizing the questions for the global warming example. Notice that the question "when did global warming begin?" was changed to "when was it first noticed as a problem?" The revised question communicates the message better. The question "has it ever occurred in the past?" can be used as a detail to answer "when was it first noticed?" The question "who says there is global warming?" was not selected. If this was your paper, you might prefer a different question arrangement. As long as the answers to the questions flow from one to the next, then the map will work.

Mapping with the 5Ws and H is very effective for quickly organizing your thoughts for essay tests. You can create your spider map in the margin or on a separate piece of paper. This does not take long and is well worth the benefit of having your thoughts organized before you begin writing.

4. **Checking for Idea Flow**. When you have finished using, changing, or eliminating your questions, read them to see if your order makes sense. If you can easily see the organization of your paper in your questions, then you have succeeded in creating the framework of your outline. Does rearranging the questions help? Does adding more questions or taking any out help? Make changes as you see fit.

5. **Fill in the details**. Once the flow of ideas is established, then it is time to fill in the details. Using the body of the summary paper and key words, fill in the details relating to or answering each question. Include any statistics, names, quotes, or

important dates. If you did not do any research, fill in any details you would want to include in your writing.

If you do not have enough information to answer a question and the question is important to your paper, then do a little more research looking for the answer. Figure 13-7 shows some details for each of the questions asked in the global warming example.

After filling in the details, you may need to reorganize their order. In the end, you will have completed your writer's road map. Make changes to the map as you develop the paper. Now you are ready to begin writing your rough draft.

Figure 13-6
Organizing Questions from Your Map

8. How is ti a threat to people and the environment?	
9. How will global warming effect:	
* weather	
* people	
* plants	
* animals	
10. Where are the effects felt the most?	
11. Why Now?	
12. What about the future?	
* consequences	
* predictions	
* actions	

Thesis Statement	Global Warming is a threat to people and the environment
1. What is global warming? (GW)	
2. Why is GW such a talked about issue?	
3. When was it first noticed as a problem?	
4. What causes GW?	
5. Who is responsible?	
6. What evidence is there to support GW?	
7. Who is doing research?	

8. How is ti a threat to people and the environment?	- breathing disorders/asthma - skin cancer from sum exposure - increase in diseases carried by animals - food supply contaminated
9. How will global warming effect:	temp's up 9° fareinheit from 25 & water supply upply arth theory R flooding (rising sea levels) pply

Thesis Statement	Global Warming is a threat to people and the environment	
1. What is global warming? (GW)	- also known as "Greenhouse Effect" - depletion of ozone layer.	
2. Why is GW such a talked about issue?	- effects on people - effects on environment - effects on layer shrinking	
3. When was it first noticed as a problem?	- ozone layer & sun harmfulness - warmer night temperatures - changing weather patterns - has it ever occurred in the past	on of causes on dioxide causing change phere ppers no more
4. What causes GW?	- chemicals in environment/factor - aerosol cans - cutting down of trees in rainforest - car emissions	ric bills up ather in New England.
5. Who is responsible?	- those involved in the cause: - others: - - - - - -	
6. What evidence is there to support GW?	See #5 - use some examples:	
7. Who is doing research-	- scientists environmentalists - of public health/gov't - Earth summit 1992 in Rio de Janiero	

Figure 13-7
Filling in the Details

Success Skills

Using the topic and thesis statement you chose earlier in this chapter, proceed through the five steps for mapping with the 5W's and H. You can work independently or solicit the help of a partner. Partners are especially helpful in the brainstorming process. When you finish, you should have an outline of questions and some details for your writing task.

Topic _____

Thesis Statement _____

who, what, when, where, why and how

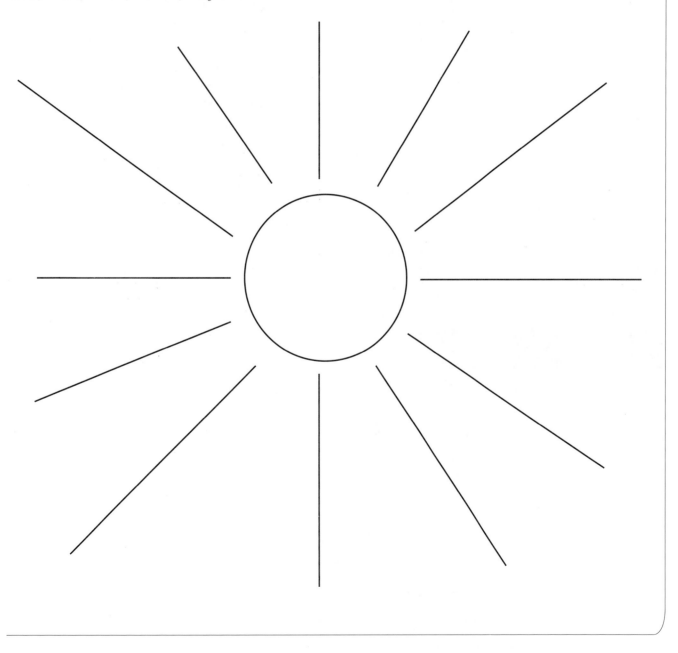

Step 6 Writing the Rough Draft

The **rough draft** of your paper is just that: rough. It is your first attempt at getting your ideas down on paper. This means you should not expect to have a finished smooth-flowing paper ready to hand in after this step. You need not worry about making mistakes, including spelling and punctuation, at this time. This draft is not supposed to be perfect. You will have an opportunity to revise your rough draft in the next step.

When writing your rough draft, make sure to leave a double or triple space between each line you write. This will give you room for making changes and revising later.

Every essay or paper you write should have three parts: an *introduction*, a *body*, and a *conclusion*. Each of these parts serves a specific purpose.

The introduction

The **introduction** *tells* a reader what the paper is about. It should be interesting, creative, and catch the reader's attention. The introduction includes a thesis statement and identifies what will be proved or discussed. If you are writing an essay, the introduction can be a paragraph or so in length. If you are writing a ten-page paper or report, the introduction should be at least several paragraphs long and total at least a page or more.

Using stories, analogies, personal examples, or interesting information you found while researching will help in writing your introduction. Using the global warming example, a possible introduction to a short essay is given below.

Imagine that every year the summer season will be a little hotter than the summer before. Imagine that it no longer snows in the United States. Imagine that going outside with skin exposed to the sun increases the chances of getting cancer by 25 percent. Imagine having to wear an oxygen mask every day just to survive. Why would anyone want to imagine these situations? Probably because they could happen. Global warming is the cause of each of these problems and is a threat to people and the environment.

ACTIVITY 5

Now it is your turn to come up with a possible introduction for your discussion. Think about how you can make it interesting for the reader.

_____

_____

_____

_____

_____

_____

_____

Success Skills

The body

The body of your paper shows the reader that you can support and document your position. This is where you discuss your point of view and back up your thesis with facts and specific information. The body of a paper should contain background information about your topic, including important points, historical information, and definitions of key words relating to the topic. In addition to your own point of view, the body is where you state other possible points of view. Most of the material you created in your informal outline should be used in the body.

Use the following information to help you create the body of your paper.

1. **Remember to write for your audience.** Your audience may be an instructor, a boss, or a work team. Though the people in your audience may be familiar with your topic, it is helpful to assume that they know nothing. Write as if you were an instructor providing the information to a student. This forces you to communicate clearly and fully.

    For example, if you were writing a paper on global warming, you might assume that the instructor is familiar with the term "ozone layer." By pretending he or she is not, however, you are forced to define the term, making the paper easier for the reader to understand.

2. **Write freely and simply.** While writing your rough draft, don't worry about grammar, spelling, or punctuation. It is more important to get your ideas on paper now and revise them later. The following acronym is used by many writers to guide their writing process. It means to avoid long sentences with big words.

    KISS = Keep it simple and short.

3. **Use connecting words. Connecting words** help to bridge the relationship between sentences. For instance, the word "however" means you are making an exception to something you just said. The words "in addition to" mean you are adding more to what is already said.

> " We do not know who we are until we see what we can do. "
>
> —Martha Grimes
> Contemporary mystery writer

Smart Tip

Writing an essay is far different from writing a news story or report. The first allows for opinion, the latter for detailing.

ACTIVITY 6

Below is a list of common connecting words. Try to figure out what they mean and how they are used. Use the right side for your suggestions.

Connecting Words	Suggestions for Usage
however	*making an exception*
in addition to	*adding more to what was just said*
in other words	*restating to explain better*
most of all	*pointing out the most of something*
furthermore	
consequently	
on the other hand	
as a result	
besides	
therefore	
to sum up	
for example	
first, second, third	
for this reason	
above all	
in conclusion	
in short	
although	
because	
since	
previously	
ultimately	
afterwards	
meanwhile	
similarly	
presently	
subsequently	

Success Skills

4. **Document your sources**. Documenting where you found your information is required for academic papers and suggested for all other lengthy writing. This lends credibility to your words and recognizes others whose information you used. Simply include the author's last name and the pages where you found the specific information you quoted. Then, in the bibliography include the remaining information.

You may be asked to document your sources according the guidelines of the American Psychological Association (APA), the Modern Language Association (MLA), Campbell's, or other documenting source. Your school or local library will have the information you need. Three examples of documenting a book source according to "*A Guide to MLA Documentation Style for Research Papers*" are shown below:

Brooks, John. *Telephone: The First Hundred Years*. New York: Harper, 1976.

a. Cite the author's last name and page number(s) in parentheses. For example:

One historian argues that the telephone created "a new habit of mind—a habit of tense alertness, of demanding and expecting immediate results." (Brooks 117-18)

b. Use the author's last name in your sentence and place only the page number(s) of the source in parentheses. For example:

Brooks points out that the telephone created "a new habit of mind—a habit of tense alertness, of demanding and expecting immediate results." (117-18)

c. Give the author's last name in the sentence when you cite the entire work. For example:

Brooks argues that the history of the telephone is characterized by innovations that have changed public attitudes toward technology.

For documenting Internet research, you can document resources in a variety of ways. See Appendix G for some guidelines from the Andrew Mellon Library.

Factoid

Gibbon spent 20 years writing *The Decline and Fall of the Roman Empire*. Noah Webster spent 36 years writing his dictionary.

5. **Keep your research notes**. When you finish using the research notes for your rough draft, do not throw them away. You may need them for checking a source or making sure you wrote the right information.

The conclusion

The **conclusion** is a summary of your important points. It lets a reader know you are finished with your argument. The conclusion also allows you to restate your position and to explain why you believe what you believe. The conclusion for a five- to ten-page paper is usually more than one paragraph, while shorter papers may be just one paragraph.

ACTIVITY 7

Begin writing the rough draft of your paper using the information in the preceding section. If you have done some research on the topic, make the paper at least three pages long. If you have not completed the research, then make your paper one to two pages long.

Step 7 Revising the Rough Draft

At this point in the writing process, the hardest work is done. You have decided on a topic, completed your research, created a thesis statement and outline, and written the rough draft. Now is the time to prepare for the final draft. People who try to cram their writing in the day or night before it is due miss out on this valuable part of the writing process.

Before beginning to revise your rough draft, set it aside for a day or more. Getting away from it for a while refreshes your thought process and allows you to continue with a new perspective. Revising your rough draft means editing it. **Editing** is the process of correcting, adding, eliminating, or rearranging your information so that it makes sense to the reader. This also includes changes in grammar, spelling, and punctuation.

> " Great works are performed not by strength but by perseverance. "
>
> —Samuel Johnson
> British poet and essayist

Factoid

The average adult with Internet access will spend 5.3 percent of the rest of his or her life online, according to research firm Cyber Dialogue. The results of an extensive survey of Internet users showed that the average adult will spend a total of 23.5 months of his or her life online. That's 17,500 hours.

The questions below are provided as a guide for revising your paper. Read each question, then go back to your paper, and check for the answer. If the answer to any question is No (which many will be), you need to correct, add, eliminate, or rearrange the information. If the answer to a question is yes, then you have completed the revision for that question.

For the Introduction:

Is the thesis statement included? _____

Is the thesis statement interesting or catchy? _____

Is the thesis statement long enough or complete enough? _____

Is the thesis statement clear? _____

For the Body:

Does the body follow an outline or writer's road map? _____

Is the first sentence of every paragraph a main idea (topic sentence)? _____

Does each paragraph support the main idea? _____

Are the ideas easy to follow? _____

Are each of the main ideas backed up by research, quotes, or other experiences? _____

Are the sources quoted properly? _____

Are the key points clearly stated?_____

Is the content specific enough? _____

Are the examples appropriate to the topic? _____

Did you avoid using the same word over and over again? _____

Is the grammar correct? _____

Is the spelling correct? _____

Is the punctuation correct? _____

For the Conclusion:

Is the thesis restated in the summary? _____

Does the conclusion summarize your point of view? _____

Step 8 Creating the Final Draft

Creating the final draft is the easy part. This is where you format the paper for its final readers. Review the following guidelines for preparing a research paper and adapt them to your needs.

♦ Leave a one-inch margin on the top, bottom, and sides of your paper. Double-space and paginate the paper.

♦ Create a cover sheet or title page. Key your title in the middle of a blank piece of paper. Then, for school papers, on the bottom right side, include your name, the class number and name, your instructor's name and the date. (See Figure 13-8.)

♦ Use a clean, readable font, such as 10 or 12 point Times Roman or Arial.

♦ Start the first page of a paper after the cover sheet approximately three inches from the top.

♦ Indent the first line of every paragraph.

♦ Indent and single space any quotes.

♦ Prepare the bibliography and works cited list on separate pages with appropriate headings.

Now that you have keyed your paper, *read it aloud, either to yourself or to someone else*, to quickly find anything that does not make sense. Listen for grammatical problems and look for incorrect spelling and punctuation. Your final draft should be clean and neat.

Figure 13-8 Sample Cover Sheet

Global Warming
A Threat to People and the Environment

Jane Gomez
SCI 101 - Environmental Science
Professor Jack Handey
May 20, 2001

ACTIVITY 9

Prepare the final draft of the paper now. When you finish, reward yourself for a job well done!

Checkpoint 13.2

1. Describe the three parts of any essay, paper or report.

2. What are the eight steps in the writing process?

3. What is the easiest part of the writing process for you? the hardest?

13.3 WRITING E-MAIL

E-mail is one of the most common and important writing activities for professional workers, online learners, and other Internet users. It is increasingly becoming the preferred mode of communication over face-to-face meetings, telephones, and faxes.

E-mail connects you to people, information, and the Internet. It allows you to get a short message out quickly and effectively to a lot of people at once, especially to people who are far away. E-mail can help you manage your time better by limiting time-consuming phone conversations and face-to-face meetings.

Because facial expressions, body language, and tone of voice are missing from e-mail, you lose valuable clues to the message. Therefore, the words you choose, and the way you use and present them are extremely important. Misusing words leads to a misunderstanding of the message by the reader, which can lead to a situation you never intended.

ACTIVITY 10

Research news magazines to find at least one story reported in the press about the misuse of e-mail. You may be shocked at what you find. Share the stories with others so they may avoid making e-mail mistakes!

_____

_____

_____

_____

_____

_____

_____

_____

_____

_____

_____

_____

Wilma Davidson, author of *Business Writing*, suggests the following e-mail writing guidelines. Review them and identify which ones you already use and which you might want to use in the future.

Send E-mail to the Right People

For the primary recipients of your message—people from whom you want action—key the receiver's address into the TO field.

For people who are to be courtesy copied—meaning they are not expected to take action—use the CC field for the address. TO and CC recipients can see all the names and addresses in the TO and CC fields.

If your program has the BCC option (blind courtesy copy), use it to share information with a recipient from whom you do not expect a response. Some believe BCC hints that a message is being sent behind someone's back, since all the recipient addresses are not listed. Many spammers—those who send junk e-mail—use the BCC field.

Write an Informative and Engaging Subject Line

An e-mail should prove to the receiver as quickly as possible why it should or should not be read. When people look at their e-mail in-box, one way they decide which ones to read first are those with the most informative and engaging subject lines. Which subject line tells you more or gets your attention first?

a. Meeting Info   a. Meeting postponed till Tuesday

b. I have a question   b. What is dress code for the party?

c. (no subject)   c. any subject

ACTIVITY II

Try your hand at revising these e-mail subject lines to make them more informative and engaging.

Original Subject Line	Revised Subject Line
1. FYI	
2. It's Late	
3. Thoughts	
4. Tires	
5. The New Year	
6. Are You Free?	

Bottom-Line Your Message

Place the key point or question first in the e-mail communication. Too many people ramble, explaining why they need what they want, and don't come to the point until the end. To be a good e-mail writer, help the reader get your message sooner.

Be Brief

When writing e-mail, longer is not better. Ideally, e-mail messages should resemble a postcard more than a letter. Keep the KISS rule in mind (Keep It Simple and Short).

Use Spaces and Paragraph Breaks for Readability

Many people write lengthy e-mails using one long paragraph. This makes the message difficult to read. Though the format options are limited on e-mail, try creating smaller paragraphs and putting a line space between each one. The reader will thank you. Never use all capital letters to emphasize an entire paragraph. This is difficult to read and is interpreted as "yelling."

Provide the Reader with an Easy Way to Reply

This means being specific in your request, whenever possible, with a yes or no response.

Be as Personal as the Situation Allows

When communicating with a professor, boss, or coworker, you might need to be more formal than writing to a friend or relative. Use your judgment.

Avoid Sarcasm

It is often misinterpreted.

Proof It

Making a keying error or spelling mistake is easy with e-mail. This makes your communication look sloppy and gives the reader the wrong impression of you. How you look on screen is a direct reflection of you.

Wait a Moment before Pressing Send

Double-check your message before you send. Also make sure you have attached any documents that are needed. Make sure the tone, topic, and appearance of your e-mail won't embarrass you.

Smart Tip

E-mail should not be used for lengthy or complicated messages, indiscreet messages, confidential messages, angry exchanges, or any message you wouldn't want to be viewed publicly or have forwarded.

ACTIVITY 12

With a partner, create a situation where you need to communicate with each other by e-mail, such as for planning a party, getting together to study, proposing ideas for a work project, or another reason. Have one person begin by writing the first e-mail message according to the guidelines described above. The message can be written on paper, or online if you have access to e-mail. Print your messages out for later use in this activity. Ask the second person to reply and continue with at least three communications each. When you complete the e-mail chain, share your messages with others in your class. Discuss how the messages are effective and how they can be improved. You may use the space below to draft your first two exchanges.

First message _____

_____

_____

Reply _____

_____

_____

Second message _____

_____

_____

Reply _____

_____

_____

_____

> "As e-mail has become more entrenched, the people that use e-mail effectively tend to wield more influence than those who write badly or annoy people with their messages."
>
> —Joan Tunstall
>   Author of *Better Faster E-mail*

Checkpoint 13.3

1. How is writing an e-mail and writing a letter different?

2. Why is writing an informative subject line important?

3. Which of the e-mail writing guidelines make the most sense to you?

Focus on Ethics

Nancy, a shoe manufacturing marketing analyst, was asked by her boss to come up with some research on the company's competitors. While searching the Internet, she found a web site that included what was needed. It had been developed by an independent marketing consultant. She copied it, edited it, and submitted it as her report. Is this ethical? Why or why not?

WEB LINK

http://weblications.net/abrain.htm

A look at Left brain/Right Brain functions and how they relate to writing. A step-by-step process to help you relax before writing.

http://www.coun.uvic.ca/learn/essay.html

More on writing essays and reports

http://www.motivationalquotes.com

A site dedicated to personal and professional motivation and inspiration, perfect to add to any writing or oral presentation.

Key Terms and Concepts

conclusion	KISS	thesis statement
connecting words	mapping	topic
editing	position	writing process
introduction	rough draft	
issue	thesis	

Chapter Summary

1. Communicating your thoughts on paper effectively is very important for your success in the real world.

2. Writing essays, papers, and reports require an 8 step process.

3. The first steps of the 8 step process include finding time to write, deciding on a topic, doing research, and creating a thesis statement. The next steps include creating an outline using the 5W's and H and writing a rough draft to include an introduction, the body, and a conclusion. The final steps include revising the rough draft and creating your final draft.

4. Writing effective e-mail correspondence enhances your position with others. E-mail carries its own set of guidelines that, when followed, make for effective written communication.

Based on the information you learned in this chapter, answer the following questions using your own words.

1. Pick an occupation—one in which you currently work or one in which you want to work—and describe the types of writing required to do this job.

2. Describe the writing process in your own words without looking back at this chapter.

3. What can you do to select a topic for a paper? What are some points to consider?

4. What is a thesis statement? How do you create a thesis statement?

5. What are the 5Ws and H? How can they be used to generate ideas for your essay or paper?

6. Describe mapping in your own words.

7. What are the three parts of any essay or paper? What purpose does each part serve?

8. What is involved in revising a rough draft?

9. How can you use the e-mail guidelines in this chapter to write better e-mails?

10. Why is learning to communicate well on paper beneficial for you?

Case 1

Aimee's boss asked her to write an evaluation of customer service for their department head. He told her he wanted a thorough report covering (1) the importance of keeping customers happy, (2) what customer services the department currently provide, (3) recommendations of what her department should do to improve, (4) what other organizations are doing, (5) how customers are changing, and (6) a history of the department's customer service activities. It sounded very overwhelming to Aimee, even though she had spent several years as a customer service representative and was interested in the topic.

1. What would you recommend to Aimee to get her started on writing this evaluation?

2. Aimee brings her rough draft to you, which is organized exactly as her boss outlined it originally. You suggest she rearrange it in more logical fashion so that each issue leads to the next one. What order would make more sense and why?

Case 2

Art was writing a letter to a newspaper to complain about a local trucking service. He felt that the trucks roared down his street faster than the speed limit. Often several trucks travelled together, which created dust in the summer and bothered his asthma. He thought that, occasionally, they did not come to a full stop at the stop sign, and now he had found tire marks on his newly seeded lawn. He was also afraid for the safety of kids across the street, two of whom were under school age and sometimes played in their yard unsupervised.

1. Which of Art's concerns should he research to be sure his observations and statements are accurate before he writes the letter?

2. What might Art write in a letter to get the newspaper's attention about his problem with the trucks?

SELF-CHECK PROGRESS CHART

	Chapter 1	Chapter 2	Chapter 3	Chapter 4	Chapter 5	Chapter 6	Chapter 7	Chapter 8	Chapter 9	Chapter 10	Chapter 11	Chapter 12	Chapter 13
1000													
950													
900													
850													
800													
750													
700													
650													
600													
550													
500													
450													
400													
350													
300													
250													
200													
150													
100													
50													

	Begin End 1	Begin End 2	Begin End 3	Begin End 4	Begin End 5	Begin End 6	Begin End 7	Begin End 8	Begin End 9	Begin End 10	Begin End 11	Begin End 12	Begin End 13

Final Self-Evaluation

This final self-evaluation will give you an idea of how much progress you have made from the beginning of the course to the present. It helps you to see which active learning habits and behaviors you have learned and which you may still need to improve. As you have done in every chapter throughout the book, read each statement and then circle the letter (Y, S, or N) most appropriate to your answer. Remember to answer honestly, rate yourself at the end of each chapter section and then complete the Self-Check Progress Chart on page 351.

Chapter One - Learning by Doing

1.	I generally have a positive attitude while learning.	Y	S	N
2.	I sit near the instructor or meeting leader.	Y	S	N
3.	I actively and fearlessly participate in discussions.	Y	S	N
4.	I listen carefully and take good notes.	Y	S	N
5.	I work or study in an appropriate environment for learning.	Y	S	N
6.	I take good notes and write questions while reading.	Y	S	N
7.	I am prepared and complete my work on time.	Y	S	N
8.	I keep a calendar and follow a schedule.	Y	S	N
9.	I ask for and get help when needed.	Y	S	N
10.	I learn from my mistakes.	Y	S	N

Rate Yourself

Number of Ys _____ X 100 =

Number of Ss _____ X 50 =

Number of Ns _____ X 0 =

Total =

Chapter Two - Discovering Your Learning Style

1.	I know what learning styles are.	Y	N
2.	I know my learning style preferences.	Y	N
3.	I am familiar with how a sequential learner prefers to learn.	Y	N
4.	I am familiar with how a sequential instructor prefers to teach.	Y	N
5.	I am familiar with how a random learner prefers to learn.	Y	N
6.	I am familiar with how a random instructor prefers to teach.	Y	N
7.	I know if I am a more visual, auditory, or tactile learner.	Y	N
8.	I know several learning strategies that will help me learn best.	Y	N
9.	I am aware of the learning styles of others.	Y	N
10.	I know how to adjust my learning styles to the teaching styles of my instructors.	Y	N

Rate Yourself

Number of Ys _____ X 100 =

Number of Ns _____ X 0 =

Total =

Chapter Three - Creating Concentration

1.	I learn in a quiet, distraction-free environment.	Y	S	N
2.	I learn without a radio or television on.	Y	S	N
3.	I resist taking phone calls or checking e-mail while studying.	Y	S	N
4.	I work at an uncluttered desk or table with good lighting.	Y	S	N
5.	I am aware of the room temperature and can make myself comfortable.	Y	S	N
6.	I am aware of, and try to reduce, mental distractions before learning.	Y	S	N
7.	I am usually relaxed when I have a lot of studying to do.	Y	S	N
8.	I know several ways to increase my concentration while studying.	Y	S	N
9.	I reserve most of my learning for the time of day when I am most alert.	Y	S	N
10.	I enjoy learning.	Y	S	N

Rate Yourself

Number of Ys _____ X 100 =

Number of Ss _____ X 50 =

Number of Ns _____ X 0 =

Total =

Chapter Four - Learning Time Management

1. I know what is important to me.	Y	S	N
2. I make time for those things I feel are most important.	Y	S	N
3. I know how I spend my time.	Y	S	N
4. I know that learning requires time and repetition.	Y	S	N
5. I keep and follow a monthly calendar.	Y	S	N
6. I keep and follow a weekly planner.	Y	S	N
7. I plan ahead for project due dates and future events (writing projects, tests, presentations).	Y	S	N
8. I set goals for myself.	Y	S	N
9. I reward myself when I reach a goal.	Y	S	N
10. I know what procrastination is and how it affects my ability to manage my time.	Y	S	N

Rate Yourself

Number of Ys _____ X 100 =

Number of Ss _____ X 50 =

Number of Ns _____ X 0 =

Total =

Chapter Five - Studying Smart

1. Before the day of a test, I know what material will be covered.	Y	S	N
2. Before the day of a test, I know what type of test will be given (multiple choice, essay, and so on).	Y	S	N
3. I eat healthy foods, get enough sleep, and exercise regularly.	Y	S	N
4. I know the difference between memorizing and learning.	Y	S	N
5. I avoid cramming for tests.	Y	S	N
6. I do the most difficult and challenging work first.	Y	S	N
7. I study for a test a little each day for several days or weeks before the testing date.	Y	S	N
8. I am good at predicting test questions from my notes and reading material.	Y	S	N
9. When learning new information, I use memory devices.	Y	S	N
10. I learn from my testing mistakes and take action to prevent them in the future.	Y	S	N

Rate Yourself

Number of Ys _____ X 100 =

Number of Ss _____ X 50 =

Number of Ns _____ X 0 =

Total =

Chapter Six - Taking Notes from Lecture

1. I come prepared to meetings and classes with the tools for note taking.   Y   S   N
2. I can pick out the important information from a lecture or meeting to take notes on.   Y   S   N
3. I take notes from others using key words, not full sentences.   Y   S   N
4. I abbreviate often when I take notes.   Y   S   N
5. I frequently use my own words when taking notes.   Y   S   N
6. At work, I have occasion to take some form of notes while on the phone.   Y   S   N
7. I know at least four effective note taking habits.   Y   S   N
8. I am aware of personality clues of speakers.   Y   S   N
9. I am aware of verbal clues of speakers.   Y   S   N
10. My class or meeting notes are easy to study and learn from.   Y   S   N

Rate Yourself

Number of Ys	_____	X	100	=
Number of Ss	_____	X	50	=
Number of Ns	_____	X	0	=
			Total	=

Chapter Seven - Taking Notes from Reading Material

1. The notes I take from my reading are easy to study and learn from.   Y   S   N
2. When reading material that I need to learn or refer to later, I usually take some form of notes.   Y   S   N
3. I know how to study without a lot of rereading.   Y   S   N
4. I take notes from reading using key words, not full sentences.   Y   S   N
5. I mark areas I don't understand in my text so I can ask questions about them.   Y   S   N
6. I know how to use a highlighter effectively.   Y   S   N
7. I know how to create margin notes.   Y   S   N
8. I can locate the important information from reading material and take effective notes from it.   Y   S   N
9. I use note taking as an active way to concentrate and learn when I read.   Y   S   N
10. I learn more when I take effective notes.   Y   S   N

Rate Yourself

Number of Ys	_____	X	100	=
Number of Ss	_____	X	50	=
Number of Ns	_____	X	0	=
			Total	=

Chapter Eight - Reading Comprehension Skills

1.	I understand what active readers know and do.	Y	S	N
2.	I know the difference between nonfiction and fiction material.	Y	S	N
3.	I am aware of my purpose and responsibility before I read.	Y	S	N
4.	I know how to pre-view a nonfiction book or magazine.	Y	S	N
5.	I know how to pre-view a nonfiction chapter or article.	Y	S	N
6.	When I come across a word I don't know, I use context clues to understand its meaning.	Y	S	N
7.	When I come across a word I don't know, I use prefixes, roots, and suffixes to identify its meaning.	Y	S	N
8.	When I come across a word I don't know, I use a dictionary effectively.	Y	S	N
9.	I have a system for tracking new words.	Y	S	N
10.	I can manage my reading workload.	Y	S	N

Rate Yourself

Number of Ys _____ X 100 =

Number of Ss _____ X 50 =

Number of Ns _____ X 0 =

Total =

Chapter Nine - Survival Reading Skills

1.	I can handle my reading workload with ease.	Y	S	N
2.	I know how to effectively increase my reading speed.	Y	S	N
3.	I know how to locate and read key words.	Y	S	N
4.	I know how to locate and read in phrases.	Y	S	N
5.	I know how to use my hands or a white card to help me increase my reading speed.	Y	S	N
6.	I know how to adjust my reading speed according to my purpose and background knowledge.	Y	S	N
7.	I know the difference between skimming and scanning.	Y	S	N
8.	I know how to skim effectively.	Y	S	N
9.	I can scan accurately.	Y	S	N
10.	I know that reading everything all the time is not an efficient use of my time.	Y	S	N

Rate Yourself

Number of Ys _____ X 100 =

Number of Ss _____ X 50 =

Number of Ns _____ X 0 =

Total =

Success Skills

Chapter Ten - Mastering Tests

1. I know that a low test grade does not make me a failure.	Y	S	N
2. I realize that it is okay not to know everything on a test.	Y	S	N
3. I follow both written and oral test directions carefully.	Y	S	N
4. Before I begin a test, I pre-view it by looking for the point spread.	Y	S	N
5. I pre-view my tests by looking for answers to other questions.	Y	S	N
6. I budget my time effectively when I take a test.	Y	S	N
7. On paper tests, I do the easiest questions first and come back later to the harder ones.	Y	S	N
8. I am aware of the differences between computer-based and paper tests.	Y	S	N
9. I review returned tests for topics I need to understand better.	Y	S	N
10. I learn from my testing mistakes.	Y	S	N

Rate Yourself

Number of Ys _____ X 100 =

Number of Ss _____ X 50 =

Number of Ns _____ X 0 =

Total =

Chapter Eleven - Using Your Critical and Creative Mind

1. I regularly analyze my thinking process.	Y	S	N
2. I can define critical thinking and creative thinking.	Y	S	N
3. I know what metacognition means.	Y	S	N
4. I know the difference between divergent and convergent thinking.	Y	S	N
5. I know four guidelines for critical thinking.	Y	S	N
6. I can identify common thinking errors in advertising and political speeches.	Y	S	N
7. I can recognize the difference between facts and opinions.	Y	S	N
8. I take time to use thinking skills when I solve problems.	Y	S	N
9. I know the four rules of brainstorming.	Y	S	N
10. I realize that know-how and practice can improve thinking.	Y	S	N

Rate Yourself

Number of Ys _____ X 100 =

Number of Ss _____ X 50 =

Number of Ns _____ X 0 =

Total =

Chapter Twelve - Finding Information on the Web

1.	I understand what the World Wide Web is and what kind of information can be located on it.	Y	S	N
2.	I know the difference between a search engine and a directory.	Y	S	N
3.	I know how to use the basic search features of the Web.	Y	S	N
4.	I know how to refine searches to locate exact information.	Y	S	N
5.	I am able to analyze and compare the search results from different web services.	Y	S	N
6.	I understand the copyright restrictions of downloading text and images from web sites.	Y	S	N
7.	I know how to evaluate the validity of web sources.	Y	S	N
8.	I know how to look for a job on the Web.	Y	S	N
9.	I know how to create an educational report using web site sources.	Y	S	N
10.	I feel confident that I know how to find information on the web.	Y	S	N

Rate Yourself

Number of Ys	_____	X	100	=
Number of Ss	_____	X	50	=
Number of Ns	_____	X	0	=
			Total	=

Chapter Thirteen - Writing in the Real World

1.	I know that writing is an important part of school, work, and personal life.	Y	S	N
2.	I understand that good writing follows a process.	Y	S	N
3.	I schedule time ahead for my longer writing projects.	Y	S	N
4.	I know how to use the Internet for research.	Y	S	N
5.	I know how to decide on a topic.	Y	S	N
6.	I know how to write a good thesis statement.	Y	S	N
7.	I can create an organized outline for my writing by using the mapping process.	Y	S	N
8.	I can describe the three parts of most written communication.	Y	S	N
9.	I know how to effectively present the final draft of my writing.	Y	S	N
10.	I know how to write effective e-mail.	Y	S	N

Rate Yourself

Number of Ys	_____	X	100	=
Number of Ss	_____	X	50	=
Number of Ns	_____	X	0	=
			Total	=

Success Skills

EFFECTIVE NOTE-TAKING HABITS
(For use with Chapters 6 and 7)

You should know about several effective note taking habits that are easy to use. Some are specific for classroom learning while others are for self-learning or business use. As you read through each, decide which are best for your situation.

Pre-view Reading Before a Class or Meeting

If, according to your syllabus or your instructor's comments, you know that Chapter 4 will be discussed in your next computer programming class, it is an excellent idea to spend a few minutes previewing or skimming the chapter (see Chapter 8) before class. If your boss says the focus of an upcoming meeting is the new procedure manual, then looking over it ahead of time gives you some background knowledge which will help you to take good notes as well as actively participate in the discussion. You will also understand the information better.

Start Each Day with a Fresh Piece of Paper

Every page of your notes is like a photo of what happens on a given day. By starting each day with a fresh piece of paper, you will keep your "photos" separate and leave room to add information.

Write on Only One Side of the Paper

Writing on one side of the paper gives you open space on the other side to summarize the notes. Write notes from related reading, or draw mind maps.

Always Date and Title Every Page

If you write the date and the title of topics being covered at the top of each page, you will have an easy reference to turn to later. If you take more than one page of notes, number the pages in order on the top right-hand side as pg. 1, pg. 2, pg. 3, or other numbering you prefer.

Write in the Shortest Form Possible

When taking notes from an instructor or in a meeting, you do not have a lot of time to write all that is said, nor should you. Since people do not remember complete sentences, it is a waste of time to try to write full sentences. Instead, by using abbreviations and key words, you will be able to get the important information in a shortened form.

Use Abbreviations

Using abbreviations, or shortened words or phrases, makes note taking easier. They are easy to use once you establish your own style of abbreviating. You are already familiar with some abbreviations, but you will want to create others of your own. A simple way of creating your own abbreviations is to either shorten the word, use a symbol, or omit vowels. For example, if you are discussing "forms of communication" and the word "communication" is often repeated in your notes, you can shorten the word to "comm." If you are discussing a topic having to do with money, you can use the symbol "$" in your notes. If you are discussing "management," you can omit vowels and use "mngmnt" or an even shorter term "mgmt."

Activity 1 Creating Abbreviations

In the following list, the left side gives you a common word and the right side is for your shortened version of the word. Some are very simple while others will make you think. Use your imagination in creating the abbreviations, but be sure to remember what you have written. Can you think of any other abbreviations you can use? Write them on a separate piece of paper.

Common Word or Term	My Abbreviation	Common Word or Term	My Abbreviation
abbreviation	_abbrev._	decrease	_____
communication	_comm._	equals	_____
money	_$_	and	_____
management	_mgmt_	definition	_____
chapt	_____	plus	_____
North	_____	with	_____
South	_____	without	_____
East	_____	therefore	_____
West	_____	for example	_____
pages	_____	percentage	_____
and so forth	_____	number	_____
government	_____	computer	_____
introduction	_____	important	_____
association	_____	building	_____
paragraph	_____	something	_____
greater than	_____	business	_____
less than	_____	employer	_____
increase	_____	employee	_____

Use Key Words

Using key words, as you learned in Chapter 9, is another good way of taking notes in a short form. Key words are the larger, more important words in a sentence. By writing only key words, you save time, concentrate on the main ideas, and end up with fewer words.

Learning to write key words definitely takes concentration as well as some practice, but the time and energy you use to learn this skill will save time and energy when you review your notes or study for exams.

Activity 2 Key Words

Read the following complete sentence. Then read the key words that could serve as your notes. Notice how easy it is to go from writing seven words to only three without losing meaning.

Complete Sentence

The results of the test were conclusive.

Key Words

Test results conclusive.

Now it's your turn to try to come up with your own key words for the following sentences. You can use abbreviations or bullet points to make them as short as possible. Afterwards, reread your notes to see if they are understandable. If not, make changes.

Example Sentence: Advertising is the most expensive part of a new business venture.

Key words: Advrtsng = most $ new business

1. An encyclopedia article is the best place to start researching a topic. _____

2. Daily sales figures need to be completed by closing time. _____

3. Computers have eliminated many jobs, but also made people work longer hours. _____

4. Your most important job-hunting tool is your resume. _____

5. As a secretary, you will have to take notes of important meetings and type them up for the record. _____

Use Your Own Words

When you take notes, it is not necessary to write word for word what a person or the reading says. If you are instructed to write something exactly as it is stated, do so; but if you are writing notes on your own, learn to use your own words.

Abbreviations and key words make this possible. Writing your own words forces you to understand what is said before you write.

Activity 3   Informal Outline

Text samples for you to begin practicing your own informal outlines are shown. Use summary paper and write your notes only on the right side of your margin. You can work individually or with other classmates. Remember to use as many effective note-taking techniques as possible.

Read each text first before writing anything. This will help you decide which ideas are more important than others and what information you actually want to take notes on. This is similar to what you have to do in a class or meeting—listen first, then write.

While you are working, ask yourself which ideas seem to be the most important? Which are less important? Why? What do you think is the best way to write the notes? (Keep in mind that no two note takers are the same.) By sharing your ideas with others, you may get ideas that will help make your note taking easier.

Text 1

Learning is an activity of a person who learns. It may be intentional or random; it may involve acquiring new information or skills. It is usually accompanied by a change in behavior and goes on throughout life

Text 2

Success in your classes depends upon effective note-taking and study techniques. To be successful, you must be able to record and to study a variety of lecture information presented in many different formats. Some instructors prefer to give main ideas with details; others prefer to build vocabulary with related examples. Some enjoy using a variety of visual aids, like handouts or overheads, while some just use the blackboard. The Cornell Method of Note Taking can he used with all lecture formats. It helps students simplify their record of the lecture material, while providing a simple study technique at the same time.

Text 3

American public schools did not always exist. Education actually began in the home with the mother being the first teacher. Mothers taught their children reading, writing, and arithmetic as well as Bible education. They were also in charge of teaching their children discipline. As the youngsters grew, the mothers continued teaching their daughters in sewing, cooking, and homemaking, while the sons learned the apprenticeship of their fathers.

Text 4

People are not born with background knowledge. It starts accumulating at birth and is the result of whatever the person is involved in, who influences them, what they learn in school, what they read, what they see on television, who their friends are, and so on. This background knowledge is a valuable tool, especially for reading. Possessing background knowledge helps people read faster and with higher levels of concentration and comprehension.

Success Skills

To build background knowledge while reading, good readers ask themselves three simple questions. The first question is "What do I need to know?" If readers can answer this question, they have a purpose in mind. The second question is 'How well do I already know it?" or "How much background knowledge do I already have?" People with background knowledge read faster and with greater interest than a person who has none. The last question is "What do I need to know?" It is the responsibility of the reader to seek out information when he or she is unfamiliar with a topic. This is the key to building background knowledge.

Text 5

What makes people successful? The behavior most common to successful people is that they listen respectfully to everyone. Close observation reveals that listening is a set of behaviors that involves more than simply hearing another's words. It includes making eye contact with the speaker, which is important because the person wants to know you are hearing what he or she says. Responsive facial expressions, such as a quizzical look when you don't understand what a person is saying or a widening of your eyes when you are skeptical, are appropriate because they also let the speaker know you are listening. Nodding your head and saying "Uh-huh" or "I see" from time to time lets the speaker know you are hearing him or her. Shifting positions or standing in an attentive postures tells the speaker you are prepared to receive his or her message. Asking the speaker questions will help clarify your understanding of what is being said and will let the speaker know you really heard what was said.

Appendix C

PRE-VIEWING FICTION
(For use with Chapter 8)

Pre-viewing fiction takes more guesswork than non-fiction. (For information about pre-viewing non-fiction, see Chapter 8.) Because fiction writers have the freedom to use any writing style and format they choose, fictional material doesn't have an outline that you can easily follow. Your job then is to use the information available to follow the author and understand what is written.

You can use this process when trying to decide what book you want to buy or take out of the library. The short time you spend appropriately choosing your material will result in a more pleasurable reading experience.

Pre-viewing Fiction Material

Pre-viewing fiction material familiarizes you with some of the important aspects of the writing and helps you to read the material more actively.

The Title. Though the title of a novel can tell you what the subject is, it can sometimes be misleading. For example, *The Eye of the Needle* by Ken Follet might lead you to believe that it is a book about sewing, but in reality it is a spy novel that uses the "eye of a needle" as a symbol in the plot. A title of a novel can at best give you a clue to the theme of the book, rather than its main idea.

The Author. Knowing some information about the author will help you to better understand your story. This information can often be found on either the inside or back cover of the book jacket. For instance, a copy of *The House of the Seven Gables* by Nathaniel Hawthorne might tell you that he was born in Salem, Massachusetts in 1804, that he lived near Boston, and that he died in 1864 after writing several novels. Even this cursory information tells you what era he lived in and what influences he might have had.

Some novels have a preface or introduction written by the author. By reading this you can get more clues to the writer's personality. Other questions to think about when learning about an author include: Have they published before? What is their reputation? What is their point of view?

The Copyright Date. The copyright date is found within the first few pages of a book. Learning the date the book was written and/or published can give you clues about what to expect.

Example 1: *The House of Seven Gables* by Nathaniel Hawthorne was originally published in 1851, but the current edition reads 1981. This tells you that the book has been very popular and has withstood the test of time. Since it is still read today, then it must be an admired piece of writing as well as popular.

Example 2: *To Kill a Mockingbird* by Harper Lee has a copyright of 1960. This information would tell you that you would NOT read about things that were developed or happened since then, including computers, video games, or McDonald's.

The Publisher's Information. A publisher will provide you with several pieces of information that are helpful in the pre-view process. A short plot summary can sometimes be found on the back cover, inside cover, or book jacket. This will give you an idea of what the story is about as well as what kind of story it is: mystery, romance, thriller, classic novel, etc.

Testimonial quotes, written by famous, well-known, or popular people are sometimes provided on the back cover or within the first few pages of a novel. These quotes attest to the quality of the writing and/or the story. Be wary of these, however. Remember that publishers are out to sell books, so their quotes are like advertising. Have you ever read an unfavorable quote? Use these for general information only.

The cover design is also advertising for the book. Some books are more pleasing to the eye than others, but they usually offer little indication as to how good the book really is. A table of contents, though not regularly found in a novel, can be helpful as well for referencing a chapter for study purposes or review.

The First Few Pages. By reading the first few pages of a story, you can get a better feel for the writer's style. The setting, or where the story takes place, is an important piece of information. If the story takes place on a desert island, it sets your mood to think of an isolated place with lots of sand and ocean. This is quite different than a setting in the middle of New York City.

The tone, or the mood of the story, adds information to the setting. The story could take place on a bright, sunny day in a park filled with happy children, or on a dull rainy afternoon in the back room of a dusty office. Each sets a different tone for the part of the story being read.

Notice the character names. Are they easy or difficult to remember? It may be helpful to write them down on separate pieces of paper. You can also write some information about who they are related to, in what incidents they were involved, etc., to help you keep track of the characters. (For tips on taking notes from fiction material, see page 176 in Chapter 7.)

Length of Book. Do you want a short novel or a long one? Do you want a book broken up into chapters or no chapters? Check the length and layout to make your decision.

At this point, you should feel ready to begin reading your fiction material. Keep the information you obtained from pre-viewing in mind as you read the story.

Activity 1   Fiction Material

For this activity, you will be pre-viewing a novel. This will familiarize you with the process by going through it step-by-step. Locate a novel you haven't read before.

1. Look at its title. What do you think may be the theme based on the title? _____

   If you read the novel, return to this page when you are finished and see how accurate you were.

2. Looking at the information in your novel, what do you know about its author?_____

   _____

3. What is the copyright date? _____What does it tell you?_____

4. Look for the publisher's information in your book. What does it tell you?_____

5. Read the first few pages of your story. What can you tell about the author's style? _____

   Do you like the story? _____Why?_____

6. How long is your book?_____Is this a good length for you?_____

BUILDING VOCABULARY
(For use with Chapter 8)

Activity 1   Common Prefixes

1. On each of the following lines, you are given a prefix, its meaning, and an example using the prefix. If you are unsure of the meaning of the example word, use a dictionary to get its exact meaning. Write down the word and its meaning on a separate piece of paper for future use. Notice how the meaning relates to its prefix meaning.

2. Then, in the blank space to the right of the example, give your own example of a word that begins with the prefix and which uses the prefix meaning. If you can think of more than one example, make a list of them on a separate piece of paper. Be aware that your example may not carry the meaning of the prefix. Look up your example in a dictionary if you are unsure.

Prefix	Meaning	Example	Your Example
ab	from, away from	abduct	_____
ad	to, forward	admit	_____
ambi	both	ambiguous	_____
an, a	without	anemia	_____
ante	before	antecedent	_____
anti	against, opposite	antipathy	_____
arch	chief, first	archetype	_____
be	over, thoroughly	befuddle	_____
bi	two	bicycle	_____
cata	down	catapult	_____
circum	around	circumspect	_____
com	with, together	communicate	_____
co	with	coeditor	_____
contro (a)	against	controversy	_____
de	down, away	descend	_____
demi	partly, half	demigod	_____
di	two	dichotomy	_____

dia	across	diagonal	_____
dis, dif	not, apart	difference	_____
dys	faulty, bad	dyspepsia	_____
ex, e	out	eject	_____
extra, extro	beyond, outside	extracurricular	_____
hyper	above, excessively	hyperventilate	_____
hypo	beneath, lower	hypoglycemia	_____
in	not	inefficient	_____
im	not	impeccable	_____
inter	between, among	interjection	_____
intra, intro	within	intramural	_____
macro	large, long	macrocosm	_____
mega	great, million	megalomania	_____
meta	involving change	metamorphosis	_____
micro	small	microcosm	_____
mis	bad, improper	misnomer	_____
mono	one	monotheism	_____
multi	many	multitudinous	_____
neo	new	neophyte	_____
non	not	nonentity	_____
ob, of	against	obtrude	_____
pan	all, every	panorama	_____
para	beyond, related	parallel	_____
per	through, completely	pervade	_____
peri	around, near	periphery	_____
poly	many	polyglot	_____
post	after	posterity	_____
pre	before	premonition	_____
prim	first	primordial	_____

pro	forward, in favor of	proponent	_____
proto	first	prototype	_____
pseudo	false	pseudonym	_____
re	again, back	reimburse	_____
retro	backward	retrospect	_____
se	away, aside	seclude	_____
semi	half, partly	semiconscious	_____
sub	under, less	subjugate	_____
sup	under, less	suppress	_____
super	over, above	supervise	_____
sur	over, above	surtax	_____
syn, sym	with, together	synchronize	_____
tele	far	telegraphic	_____
trans	across	transpose	_____
ultra	beyond, excessive	ultramodern	_____
un	not	unwitting	_____
under	below	underling	_____
uni	one	unison	_____
with	away, against	withhold	_____

Activity 2   Common Roots

1. On each of the following lines you are given a root, its meaning, and an example using the root. If you are unsure of the meaning of the example word, use a dictionary to get its exact meaning. Write down the word and its meaning on a separate piece of paper for future use. Notice how the meaning relates to its root meaning.

2. Then, in the blank space to the right of the example, give your own example of a word that begins with the root and which uses the meaning. If you can think of more than one example, make a list of them on a separate piece of paper. Keep in mind that roots are not only found in the middle of a word, but also in its beginning. Be aware that your example may not carry the meaning of the root. Look up your example in a dictionary if you are unsure.

Root Word	Meaning	Example	Your Example
ac	sharp	acerbity	_____
aev, ev	age, era	medieval	_____
agog	leader	demagogue	_____
agri	field	agriculture	_____
ali	another	alienate	_____
alt	high	altimeter	_____
alter	other	alterego	_____
am	love	amicable	_____
anim	mind, soul	magnanimity	_____
ann, enn	year	perennial	_____
anthrop	man	misanthrope	_____
apt	fit	aptitude	_____
aqua	water	aquatic	_____
arch	ruler, first	archeology	_____
aster	star	asterisk	_____
aud	hear	audible	_____
auto	self	autonomy	_____
belli	war	rebellious	_____
ben	good	benefactor	_____
bon	good	bonus	_____
biblio	book	bibliography	_____
bio	life	biography	_____

breve	short	abbreviate	_____
cap	to take	capture	_____
capit, capt	head	decapitate	_____
carn	flesh	carnage	_____
ced	to yield, to go	antecedent	_____
cess	to yield, to go	process	_____
celer	swift	celerity	_____
cent	one hundred	centipede	_____
chron	time	anachronism	_____
cid, cis	to cut, to kill	homocide	_____
cit	to call, to start	excite	_____
civi	citizen	civilization	_____
clam	to cry out	clamorous	_____
claus, clud	to close	claustrophobia	_____
cognit	to learn	incognito	_____
compi	to fill	complement	_____
cord	heart	cordial	_____
corpor	body	incorporate	_____
cred	to believe	incredulous	_____
cur	to care	curator	_____
curr, curs	to run	excursion	_____
da, dat	to give	data	_____
deb	to owe	indebtedness	_____
dem	people	epidemic	_____
di	day	diary	_____
dic, dict	to say	verdict	_____
doc, doct	to teach	document	_____
domin	to rule	dominant	_____
duc, duct	to lead	viaduct	_____

Success Skills

dynam	power, strength	dynamic	_____
ego	I	egocentric	_____
erg, urg	work	ergonomics	_____
err	to wander	erratic	_____
eu	good, well	eupeptic	_____
fac	to make, do	factory	_____
fic	to make, do	fiction	_____
fec, fect	to make, do	affect	_____
fall, fals	to deceive	fallacious	_____
fer	to bring, to bear	transfer	_____
fid	belief, faith	infidel	_____
fin	end, limit	confine	_____
flect, flex	bend	deflect	_____
fort	luck, chance	fortuitous	_____
fort	strong	fortitude	_____
frag, fract	break	infraction	_____
fug	flee	fugitive	_____
fus	pour	effusive	_____
gam	marriage	polygamy	_____
gen, gener	class, race	generic	_____
grad	go, step	gradual	_____
graph	writing	stenography	_____
gram	writing	telegram	_____
greg	flock, herd	gregarious	_____
gress	go, step	digress	_____
helio	sun	heliograph	_____
it	journey, road	exit	_____
itiner	journey, road	itinerary	_____
jac, jec	to throw	projectile	_____

jur,jurat	to swear	perjure	_____
labor	to work	collaborate	_____
lat	to bring, to bear	translate	_____
leg	to choose, to read	legible	_____
lig	to choose, to read	eligible	_____
leg	law	legitimate	_____
liber, libr	book	libretto	_____
liber	free	liberation	_____
log	word, study	etymology	_____
loqu	to talk	loquacious	_____
luc	light	translucent	_____
magn	great	magnanimity	_____
mal	bad	malevolent	_____
man	hand	manuscript	_____
mar	sea	maritime	_____
mater, matr	mother	matrilineal	_____
mit, miss	to send	dismiss	_____
mob, mov	move	mobilize	_____
mon, monit	to warn	premonition	_____
mori, mort	to die	moribund	_____
morph	shape, form	anthropomorphic	_____
mut	change	immutable	_____
nat	born	innate	_____
nav	ship	circumnavigate	_____
neg	deny	renege	_____
nomen	name	nomenclature	_____
nov	new	renovate	_____
omni	all	omnivorous	_____

oper	to work	cooperation	_____
pac	peace	pacifist	_____
pass	feel	impassioned	_____
pater, patr	father	patriotism	_____
path	disease, feeling	apathetic	_____
ped, pod	foot	impediment	_____
ped	child	pedagogue	_____
pel, puls	to drive	compulsion	_____
pet, petit	to seek	petition	_____
phil	love	philanderer	_____
pon, posit	to place	postpone	_____
port	to carry	export	_____
poten	able, powerful	omnipotent	_____
psych	mind	psychosis	_____
putat	to trim, to calculate	amputate	_____
ques, quir	to ask	inquisitive	_____
reg	rule	regent	_____
rid, ris	laugh	ridiculous	_____
rog, rogat	to ask	interrogate	_____
rupt	to break	interrupt	_____
sacr	holy	sacriligious	_____
sci	to know	omniscient	_____
scop	watch, see	microscope	_____
scrib, script	to write	mistranscribe	_____
sect	cut	bisect	_____
sed	to sit	sedentary	_____
sent, sens	to think, to feel	sensitive	_____
sequi, secut	to follow	consecutive	_____
solv, solut	to loosen	dissolute	_____

somn	sleep	insomnia	_____
soph	wisdom	sophisticated	_____
spec	to look at	spectator	_____
spir	breathe	respiratory	_____
string, strict	bind	stringent	_____
stru, struct	build	constructive	_____
tang, tact	to touch	tangent	_____
tempor	time	extemporaneous	_____
ten, tent	to hold	retentive	_____
term	end	interminable	_____
therm	heat	thermostat	_____
tors, tort	twist	tortuous	_____
tract	drag, pull	attraction	_____
trud, trus	push, shove	protrusion	_____
urb	city	suburban	_____
vac	empty	vacuum	_____
vad, vas	go	invade	_____
ven	come	intervene	_____
ver	true	verisimilitude	_____
verb	word	verbatim	_____
vers, vert	turn	diversion	_____
via	way	deviation	_____
vid, vis	to see	evidence	_____
vinc, vict, vanq	to conquer	invincible	_____
viv, vit	alive	vivacious	_____
voc, vocat	to call	invocation	_____
vol	wish	voluntary	_____
volv, volut	to roll	convolution	_____

Success Skills

Activity 3   Common Suffixes

1. On each of the following lines you are given a suffix, its meaning, and an example using the suffix. If you are unsure of the meaning of the example word, use a dictionary to get its exact meaning. Write down the word and its meaning on a separate piece of paper for future use. Notice how the meaning relates to its suffix meaning.

2. Then, in the blank space to the right of the example, give your own example of a word that begins with the suffix and which uses the suffix meaning. If you can think of more than one example, make a list of them on a separate piece of paper. Be aware that your example may not carry the meaning of the suffix. Look up your example in a dictionary if you are unsure.

Suffix	Meaning	Example	Your Example
able, ible	capable of	portable	_____
ac, ic	like, pertaining to	dramatic	_____
acious, icious	full of	avaricious	_____
al	pertaining to	logical	_____
ant, ent	full of	eloquent	_____
ary	like, connected with	dictionary	_____
ate	to make	consecrate	_____
ation	the act of	exasperation	_____
fic	making, doing	terrific	_____
fy	to make	beautify	_____
iferous	producing, bearing	vociferous	_____
il, ile	capable of	puerile	_____
ism	doctrine, belief	monotheism	_____
ist	dealer, doer	realist	_____
ity	state of being	annuity	_____
ive	like	expensive	_____
ize, ise	make	harmonize	_____
oid	resembling, like	anthropoid	_____
osis	condition	neurosis	_____
ous	full of	nauseous	_____
tude	state of	certitude	_____

READING EXERCISES
(For use with Chapter 9)

Timing Instructions

Several kinds of reading exercises in this book require that you time yourself so that you can measure your progress in speed. Here is the best method for timing yourself when you are not in a classroom and when you do not have a stop watch.

1. Use a watch or clock with a sweep second hand. With a pen and paper handy, wait until the second hand is about ten seconds before the 60 second mark. Then write down the exact time in minutes. This is your beginning time. (The hour is unimportant for these short exercises.) When the second hand crosses the 60, begin the reading exercise.

2. As soon as you have finished reading, look at the second hand and write down the exact time in minutes and seconds above your beginning time. This is your ending time. Your record will look something like this:

Ending Time:	41 min. 22 sec.
Beginning Time:	39 min. 00 sec.
Total Time:	2 min. 22 sec

3. Subtract your beginning time from your ending time to get your reading time in minutes and seconds. In the above example, the reading time is 2 minutes and 22 seconds.

Ending Time:	_____
Beginning Time:	_____
Total Time:	_____

Figuring Words–Per–Minute

Once you have your reading time, you can figure the words-per-minute.

1. Using the chart below, first translate your seconds into one of the numbers listed under "translated time." This makes it easier to figure words-per-minute. With the example of 2 minutes, 22 seconds, the 22 seconds falls between the 19 and 24 seconds making your translated time into .3. Your reading time is now 2.3 minutes.

Seconds	Translated Time	Seconds	Translated Time
0-6	.0	31-36	.5
7-12	.1	37-42	.6
13-18	.2	43-48	.7
19-24	.3	49-54	.8
25-30	.4	55-60	.9

2. Using the simple formula of *Words Per Minute (WPM) = No. of words ÷ your translated time*, take the number of words in the reading and divide it by your time. You can use a calculator if you have one. If the number of words was 575 and your time was 2.3 minutes, your words-per-minute would be 250 words-per-minute.

Figuring Percentage of Comprehension

1. Compare your answers to those on page 391 in this Appendix. If you have an incorrect response, write down the correct one and go back to see where you might have had a problem. Learning from your mistakes is a far better education than getting everything right all the time!

2. Now multiply the number of answers you had correct by 10% to get your percent of comprehension. For example, 5 correct answers is 50%, 7 correct is 70%, and 10 correct is 100%.

Practice Readings

For these Practice Reading exercises, follow the order of activities as listed below:

1. Write down your Beginning Time.

2. Read the article using key words, phrases, and/or a pacer.

3. Write down your Ending Time.

4. Answer the ten questions that follow without looking back at the reading.

5. Figure words-per-minute.

6. Figure your comprehension percentage by checking your answers against those in this Appendix.

You will now see short informational readings on several different topics. Without looking at the questions on the following pages, read the information using any or all of the three reading tools you have just learned about while timing yourself.

Reading Exercise No. 1—Labor Unions

Ending Time: _____

Beginning Time: _____

Total Time: _____

A little less than twenty percent of the American workforce are members of labor unions. A labor union is a group of workers who have joined together to protect their rights.

The two main types of unions are craft and industrial. A craft union is made up of skilled workers in a craft or trade, such as plumbers, musicians, or barbers. Workers in the same industry often belong to an industrial union. Perhaps you have heard of the United Auto Workers or the United Mine Workers. These are industrial unions.

Throughout its history, organized labor has fought for three main goals. These have been improvements in:

1. Wages, hours, and benefits
2. Job security
3. Safe and healthful working conditions

Unions do other things besides working for these goals. One is to provide apprenticeship programs that teach work skills to young union members. Some unions have hiring halls where workers can go to find out about job openings. Political involvement is often an important labor goal. Unions frequently give money to favorite candidates and provide campaign workers.

The presence and strength of unions varies among geographic areas. Most unions are in the Midwest and Northeast parts of the United States. These areas have large construction, manufacturing, transportation, and mining industries.

A company that has an agreement with a union is called a union shop. In a union shop, the employer can hire whomever he or she chooses. However, the employee must join the union within a certain period of time. About twenty states, most of them in the South, have so-called "right-to-work" laws that don't allow union shops. These states have open shops in which an employee doesn't have to join a union. Open shops may exist in the other thirty states as well, but employees are often under pressure to unionize.

When you start a job, a co-worker or supervisor may ask you to join a union. Members of the local union must vote on your membership. Usually, though, anyone who applies is accepted. You will probably pay an initiation fee to join and you must pay regular dues.

Source: Bailey, Larry. *Working: Learning a Living*. © 1995 South-Western. Reprinted with permission.

Without looking back at the information you just read, answer the following ten questions to the best of your ability. Make a guess when you are not sure. Decide whether the following statements are true (T), false (F), or not mentioned (N). A true statement is a fact based on the information you read. A false statement is one that is mentioned but not correct. A statement that is not mentioned was not discussed at all.

_____ 1. Approximately 20 percent of the American work force are members of labor unions.
_____ 2. A labor union is a group of workers who have joined together to protect their rights.
_____ 3. There are craft unions and mine unions.
_____ 4. A craft union member would be a machinist.
_____ 5. Only men can be a member of a union.
_____ 6. Unions seek to improve an employee's job security.
_____ 7. Unions are strong in all areas of the country.
_____ 8. A union shop is a company that has an agreement with a union.
_____ 9. An employee must be a member of the union before working in a union shop.
_____ 10. Union members are required to wear the union logo on their work clothes.

Once all ten questions are answered, compare your answers to those on page 391 in this Appendix to figure your words-per-minute and percentage of comprehension.

Reading Exercise No. 2—The Changing Workplace

Ending Time: _____

Beginning Time: _____

Total Time: _____

When this country was founded in 1776, most people lived and worked on small, family-owned farms. The farm family raised livestock, poultry, and grain. Surplus food was traded for other products.

As trading increased, small villages grew along rivers and other transportation routes. The growth of towns provided new jobs for shop owners, bankers, blacksmiths, and others. Employment in nonagricultural occupations grew steadily. Agriculture, however, still remained the base of the economy.

In 1876, the share of the labor force working in agriculture stood at about fifty percent. Gradually, the number of farmers decreased as more and more people moved to cities. Meanwhile, agricultural production increased due to better equipment, improved plant and animal strains, and new farming methods. By 1990, the number of workers employed in agriculture had shrunk to less than three percent of the labor force.

In the second half of the 1800s, U.S. industry expanded rapidly. Growing towns and cities needed more and more goods. Typical workers in the early 1900s had factory jobs. They produced steel, machinery, and other manufactured goods. By 1920, over sixty percent of all workers were employed in goods-producing industries.

Growing industry and a growing population needed many kinds of business, transportation, communication, personal, and government services. In response to these demands, service industries began to expand. About 1955, the number of workers providing services passed the number of workers producing goods. Typical service occupations included secretary, clerk, salesperson, and manager.

The shift to service industries and occupations has continued. In 1990, over seventy percent of all workers were employed in services. This service economy, however, is also undergoing change. A new economy is evolving based on knowledge and information.

New ways of dealing with information are changing many types of industries. Here are some examples. Not long ago, communications meant sending information through cable or between ground-to-ground stations. Now, orbiting satellites beam communications around the world.

The use of robots in auto manufacturing is another example. Before robots, skilled workers used hand-held spray guns to apply paint finishes. Now robots do this, receiving their instructions from computers.

Computers haven't just changed the communications and auto industries. Computers are influencing almost all industries and occupations. In many offices, for example, computers are replacing typewriters. Computers are the backbone of the information society.

Source: Bailey, Larry. *Working: Learning a Living.* © 1995 South-Western. Reprinted with permission.

Without looking back at the information you just read, answer the following ten questions to the best of your ability. Make a guess when you are not sure. Decide whether the following statements are true (T), false (F), or not mentioned (N). A true statement is a fact based on the information you read. A false statement is one that is mentioned but not correct. A statement that is not mentioned was not discussed at all.

_____   1. In 1776, most people lived and worked on a farm.
_____   2. Small villages grew because the farming industry grew.
_____   3. One hundred years after the country was founded, about 3 percent of the labor force were working on farms.
_____   4. It can be assumed that advancements in technology have shrunk the farming work force.
_____   5. Industry grew because towns and cities needed more goods.
_____   6. Farmers were retrained to work in industry.
_____   7. The population has grown faster than industries.
_____   8. Service occupations have come about because of the growth of the population.
_____   9. Industries have basically remained the same over the years.
_____   10. The economy of the 1990s is based on knowledge and information.

Once all ten questions are answered, compare your answers to those on page 391 in this Appendix to figure your words-per-minute and percentage of comprehension.

Reading Exercise No. 3—The Attraction of Place

Ending Time: _____

Beginning Time: _____

Total Time: _____

People have always traveled. Curiosity, a basic characteristic of humans, has led people of all eras to explore new environments, seek new places, discover the unknown, search for different and strange places, and enjoy other experiences. This suggests that one place is different from another place, or there would he no curiosity about other places. The *National Geographic* magazine, for example, is considered one of the truly fine magazines in the world today. It adorns many libraries, public and private. It expends considerable effort to illustrate the differences that exist in the world between places. Its popularity reflects people's curiosity about other places and cultures.

While people have always traveled, tourism as we know it today is a recent phenomenon. It has only been since World War II that tourism, particularly international tourism, has developed as a major activity in the world. Early travelers and early tourism were reserved for a few: for the rich or the very brave. One important impetus for tourism resulting from World War II was that the war brought many people in contact with other people and places. They became more interested in the world. The events in one part of the world have an important impact on residents in another part of the world. Growth and change in modes of transportation have also encouraged travel. Replacement of transatlantic ships by airplanes was followed by the jet age from the 1960s to today. Fast, cheap transportation has make world travel a possibility for millions of people.

There are well-developed links between tourism and geography, in that the uniqueness of a place (whether it be an Indian periodic market, a tremendous waterfall, a snowy mountain village, or a resort on a sunny sandy coast) is the result of the geographic relationships at that place. Geography is the study of the earth as the home of humans. It is concerned with the combination of factors that make each individual place on the face of the earth somehow unique. Study of geography represents an attempt to gain an understanding of the causes of the uniqueness that characterizes each place. Uniqueness results from the combination of the natural (or physical) setting of climate, landform, and resources, and the features created by the residents of that place such as buildings, economy, dress styles, or other cultural features. The combination of physical and cultural factors that make each place different is the basis for human curiosity about other places, which causes the growth and development of tourism.

The process of tourism itself has contributed to the uniqueness of place. Every place on the earth's surface changes over time. Changes in economy, political organizations, culture, population size, and the physical environment constantly alter the texture and fabric of the complex mosaic that makes up a place. The invasion or migration of large numbers of people from another place for a short period of time will have an impact on the visited place, changing the uniqueness, creating a new and different cultural, political, economic, and physical landscape.

Source: Hudman, Lloyd, and Richard Jackson. *Geography of Travel and Tourism*. © 1998 Delmar Publishers Inc. Reprinted with permission.

Without looking back at the information you just read, answer the following ten questions to the best of your ability. Make a guess when you are not sure. Decide whether the following statements are true (T), false (F), or not mentioned (N). A true statement is a fact based on the information you read. A false statement is one that is mentioned but not correct. A statement that is not mentioned was not discussed at all.

_____   1.   People travel when they get bored with their surroundings.
_____   2.   The only magazine mentioned by name in this reading was the *National Geographic* magazine.
_____   3.   Tourism as we know it today is the same as when traveling began.
_____   4.   A benefit of World War II is that it brought many people in contact with other people and places.
_____   5.   The cost of traveling has increased with the growth and change in modes of transportation.
_____   6.   Women are better travelers than men.
_____   7.   Geography, as it is defined in the article, is the study of earth as the home of humans.
_____   8.   Detailed geographical maps tell a lot about a place.
_____   9.   Human curiosity causes the growth of tourism.
_____   10. The uniqueness of each place is advertised in the travel brochures.

Once all ten questions are answered, compare your answers to those on page 391 in this Appendix to figure your words-per-minute and percentage of comprehension.

Skimming Exercise

For this skimming exercise, follow the order of activities as listed below:

1. Write down your Beginning Time.

2. Skim the reading to your satisfaction looking for general or main ideas.

3. Write down your Ending Time.

4. Answer the ten questions that follow without looking back at the reading.

5. Figure words-per-minute.

6. Figure your comprehension percentage by checking your answers against those on page 391 in this Appendix.

Remember, skimming is done at a fast speed with lower than normal comprehension. You are not required to get 100 percent comprehension, so do not read everything. Read looking for the general ideas with a few specifics.

Skimming Exercise—The King of the Pests

Ending Time: _____

Beginning Time: _____

Total Time: _____

Every homeowner, no matter how fastidious, sometimes finds a bug or two in the house—a roach, some ants, water bugs, etc. It is generally acknowledged that it is no disgrace to find these pests; but, it is also admittedly bad manners, to say the least, to keep them! Hence it is important to (1) understand pest control, (2) be aware of the need of protecting oneself against the few unethical pest control companies that may be operating in the community, and (3) realize the need for controlling the king of all pests, the terrible termite!

For most minor invasions, for such pests as the roach, there are many effective "do-it-yourself" commercial products on the market. Consistent use of these products generally rids the premises of the nuisances. But extreme caution should be employed in their use. Great care should be taken to make certain that poisonous substances are kept out of reach of young children and household pets. Follow label directions carefully; use normal caution; and no problems should arise. If an infestation seems to get out of hand, then professional help may be solicited. A whole-house treatment by a pest control company is sometimes advisable and usually is effective over a long period of time.

The King of the Pests

Most little bugs don't eat much, but the king of the pests—the termite—that's another story. Termites have been known to eat whole houses—quietly and often undetected until major damage has been done.

Termite control can present major problems. A case in point: A stranger called on the modest home of a retired minister and his wife, introduced himself as a representative of a termite control company, and asked to make a free inspection of their home for termites. The man went under the house, returned shortly with a board full of insects, and told them their house was near collapse. He offered to treat the house and save t from ruin, the price depending "on the number of gallons of poison I have to use." The result: the couple was swindled out of $550 of their savings.

The swindler was one of scores of such transients who roam the nation from coast to coast, fleecing uninformed people of substantial sums on worthless termite control jobs. In many cases the homes of the victims are not even infested with the pests; in others, the treatment is worthless—or worse than worthless because the victim is lulled into a sense of security while the unharmed insects continue to chew away the house.

What Are Termites?

First of all, just what ARE termites? How do they enter your home? How do they multiply so rapidly when they do enter? How do they operate? And how can you get rid of them?

The termite family is a highly specialized caste organization, each member of which is physically adapted to perform one special function of family life. They are (1) the workers, who do the damage and make up some 90% of the colony; (2) the soldiers, who guard the colony against natural enemies; (3) the reproductives, who perpetuate the life of the colony. At the head of each colony are a king and a queen.

Termites are not "white ants" or "flying ants" as they are sometimes erroneously called, nor are they related to the ant family. In the United States, there are 56 species of termites which fall into three groups: dry wood termites, damp wood termites and subterranean termites. The latter causes nearly all termite damage in this country.

How to Detect Termites

Some evidences of the existence of a termite colony include the appearance of winged swarms during the migration season and presence of shelter tubes on walls of the foundation of the house. You may also discover worker termites in wood scraps lying on or in the ground.

How Termites Enter Your Home

Headquarters of the termite is the nest, located well below the surface of the earth. They have been found as deep as 25 feet.

The workers tunnel up through the earth to make contact with a supply of wood on which to feed. If they can find wood touching ground, such as porch steps or posts, they bore in and start working. Brick, stone or concrete foundations do not stop them. To reach wood, they build mud tubes up the side of the foundation walls or piers or through cracks, mortar joints or hollow masonry units in the foundation.

Contact with the wood understructure at only one small point enables them to eventually infest and damage woodwork throughout the building. In steady streams they relentlessly travel up to the wood for food and back down to the ground for moisture.

Their attack may not be confined to any one portion of a building. While one group of workers is eating away at one corner of a house, another may be burrowing exploratory tunnels or building tubes toward another point of attack. They constantly seek new sources of food supply for their expanding colony. Some buildings have become severely damaged in a relatively short time. Others have harbored termite infestation for years with only minor damage occurring.

Success Skills

Methods of Prevention and Treatment

Insecticides used in killing household pests such as flies, mosquitoes, etc. are of no value in termite control because they do not come in immediate contact with the termites which are out of sight and hidden deep in the ground. Attempts to stop termites by fumigation also have proven useless. Such methods of termite control fail because they attempt the impossible task of exterminating all the insects.

On the other hand, modern scientific methods attack the problem by seeking to cut off the termites within the building from returning to their ground nests and to block new invasions from the ground. Both results are accomplished by placing an unbroken, effective barrier in the path of the termites. Termites above the barrier soon die for lack of moisture; those below can do no damage. The barrier may be either mechanical or chemical or a combination of both.

Regardless of the type of control selected, approved methods also require that loose wood and general debris under the building be removed. Stumps within the limits of the foundation should be removed when possible.

Responsible termite control operators usually do not price a job by the number of gallons of chemical or "poison" used. Since this is frequently the method used by swindlers, it may be a caution signal. Any doubts about whether you really have termite infestation can be dispelled by having two or three reputable termite control operators inspect the property. And, lastly but most important, you can check the firm's reliability with the Better Business Bureau without charge or obligation.

Source: Adapted from a non-copyrighted Bliss Exterminating public information brochure.

Without looking back at the information you just read, answer the following ten questions to the best of your ability. Make a guess when you are not sure. Decide whether the following statements are true (T), false (F), or not mentioned (N). A true statement is a fact based on the information you read. A false statement is one that is mentioned but not correct. A statement that is not mentioned was not discussed at all.

_____ 1. Keeping a dirty house almost always guarantees a termite infestation.
_____ 2. Some pest control companies fake termite infestations making homeowners pay to get rid of imaginary pests.
_____ 3. Roaches look like termites.
_____ 4. Tiny termites eat houses.
_____ 5. Termites are related to the ant family.
_____ 6. Termite nests can be 25 feet deep.

_____   7.   Termites travel through mud tubes.

_____   8.   Spiders help eliminate termites by eating them.

_____   9.   Household insecticides are effective in killing termites.

_____   10.   One way to reduce a termite infestation is to remove all tree stumps from around the foundation.

Scanning Exercises

For each of the following exercises, you will be able to practice your scanning ability. Time yourself to see how long each exercise takes. (See "Timing Instructions" in this appendix if needed.) Though there are no words-per-minute to figure, the quicker you locate the information with accuracy, the better!

First, read a question below the listing and then search above, using your hands or a white card pacer, looking for the correct answer. When you have found the correct answer, write it down in the blank provided next to the question. Notice how quickly your eyes and brain are communicating to each other to eliminate the incorrect information and focus on the correct information.

Scanning Exercise No. 1—Nursing Course Listing

Ending Time: _____

Beginning Time: _____

Total Time: _____

NUR 216 Health & Physical Assessment in Nursing   3.0 cr
Prerequisite: NUR 215

| 6860 | 70 | 04:00p-06:50p M Staff | **** | 01/25-05/22 |

Special Information: Meets Lawrence & Mem. Hosp.

| 8389 | 71 | 04:00p-06:5Op M Staff | **** | 01/25-05/22 |

Special Information: Meets Hosp. of St. Raphael

| 5180 | 72 | 04:00p-06:50p M Staff | **** | 01/25-05/22 |

Special Information: Meets Manchester Hospital

| 2959 | 73 | 04:00-06:50p M Staff | **** | 01 /25-05/22 |

Special Information: Meets St. Francis Hospital

| 9958 | 74 | 04:00p-06:50p M Staff | **** | 01/25-05/22 |

Special Information: Meets St. Mary's Hospital

| 0315 | 75 | 04:00p-06:50p M Staff | **** | 01/25-05/22 |

Special Information: Meets Central CT ST Univ

| 5400 | 76 | 04:00p-06:50p M Staff | **** | 01 /25-05/22 |

Special Information: Meets Backus Hospital

1. What is the name of the course listed?   _____

2. What is the course number?   _____

3. What time and day does Section 75 meet?   _____

4. How many class sections are there?   _____

5. Where does Section 72 meet?   _____

6. Where does Section 76 meet? _____

7. How many credits does this course offer? _____

8. What is the prerequisite to this course? _____

9. From what date to what date do all the classes meet? _____

10. Where does Section 75 meet? _____

(To check your answers, see the answers on pages 391 and 392 in this appendix.)

Scanning Exercise No. 2—Telephone Listing

    Ending Time: _____

    Beginning Time: _____

    Total Time: _____

555-7998	Williams Anne M Mrs 80 Henry Hudson
555-1022	Williams Antique Shop 179 Bayshore Rd
555-2933	Williams B E 7 Eastern Ave
555-9016	Williams Barbara S Westbury
555-4810	Williams Basil & Christine 10 Freeland
555-8993	Williams Beryl 296 Palmer Farms Rd
555-1248	Williams C 790 Lake Rd
555-4208	Williams C Webb Taconic Rd
555-9084	Williams Christopher B 4 Eastern Ave
555-7379	Williams Claude H 92 Pickford
555-0225	Williams & Co 251 Waller
555-7561	Williams David 5 Pilot Rock Rd.
555-1114	Williams Elizabeth C North Pine
555-1286	Williams Francis S 35 St Andrews Rd.
555-0635	Williams George & Kathi 24 Lake Drive N
555-7175	Williams Geo R D 133 Prospect Dr
555-4228	Williams Gwynne 43 Bloomfield Rd
555-8993	Williams Howard 0 Jr Dr 296 Palmer Farms Rd
555-0848	Williams—Children Phone 296 Palmer Farms Rd
555-2331	Williams J Bryan III 10 Stansbury P1
555-1 766	Williams J R 34 Covert
555-7187	Williams John F 102 Calvert Dr
555-1391	Williams John I 91 Cedar Dr
555-1995	Williams Joseph L III 50 Cleveland Ave
555-9283	Williams Jos L Jr 141 Dairy Rd
555-6800	Williams Joseph L Jr rl est 32 Park P1
555-2892	Williams Joseph S Parsons Dr
555-6800	Williams Josephine C rl est 32 Park P1
555-5061	Williams K & R 171 Versailles Ave

555-8376	Williams K R 182 Lake Rd
555-3800	Williams Karen L atty 100 Kuntsler Rd
555-1941	Williams Keith 40 Dairy Rd
555-9443	Williams Ken 16 Madison Ave
555-1687	Williams Lincoln A 44 Hudson
555-0870	Williams Lou 5 Kings Rd
555-2341	Williams Philip 155 Taconic Rd
555-0671	Williams Philip J 2 Mendota
555-3383	Williams R E 140 Westbury
555-5061	Williams R & K 171 Kingsway Plaza Dr
555-8570	Williams Richard A 6 Allwich Ave
555-1012	Williams Richard A atty 1 Beth Blvd
555-7282	Williams Roger J 15 Prospect Park Dr
555-9198	Williams Staunton Jr 184 Eastern Ave
555-4826	Williams Sydney M 795 Leslie Lane
555-6233	Williams Thos R 205 S Maine Maid Rd

1. Whose phone number is 555-7379? _____

2. Who lives at 2 Mendota? _____

3. How many listings does 296 Palmer Farms Rd. have? _____

4. What is the business phone of Joseph L. Williams, Jr.? _____

5. Whose phone number is 555-3383? _____

6. Who lives at 182 Lake Rd.? _____

7. What is the phone number of 205 5 Maine Maid Rd.? _____

8. What is the business address of Richard A. Williams? _____

9. Whose phone number is 555-1391? _____

10. Who lives at 795 Leslie Lane? _____

(Check your answers on page 392 in this Appendix.)

Scanning Exercises No. 3A–E—Scanning Text

For each of the following paragraphs, there are one or two questions to answer. Read the question(s), then scan through the paragraph looking for the answer(s). When you find the answer(s), write it in the blank next to the question. Time yourself once for all five questions.

Ending Time: _____
Beginning Time: _____

Total Time: _____

No. 3A: What is the function of the eyelashes?_____

Hair protects the body in several ways. The eyebrows keep sweat from falling into the eyes. The tiny hairs inside the nose and ears stop small particles from entering and causing damage. The eyelashes keep small objects from getting into the eye. These hairs all act very much like a screen door on a house in keeping out unwanted organisms. The skin itself screens out harmful rays from the sun which may cause bums and harm the body.

No. 3B: What is being described in this paragraph? _____

Picture an immense room, segmented by brilliant blue draperies, flashes of color, neon lights, video presentation, models in sequined gowns, men and women in business attire and in the aisles, crowds of people of all ages in varied attire strolling and stopping frequently to view the booths. This would he a typical trade show. What is seemingly a random gathering of action and bodies, is in reality a carefully choreographed production. An air of excitement is deliberately created by the exhibit management company and exhibitors are encouraged to present a show.

No. 3C: How many types of cancer are there? _____

No. 3D: What is the leading cause of death in the United States? _____

It has been estimated that in the United States alone over 1,000 people a day die from some form of cancer. Since 1949 there has been a sharp rise in the number of men who develop cancer. Cancer of the lung has risen sharply in men. Cancer of the breast, colon and rectum occur most often among women. There are over one hundred types of cancer. Cancer is second only to heart disease as the leading cause of death each year. However, statistics also show that deaths due to cancer are increasing whereas those due to heart conditions are decreasing. Research continues into the cause and cure for cancer.

No. 3E: Where is optical center? (be specific) _____

When someone looks at a page, two things happen. First, the reader's eye will automatically go to the optical center. The optical center is defined as the place on the page where one's eye falls naturally. This is considered to be about three-eighths of a page from the top. Second, the reader's eye scans a page in the shape of a Z. This means that the eye moves across the top, diagonally down the page from right to left, and then across the bottom. For this reason, illustrations placed at the tops and bottoms of pages make them look appealing. Understanding and remembering these two ways in which the eye naturally sees a page are critical to the page makeup.

Adjusting Reading Speed

Things that help me SPEED UP

Reading for main ideas (my purpose)

Easy vocabulary

Some background knowledge

For class discussion (responsibility)

Interest

Narrow column width

Quiet

Good light

Comfortable temperature

Don't have a lot of time

Bigger print style

Author's style

Well-rested

Early in the day

Pre-viewing

Reading key words

Reading phrases

Using pacers

Things that cause me to SLOW DOWN

Reading for details (my purpose)

Difficult vocabulary

Little background knowledge

For quiz or test (responsibility)

Lack of interest*

Wide column width

Noisy

Poor light

Too hot or too cold

Have plenty of time

Smaller print style

Author's style

Tired*

Late in the day

Not pre-viewing

Not reading key words

Not reading phrases

Not using pacers

*If you are not interested or you are tired, you tend to read slowly, but with the reading tools and other speed-up factors, you can speed up and get your work done quicker.

Practice Reading Answers

Reading Exercise No. 1—Labor Unions

350 words ÷ _____your translated time* = _____WPM

Answers

1. T, 2. T, 3. F, 4. F, 5. N, 6. T, 7. F, 8. T, 9. F, 10. N

No. of correct responses _____x 10 % = _____% comprehension

Reading Exercise No. 2—The Changing Workplace

381 words ÷ _____your translated time* = _____WPM

Answers

1. T, 2. F, 3. F, 4. T, 5. T, 6. N, 7. N, 8. T, 9. F, 10. T

No. of correct responses _____x 10 % = _____% comprehension

Reading Exercise No. 3—The Attraction of Place

504 words ÷ _____your translated time* = _____WPM

Answers

1. F, 2. T, 3. F, 4. T, 5. F, 6. N, 7. T, 8. N, 9. T, 10. F

No. of correct responses _____x 10 % = _____% comprehension

Skimming Exercise Answers

Skimming Exercise No. 1—The King of Pests

1,133 words ÷ _____your translated time* = _____ WPM (skimming)

Answers:

1. F, 2. T, 3. N, 4. T, 5. F, 6. T, 7. T, 8. N, 9. F, 10. T

No. of correct responses _____x 10 % = _____% comprehension

*See "Figuring Words-Per-Minute" on page 376 of this appendix if you need more information.

Scanning Exercise Answers

Scanning Exercise No.1—Nursing Course Listing

1. Health and Physical Assessment in Nursing
2. NUR 216
3. 4 pm on Mondays
4. 7 class sections
5. Manchester Hospital
6. Backus Hospital
7. 3 credits
8. NUR 215
9. From 1/25 to 5/22
10. Central CT ST Univ

Scanning Exercise No. 2—Telephone Listing

1. Claude H.
2. Philip J.
3. 3 (Beryl, Howard 0. and Children's Phone)
4. 555—6800 (business is "rl est", or real estate)
5. RE
6. KR
7. 555—6233
8. Belli Blvd. (business is "atty" or attorney)
9. John I.
10. Sydney M.

Scanning Exercise No. 3—Scanning Text

3A: keep small objects from entering the eye

3B: a typical trade show

3C: 100 (types of cancer)

3D: heart disease

3E: 3/8ths of a page from the top

ACTIVITY ANSWER KEYS
Chapter 10

Answers to Activity 5

1. **C**—Both Paris and London are mentioned twice in the answers while the other cities are only mentioned once. If you only remembered one of the two cities, you had to make a choice.

2. **C**—Using background knowledge, you would hopefully know that Italy is a peninsula surrounded by water on three sides, thus making "a lack of adequate ports" not possible.

3. **D**—First, use the process of elimination. By looking at the five answers, you will see three that are similar (C, D, E). This could indicate that one of the answers lies within as in this case it does. If you didn't know the math for figuring out the answer, at least you could narrow down the possibilities. By knowing the answer is probably in l6ths, then figuring 1/3 into l6ths seem an efficient use of your test-taking time.

4. **B**—The key word is *mismatched*. In order to find the answer, you need to first find the matching ones. This can help eliminate some of your choices. By matching the city correctly to its state, then A, C and D are not the mismatched one. Letter B is.

5. **A**—Because "cluss" is in the answer.

6. **B**—There are two reasons why letter B is the correct one.
    1. It is the longest answer.
    2. It satisfies the condition presented in the question (. . . is true when.. .) by the word *if*.

7. **C**—Letters A, B and D uses definite terms such as *all*, *always* and *no*. The question uses the word *frequently* making letter C with the word "usually" a better answer.

8. **D**—Letter D best satisfies the grammar rule that a vowel must come after a consonant when using the word *an*. Most instructors don't make it this easy for you but if they do, be aware of it.

9. **A**—Letter A is the only answer that satisfies the plural question of "conditions".

10 **B**—The key word is *always*. Vost is "always" present in all of the answers.

11. **C**—The answer is given in question 8. (Remember that pre-viewing the playing field can help find answers within a test!)

12. **C**—According to studies of instructor created exams (not stan-dardized tests), this is the most common answer given on multiple-choice exams, followed by B, then A, then D. When all else fails, a "C" guess is better than no answer at all!

Answers to Activity 8

E.	1.	Active Learning	Learning like a sponge
C.	2.	Background Knowledge	What you already know
F.	3.	Cornell Method	Notetaking method best used by sequential learners
K.	4.	Critical Thinking	Thinking about thinking

A. 5.   Previewing   A reader's road map
H. 6.   Passive Learning   Learning like a rock
B. 7.   Mind-Mapping®   Notetaking method best used by a random learner
I. 8.   Mind-wandering   Can only be reduced, not eliminated
G. 9.   Learning Influences   Those things that affect your study concentration
D. 10.   Skimming and Scanning   High/fast reading gears

Answers to Activity 9

1.   <u>an</u> active
2.   passive
3.   sequential; random
4.   procrastination
5.   background knowledge
6.   purpose and responsibility
7.   concentration
8.   key words, phrases, pacers
9.   body, recall column
10. smarter, harder.

Chapter 11

Answers to Activity 4

1. d, 2. a, 3. h , 4. b, 5. f, 6. c, 7. e, 8. j, 9. g, 10.i

Answers to Activity 7

1. Incubation, 2. Insight, 3. Inspiration, 4. Preparation, 5. Actualization

CITING ELECTRONIC SOURCES

When presenting your online research, you must cite the sources you consulted to locate your information. Several correct styles exist for naming the sources used, and various fields of study and various publications have their own accepted styles. All accepted styles of reference include the same general information, though the information may be arranged differently. No matter what format you choose, the objective is to provide enough information so that your reader could locate your original source. The Andrew Mellon Library suggests the following formats for citing information from the Internet and other electronic sources:

INTERNET
World Wide Web

DiStefano, Vince. Guidelines for better writing. (Online) Found at http://www.usa.net/-vinced/hom/better-writing.html. on (May 8, 1996)

MIT Business Database. (Online) Found at http://www.prnewswire.com/ on (August 15, 1996).

INTERNET
Gopher

Chalmers, Andrea. Bosnia: A Country in Transition. (Online) Found at gopher:nywer.net. Today's News/World News/Bosnia-Herzegovina/on (March 6, 1996).

INTERNET
Usenet Newsgroups

Dey, Tom. Education Insights. (Online) Found at usenet.k12ed.research/ on (May 1, 1996).

INTERNET
Online Image

Hubble Space Telescope release in the Space Shuttle's Payload Bay (Online Image). Found at ftp://explorer.arc.nasa.gov/pub/SPACE/GIF/s31-04-015.gif on (June 16, 1996).

Newspaper Article
(full-text)

Hirsh. Kim S. "Pregnant and Poor: Reducing the Risks." The New York Times 1993. March 29, Sec. 13CN (CD-ROM) UMI: New York Times Ondisc, 1993.

Newspaper Article
(abstract)

Hays, Constance L. "Free Care For the Poor and Pregnant Comes on Wheels," New York Times 1992, Jan. 21, Sec. 5CN (CD-ROM) Abstract from UMI: National Newspaper Abstracts, 1992.

Magazine Article
(full-text)

Kozol, Jonathan. "Romance of the Ghetto School." Nation 1994, May 23, pp. 703+ (CD-ROM) Ebsco: Magazine Article Summaries Full Text Elite, 1994.

Magazine Article
(abtract)

Subramanian, Pramilla N. "Atrial fibrillation: Indications for anticoagulation." Primary Cardiology,1994, June (CD-ROM) Infotrac: Health Reference Center, Nov. 1991-Nov. 1994.

RECOMMENDED READING

GETTING MOTIVATED

Brim, Gilbert. *Ambition: How We Manage Success and Failure Throughout Our Lives*. New York, NY: BasicBooks, 2000.

De Bono, Edward. *Serious Creativity: Using the Power of Lateral Thinking to Create New Ideas*. New York, NY: Advanced Practical Thinking, 1993.

McWilliams, John-Roger and Peter McWilliams. *Do It! Let's Get Off Our Buts*. Los Angeles, CA: Prelude Press, 1997.

Ottens, Allen J. *Coping with Academic Anxiety*. New York, NY: Rosen Publishing Group, 1991.

Robbins, Anthony. *Personal Power!* Chicago, IL: Nightingale-Conant Corporation, 1992. Audiocassettes.

Robbins, Anthony. *Awaken the Giant Within: How to Take Immediate Control of Your Mental, Emotional, Physical & Financial Destiny*. New York, NY: Fireside, 1993.

Waitley, Denis. *The Psychology of Human Motivation*. Chicago, IL: Nightingale-Conant, 1991. Cassette recording. Includes a workbook entitled *Psych Up!*

Wexler, Phillip S., W.A. Adams and Emil Bohn. *The Quest for Quality: Prescriptions for Achieving Excellence*. New York, NY: St Martin's Press, 1996.

BUILDING SELF-ESTEEM

Helmsteter, Shad. *The Self-Talk Solution*. New York, NY: Dove Audio, Inc., 1998. Audio cassettes.

Martarano, Joseph T. and John P. Kildahl. *Beyond Negative Thinking: Breaking the Cycle of Depressing and Anxious Thoughts*. New York, NY: Perseus Publishing, 1989.

McWilliams, Peter. *You Can't Afford the Luxury of a Negative Thought*. Los Angeles, CA: Prelude Press, 1995. Also available on cassette recording.

Robbins, Anthony. *Personal Power!* Chicago, IL: Nightingale-Conant Corporation, 1992. Audiocassettes.

Robbins, Anthony. *Awaken the Giant Within: How to Take Immediate Control of Your Mental, Emotional, Physical & Financial Destiny*. New York, NY: Fireside, 1993.

REACHING YOUR GOALS

Covey, Stephen R. *The Seven Habits of Highly Effective People*. New York, NY: Fireside, 1990. Also on audio cassette and CD from Covey Leadership Center, Provo, UT.

Lakein, Alan. *How to Get Control of Your Time and Your Life*. New York, NY: New American Library, 1996.

Leonard, George. *Mastery: The Keys to Success and Long-term Fulfillment*. New York, NY: Plume, 1992.

EXPLORING CAREERS

Bolles, Richard Nelson. *What Color is Your Parachute?: A Practical Guide for Job-Hunters and Career Changers*. Berkeley, CA: Ten Speed Press, 2000.

Encyclopedia of Careers and Vocational Guidance. Chicago, IL: Ferguson Publishing Company 10th Edition, 1996.

Kleiman, Carol. *The 100 Best Jobs for the 1990's and Beyond*. New York, NY: Berkley Publishing Group, Reprint edition, 1994.

Tieger, Paul D. *Do What You Are: Discover the Perfect Career for You Through the Secrets of Personality Type*. Boston, MA: Little, Brown, 1995.

IMPROVING YOUR WRITING

(Also, ask your instructors for their personal favorites)

Davidson, Wilma. *Business Writing*. New York, NY: St. Martins Press, 2000.

Kirszner, Laurie G. and Stephen R. Mandell. *Holt Handbook*, 4th Edition. Orlando, FL: HBJ College Publications, 1997.

Leggett, Glen et al. *Prentice Hall Handbook for Writers*, 12th Edition. New York, NY: Prentice-Hall, 1994.

Strunk, William and E.B. White. *The Elements of Style*, 4th Edition. Boston, MA: Allyn & Bacon, 2000.

Tyner, Thomas E. *Deep in Thought: A Thematic Approach to Thinking and Writing Well*. Belmont, CA: Wadsworth Publishing Company, 1992.

IMPROVING YOUR READING SPEED

Marks-Beale, Abby. *10 Days to Faster Reading*. New York, NY: Warner Books, 2001.

Timed Reading Series, NTC Publishing (formerly Jamestown Publishers), Lincolnwood, IL: Call 1-800-USA-READ for a catalog.

CITING SOURCES FROM THE INTERNET

Xia Li and Nancy Bererme. *Electronic Styles: A Handbook For Citing Electronic Information*. Medford, NJ: Information Today, 1996.

Janice R Walker and Todd Taylor. "The Columbia Guide to Online Style." New York, NY: Columbia University Press, NY 1998.

Bibliography

Apps, Jerold W. *Study Skills for Today's College Student*. New York, NY: McGraw-Hill Inc., 1990.

Augarde, Tony. *The Oxford Dictionary of Modern Quotations*. New York, NY: Oxford University Press, 1993.

Baugh, L. Sue. *How to Write Term Papers & Reports*. Lincolnwood, IL: NTC Publishing Group, 1996.

Buzan, Tony. *Use Both Sides of YourBrain*, 3rd Edition. New York, NY: The Penguin Group, 1991.

Christie, Chris. *AHA: CPS Process: Concepts*. Syracuse, NY: Challenge Institute, 1989.

Coman, Marcia and Kathy Heavers. *How to Improve Your StudySkills*, 2nd Edition. Lincolnwood, IL.: NTC Publishing, 1997.

Dictionary of Contemporary Quotations. Gaylord Professional Publications; Vol. 1-3.

Effective Study Strategies. Acton, MA.: Academic Resources Corp.,1987. Audiocassettes with workbook.

Fobes, Richard. *The Creative Problem Solver's Tool Box*. Corvallis, OR: Solutions Through Innovation, 1993.

Fry, Ron. *How to Study Program (Book Series)*, 5th Edition. Hawthorne, NJ: Career Press, 2000.

Galica, Gregory S. *The Blue Book: A Student's Guide to Essay Exams*. San Diego, CA: Harcourt, Brace, Jovanovich, 1991.

GED High School Equivalency Exam Review Book. Englewood, NJ: Cambridge Adult Education, Prentice Hall Regents, 1987.

Gibbs, J.J. *Dancing With Your Books: The Zen Way of Studying*. New York, NY: Penguin Group, 1990.

Goleman, Daniel. *Emotional Intelligence*. New York, NY: Bantam Books, 1995.

Gross, Ronald. *Peak Learning*, Revised Edition. Los Angeles,CA: Jeremy P. Tarcher, Inc., 1999.

Harnadeck, Anita. *Critical Thinking Book One*. Pacific Grove, CA: Midwest Publications Company, 1981.

Hermann, Ned. *The Creative Brain*. Lake Lure, NC: Brain Books, 1989.

Herold, Mort. *Memorizing Made Easy*. Chicago, IL: Contemporary Books, 1982.

Jensen, Eric. *Barron's Student Success Secrets*, 3rd Edition. New York, NY: Barron's Educational Series, 1989

Jensen, Eric. "Learning Styles in the 90's: How to Read Them and What to Do About Them". DelMar, CA: Turning Point, 1991. Set of 3 audiocassettes.

Kanar, Carol C. *The Confident Student*. Boston, MA: Houghton Mifflin Company, 1991.

Kesselman-Turkel, Judi and Franklynn Peterson. *Getting It Down: How to Put Your Ideas on Paper*. Chicago, IL. Contemporary Books, 1983.

Kesselman-Turkel, Judi and Franklynn Peterson. *Research Shortcuts*. Chicago, IL: Contemporary Books, 1982.

Kesselman-Turkel, Judi and Franklynn Peterson. *Study Smarts: How to Learn More in Less Time*. Chicago, IL: Contemporary Books, 1981.

Kesselman-Turkel, Judi and Franklynn Peterson. *Test-Taking Strategies*. Chicago, IL: Contemporary Books, 1981.

Success Skills

Killaritsch, Jane. *Reading & Study Organization Method for Higher Learning*. Columbus, OH: Reading Study Skills Center, Office of Developmental Education, Ohio State University.

Knowles, Malcolm S. & Associates. *Andragogy in Action: Applying Modern Principles of Adult Learning*. San Francisco, CA: Jossey-Bass Publishers, 1984.

Lakein, Alan. *How to Get Control of Your Time and Your Life*. New York, NY: Signet Book, The New American Library, 1973.

Langer, Ellen. *Mindfulness*. Reading, MA: Perseus Books, 1989.

Media Matters: Critical Thinking in the Information Age. Cincinatti, OH: South-Western Educational Publishing, 2000.

Merriam-Webster Thesaurus. New York, NY: Pocket Books, 1978.

Moore, Brooke Noel & Parker, Richard. *Critical Thinking*. Mountain View, CA: Mayfield Publishing Company, 2001

North, Vanda. *Get Ahead*. Bournemouth, England: BC Books, 1992.

Olney, Claude Dr. "Where There Is A Will, There Is An A". Chesterbrook Educational Publishers: 1988. Audiotape and Videocassette.

Paul, Walter. *How to Study in College* (4th Edition). Boston, MA: Houghton Mifflin Company, 1989.

Paul, Richard. *Critical Thinking*. Rohnert Park, CA: Center for Critical Thinking and Moral Critique, Sonoma State University, 1990.

Parnes, Sydney, Ed. *Source Book for Creative Problem Solving*. Buffalo, NY: Creative Education Foundation Press, 1992.

Patterson, Becky. *Concentration: Strategies for Attaining Focus*. Dubuque, IA: Kendall-Hunt, 1993.

Parnes, Sydney. *Optimize the Magic of Your Mind*. Buffalo, NY: Creative Education Foundation Press, 1995.

Random House Dictionary of the English Language. New York, NY: Random House, 1988.

Ruggiero, Vincent R. *Beyond Feelings*. Mountain View, CA: Mayfield Publishing, 1995.

Ruchlis, Hy & Sandra Oddo. *Clear Thinking*. Buffalo, NY: Prometheus Books, 1990.

Shepherd, James F. *College Study Skills*. Boston, MA: Houghton Mifflin Company, 1990.

Snider, Jean. *How to Study in High School*. Providence, RI: Jamestown Publishers, 1989 (Chapter 11).

VanGundy, Arthur B. *Brain Boosters for Business Advantage*. San Diego, CA: Pfeiffer & Company, 1995

Wlodkowski, Raymond J. *Enhancing Adult Motivation to Learn*. San Francisco, CA: Jossey-Bass Publishers,1990.

Warring, R.H. *Logic Made Easy*. Blue Ridge Summit, PA: Tab Books, Inc., 1984.

Wyckoff, Joyce. *Mindmapping: Your Personal Guide to Exploring Creativity and Problem Solving*. New York, NY: Berkeley Books, 1991.

Zorn, Robert. *Speed Reading*. New York, NY: Harper Perennial, 1991.

Glossary

abridged dictionary a shorter version of an unabridged dictionary

academic calendar monthly calendars, from September to August, used by individuals taking school or training courses

acronym word or words formed from the first letters of words or groups of letters in a phrase

active doing something

active reader a reader who focuses on what is being read

activities ways to learn firsthand the information in a chapter

almanac book containing facts, facts, and more facts

alphabetical going in order from A to Z

analogy making a comparison between two things

antonym words that are opposite in meaning

appeals to pity soliciting sympathy

appendix contains supplementary information that further explains a subject in the text

apple polishing playing up to another person to get something that is desired

arm-swing rule gently sweeping a semi-circle of clear space

auditory learner a person who prefers to learn by listening

background knowledge what you already know based on your previous experiences and learning

bad stress makes performing well or achieving goals challenging because of fear or worry

balanced learner a learner who has an equal preference for sequential and random learning

begging the question when a statement gets repeated with different words

beliefs interpretations, evaluations, conclusions, and predictions a person considers to be true

bias a tilted point of view

bibliography tells what reading resources the author used in writing the book

body (of summary paper) the right-hand side of summary paper

boldface words in dark print, usually pointing out a new vocabulary term or heading

Boolean search a way to search logically on the Internet

brainstorming a random, unorganized thought-generating process that results in new ideas

bottom line placing the key point or question first in an e-mail communication

browser a software program that is used to view Web pages

card stacking presenting only part of the picture

category method of classification

cause the reason something happens

CEUs continuing education units, credits required for many certified professionals

chronological information arranged in numeric order

classification the category a subject falls into

column (of summary paper) a space to write in when using the Cornell Note Taking Method

column width how wide or narrow the printed text is on a page

compare looking at things to emphasize their similarities

concentration the art of being focused

conclusion a summary of your important points

connecting words words that help bridge the relationship between sentences

context clues the word clues or hints that lead to the meaning of the vocabulary word

contrast a way to look at things that emphasizes their differences

convergent thinking looks for correct answers or guides a person toward selecting from several answers

coping attitude neither positive nor negative, but one that helps a person cope with the work or situation

copyright date tells how recent or how old the information is in a book (sometimes referred to as the publishing date)

cramming trying to memorize a lot of information in a very short period of time

creative thinking thinking about thinking in order to bring something new into existence

critical thinking thinking about thinking in order to decide what to believe and how to behave

daily activity log a simple way for individuals to see how they spend their time

dictionary a book that contains words and their meanings listed in alphabetical order

directory contains alphabetical information such as names or addresses

distractions something that divides attention or breaks concentration

divergent thinking thinking aimed at finding many possible answers

download material that can be saved from the Internet to a computer

editing process where a person corrects, adds, eliminates, or rearranges information so that it makes sense to the reader

educated guess guess based on good information

effect what happens as a result of a cause

effective being capable of producing a desired result

effective highlighting reading a complete paragraph or section before highlighting anything

effective learning environment an environment where learning occurs easily

effective recall using appropriate methods for remembering

efficient accomplishing a job with a minimum amount of time and effort

empowered feeling capable of learning something by using good study habits

encyclopedias a book, or set of books, containing articles on various subjects from A to Z

estimation an approximate amount; a guess

etymology word origins indicating where a word comes from

expose to uncover, make known, or disclose

eye span   the amount of information a person sees at a time when looking at a page

fallacies   mistakes in thinking

false dilemma   creating a dilemma where one does not exist

fiction   reading material that is imaginative in nature

5Ws and H   who, what, when, where, why, and how

flexible reader   reader who can adjust his or her reading techniques according to the reading purpose, difficulty of material, and background knowledge

footnotes   explanatory comments or reference notes that relate to a specific part of text on a page

full notes   taking all of your notes on paper, not in the textbook

glossary   a specialized dictionary at the back of a book to help a person quickly find the specific meaning of a word given in the text

goal   something that a person wants to have, do, or be

good stress   helps with motivation and energy

handbooks   contain technical information

hasty generalization   making a decision too quickly

headings   provide specific information about the chapter as well as the outline of the information

hemisphericity   a theory that suggests the brain has two hemispheres, left and right, with each representing certain qualities

highlighting   using a colored marker to

underline the important information in reading material

horizontal   something going across from left to right

horse laugh   making fun of someone or something when you disagree

hyperlink   an address or URL that links one web site to another

illustration   photos, figures, graphs, tables, or charts that explain the content

incorporate   to combine into one

independent learner   a person who prefers to learn alone

index   alphabetical listing of names, places, and topics along with the numbers of the pages on which they are mentioned

ineffective   being unable to produce the desired result

ineffective learning environment   an environment that results in a waste of time and makes learning difficult

inefficient   anything that wastes time and effort

intellectual capital   a smart work force that is able to continuously learn and improve

Internet   a network that allows computers to communicate

introduction   tells the reader what a paper will be about

ISP   Internet Service Provider; company through which access to the Internet is gained.

issue   an unresolved question about a topic

italicized   words in slanted print, usually

meaning something important, *slanted print like this*

jargon   vocabulary or terminology specific to a profession or trade

just reading   the most passive reading method

key words   the most important words in text

key term list   a vocabulary list

kinesthetic learners   people who prefer using their sense of touch and inner feelings to learn

KISS   Keep it simple and short

learning   a natural and constant process of gathering and processing information

learning goal   completing projects and assignments on time

learning influences   things that affect the way you learn

learning environment.   the combination of learning influences that are present while a person studies

learning goal   the desire to complete projects and assignments in a reasonable time

learning styles.   how people prefer to gather information and what they do with it

long-term goal   something that takes longer than six months or a year to achieve

mapping   a pre-writing thought process that helps a person organize thoughts and information on paper and results in an informal outline

margin notes   summary notes or questions listed in the margin of reading material

memorizing   trying to commit information to memory by rote, or by mindless repetition

memory devices   ways to recall information

mental learning environment   what your mind thinks about while you are studying

metacognition   conscious attention to thinking

Mind Mapping ®   a creative way to take notes that organizes ideas through visual patterns and pictures

mind wandering   a momentary lack of concentration or focus

mnemonic sentences   an aid to organizing ideas in which people make up a sentence using their own words

monthly calendar   helps you keep track of appointments

multiple guess   taking a wild guess when the answer is unknown

multiple intelligences   eight natural intelligences that people may be strong in

name calling   substitutes a personal insult for a direct response

nonalphabetical   not in a, b, c order, such as a television listing

nonfiction   reading material that is factual in nature

objective tests   tests that have a single correct answer, such as multiple choice, matching, true-false, or fill-in-the-blank

observer   a person who learns by paying careful attention to what is visible

on-line databases   computerized indexes in which a microcomputer is connected to a large computer in another location

osmosis   a passive process by which a person learns information or ideas without conscious effort

pacer a device, such as a person's hand or a white card, that can be used to force the reader's eyes to move down the page faster

palmtop calendar electronic handheld organizer

panic pushers people who ask questions about the material you are about to be tested on

participants people who learn by getting involved in the learning process

passive doing nothing

passive reader a reader who does nothing to focus on the reading material

peer pressure that which causes a person to go along with the crowd

performance test measures how well a person can execute, or perform, a certain task or activity

peripheral vision the wide distance a person is able to see on the left and right while staring straight ahead

perspective a person's point of view

phrase a group of words that express a thought

physical learning environment the place a person chooses to study

physiology generally, the way a person feels

plagiarism using another person's words without giving credit

position a person's point of view on an issue

possess to have as one's own

preface tells why an author wrote a book or what the reader needs to know about how the book is organized (usually found after the title page)

prefix a part of the word that is added to the beginning

pre-viewing looking over material before reading it to discover clues to its contents

process a series of related steps or actions taken to achieve an end

procrastination putting off doing something unpleasant or burdensome until a future time

productive time time spent in an activity that leads to a goal

projects ways to learn firsthand the material in a chapter

publisher a person or company whose business is to reproduce books and periodicals, for sale

purpose the reason why you do your assignment

purpose for reading the reason why a person reads

random learner a less logical, more haphazard approach to taking in information (compare to sequential learning style)

reading actively includes previewing, reading key words, reading phrases, and using pacers

reading responsibility being accountable for the information you are reading

recall to remember

recall column of summary paper the left hand side of summary paper

research locating usable information for a paper or project

responsibility how a person is accountable

reward something people give themselves in return for their efforts

rough draft   a person's first attempt at getting ideas down on paper

scanning   looking only for a specific fact or piece of information without reading everything

scare tactics   causing fear in another person

search engine   a computer program that recognizes keywords then locates specific web pages

sensory learning preference   visual, auditory and tactile preferences for learning

sequence   the following of one thing after another

sequential learner   a person who learns in a logical, step-by-step way while taking in information (compare to random learning style)

short-term goal   something to be achieved within the next six months or a year

significant   important

skimming   reading in high gear; looking only for the general or main ideas

slippery slope   when a claim is made that one change will lead to more changes and end in a bad result

social learner   a person who prefers to learn in a group

straw person   disagreeing by changing a person's statement

stress   the body's reaction to something that happened or is about to happen

strategy   a plan or method for obtaining a goal or result

study goal   completing an assignment in a reasonable time frame

study order   the order in which a person does assignments

subheadings   specific information about a chapter, as well as the outline of the information

subject directory   a database of hand-chosen sites that have been reviewed and selected by people rather than by a computer program

subject line   the space that identifies the overall message in an e-mail

subjective test   a test that evaluates overall understanding of material by requiring the test taker to write opinions or comments, such as short answer or essay

subtitle   gives additional information

suffix   the part of a word added at the end

summary   a brief statement or restatement of main points

summary paper   used for the Cornell Method of Note Taking; has a 3-inch left margin

syllabus   a schedule of assignments

synonym   a word that is similar in meaning to another word

table of contents   the outline of the text

tactile learner   a person who prefers to use the body to learn

testimonial   convincing others by using a quote from someone of status

testing success factors   something that contributes to a successful test result

textual   information located within the paragraphs of the text

thesaurus   a type of dictionary that contains only synonyms and antonyms

thesis   the conclusion you draw from what you study; the main point of a paper

thesis statement   a summary of the thesis

title   identifies the topic or main idea

topic sentence   the main idea of a paragraph, usually the first sentence of every paragraph

topics   he subjects you study

transform   to change in form, appearance, or structure

two wrongs make a right   returning an insult with an insult

unabridged dictionary   the most complete type of a dictionary because it includes all words and definitions

unproductive time   time spent in an activity that does not lead to a goal

URL   uniform resource locator, the address of a Web site

vertical   something going up and down, from top to bottom

visual learner   people who prefer to use their eyes to learn

visualization   creating or recalling mental pictures relating to what you are learning

walking dictionary   a person you ask to help you figure out a word you don't understand

weekly activity log   the same as a daily activity log, except it is completed for a full week, or seven days in a row

weekly project planner   an effective way to keep track of assignments and plan study time according to a term calendar

word structures   prefixes, roots, suffixes, and other parts of words

working bibliography   a list of all the books and articles that are used for a paper

World Wide Web   a huge system of linked resources that contain hyperlinks to other resources or web sites

writing process   a series of related writing steps

Success Skills

Subtitle, 188
Suffix, 181, 200-201
Summary, 170
Summary-in-the-margin notes, 170
Summary (concluding) paragraphs, 193
Syllabus, 87
Synonyms, 205

T

U

Success Skills

Checkpoint 3.1

1. What is a learning influence?
2. What influences you positively when you learn?
3. What influences you negatively?

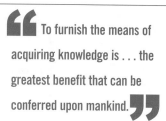

" To furnish the means of acquiring knowledge is . . . the greatest benefit that can be conferred upon mankind. "

—John Quincy Adams
   Sixth president of the
   United States

Focus on Ethics

You have a job working for a great boss who challenges you and makes you feel valued. Of your many job functions, you check your boss's e-mail when she travels and only forward those messages that are of the most importance. You have been told not to open messages marked "personal." This day, your mind wanders and you inadvertently open a personal message. It is from a recruiting firm providing job openings outside of your company that she might have interest in. As you stare at the screen, you must decide whether or not to pass this message along. What would you do? Why?

WEB LINK

www.utexas.edu/student/lsc/handouts/1442.html

This is a page entitled "Concentration and Your Body" from the University of Texas at Austin. It reinforces and supplements the information in this chapter. Access the main site to search other learning skills pages.

Smart Tip

According to R. Alec MacKenzie, a time management guru, for every minute you plan, you save two minutes in execution. For example, if you take 15 minutes at the end of each day to plan the following day, you would then save 30 minutes that next day because of the forethought and planning. How might this affect your life?

Key Terms and Concepts

arm-swing rule
concentration
effective learning environment
ineffective learning environment

learning environment
learning influences
mental learning environment

mind wandering
physical learning environment
physiology